Education, Equality and Human Rights

'Addressing issues that include the challenge of disability discrimination in schooling, gender and equality, "race" and racism, sexuality and social justice, and class analysis and knowledge formation, *Education, Equality and Human Rights* is an urgent and important contribution to the social justice literature as it intersects with current educational debates and struggles.'

Professor Peter McLaren, University of Auckland, New Zealand

Education, Equality and Human Rights traces the history of diverse equality issues up to the present, and enables readers to assess their continuing relevance in the future. Written by experts in their particular field, each of the five equality issues of gender, 'race', sexual orientation, disability and social class are covered as areas in their own right as well as in relation to education. This third edition has been fully revised to reflect major changes in law and policy, and offers contemporary perspectives on worldwide equality issues.

Key issues explored include:

* human rights and equality;
* gender;
* gender and education;
* racism;
* racism and education;
* sexuality and identity;
* sexuality and homophobia in schools;
* the struggle for disability equality;
* inclusive education;
* social class;
* social class and education.

With a new Foreword by leading educationist Peter McLaren, this comprehensive, accessible and thought-provoking book will be of interest to teachers, student teachers, education students and all those more generally interested in issues of equality and human rights.

Mike Cole is Emeritus Research Professor in Education and Equality at Bishop Grosseteste University College Lincoln, UK. He has published a number of books in the field of education and equality and is well known for his research into issues of Marxism and educational theory.

Peter McLaren is Professor in the School of Critical Studies in Education, Faculty of Education, University of Auckland.

Education, Equality and Human Rights

Issues of gender, 'race', sexuality, disability and social class

Third edition

Edited by Mike Cole

Routledge
Taylor & Francis Group

LONDON AND NEW YORK

First edition published 2000
by Routledge

Second edition published 2006

This third edition published 2012
by Routledge
2 Park Square, Milton Park, Abingdon, Oxon OX14 4RN

Simultaneously published in the USA and Canada
by Routledge
711 Third Avenue, New York, NY 10017

Routledge is an imprint of the Taylor & Francis Group, an informa business

British Library Cataloguing in Publication Data
A catalogue record for this book is available from the British Library

Library of Congress Cataloging in Publication Data
Education, equality and human rights : issues of gender, 'race', sexuality,
disability and social class / edited by Mike Cole. — 3rd ed.
    p. cm.
    1. Educational equalization—Great Britain. 2. Discrimination in
    education—Great Britain. 3. Human rights. 4. Critical pedagogy—Great
    Britain. I. Cole, Mike, 1946–
    LC213.3.G7E334 2012
    370.11′5—dc23   2011022246

ISBN: 978-0-415-58417-3 (hbk)
ISBN: 978-0-415-58416-6 (pbk)
ISBN: 978-0-203-15552-3 (ebk)

Typeset in Bembo
by Keystroke, Station Road, Codsall, Wolverhampton

MIX
Paper from
responsible sources
FSC
www.fsc.org   FSC® C004839

Printed and bound in Great Britain by
CPI Group (UK) Ltd, Croydon, CR0 4YY

Contents

Notes on contributors

Mike Cole is Emeritus Professor in Education and Equality at Bishop Grosseteste University College Lincoln, UK. He has written extensively on equality issues. Recent books include *Marxism and Educational Theory: Origins and Issues* (Routledge, 2008); *Critical Race Theory and Education: A Marxist Response* (Palgrave Macmillan, 2009); *Equality in the Secondary School: Promoting Good Practice Across the Curriculum* (Continuum, 2009); and *Racism and Education in the U.K. and the U.S.: Towards a Socialist Alternative* (Palgrave Macmillan, 2011).

Viv Ellis is Co-convenor of the Oxford Centre for Sociocultural and Activity Theory Research (OSAT) and a Fellow of St Cross College. He was a teacher in comprehensive schools before moving into teacher education and educational research. His most recent book is *Cultural-Historical Perspectives on Teacher Education and Development* (Routledge, 2010).

Simon Forrest works in the Medical School at Durham University. He has a background in school teaching and research related to young people's sexual lifestyles, risks, relationships and identities. He has co-authored a book supporting teaching about homosexuality in the context of schools, *Talking About Homosexuality in the Secondary School* (AVERT, 1997), and has since published numerous papers and other articles in the field of young people's sexual attitudes and lifestyles. He is now a trustee of AVERT, which is a leading global AIDS charity, and contributes to local and national initiatives aiming to support boys and young men.

Richard Hatcher is Professor of Education in the Faculty of Education, Law and Social Science at Birmingham City University, UK. He has written widely on issues of education policy and social justice. He is also involved in activity on these issues within the National Union of Teachers. He is currently researching the education reforms of the Conservative–Liberal Democrat coalition government, with a particular focus on aspects of privatisation in the school system.

Jane Kelly retired from Kingston University where she had taught Art History and Women's Studies in 2002. She is an active campaigner on rights of asylum seekers and Chair of Southwark Day Centre for Asylum Seekers. She is also on the editorial board of *Socialist Resistance*, the journal of the British section of the Fourth International.

Jane Martin is Professor in Social History of Education and Head of Department of Educational Foundations and Policy Studies at the Institute of Education, University of London. She has previously lectured in History, Sociology and Education Studies at the University of Northampton and London Metropolitan University. Her publications include *Women and the Politics of Schooling in Victorian and Edwardian England,* winner of the History of Education Society Book Prize, 2002. Her most recently published work is *Making Socialists: Mary Bridges Adams and the Fight for Knowledge and Power, 1855–1939* published by Manchester University Press. Currently, she is President of the UK History of Education Society.

Peter McLaren was formerly Professor in the Graduate School of Education and Information Studies, University of California, Los Angeles, and is now Professor, School of Critical Studies in Education, Faculty of Education, University of Auckland. He is the author and editor of over 40 books in critical pedagogy, critical ethnography and the political sociology of education. Professor McLaren lectures worldwide, and his writings have been translated into 20 languages. He is the inaugural recipient of the Paulo Freire Social Justice Award at Chapman University. Scholars and activists in Tijuana, Mexico have created la *Fundación McLaren de Pedagogía Crítica* as an institution to advance Professor McLaren's work throughout Mexico and the Americas as well as the work of critical educational scholars worldwide. *La Catedra McLaren* was established at the Bolivarian University, Caracas, Venezuela. Recently, *Instituto Peter McLaren* was created in Ensenada, Mexico. Professor McLaren's most recent books include *Pedagogy and Praxis in the Age of Empire* (with Nathalia Jaramillo), *Capitalists and Conquerors, A Critical Pedagogy of Consumption*, and *Academic Repression.*

Richard Rieser is a disabled teacher and educationalist who has spent the last 25 years struggling for disability equality and inclusion in the education system. He currently runs the international consultancy World of Inclusion www.worldofinclusion.com. Richard represented the UK Disability Movement in New York during the United Nations Ad Hoc Committee that drafted the UNCRPD. He splits his time between championing parents who want inclusion for their children, training schools and teachers on inclusion and working to develop the capacity for inclusion and disability equality around the world. Recently he has led projects in Papua New Guinea, Saudi Arabia, Ukraine, Russia, Spain and France and South Africa. Richard is currently also coordinator of UK Disability History Month. He has written a number of books and produced several films about inclusion and advised the UK government.

Foreword

Capital unchained: the decomposition of world civilization[1]

It is evident everywhere that progressive educators around the world are harboring an anticipatory regret at what the world will surely be like if unbridled capitalism has its way. Great swathes of the globe are imploding from the expansion of the world capitalist system. And even during capitalism's current deceleration it is still lurching forward like Nosferatu in the German expressionist horror film, furtively picking its way through the murky catacombs of humanity, searching for new victims upon which to feed, as well as rectifying missed opportunities. Like the cybernetic hunter-killers from the *Terminator* films, pulverized by repeated assaults, capitalism keeps crawling forward, seemingly unstoppable. Already the juggernaut of neoliberal capitalism has left in its wake life-threatening poverty, ecological havoc, the amassing and concentration of wealth in fewer and fewer hands, a ceaseless advancement of insecurity and unemployment for already aggrieved communities, and worsening living standards and quality of life for the mass of the world's population. Capitalist globalization has meant a worldwide empowerment of the rich and devastation for the ranks of the poor as oligopolistic corporations swallow the globe and industry becomes dominated by new technologies. The transnational private sphere has been colonized by globalized capital, as corporations, financial institutions, and wealthy individuals seize more and more control of the production and distribution of surplus value. The creation of conditions favorable to private investment has increasingly become the cardinal function of governments. Deregulation, privatization of public service, and cutbacks in public spending for social welfare have been the natural outcomes of this process. The signal goal here is competitive return on investment capital. In effect, financial markets controlled by foreign investors regulate governments' policies and not the other way around, since investment capital is for the most part outside all political control. Even when countries such as the United States and its NATO allies wage brutal war on behalf of capitalist and geopolitical assets, citizens in the affluent West can no longer be offered any assurance that they will be able to find affordable housing, education for their children, or medical assistance. It is the International Monetary Fund and the World Trade Organization who oversee regulatory functions outside the purview of democratic decision-making processes. It is these bureaucratic institutions – including the World Bank – that have set the rules and that arbitrate between the dominant economic powers, severely diminishing the power of governments to protect their citizens, and drastically undermining the democratic public sphere in the process. Increasingly youth have been forced to sacrifice their futures in order to fund the endless wars on terror, to fund a crisis-response program of bailing out the banks and to bolster the extravagant lifestyles of the financial elite. This calls for a revolutionary upsurge on the part of youth, with teachers playing a vital role in educating for socialism as state officials consistently refuse to consider increasing taxes on corporations and the rich to prevent public service and wage cuts.

We are now in the midst of 'epidemics of overproduction', and a massive explosion in the industrial reserve army of the dispossessed that now live in tent cities – or *casas de cartón* – in the heart of many of our metropolitan centers. As we recoil from the most vicious form of deregulated exploitation of the poor that history has witnessed since the Great Depression, we continue to witness a re-feudalization of capitalism, as it refuels itself with the more barbarous characteristics of its robber baron and Dickensian-era past. As social 'actors' in the labor process, we have become the oxygen for the machines of capital accumulation, grist for the satanic post-industrial mills of the transnational capitalist class and bloodless pulp for the high-tech jaws of the corporate hyenas whose driving compulsion is to devour living labor; we are remodeled as the living dead, a personification of dead labor in the theater of the damned. We do not live with the global anxiety of impending catastrophe. We are this catastrophe waiting for a change of course.

The left's struggle against what appears to be an intractable and immovable force reflects the world-historical antagonism between socialism and barbarism, only this time such a battle is occurring at a time of unparalleled advantage for capital in a world where a single superpower has set its military into furious motion as neoliberalism's global enforcer. In short, our guardians of democracy have become icons of destruction in this age of terror. Efforts by the transnational ruling class that range from attempts at smashing unions everywhere, increasing utilities costs in townships such as Soweto, privatizing the water system in Bolivia's Cochabamba, to the marketing of antibiotics to pediatric patients by drug companies whose marketing researchers help them exploit the developmental vulnerabilities of children, have made it clear that it would sell the tears of the poor back to the poor themselves if it would result in a high enough profit margin. Here in the United States, do the vigilante patriots who patrol the Southern border and pistol whip with their newly minted glocks undocumented Mexicans even know that most US flags that have peppered the homes, storefronts, and cars across the country since 9/11 are made in China, and that Steve Walton, the poster-boy for the phrase, 'Buy American', now watches the WalMart chain he founded import 60 percent of its merchandise from China? But does outsourcing to China really matter to most Americans, given that much of their own apparel industry is made under similar sweatshop conditions, when even the Department of Defense buys some of its uniforms from sweatshop industries?

Clearly at this time of globalized financialization, we are suffering one of the worst moments in the crisis of capitalism. Accumulation by dispossession has marked the entire history of capitalism and we are now seeing the results of a very long crisis that began in the 1970s. We have to understand this as a serious systemic crisis. It is no runic mystery that the current system of world capitalism is unsustainable. The survival of humanity requires a new cultural compact and a new productive system that opposes the logic of capital and that creates a new social metabolism rooted in egalitarianism, community, and human development and a new metaphrastic liaison between theory and practice. One where we can prevent bureaucracy from rupturing our attempts at creating a socialism for the twenty-first century. Of course, discussions about socialism are not present in the United States except in small, specialized publications and among small groups. There are very few educators – even critical educators – that explicitly address socialism, or even use the word. The dominant political culture here is Paleolithic in its ideology and hence the struggle for democracy has become a parergon. Conservatives want the United States to assert its domination in world markets, even if it means asserting military strength.

In the United States today we have at the helm of the nation the first African-American president, elected with the highest popular vote percentage of any candidate of either party in 20 years, and the highest for a non-incumbent in a half-century – but he accomplished this with only 43 percent of the white vote. Many liberals thought this election to be a handsel, a sign that a new period of profound political renewal was at hand, emerging from the fetid swamplands of the George W. Bush disaster. While tacking to the center-right on most domestic and foreign issues – including his egregious handling of an unprecedented economic crisis by bailing out the banks and pandering to the financial sector to the detriment of working people – he has unchained a racist fury across the US mediascape on the part of right-wing pundits who have accused him of being 'demonstrably a racist', of caving in to the requests of people of color,[2] of being a race-baiter, of being the 'most racial president', of having appointed a 'racist administration', of using a 'black accent' when he addresses groups of African Americans, of preying on 'white guilt' and using 'racial anxiety' to get himself elected, of 'defending racism', of supporting civil rights groups that are nothing more than 'race-baiting poverty pimps'. Other pundits have argued that they are fed up with refraining from criticizing the president because he is of 'mixed-race'. Michelle Obama was accused of not attending the funeral of white senator Robert Byrd because she has 'authentic slave blood' whereas Obama does not possess such blood. Some media pundits argued that private businesses 'ought to get to discriminate' and 'it should be their right to be racist'. These are not isolated comments from the fringe internet but rather from popular radio and television personalities who not only echo the pre-civil rights–era racism but have spawned a new species of racism, which suggests anyone belonging to an ethnic minority group is racist if they happen to highlight the problems within their own communities. Any discussions that are not dominated by white men or women are considered to be racist. Now it is white people that are the supposed victims of the racism of people of color. Not only has capitalism grown a second set of jaws and is undergoing a ferocious re-feudalization by means of 'accumulation by dispossession' (Harvey, 2003), but US-based racism has intensified under neoliberal conditions fostered by privatization, financialization and the management and manipulation of crises and state redistributions. Moroever, as Steve Martinot (2010) notes, with the rise of twentieth-century US colonialism and imperialism, there is now an international third-world working class.

Attacks on progressive educators have been much more virulent since Obama was elected, partly because Obama is perceived as a socialist, which of course reveals how little Americans in general know about socialism and its history of development. While Republican members of the US Congress have accused Obama of being a socialist, Obama is being perceived by many right-wing extremists as part of a communist takeover of Washington. The country is becoming increasingly polarized; some have even compared it to fighting the Civil War all over again in ideological terms. So, of course, the left is further demonized by neo-Confederate ideologues along with the center-left, and Obama begins to lurch, politically rudderless, towards the right. Meanwhile people of color still lag well behind whites in almost every major social, economic, and political indicator. Social movement politics and not electoral politics is the vehicle for achieving racial justice. So it is unlikely there will be much change with Obama. Obama's policies on health care, immigration, jobs, racism, the jus belli wars of 'humanitarian necessity' in Afghanistan and Iraq (and now Libya), and the Palestinian question have not only fallen short of his promises; many of them have fallen into line with his loathed and failed predecessor. Obama doesn't like to talk about racism (and when he does he likes to remind people he is half white) and even suggests that America is now beyond race, fueling the eschatological myth that racism is now dead and the US has transmogrified into a post-racial society.

Obama wants to expand the military by 90,000, has redeployed troops from Iraq to Afghanistan, is a big supporter of free-market capitalism, and his policies on Cuba, Venezuela, North Korea, and Palestine are hawkish. Even while Obama denounced the human rights abuses of the Qaddafi regime, it was revealed through documents left behind as Tripoli fell to the rebel army that the CIA and MI-6 had a longstanding relationship with Qaddafi's spymaster office, and from 2002 to 2007, the CIA would send terrorist suspects to Libya to be tortured.

While clearly the struggle for racial justice has been banished to the hinterlands and willowwacks of contemporary political life, to its lowest point since the Kerner Commission Report announced 40 years ago that 'Our nation is moving toward two societies, one black, one white — separate and unequal', the election of Obama is unlikely to signal a permanent reversal of this trend. Has he not made speeches that excoriated black youth for a lack of 'personal responsibility?' Has he not avoided uncovering or even mentioning the real structures of institutional racism and white supremacy? In doing so has he not set the stage for the continuing demonization and incarceration of youth of color?

Obama is not pursuing prosecutions for high-level lawbreakers in the Bush administration. When, early in his presidency, he said nothing about Israel's massacre of the Palestinians in Gaza (where half the population are children) that was a telling moment. No words about the Palestinian casualties after Gaza came under sustained attack from supersonic aircraft and Merkava tanks and thousands of troops. No comments about the 40 women and children who were torn to pieces outside a school. No word about whole families ripped apart in their beds by Israel bombs that have killed hundreds of Palestinians.

Could it be that Obama has also forgotten the US-sponsored wars and military coups over the past 150 years? Has he forgotten the success of the United States in subordinating the economies and political structures of entire nations to the interests of US capital? Has he forgotten September 11? Not September 11, 2001 but the 'first' September 11. The first September 11 took place on September 11, 1973 in Chile. It was orchestrated by the United States government and succeeded in overthrowing the democratically elected government of Salvador Allende and put in its place the brutal regime of General Augusto Pinochet. What was to follow as a result of the first September 11 was the consolidation of other brutal regimes throughout Latin America with the support of Washington, creating a scenario which from 1973 until the Soviet collapse in 1990, saw the numbers of political prisoners, executions of non-violent political dissenters and victims of torture exceed those in the Soviet Union and its East European satellites (Chomsky, 2011). Could he also have forgotten the ongoing super-exploitation of the wretched of the earth, those who are trying to enter US and European borders to help support their families only to be demonized and thrust back into oblivion?

The choice of Arne Duncan as Secretary of Education by President Obama has been disastrous since Duncan is basically following many of the egregious mandates of the Bush administration, such as his immutable demand for high stakes standardized tests and value-added accountability schemes. It is a slightly softer version of Bush's No Child Left Behind Act in that it operates as a steel fist in a velvet glove. When it comes to driving present-day approaches to the crisis of public (state) schooling, Duncan abandons all pretensions to objectivity, revealing a strong ideological bent that is, no doubt, unrecognized by Duncan since it reflects the commonsense neoliberal logic of the day.

In my view, every student is endowed with the capacity for reasoning critically about his or her life and should be apprised of the opportunity for understanding the complex and multilayered context in which that life is lived; every student is capable and deserving of developing a moral conscience that respects others as active, uniquely creative, and dignified subjects of history. Every student has a right to ask: How can I change my present, in order to live in the future with courage, commitment, and a critical disposition that can make the world a better place for all those who suffer and are oppressed? Those who run the educational system in the United States care nothing about the rights and capacities of students; the system works to keep students good patriots and capitalist workers and cosmopolitan consumers, who believe their country supports and defends the cause of freedom and prosperity for all around the world. It is an education, in other words, in mystification.

During Duncan's tenure as Superintendent of Chicago Public Schools, the drop-out and literacy rate of the students worsened, the militarization of inner-city public (state) schools increased, the school system became more segregated, and schools that didn't meet the 'standards' set by state officials were shut down. In addition, mass-firing of teachers (sometimes, entire school staff) whose students didn't perform acceptably on standardized tests continued, and to replace these so-called 'failed schools' Duncan advocated the creation of charter schools, which often perform worse than public (state) schools. There is nothing on Duncan's agenda to improve the graduating rates of black and Latino students, which stand at 50 percent and 53 percent, respectively, or other racialized Americans.

The financial Katrina that has occurred within our winner-take-all economy has allowed the biggest debt bubble in history to fester without any control, causing the largest financial crisis since the Great Depression. We are currently in the midst of one of the most vicious forms of deregulated exploitation of the poor that history has witnessed since the 1920s. In virtually every country in the world, the gap between rich and poor has widened considerably as we continue to witness with dismaying regularity an obscene concentration and centralization of social, political, and, most importantly, economic power in the hands of a relatively small number of oligopolies. The combined wealth of the three richest people in the world exceeds the combined gross domestic products of the 48 poorest countries, and the combined wealth of the 225 richest people is roughly equal to the annual income of the poorest 47 percent of the world's population. Crony capitalism has ushered in the rebirth of satanic mills – child labor, slave-like conditions, young women and men working for a pittance in the export-processing zones where they are subjected to sly new forms of indentured servitude, and where trade unionists and labor organizers are routinely fired, beaten, or simply 'disappeared'. Immigrants in detention languish without lawyers and decent medical care even when they are mortally ill. Lawmakers are struggling to impose standards and oversight on a system deficient in both. Counties and towns seek federal contracts to incarcerate un-documented immigrants as prosecutions rapidly expand and as the government plans to build new family detention centers.

One in four jobs in the United States pays less than a poverty-level income. Since 2000, the number of Americans living below the poverty line, at any one time, has risen steadily. Recent statistics indicate that 37 million residents in the United States are now designated by the government as poor. Twenty-two years ago, American CEOs earned on average 42 times more than production workers. Today, they earn 431 times more. As more Americans become billionaires, the real median earnings of full-time workers continue to fall.

William K. Tabb (2008) notes the system itself created this crisis by floating the stock of new companies that promised to invest in high technology. Prices rose so high that the stock market came crashing down. When the Federal Reserve lowered interest rates and kept lowering them, it became easier for companies and individuals to borrow and it helped people pay off debt and borrow more, and low-interest mortgages made home ownership cheaper. As housing prices rose and kept rising, mortgage originators gave out easy loans with little or no down payment as well as offering low teaser-rate loans that would reset in the future, and interest-only mortgages became common. Adjustable-rate mortgages allowing borrowers to make very low initial payments for the first years became popular. The banks learned to securitize these loans by selling the collateralized debt obligations to someone else who would receive the income. You would get paid up-front with money you could lend to still more borrowers. Tabb tells us that between mid-2000 and 2004, American households took on three trillion dollars in mortgages while the US private sector borrowed those three trillion dollars from the rest of the world. Almost half of the mortgages were financed with foreign money. When the Securities and Exchange Commission changed the rules to allow investment banks to take on a great deal more risk, we saw the collapse of Wall Street as we have known it. When the big investment banks received an exemption from regulation, limiting the amount of debt they could take on, they borrowed and invested more in relation to the actual capital the bank possessed. But they ran out of money when things went bad. This is what happens when you put your faith in the magic of the market (the market is the singular most important deity in the United States) and allow banks to self-regulate. Social regulation in the public interest is, and has always been, anathematic to the ruling class, or the transnational capitalist class, however you describe the guardians of the interest of capital.

If we wish the patterns of taxation and pro-corporate policy to be transformed in the interests of greater economic equality, we need a complete rethinking of the system in terms of what economic democracy really means for the wretched of the earth.

We are entering a period where leftist educators must play an important role in the global struggle against finance capital. Financialization is not just a mistake made by greedy corporate executives, but is part of capital unleashed, part of the unrestrainment of capital. It is not so much a question of oversupply and under-consumption as it is the frictionless logic of capital in which we witness production occurring today solely for the benefit of capital in order to generate surplus value and profit, a process that effectuates to co-propriety of capital and power. While the postwar boom is now just a whiff of smoke in the rearview mirror of Hummers on their way to more current imperialist wars, America's biggest jobs program at present is the US military. Not including foreign contractors, 1,400,000 Americans are now on active duty, another 833,000 are in the reserves and another 1,600,000 Americans work in companies that supply the military (Reich, 2010). The only metro areas in which net incomes and personal earnings rose in 2009 were those with high concentrations of military and federal jobs. Sixteen of the 20 metro areas rising the fastest in per-capita income rankings since 2000 have military bases or a base nearby. Even weapons programs deemed outmoded or defunct by the Pentagon cannot be canceled because of the potentially devastating effects on the US economy.

It is interesting to note that Oliver Stone's new documentary, *South of the Border*, which interviews several left-wing leaders of Latin American countries, has included a new allegation from Argentina's former president, Néstor Kirchner, that sheds light on the US commitment to endless war. During his interview with Stone, Kirchner said he once discussed global economic problems with former President George W. Bush. According to Kirchner, when he suggested a new Marshall Plan to Bush, referring to the Second World War-era European reconstruction plan, when US$13 billion in economic and technical assistance was provided to help the recovery of the European countries that had joined in the Organization for European Economic Co-operation, Bush's response was totally negative. Here is an extract from the film:

> KIRCHNER: I said that a solution for the problems right now, I told Bush, is a Marshall Plan. And he got angry. He said the Marshall Plan is a crazy idea of the Democrats. He said the best way to revitalize the economy is war. And that the United States has grown stronger with war.
>
> STONE: War, he said that?
>
> KIRCHNER: He said that. Those were his exact words.
>
> STONE: Is he suggesting that South America go to war?
>
> KIRCHNER: Well, he was talking about the United States: 'The Democrats had been wrong. All of the economic growth of the United States has been encouraged by wars.' He said it very clearly.
>
> (Stone, 2009)

This, of course, begs the question: What kinds of jobs programs do we really need? Supplying the most powerful military in the world so that it can commandeer over 700 of its bases worldwide and continue its imperialist designs? What about jobs programs that produced light-rail trains, public parks, better school facilities, water and sewer systems, and non-carbon energy sources (Reich, 2010)? Did I say light-rail trains? Some conservative Republicans consider rail transportation to be a form of evil socialism, because it takes away the individuality enjoyed by driving a car. God Bless America.

In recent years it has become much clearer to me how and why much of the work by progressive educators in the United States has largely failed to effect the urgent and necessary advances in educational equality and social justice that are urgently demanded by the organic crisis we are facing in our schools. It is not that I have suddenly freed myself from the custody of progressive thought. Or developed an instant clarity of mind forged of the necessary revolutionary adamant to enable me to grasp ideas and do things that had previously orbited outside the precincts of my educational work. It is more the case that I have begun to take stock of the antedating achievements of the Marxist educational tradition in the United Kingdom and elsewhere, and have been engaging works that are clearly within – or at the very least indebted to – such a tradition. This is not to say that most of the educational reform movement in the United Kingdom has managed to escape the kind of despairing capitulation to the inevitability of the rule of capital and the regime of the commodity fetish that we have experienced among reform-minded educationalists here in the United States. Or that we need to misprize everything about the liberal tradition of educational reform. It has more to do with the fact that the critical tradition in the United Kingdom has begun to reemerge in important ways that its United States counterpart has not yet managed to achieve – namely, as a serious reengagement with Marxist analysis and the concept of social class.

But I would be remiss if I limited the rediscovery of Marx and Marxist analysis to leftist scholars in Great Britain. While the border that separates Marx from the academy remains, in the main, unbreached, the tradition of Marxist scholarship and the history of Marxist-driven class struggles is currently enjoying a spiked interest among some constituencies in the North American academy, including education, just as there appears to be a renewed interest in Marxism among grassroots activists, as evidenced by the various panels and sessions at the recent World Social Forums. But it is safe to say that the work being done by educators such as Mike Cole, Dave Hill, Glenn Rikowski, Paula Allman, and others has managed to stir a debate in the United Kingdom, which has so far failed to heat up with a similar intensity among the educational left here in the United States. This state of affairs is changing rapidly as the crisis of capitalism intensifies, world conditions continue to deteriorate into further criminal misuse and state terrorism, and as more Marxist and Radical Left works such as Cole's edited collection begin to attract audiences here.

It is in this context that the most recent edition of Mike Cole's *Education, Equality and Human Rights* needs to be read with renewed appreciation. Addressing issues that include the challenge of disability discrimination in schooling, gender and equality, 'race' and racism, sexuality and social justice, and class analysis and knowledge formation, *Education, Equality and Human Rights* is an urgent and important contribution to the social justice literature as it intersects with current educational debates and struggles. From the date of its original publication in 2000, this generous and luminous volume has deftly advanced the fecundating power of Marxist, neo-Marxist, and Radical Left analysis in moving educational change beyond the precincts of currently enfeebled liberal reform efforts. Its impact has been impressive and continues to wield considerable influence among theorists, policy-makers, and activists. Released in a new edition that will make it more readily available to educators, social workers, and students of sociology and the social sciences in the United States, this collection of essays could not have come at a more opportune time.

In the United States, the strategy embedded in the mainstream lines of descent emanating from Freire and his exponents and commentators of critical pedagogy has been to make the very concept of class a contestable social concept and an occasion to circumvent serious debate over the causes of exploitation and dynamics of the rule of capital, and to increase the plausibility of the liberal imperative of overcoming low 'social economic status', a notion that distantly mirrors the liberal mandate for advancing equal opportunity rather than fighting for social and economic equality. This is far from the position taken by Freire himself. We would be grievously underestimating the degree to which critical pedagogy colludes with ruling class ideology if we ignore its political inertia, theoretical flabalanche, and progressive domestication over the years.

Much (but of course not all) of the 'mainstreamed' critical educational work in the United States, along with work in related fields, now appears woefully detached from historical specificities and basic determinations of capitalist society to be of much serious use in generating the type of critique and practice that can move education reform past its log-jam of social amelioration and into the untapped waters of social transformation. What is not on offer is an alternative social vision of what the world should and could look like outside the value form of capital. What is needed is not an abandonment of critical pedagogy. What is needed is a revolutionary critical pedagogy. The construction of a new vision of human sociality has never been more urgent in a world of reemerging rivalries between national bourgeoisies and cross-national class formations, where the United States seeks unchallenged supremacy over all other nation states by controlling the regulatory regimes of supra-national institutions such as the World Bank and the International Monetary Fund.

It is a world where the working class toil for longer hours to exact a minimum wage that amounts to pin money for the ruling elite. Even if the ruling class somehow felt compelled to reconfigure its tortured relationship with the working class, it could not do so and still extract the surplus value necessary to reproduce and maintain its own class formation built upon its historical legacy of class privilege and power. It is a world where, in the United States, the percentage of youth with a summer job in 2011 was the lowest at any time since the Second World War and where tuition fees — already the highest in the world — are soaring.

It is also a world undergoing an organic crisis of capital as domestic class fractions within the United States not only struggle to avoid membership in

Marx's reserve army of labor, but are thrust, *nolens volens*, into service as the new warrior class destined to serve as capital's imperial shock troops, expected to fight wars of preemption and prevention declared by the US administration under the cover of the war on terrorism. When war is declared not only on terrorists but also on those who *might* one day become terrorists, you are, in effect, declaring war on the structural unconscious of the nation that you are supposed to be serving, nourishing the psychic roots of national paranoia. It is a war of both direction and indirection, a war without limits and without end, a war that can never be won except on the Manichean battleground that exists not in the desert of the real but in the maniacal flights of fancy of religious fundamentalism that we are witnessing more and more in the demagogic rants and spittle-flecked ravings of Republican and Tea Party politicians. The powers and principalities that duke it out with flaming swords beyond the pale of our cynical reason can only be glimpsed in the reverse mirror image of our particular liberties and values that we attribute to the resilience and successes of free market capitalism. The structural unconscious, that determinate social compulsion discovered by Marx, has been forged in the realm of capitalist unfreedom, scarcity, and deprivation (Lichtman, 1982). The structural unconscious acts behind the backs of individuals, but while doing so is wholly dependent upon the will, consciousness, and intelligence of social actors. But the structural unconscious does not coincide with the self-understanding of that will, consciousness, and intelligence possessed by members of society. The conscious intentions of US citizens have become so integrated into the social universe of capital and 'the imperial mentality' that their will and understanding has been defeated. If our social structures – including education – are irrational, then it stands to reason that the subjectivities required to reproduce them will be also. But the issue exceeds that of the role of the United States. The detritus of the transnational capitalist class is growing more and more visible throughout the world, as the poor in numerous developed and developing countries continue to be exterminated by war, genocide, starvation, military and police repression, slavery, and suicide. Those whose labor power is now deemed worthless have the choice of selling their organs, working the plantations or mines, or going into prostitution. Capital offers false hope but as it fails to deliver on its promise, the search for alternatives to its social universe continues. More false hope comes in the form of full-blown theocracies, or governments slouching towards theocratic ideals, and when these are seen for the perversities that they are, there is hope that a socialist alternative will prevail. Christian dominionists such as Congresswoman Michele Bachmann, currently a candidate for the Republican nomination in the 2012 US presidential election, believes in applying a biblical worldview to all aspects of political life and considers herself biblically mandated to occupy the presidency and to oppose humanistic statism at all costs. According to Bachmann, the Bible should be the guide for all political leaders in the United States until Christ returns. Bachmann's views are championed by the rapidly growing Tea Party movement throughout the United

States, a movement funded by the billionaire Koch brothers whose political platform corresponds to the Kochs' corporate interests. Longtime libertarians, the Koch brothers want to wipe out social security, to lower personal and corporate taxes, and to fight for less oversight of industry. In the United States, religious conservatives would like to bring all of this about in the name of Jesus.

In 1513, the *conquistadores* would read to the indigenous peoples of Las Americas a declaration of sovereignty and war, in the form of the '*Requerimiento*', to assert their domination over the entire continent. This document maintained that through St. Peter and his Papal successors, God ruled the entire earth and that Pope Alexander VI conferred title over all the Americas to the Spanish monarchs. Those indigenous peoples who did not convert to Catholicism were to be made slaves, tortured and disposed of in any manner deemed appropriate by the Spanish. If they refused, the *Requerimiento* stipulated that it was to be *their own fault*.

So instead of the *Requerimiento* being read threateningly from a brigantine anchored off the Yucatan peninsula to indigenous populations crowding the shoreline, we have gaining traction today paramilitary organizations, who volunteer to secure the border in T-shirts emblazoned with slogans such as 'Kill a Mexican Today?' and who, with the backing of politicians, businessmen, and wealthy ranchers, organize for-profit 'human safaris' in the desert. While there, ordinary citizens can join paramilitaries in catching the 'illegals' crossing the border, and if they are lucky, to have an opportunity to indulge in some savage beatings (that is, if *la migra* isn't watching).

If this situation isn't disconcerting enough, there's the bill that stipulates the banning of ethnic studies in Arizona schools, HB 2281, and SB 1070, the racial profiling law, and SB 1097, the proposed law that will require children to identify the immigration status of their parents, and HB 2561/SB 1308 and HB 2562/SB 1309 – bills that seek to nullify birthright citizenship (guaranteed by the 14th Amendment) to children whose parents cannot prove their legal status. But the most reactionary bill of them all recently introduced by state legislators is SCR 1010, a bill that seeks to exempt Arizona from international laws. Copycat legislation from Arizona is springing up throughout the United States as 15 states have introduced legislation closely modeled on Arizona's law since the beginning of 2011. Legislators in other states are waiting for clarification from the courts before introducing similar measures. New legislation has attacked the right of citizenship to so-called 'anchor babies' or children born in the US to migrant families (who might be stealth terrorists that would grow up hypnotically programmed to assassinate political figures). Fortunately, the two proposals to deny citizenship to the children of illegal immigrants faltered recently when proponents could not get the votes of a Senate panel. There was opposition from the business community who argued that, if passed, the proposals would hurt business ventures in Arizona.

Arizona lawmakers' attacks on ethnic studies programs is an attempt to preempt any opportunity to gain critical insight into the political workings of

US society that might be offered in such programs or that might compel the curious to question the status quo. Maintaining that ethnic studies programs teach hate, racial separation, and the overthrow of the US government, HB 2281 is really directed at the Mexican American studies K–12 program in Tucson. The program is dedicated to keeping Mexican-American students from being able to write an essay like the one you are reading. The Mexican-American studies K–12 program is not grounded in the revered Western canon, and its history does not commence with the pilgrim fathers; in contrast, the foundations of the program are built upon a 7,000-year-old maiz-based curriculum in which students are taught indigenous (Mayan) concepts such as In Lak Ech (you are my other self); Panche Be (to seek the root of the truth), and Hunab Ku (we are all part of creation). This program has a 97.5 percent high school graduation rate. For the stentorian sentinels of public (state) education, this program is an outrage; it amounts to sabotaging a rationally coordinated universe of multiple-choice tests with a pre-Cartesian unconsciousness, to despoiling the sacred Western monoculture and curbing its relentless spread. From the point of view of the oppressed, eliminating the ethnic studies program amounts to a form of cultural genocide, of epistemicide.

In addition to the attacks on immigrants and ethnic studies programs in Arizona, we have the inglorious case of Wisconsin. Wisconsin's Republican Governor Scott Walker signed a bill that ended collective bargaining for public employees, prompting protests by labor and student groups throughout the United States. The bill constitutes an outright assault on the solvency and quality of public (state) education. A provision of the anti-union bill that Wisconsin Republicans finally managed to pass authorizes state officials to fire any state employee who joins a strike, walk-out, sit-in, or coordinated effort to call in sick. Under the title 'Discharge of State Employees', the law states, 'The Governor may issue an executive order declaring a state of emergency for the state or any portion of the state if he or she determines that an emergency resulting from a disaster or imminent threat of a disaster exists.' Acting through an appointed body, the governor could then fire any employee who does not '(a) report to work for any three days during the state of emergency, (b) participates in a strike, work stoppage, sit-down, stay-in, slowdown, or other concerted activities to interrupt the operations or services of state government' (Eley, 2011).

In Michigan a bill has been introduced that could mitigate the powers of unions and elected officials. The bill, which has already been approved in the House, will allow the governor to declare a 'financial emergency' in towns or school districts and appoint someone to fire local elected officials, break contracts, seize and sell assets, and eliminate services. The United States is returning to a pre-civil rights era. Emancipation from the logic and practice of neoliberalism will require more than a generation to braird, and we cannot content ourselves with small victories that have forced themselves through the unexpectable fissures of neoliberalism's rust-splotched crust. We are in desperate need of a coherent philosophy of praxis. And this has never been truer than in the case of education.

The Marxist, neo-Marxist and Radical Left critiques found in the pages of *Education, Equality and Human Rights* in my mind more adequately address the differentiated totalities of contemporary society and their historical imbrication in the world system of global capitalism than progressive trends most often found in the educational literature in the United States. The text as a whole raises issues and unleashes the kind of uncompromising critique that more domesticated currents of critical education studies in the United States do not. And it brings some desperately needed theoretical depth to the tradition of critical education in general. Such theoretical infrastructure is absolutely necessary for the construction of concrete pedagogical spaces in schools and in other sites where people can be critically nourished in their struggle for educational change and social and political transformation.

Cole and his contributors collectively assert – each with their own unique focus and distinct disciplinary trajectory – that the term 'social justice' all too frequently operates as a cover for legitimizing capitalism or for tacitly admitting to or resigning oneself to its brute intractability. Consequently, it is essential to develop – as this marvelous book has done – a counterpoint to the way in which social justice is used in progressive education by inviting students to examine critically the epistemological and axiological dimensions of social democracy so that they might begin to reclaim public life from its embeddedness in the corporate academic complex. It is precisely this challenge that has been taken up and exercised with such success by the authors of this important collection.

A true renewal of thinking about educational and social reform must pass through a regeneration of Marxist theory within an eco-socialist framework if the great and fertile meaning of human rights and equality is to reverberate in the hopes of aggrieved populations throughout the world. One way to fuel the political agency of those who seek a non-capitalist future is to bring Marx out of the academic storage bins and into teacher education programs and explore the rich history of revolutionary struggle, which for me would include movements within the revolutionary or utopian romantic traditions (here I am referring to revolutionary romanticism as a critique of bourgeois modernity distinguished from its other incarnations such as restitutionist, conservative, or fascistic romanticism – see Lowy and Sayre, 2001). It is important that we should not be sidelined by cultural heterogeneities and versions of difference that the postmodern left uses to 'deflect the difference that makes all the differences: the social division of labor under capitalism' (Zavarzadeh, 2003). Marx (1972) argued that as intellectuals we must begin to engage in 'a ruthless criticism of everything existing' in addition to 'the self-clarification of struggles and wishes of the age.' This suggests an unrelenting critique of systems of intelligibility and epistemologies that are marinated in the coloniality of power, in the type of enlightened false consciousness that denies non-Western knowledges claims to truth and value (Quijano, 1991). It also suggests that as we participate in an analysis of the objective social totality: that we simultaneously struggle for a social universe outside of the value form of labor. If we are to educate at all, we must educate for this!

Capitalism continues to wreak its revenge, despite its present state of unprecedented crisis. Under the weight of neoliberalism, our historical narratives follow not a single chronology; they must live in moments at once recursive, fragmented, and entangled in the chiasmic turning points of popular struggle. Anti-systemic movements of all shapes and stripes are still around but have, for the most part, become domesticated into reformist shadows of their previous revolutionary selves, forming enfeebled and enfeebling popular fronts that fall like spent cartridges on the heels of any real challenge to capitalism. Here critical educators must take a stand, working for a political or direct democracy, for the direct control of the political process by citizens, for economic democracy, for the ownership and direct control of economic resources by the citizen body, for democracy in the social realm by means of self-management of educational institutions and workplaces, and for the ecological justice that will enable us to reintegrate society into nature (Fotopoulos, 2010). We may long for a dialectical reversal of the present crisis but unless we conjugate our longing with action and become the living loam of social change, we simply add to the bewitchment of capital. We must be devoted to fashioning the skills needed to imagine and bring about new forms of democracy that can foster rule by the people at the transnational level.

Latin America, in particular the Bolivarian Republic of Venezuela, represents a beacon of hope for such developments – for a socialism of the twenty-first century. Unsurprisingly then, it is to that continent that Mike Cole is increasingly concentrating his efforts (e.g. Cole, 2009, 2011; Cole and Motta, 2011; Cole and McLaren, 2011; Motta and Cole, 2012), in an ongoing attempt to make the case for exporting the Bolivarian Revolution worldwide. Clearly a democratic decision-making process should be utilized by those who produce and depend upon the profits from the productive enterprises of our society. If critical educational studies is to avoid being corralled into accepting the dominant ideology, or annexed to pro-capitalist forces among the left, or transformed into a recruiting ground for liberal reform efforts, or even worse, turned into an outpost for reactionary populism, it will largely be due to the efforts of people such as Mike Cole and his cadre of authors in this book. This third edition of *Education, Equality and Human Rights* will reinvigorate the debate over educational change. Not only will it become required reading for progressive educators, social workers, students, and professionals, but it will help tilt the scales of the social in the direction of real justice. We would do well to refuse the apparently inevitable and deepen our faith in the resolve, forbearance, and solidarity among the immiserated and the damned, those toilers of the world whose sweated labor can still be put to use in the graveyard of capital. We, the educators, are being educated to bring about a world that is hospitable to equality and social justice for all – a world where the prehistory of capitalism can be finally laid to rest.

Peter McLaren
School of Critical Studies in Education, Faculty of Education
University of Auckland, New Zealand

Notes

1   An expansion of some parts of an earlier version of this Foreword can be found in Peter McLaren, *Capitalists and Conquerors: A Critical Pedagogy Against Empire* (Lanham, MD: Rowman & Littlefield, 2005).
2   For the benefit of readers outside the US, it should be pointed out that 'people of color' in the US is routinely used as an inclusive nomenclature to describe people who do not self-identify as 'white'.

References

Chomsky, N. (2011). September 11 and the imperial mentality: looking back on 9/11 a decade later. In Reader Supported News, September 6, from: http://reader supportednews.org/off-site-opinion-section/423-national-security/7326-911-and-the-imperial-mentality (accessed September 6, 2011).

Cole, M. (2009) 'The state apparatuses and the working class: experiences from the United Kingdom: educational lessons from Venezuela', in D. Hill (ed.) *Contesting Neoliberal Education: Public Resistance and Collective Advance*, New York: Routledge.

Cole, M. (2011) *Racism and Education in the UK and the US: The Socialist Alternative,* New York: Palgrave Macmillan.

Cole, M. and McLaren, P. (2011) 'VENEZUELA: revolution under attack', *University World News*, February 20, No. 159, www.universityworldnews.com/article.php? story=20110218224050723&mode=print (accessed April 3, 2011).

Cole, M. and Motta, S.C. (2011) 'Opinion: the giant school's emancipatory lessons', *Times Higher Education Online,* January 14, www.timeshighereducation.co.uk/ story.asp?storycode=414858 (accessed April 3, 2011).

Eley, T. (2011) 'Wisconsin's anti-worker law: an historic attack on the working class', World Socialist Website, March 11, http://rtuc.wordpress.com/2011/03/11/ wisconsin's-anti-worker-law-an-historic-attack-on-the-working-class/ (accessed April 4, 2011).

Fotopoulos, T. (2010) 'Inclusive democracy as a political project for a new libertarian synthesis: rationale, proposed social structure and transition', *International Journal of Inclusive Democracy*, vol. 6, nos 2/3 (Spring/Summer), www.inclusivedemocracy. org/journal/vol6/vol6_no2_takis_CNT_Barcelona_2010.htm (accessed July 18, 2011).

Harvey, D. (2003) *The New Imperialism*, Oxford: Oxford University Press.

Lichtman, R. (1982) *The Production of Desire: The Integration of Psychoanalysis into Marxist Theory*, New York and London: The Free Press.

Lowy, M. and Sayre, R. (2001) *Romanticism Against the Tide of Modernity*, translated by Catherine Porter, Durham, NC: Duke University Press.

Martinot, S. (2010) *The Duality of Class Systems in US Capitalism*, unpublished manuscript, www.ocf.berkeley.edu/~marto/ClassDuality.htm (accessed July 18, 2011).

Marx, K. (1972) 'Karl Marx's 1844 Letter to Arnold Ruge entitled, "For a Ruthless Criticism of Everything Existing"', in R. Tucker (ed.). *The Marx-Engels Reader*, New York: W.W. Norton, 7–10.

Motta, S.C. and Cole, M. (2012) *Constructing Twenty-first Century Socialism in Latin America: The Role of Radical Education*, New York: Palgrave Macmillan.

Quijano, A. (1991) 'Colonialidad y Modernidad/Racionalidad', *Perú Indígena*, 29: 11–21.

Reich, R. (2010) 'America's biggest jobs program—the US Military', *The Huffington Post*, August 18, www.huffingtonpost.com/robert-reich/americas-biggest-jobs-pro_b_679426.html (accessed July 4, 2011).

Stone, O. (2009) *South of the Border*, Muse Productions.

Tabb, W.K. (2008) 'The financial crisis of US capitalism', *Monthy Review Zine*, October 28, http://mrzine.monthlyreview.org/2008/tabb101008.html (accessed July 4, 2011).

Zavarzadeh, M. (2003) 'The Pedagogy of Totality', *Journal of Advanced Composition*, 23 (1) 1–53.

Introduction
Human rights, equality and education

Mike Cole

International human rights legislation

As currently formulated, the concept of 'human rights' is a comparatively recent phenomenon. The President of the United Nations General Assembly, Dr E.H. Evatt, observed at the proclamation of the Universal Declaration of Human Rights in December 1948 that this was 'the first occasion on which the organised world community had recognised the existence of human rights and fundamental freedoms transcending the laws of sovereign states' (Laqueur and Rubin, 1979, cited in Osler and Starkey, 1996, p. 2).

Article 1 of the United Nations Universal Declaration of Human Rights states: 'All human beings are born free and equal in dignity and rights. They are endowed with reason and conscience and should act towards one another in a spirit of brotherhood' (cited in ibid., p. 173).[1] 'Brotherhood' is, of course, a sexist term. However, Article 2 affirms: 'Everyone is entitled to all the rights and freedoms set forth in this Declaration, without distinction of any kind, such as race, colour, sex, language, religion, political or other opinion, national or social origin, property, birth or other status' (ibid.). However, although Article 2 stresses 'without distinction of any kind' I would want to cite 'disability', 'sexuality' and 'age' specifically, in addition to the other examples given.

As far as education is concerned, Article 26 declares:

> Everyone has the right to education. [It] shall be free, at least in the elementary and fundamental stages. Elementary education shall be compulsory ... [and] shall be directed to the full development of the human personality and to the strengthening of respect for human rights and fundamental freedoms. It shall promote understanding, tolerance and friendship among all nations, racial or religious groups and shall further the activities of the United Nations for the maintenance of peace.
>
> (Ibid., p. 174)

Forty years later, in November 1989, the United Nations adopted the UN Convention on the Rights of the Child. Defining a 'child' as anyone under 18, 'unless by law majority is attained at an earlier age' (ibid., p. 175), the Convention reiterated the principles enshrined in the United Nations Charter and stated:

> The education of the child shall be directed towards . . . respect for the child's parents, his or her own cultural identity, language and values [and] the preparation of the child for responsible life in a free society, in the spirit of understanding, peace, tolerance, equality of sexes, and friendship among all peoples, ethnic, national and religious groups and persons of indigenous origin . . . [C]hildren of minority communities and indigenous populations [have the right] to enjoy their own culture and to practise their own religion and language.
>
> (Ibid., pp. 178–79)

In addition, 'children with disabilities' have the right to 'special care, education and training designed to help them to achieve the greatest possible self-reliance and to lead a full and active life in society' (ibid., p. 177). I would want to add to this Convention the right, when this becomes apparent, of children to their own sexuality.[2]

Human rights legislation in the UK

The Human Rights Act 1998 came into force in the UK in 2000. All public bodies (such as courts, police, local governments, hospitals, publicly funded schools) and other bodies carrying out public functions have to comply with the European Convention on Human Rights, which means, for example, that individuals can take human rights cases in UK courts and no longer have to go to Strasbourg to argue their case in the European Court of Human Rights (Equality and Human Rights Commission [EHRC]), undated a). Fundamental rights and freedoms to which individuals in the UK have access include:

- right to life;
- freedom from torture and inhuman or degrading treatment;
- right to liberty and security;
- freedom from slavery and forced labour;
- right to a fair trial;
- no punishment without law;
- respect for your private and family life, home and correspondence;
- freedom of thought, belief and religion;
- freedom of expression;
- freedom of assembly and association;
- right to marry and start a family;
- protection from discrimination in respect of these these rights and freedoms;
- right to peaceful enjoyment of your property;

- right to education;
- right to participate in free elections.

> (Equality and Human Rights Commission [EHRC], undated a)

Discussing Conservative Party suggestions to replace the Act with a watered-down version in the form of a 'British' Bill of Rights, Human Rights campaigner Peter Tatchell (2010) has argued:

> Despite its flaws and limitations, the Human Rights Act is probably the single most important piece of legislation passed by parliament in the last 30 years. It protects the individual against state intrusion and authoritarianism; asserting fundamental freedoms and liberties that a government cannot lawfully suppress.

'Thanks to the Human Rights Act', Tatchell continues, 'many government excesses have been overturned, including the detention of terrorist suspects without charge or trial and infringements on the right to protest and freedom of expression'. 'The Human Rights Act', he goes on, 'has also helped extend LGBT equal rights, such as securing "nearest relative" status for cohabiting same-sex partners (2002) and giving the surviving partner of a same-sex couple the right to inherit their deceased partner's tenancy (2004)' (see Chapters 5 and 6 of this volume for a discussion of sexuality).

Far from weakening the protections enshrined in the Human Rights Act, he makes the case that we need to expand and improve them. 'One of the flaws [of] the Human Rights Act,' he points out, 'is that it embodies all the limitations of the European Convention on Human Rights, which it copies and incorporates into UK law' (Tatchell, 2010).

The ECHR was first agreed, Tatchell explains, in 1950, when concepts of human rights were much narrower than they are now. As a result the ECHR and Human Rights Act include no explicit protection 'against discrimination on the grounds of disability, age, marital status, sexual orientation, gender identity, medical condition or genetic inheritance' (Tatchell, 2010).

> Moreover, the rights and freedoms guaranteed by the ECHR do not include economic and social rights, such as the right to a reasonable standard of living, to adequate health-care and education, and to a healthy environment. There is no specific, direct protection against discrimination in employment, housing, education, medical treatment and in the provision of other public services. These deficiencies need remedying in an expanded and strengthened version.

> (Tatchell, 2010)

It is time, Thatchell (2010) concludes, that Britain had a written Constitution with a Bill of Rights that includes an extended and strengthened version of the

Human Rights Act. Incorporating the Human Rights Act into a new Constitution and Bill of Rights would be a significant safeguard against tampering and subversion by an authoritarian or populist government.

Equality legislation in the UK

As far as equality legislation is concerned, on 12 May 2004 the government published a White Paper that paved the way for legislation to set up a single Commission for Equality and Human Rights (CEHR), which came into being in October 2007. The CEHR took over the work of the Commission for Racial Equality, the Equal Opportunities Commission and the Disability Rights Commission.

Seven years later, in April 2011, the public sector equality duty came into force. Those subject to the equality duty must, in the exercise of their functions, have due regard to the need to:

- Eliminate unlawful discrimination, harassment and victimisation and other conduct prohibited by the Act.
- Advance equality of opportunity between people who share a protected characteristic[3] and those who do not.
- Foster good relations between people who share a protected characteristic and those who do not.
              (Ibid.; Equality and Human Rights Commission [EHRC], 2011a)

Having due regard for advancing equality involves:

- Removing or minimising disadvantages suffered by people due to their protected characteristics.
- Taking steps to meet the needs of people from protected groups where these are different from the needs of other people.
- Encouraging people from protected groups to participate in public life or in other activities where their participation is disproportionately low.
              (Equality and Human Rights Commission [EHRC], 2011a)

The new duty covers the following eight protected characteristics: age, disability, gender reassignment, pregnancy and maternity, race, religion or belief, sex and sexual orientation. With respect to marriage and civil partnership, public authorities also need to have due regard to the need to eliminate unlawful discrimination against someone because of their marriage or civil partnership status. Compliance with the duty, it states, may involve treating some people more favourably than others (Equality and Human Rights Commission [EHRC], 2011a).[4]

The general principle of equalities legislation is surely supported by all progressive people. For Marxists, while socialist commitment is to a transformed world, any progressive reforms should be supported in principle (see Chapter 9 of this volume for a discussion of socialism and Marxism). However, the underlying intention of the legislation is not, of course, to transform the economic system. On the contrary, it is to make capitalism more efficient. As the EHRC admits:

> Compliance with the general equality duty is a legal obligation, but it also makes good business sense. An organisation that is able to provide services to meet the diverse needs of its users should find that it carries out its core business more efficiently. A workforce that has a supportive working environment is more productive. Many organisations have also found it beneficial to draw on a broader range of talent and to better represent the community that they serve. It should also result in better informed decision-making and policy development. Overall, it can lead to services that are more appropriate to the user, and services that are more effective and cost-effective. This can lead to increased satisfaction with public services.
>
> (EHRC, 2011a)

This is echoed by the current ConDem government (an appropriately named coalition of Thatcherite Conservatives and Liberal Democrats), which states:

> One of the key priorities of the Coalition Government is to support economic recovery and remove unnecessary burdens on business. The Equality Act 2010 is a major simplification of discrimination legislation that makes the law easier to understand and comply with and delivers significant benefits for business, public bodies and individuals.
>
> (Government Equalities Office, 2011)

While the contributors to this book would concur with benefits to public bodies and individuals, they are united in the view that equality should be pursued for its own sake and not related to 'benefits for business'.

The aims of the book

The purpose of this book is twofold; first, to create a better understanding of equality issues; second, to relate these issues to education. Hence the chapters of this book introduce the issues of gender, 'race' and racism, sexuality, disability and social class in their own right, before relating each specifically to education.

With respect to these five equality issues, five important points need to be made. First, they are all social constructs, which reflect particular social systems; they are not inevitable features of societies, but rather crucial terrains of struggle between conflicting social forces in any given society. In other words, I do not believe that societies *need* to be class-based, to have 'racialised' hierarchies, to have one sex dominating another. I refuse to accept that people are *naturally* homophobic or prone to marginalising the needs of disabled people. On the contrary, I believe that, in general we are socialised into accepting the norms, values and customs of the social systems in which we grow up, and schools have traditionally played a major part in that process. Where these social systems exhibit inequalities of any form, those at the receiving end of exploitation, oppression or discrimination have, along with their supporters, historically resisted and fought back in various ways, as the chapters of this book bear witness. Schools do not have to be places where pupils/students are encouraged to think in one-dimensional ways. Indeed, were this the case, there would be no point in this book. They can and should be arenas for the encouragement of critical thought. From a Marxist perspective, education should include a serious consideration of twenty-first-century democratic socialism. Elsewhere (e.g. Cole, 2011), I have referred to such education as 'the last taboo'.

Second, each of the issues under consideration in this book has a personal and an institutional parameter. In other words, people are affected by equality issues both individually and in the various institutions in society in which they interact.

Third, these inequalities are interrelated and need to be considered in a holistic way. Every human being has multiple identities. To take one example, there are, of course, lesbian, gay, bisexual and transgendered people in all social classes; among the Asian, black and other minority ethnic communities and among the white communities. There are lesbian, gay, bisexual and trans-gendered people with disabilities and with special needs.

Fourth, while recognising the interrelation of various inequalities, at the same time, their separateness must also be acknowledged. As will become clear in the chapters of this book, people are not only exploited and oppressed in similar ways, they are also exploited and oppressed in different and specific ways.

Fifth, rather than entertaining notions of 'fixed ability', I am committed to the belief, following Hart et al. (2004), that, rather than being constrained in their potential as a result of any aspect of their identity or identities, people are capable of learning without limits.

Since each chapter is introductory in its own right, I do not discuss each equality issue here. However, there is one final point to make in this Intro-duction.[5] It is necessary to make a distinction between equal opportunities and equality – the former the province of those who want a fairer and/or more cost-effective capitalism; the latter advocated by egalitarians such as socialists. Equal opportunities policies, in educational institutions and elsewhere, seek to enhance social mobility within structures that are essentially unequal. In other words, they seek a meritocracy where people rise (or fall) on 'merit', but to grossly unequal levels or strata in society – unequal in terms of income, wealth, lifestyle, life chances and power. Policies to promote equality, on the other hand, seek to go further. For example, egalitarians within education attempt to develop a systematic critique of structural inequalities, both in society at large and at the level of the individual school. Second, socialists are committed to a transformed economy, and a more socially just society, where wealth is redistributed and ownership is communal, and where citizens (whether young citizens or teachers in schools, economic citizens in the workplace or political citizens in the polity) exercise democratic controls over their lives and over the structures of the societies of which they are part and to which they contribute.[6] While equal opportunity policies in schools and elsewhere are clearly essential, it is the view of the contributors to this volume that they need to be advocated within a framework of a longer term commitment to equality. It is in this spirit that the book is written.

Notes

1   This citation from the Universal Declaration of Human Rights and the following citations from the Universal Declaration of Human Rights and the Summary of the UN Convention on the Rights of the Child are taken from Osler and Starkey (1996), Appendices 1 and 2 respectively. I have indicated the page number of Osler and Starkey's book on which each citation occurs. More recently Audrey Osler and Hugh Starkey (2010) have highlighted the struggle by groups historically subjected to discrimination for further legal measures to address specific issues. Their struggles have resulted in the UN's adoption of nine core instruments that now cover: the human rights of women, children, migrants and persons with disabilities; and the outlawing of racial discrimination, torture and enforced disappearances. The extent to which all the above human rights are fulfilled varies dramatically from country to country. Suffice it to say that the overall aims of human rights legislation have most definitely not been accomplished.

2   There are currently nine protected characteristics: age (referring to a person of a particular age or to people in a range of ages); disability (the possession of 'a physical or mental impairment that has a substantial and long-term adverse effect on that person's ability to carry out normal day-to-day activities'); gender reassignment (the 'process of transitioning from one gender to another'); marriage and civil partnership (marriage is defined as a 'union between a man and a woman' – civil partnerships apply to same-sex couples: 'Civil partners must be treated the same as married couples on a wide range of legal matters'); pregnancy and maternity (maternity is linked to maternity leave in the employment context – in the non-work context: 'protection against maternity discrimination is for 26 weeks after giving birth, and this includes treating a woman unfavourably because she is breastfeeding'); 'race' (also incorporates colour, nationality – including citizenship, ethnic or national status); religion and belief (generally as they affect your life choices [including philosophical beliefs and atheism] – normally in the definition only if they affect one's life choices); sex; and sexual orientation (Equality and Human Rights Commission [EHRC], undated b). Social class is not one of the 'protected characteristics'. For Marxists, social class equality is an oxymoron, since capitalism is fundamentally dependent on the exploitation of one class by another. The end of this exploitation would herald the end of capitalism and its replacement by socialism (see Chapter 9 of this volume for a discussion of socialism and Marxism; see also Cole, 2008, 2011). However, it is my view that discrimination with respect to social class origin (classism) should be part of the legislation.

3   As far as the private sector is concerned, a 'lighter touch' is applied. A private (or a voluntary) body is 'subject to the general duty in respect of any public functions which it has. The duty only applies to those functions, not to any private functions

the organisation carries out' [EHRC, 2011b). The EHRC gives the example of a security firm. If such a firm has a contract with a public body to transport prisoners, this would be covered by the general duty, but any security work it undertakes for a supermarket, for example, would not be covered (ibid.).

4   The rest of this Introduction draws on and develops Cole and Hill (1999).

5   Essential to this is the concept of participatory democracy, which is discussed in Chapter 9 of this volume.

6   Essential to this is the concept of participatory democracy, which is discussed in Chapter 9 of this volume.

References

Cole, M. (2008) *Marxism and Educational Theory: Origins and Issues,* London: Routledge.

Cole, M. (2011) *Racism and Education in the U.K. and the U.S.: Towards a Socialist Alternative,* New York: Palgrave Macmillan.

Cole, M. and Hill, D. (1999) 'Introduction', in D. Hill and M. Cole (eds), *Promoting Equality in Secondary Schools,* London: Cassell.

Equality and Human Rights Commission (EHRC) (undated a) *The Human Rights Act,* www.equalityhumanrights.com/human-rights/what-are-human-rights/the-human-rights-act/ (accessed 13 April 2011).

Equality and Human Rights Commission (EHRC) (undated b) 'Protected characteristics: definitions', www.equalityhumanrights.com/advice-and-guidance/new-equality-act-guidance/protected-characteristics-definitions/ (accessed 2 May 2011).

Equality and Human Rights Commission (EHRC) (2011a) 'Introduction to the Equality Duty', www.equalityhumanrights.com/advice-and-guidance/public-sector-equality-duty/introduction-to-the-equality-duty/ (accessed 10 April 2011).

Equality and Human Rights Commission (EHRC) (2011b) 'FAQs on the equality duty', www.equalityhumanrights.com/advice-and-guidance/public-sector-equality-duty/faqs-on-theequalityduty/#Are_private_bodies_covered_by_the_public_sector_Equality_Duty_ (accessed 10 April 2011).

Government Equalities Office (2011) 'Equality Act 2010', www.equalities.gov.uk/equality_act_2010.aspx (accessed 10 April 2011).

Hart, S., Dixon, A., Drummond, M. J., and McIntyre, D. (2004) *Learning without Limits,* Maidenhead: Open University Press.

Osler, A. and Starkey, H. (1996) *Teacher Education and Human Rights,* London: David Fulton.

Osler, A., and Starkey, H. (2010) *Teachers and Human Rights Education,* Stoke-on-Trent: Trentham.

Tatchell, P. (2010) 'Human Right Act needs strengthening, not weakening', keynote address to Salford University's Human Rights Conference on 4 and 5 June 2010, held to mark the first decade of the Human Rights Act, http://petertatchell.net/civil-liberties/human-rights-act-needs-strengthening-not-weakening.html (accessed 17 April 2011).

Chapter 1

Unfinished business

Women still unequal after 40 years

Jane Kelly

Introduction: women's liberation or post-feminism?

A superficial glance at the position of women in Britain 40 years since the first Women's Liberation Conference, held at Ruskin College, Oxford, in 1970, might suggest that there is little disparity between the positions of women and men, that equality has been achieved. After all, we have had a woman Prime Minister, many women have positions in the City, there are women chief executives of big companies, women vice chancellors in universities. Young women now outclass boys in exam results in schools and many subjects in university. Culturally young women have confidence, behave rather like men in their social life, they have choices that are light years away from those of women during the first half of the twentieth century.

However, if we look at some of the demands of the 1970 conference, it is evident that we are still far from having achieved equality. The right to equal pay, 24-hour childcare,[1] and free contraception and abortion on demand have not been achieved, despite legislative changes such as the Equal Pay Act of 1973. Some later demands – the right to determine one's own sexual orientation, the rights of black women, including the right to determine their own demands autonomously, reproductive rights, and the right to education have been partially achieved.

Although over 70 per cent of women are in paid work, a figure unchanged since 1999, women still only earn around 80 per cent of the male wage and these figures are based on full-time work.[2] Of course the high proportion of women working part-time do not earn anything like that percentage. The highest number of part-time women workers is to be found amongst those with dependent children because the high cost of nursery provision means that part-time work is often the only option for women.

The previous Labour government put in place a policy of a nursery place for every three- and four-year-old by 2004 and there was a threefold increase in spending from £66 million in 2001 to £200 million in 2003–04, creating one million new childcare places by March 2004. From September 2010 the free childcare entitlement for three- and four-year-olds was supposed to increase to

15 hours per week. However, since large proportions of mothers are returning to work soon after the birth of their child, the cost of childcare for the under threes remains very high.[3] So the Labour government's increase in spending on childcare was scarcely an adequate response to the needs of mothers for preschool childcare, whether they are raising children on their own or not. Furthermore, with the election of the Conservative and Liberal Democrat Coalition in May 2010 massive public sector cuts are likely so that the proposed increased hours of free childcare may not happen.

As for free abortion on demand, while abortion rights are less threatened by legal attacks than they were in the 1970s and 1980s, the service is still geographically patchy. Recent discussion to reduce the time limit because of medical advances in saving very premature foetuses has not yet led to legislation, but the threat to investigate a doctor for carrying out an abortion for a woman carrying a foetus with a cleft lip and palate shows that 43 years after the 1967 Abortion Act was passed, women still do not have a right to choose whether to have a baby. The provision for in vitro fertilisation (IVF) is also a geographical lottery with couples, including same-sex couples, often having to pay for private treatment because of poor NHS provision.

Postmodern feminism

Postmodern theory, though now less 'fashionable' than in the 1990s, has had a profound impact on analyses of the position and role of women and is quite incapable of explaining why, 40 years after the founding of the modern Women's Liberation Movement and the achievement of several pieces of equal rights legislation, such as the Equal Pay Act of 1973 and the Sex Discrimination Act of 1975, the original demands have not been met. The adoption of various post-feminist frameworks by many feminist writers and theorists has not helped us to understand why this should be the case. Postmodernism's refusal to analyse society as an entity and its determination to concentrate on the local situation means it is unable to understand women's oppression. Some feminists who have adopted postmodernism even encourage the use of distinct and often contradictory theories to look at different elements (e.g. Fraser and Nicholson, 1990, p. 26), which leads to incoherence and an inability to understand the interrelation between these different elements of the oppression of and discrimination against women.

Ever since the 1980s, the writings of the French female psychoanalysts Luce Irigaray and Julia Kristeva, who had been students of Jacques Lacan, have been increasingly adopted by feminists, along with the writings of Michel Foucault, Jacques Derrida and Roland Barthes. The stress these writers put on the place and role of the individual in society leads to real difficulty in analysing the position of women. They argue that individual consciousness is in a state of constant change, unstable and in flux; that the female subject enters the conscious world of male-dominated language and is thus inevitably discriminated against, forced to speak an alien language; that power is not centralised, for example, in the state, or some other recognisable authority, but is located within the individual herself. Consequently, the acquisition of knowledge or the ability to judge truth from falsity is an impossible ideal, best forgotten.

At the same time, many one-time feminists have assumed that so much has been achieved that there is little left to fight for. Successful careers have been built – as journalists, as politicians, as academics – from analyses once made of the rights and roles of women, but, whether out of pessimism that little can now be changed, or through a misunderstanding that their own lives represent all women's lives, a certain smugness has set in so that actual investigations into the real lives of ordinary working women are rare today. Instead the notion that women can make it if they try hard enough has taken hold, leaving the lives of the vast majority of working women unrepresented and invisible.

Despite the necessity of strategic thinking when dealing with something as pervasive as women's oppression, we have been left with a choice between post-feminists who deny that anything much needs changing or postmodernists who recognise women's oppression but whose framework is incoherent and contradictory. However, there is now some evidence of a revival of interest in feminism, including socialist feminism. This revival is still at a very early stage, but it seems likely that the effects of the financial crisis from 2008 and its impact on women's lives, especially their employment prospects, will reawaken research, activities and campaigns around women's issues.[4]

The refusal of postmodernism and post-feminism to think about the whole world and its relationships is thoroughly pessimistic and totally inadequate when it comes to changing the lives of half the world's population – namely women. In the current context of the twin crises of capitalism – the financial crisis leading to recession and public sector cuts and the environmental crisis – now more than ever we need an overarching theory in order to understand the problems, the position of women within the crises and some ideas to overcome them. I want to suggest that Marxism is much better placed to analyse these crises and to explain why women have not been able to achieve equality over the last 40 years.[5]

Against those who say that Marxist and socialist theory is gender- and colour-blind, that it 'has used the generalising categories of production and class to delegitimise demands of women, black people, gays, lesbians, and others whose oppression cannot be reduced to economics' (Fraser and Nicholson, 1990, p. 11), I want to argue for a return to the ideas of socialism and Marxism, to reject the criticism that it ignores and is ignorant of the position of women (and other oppressed groups), in order to discuss the position of women today in Britain. I think it is important to relate the ideological offensive against women, carried out by the Tory governments since 1979 and continued by New Labour after 1997, to the real position of women, at home and in the paid workforce, and to sketch out some areas of fruitful campaigning activity for the development of feminism and to fight for equal rights (see, for example, Kelly, 1992, 1999).

In this chapter I am going to look first at some examples of discrimination against women in the nineteenth century, as well as various struggles resulting in legislative or women's rights, including for both middle- and working-class women. Second, I will discuss some issues relating to women, work and the labour market today. I will explain why equal rights legislation has failed to alter women's position at work, and ask whether discrimination and inequality are direct results of biology – in the famous phrase: is biology destiny? – or whether the social position of women, especially the role played by women in the family, is more influential. Finally, I want to suggest one or two theories based on Marxism that may help us understand these problems, to put us in a better position to continue the struggle for equality.

Gendered divisions: women in the nineteenth century

While we should continue to press for the demands made in the early 1970s, we should not assume that nothing has been gained, and if we look back to the position of women in nineteenth-century Europe, we can see just how many reforms have changed women's lives since then. The Industrial Revolution, which moved production out of the home into the factory, had profound effects on both middle- and working-class women. It resulted in different spheres of influence and a gendered division, at least for middle-class women, between the domestic or private space of the home – the woman's world – and the public world of men.

In Victorian Britain, sexual hypocrisy meant that middle-class women were not supposed to enjoy sexual contact, while their husbands, partners in promoting the family values of thrift, sobriety and piety, used prostitutes in their thousands. The secondary position occupied by both middle- and working-class women in Britain in the nineteenth century is symbolised by the so-called 'rule of thumb'. Nowadays this means a more or less accurate measurement; then it meant that a man was legally entitled to hit his wife or partner, as long as the stick was no thicker than his thumb.

In Austria, too, Freud's discovery that many middle-class women suffered from what he described as 'hysterical symptoms', including temporary paralysis of limbs, has also been partially explained by reference to their seclusion within the home. Oppressive domesticity, daily unchanging routines, complete economic and social dependence on men led some women to rebel in the only ways open to them. Whether such hysterical symptoms were the result of real sexual abuse by their fathers, other male relations or close family friends, or whether the experiences had been fantasised is open to question; that the women experienced extreme physical symptoms for which there were no physiological explanations cannot be denied.

While the Industrial Revolution constructed a norm of oppressive domesticity for middle-class women, it also led to the growth of a new class, the proletariat, or working class, which included men, women and initially children as well. The contradiction between the ideal of a genteel, domestic femininity for women and the reality of working women's lives, satisfying the needs of the capitalist economy, produced a number of struggles for women's rights, fought for by both middle- and working-class women, most notably for female suffrage – the right to vote.

The demand for women's suffrage in Britain was fought for on and off during the whole of the second half of the nineteenth century and the first decades of the twentieth, and divided the British labour movement. The Chartist demands in the 1840s for annual parliaments, proportional representation and universal suffrage did not include the vote for women: they were opposed to female suffrage, as were many in the Independent Labour Party (ILP) during the last decade of the nineteenth century and the first of the twentieth, as well as the Labour Representation Committee (LRC), the early form of the modern Labour Party.

Conversely, at the turn of the century Keir Hardie, a supporter of women's right to vote and a radical member of the ILP, said that:

> he valued the zeal of middle and upper class suffragettes, but felt that 'without the active support and cooperation of working women they will have no chance whatever of being successful.' Much of his speech [in 1902 to suffragettes at Chelsea Town Hall] was devoted to countering the arguments against women's suffrage he had come across on the Labour Representation Committee. Socialists were fearful of the influence of the priest and the parson if women got the vote: Hardie said he preferred that to the influence on men voters of the publican (usually Tory) and the bookmaker. Trade unionists sometimes argued that votes for women could lead to domestic discord: what sort of domestic peace is it, Hardie asked, if it is based on the wife being treated as an 'inferior domestic animal'?
>
> (Liddington and Norris, 1978, p. 153)

The vote for women aged 30 years and over was eventually won in Britain in 1918 and in 1928 for those over 21, but it should be remembered that in France women only gained suffrage in 1944.

Other feminist campaigns in Britain produced reforms such as the Married Women's Property Acts, in 1870, which gave women the right to keep their inheritance and earnings; the Custody of Infants Act of 1886, which gave widowed mothers rights over their children, previously the responsibility of a male guardian after the husband's death; and in 1888 maintenance for deserted wives as long as the husband was at fault.

There were changes in education too, especially with regard to middle-class women. In 1850 North London Collegiate School, the first academically oriented day school for the daughters of the middle class, was opened, and in 1873, along with a number of general changes in education, Girton College, Cambridge, the first college for women, was founded. The setting up of mass education in the last decades of the nineteenth century is a telling example of the institutionalisation of inequality. Always related both economically and ideologically to the needs of the state, mass education was set up with class and gender divisions structured in. From the 1870s to the end of the century, working-class girls' education was dominated by training in domestic economy, in cookery and laundry – education for marriage and motherhood. In the early twentieth century, childcare was added.[6] In this same period the majority of middle-class girls were educated at home or in small private boarding schools, apart from the few more academic schools like North London Collegiate School and Cheltenham Ladies College (1854). These two had a broader educational content than schools for working-class girls, but like other middle-class girls' education, this content too was primarily training for marriage and homemaking.[7]

Until the end of the nineteenth century most changes pertained solely to middle-class women, since working-class women could afford access to neither education nor the law. However, legislation was passed that altered the lives of working-class women. In the 1870s and 1880s laws restricting the conditions of work for women were gradually introduced; for example, women (and children) were banned from working in the mines and from night work. This latter was a double-edged sword: women were only barred from night work where men were also employed, and this was usually better-paid work; they were allowed to work at night in the caring professions – nursing – and in places of enter-tainment, for example, bars and music halls. The exclusion from better-paid night work was achieved in the name of reform with the connivance of the male-dominated trade union movement that used the argument that a man was entitled to a 'family wage', enough to keep his wife and children so that the former should not have to take paid work.

In trying to emulate the middle-class ideal, the working-class wife and mother was made dependent on the male wage earner, and the man was made responsible for his whole family. In practice, of course, women continued to take paid work, but in the less well-paid and less protected areas.

This contradictory reform was not accepted without a fight. For example, in 1874 the Women's Protective and Provident League (WPPL) was formed to oppose both restrictive legislation for women as well as their exploitation at work. Launched by Emma Paterson, who was a bookbinder from Bristol, with the help of Mrs Mark Pattison (later Lady Dilke), the WPPL sought:

> 'the protection afforded by combination', thereby avoiding exploitation by employers and the hostility of working men who, fearful 'that the employ-ment of women . . . [would] lower their wages', were 'forbidding their members to work with women' and agitating 'to limit the hours of women's work in factories and workshops'. To Paterson, such legislation was offensive because it both reduced female earning power and put women on a par with children, for whom protection was also sought.
>
> (Bolt, 1993, p. 175)

But the legislation was passed anyhow.

This is not merely a matter of historical debate in the nineteenth century, for as recently as the 1970s trade unionists at the Cowley car plant in Oxford fought a long battle for the right of women to work nights, alongside men and for better wages than daytime work offered. This debate is part of the equality versus difference debate: do you fight for women's rights on equal terms with men – for example, making pregnancy and childbirth a temporary disability akin to breaking your leg – or do you argue that women's lives are fundamentally different from men's so that they need different rights and legislation to men, including protection from certain types of work, and in particular circumstances, during pregnancy, for example? Alexandra Kollontai, a leading member of the Bolshevik Party, took the latter view. In the period after the 1917 revolution in Russia she took up these issues and wrote a number of papers on them. As Alix Holt writes in her introduction to Kollontai's writings:

> Some of the first laws prepared by the commissariat related to the protection of maternity: women were given a legal equality that took their reproductive function into consideration. Women were not to be employed in various jobs harmful to their health, they were not to work long hours or night-shifts, they were to have paid leave at childbirth.
>
> (Holt, 1977, p. 117)

Kollontai had been discussing the needs of women in pregnancy and after childbirth well before 1917, including in a 1914 pamphlet entitled 'Working Woman and Mother'. Some of the demands she developed here included maternity insurance schemes to provide benefits for women for 16 weeks, or longer if the doctor thought necessary, both before and after the birth of a child. These were to be given directly to the mother, whether there was a live birth or not, and were to be one and a half times the woman's normal wage, or of the average wage if the woman was not employed. She was also to be entitled to benefits, equalling one-half of the normal wage, for the whole period of breastfeeding, and for at least nine months (Holt, 1977, pp. 137–38). For Kollontai, the reproductive capacity of women had to be taken into account as a special circumstance, not only for the sake of the mother but for the child's health as well.

Compared to nineteenth-century legislation in Britain, framed by the demand for a 'family wage', and leading to the exclusion of women from well-paid work, the changes introduced into the new Soviet Union were based on the equality of women, and their right not to be discriminated against because of reproduction.[8]

Women and work

Economic independence, paid work outside the home, has been seen by many as a prerequisite of freedom for women. The ability to take paid work depends on the control of fertility. From the outset the modern Women's Liberation Movement recognised the centrality of choice in matters of reproduction in the fight for equality for women. The development and introduction of the contraceptive pill, while it carried some unacceptable health risks, was still the first contraceptive method that could be relied upon to be effective, and meant that women could increasingly control their fertility: sexual intercourse did not any more lead inevitably to pregnancy and childbirth. The Abortion Act of 1967 also helped women in their right to choose whether, when, where and how to have children.

The control of fertility was an important development in the process of the incorporation of women into the workforce from the 1960s onwards. Women had been drawn into the workforce during the Second World War but were moved out of heavy industry and munitions afterwards. Although immigration from the Caribbean and from the Asian subcontinent was initially used to fill the labour gap, by the early 1960s this immigration was being restricted, and women were once again drawn into the workforce in increasing numbers.[9]

Today in Britain women make up 50 per cent of the workforce, an increase of 10 per cent since 1973. The largest proportion of women ever now works for a great part of their lives.[10] However, in the main, women's work is different from men's; it is within a segregated labour market, in worse conditions, for less pay and is more frequently part-time. The suggestion made by some who have adopted a post-feminist agenda that women have achieved equality at work is far from the truth. Even for middle-class women in such jobs as company financial managers and treasurers, where women's average hourly earnings amount to only around 60 per cent of men's, equality remains far away. It is true that in some professions and especially in the public sector women's pay is nearer to men's, but in most cases women are paid well below their male counterparts. Ironically the difference is at its narrowest at the bottom of the low pay scale, for example, among check-out operators and retail cashiers where women's average hourly earnings amount to more than 99 per cent of men's.[11]

In addition, the majority of women at work are segregated both horizontally and vertically. They are in different jobs from men, for example, in nursery and primary teaching, where the majority of workers are women; and in jobs that men do as well, but where women are usually lower down the scale or career ladder.

All this has an impact on the lower pay women receive. In the segregated labour market 49 per cent of women are employed in three areas of work: secretarial and personal assistants, sales and customer services, and personal services such as childcare, all of which are poorly paid. For example, childcare workers, who are 98 per cent female, earn on average £8,000 in a private day nursery, rising to between £10,000 to £14,000 for a qualified worker in an educational or social services setting. The average age of these workers is 32; many will be parents themselves. Such segregation leaves women in poorly paid work, in the service sector, in the caring professions, replicating expectations of women's work in the home.

One change that has taken place over the last ten years or so is the significantly higher number of mothers who return to work after maternity leave, though this is often into part-time employment. In 2008 two-thirds of working-age women with dependent children were in employment compared to 73 per cent of women without children. For women with children under five years of age 57 per cent were in employment, compared to 90 per cent of men. But large numbers of these women are working part-time (or in 'flexible work' as part-time work is euphemistically called). Thirty-eight per cent of women with dependent children worked part-time compared to 22 per cent of women without children.[12] A smaller proportion of lone mothers are in employment than mothers who are married or cohabiting. Fifty-six per cent of lone mothers were in employment, compared with 72 per cent of married or cohabiting women with dependent children. This figure for lone mothers has greatly increased since 2003 when it was 33 per cent.

The age of the youngest dependent child has an impact on the employment rate of lone mothers. Thirty-five per cent of those with a child under the age of five were in employment compared with 59 per cent of those with a child aged five to ten. The difference in employment rates between lone mothers and married or cohabiting women narrowed as the age of the youngest child rises, almost disappearing for women with dependent children aged 16 to 18.[13]

It is still the case that women rather than men take a break for childrearing – euphemistically called a career break – which also interrupts work patterns, affecting work and career prospects.

Where women work in sectors alongside men, they work in the lower grades with less pay. For example, the majority of teachers are women, but the majority of head teachers are men. This is replicated in the teaching unions: the National Union of Teachers has a majority of women members but only recently has a woman, Christine Blower, for the first time, become the General Secretary.

The Dual Labour Market thesis (Barron and Norris, 1976) describes this segregated labour market, pointing to the way women workers are segregated into areas of work associated with their domestic roles and responsibilities, but it does not explain why women are in this situation, why they have accepted this secondary position, why it is seen as normal, nor what employers gain from hiring women rather than men.

Women now represent around 50 per cent of the workforce, and the right to work and the right to choose both seem firmly embedded in contemporary thinking, yet women still only earn 80 per cent of the male wage. Why have the Equal Pay Act and the Sex Discrimination Act of 1975 not eradicated inequality?

To understand all this we need to look at the history of the last 30 years. The attacks by the Tory governments of the 1980s and 1990s that continued under New Labour are now being reinforced by the Coalition government of Tory and Liberal Democrats. I deal with this later in the chapter. The neo-liberal economic agenda, along North American lines, has led to cuts in the welfare state, increasing privatisation of public sector provision, worsening working conditions, including working very long hours or having more than one job: all this affects the position of women for the worse. At home, women are now responsible for more caring than in the past, including for the sick, the disabled and the elderly, picking up the pieces of the disintegrating welfare system. It is estimated that six million people (58 per cent women) are carers, often holding down a paid job as well. This saves the state £87 billion pounds a year, and as we face public sector cuts following the financial crisis these numbers can only increase.[14] In their paid work outside the home, women are the majority of workers in the public sector – in the NHS, in education, in social services – where conditions have worsened considerably.

Dramatic and startling changes in employment took place in Britain in the 1980s and 1990s. There was a massive loss of traditional jobs in engineering, mining and manufacturing. These were jobs with high status, good conditions and pay, full-time and unionised, with trade unions that fought to improve conditions, such as the installation of pit-head baths for miners, and they were jobs for men. There was a parallel increase in the service sector, jobs with flexible hours, part-time and short-term contracts, poorly paid and non-unionised: these are women's jobs.[15]

These structural changes go some way to explaining why women have not achieved equal pay: there is both horizontal and vertical segregation between men and women at work. Women work in the segregated labour market and in jobs at the bottom of the ladder. Assumptions about women's wider roles of responsibility for home and children make their paid work secondary. This not only includes women with husbands or partners but single women and female single parents.

Does this mean, therefore, that the oppression of women is based on biological difference? Does the biological fact of women's procreative capacity inevitably lead to this position of inequality? Is this position unalterable? Or is it rather a result of the particular ways in which our society operates, and therefore would another type of society have different solutions? I will now turn to elements of Marxist theory to offer some possible explanations for women's inequality that suggest this is not simply a function of biology, but is fundamentally determined by the economic and social demands of capital, which uses biology to reinforce the secondary role of women and sustains gender divisions to maintain its rule.

Divide and rule: production, reproduction and the reserve army of labour

Capitalist society divides not only by class, but takes advantage of other divisions, including sex and 'race', to maintain its rule. Engels linked together the production of goods for use or sale and the reproduction of life, recognising that women's oppression had been used by the ruling class to maintain power in all societies. 'The decisive element of history is pre-eminently the production and reproduction of life and its material requirements' (Engels, 1978 [1884], p. 4). In *The Origin of the Family, Private Property and the State*, Engels shows that the way in which a society reproduces itself (makes things, provides food and shelter, and so on) will affect everything about that society.[16] Thus he argues that where the capitalist mode of production predominates, where the law of value reigns, where production for profit supersedes production for use, the same ideas also influence such intimacies as marriage and family life. Within the family, he says, women are oppressed as a secondary partner – within the family he is the bourgeois and the wife represents the proletariat – used to reproduce both the present and future labour force cheaply, as well as providing a source of cheap labour outside the home.[17]

Women are expected to reproduce the future labour force by childbearing. In addition, they are expected to 'service' the other members of the family for free: shopping, preparing food, cooking, cleaning, giving emotional support; all these are the responsibility of women, to such an extent that women often find themselves without any knowledge or understanding of their own emotional and practical needs.

As socialist feminists have pointed out, Marx and Engels gave insufficient weight to the way in which a woman's entry into the workforce is determined by her role in the family; instead they analysed the family and paid work separately.

> Marx's analysis of the general tendencies within capitalism provides the foundation for the analysis of female wage labour, but . . . his specific, and extremely fragmentary, allusions to the position of women are unsatisfactory because he, like Engels, does not adequately analyse the relationship between the family and the organisation of capitalist production.
>
> (Beechey, 1987, p. 56)

Domestic roles played by women clearly influence the way they work and the kinds of jobs they do. Putting women's reproductive and domestic roles first, women's paid work outside the home is less valued than male work. Even when the woman is in fact the sole wage earner and where women make up half the workforce, it is assumed that their work is secondary to a male wage. This devaluing of women's work is based on the idea of the 'family wage' referred to above, a wage earned by the man, enough to cover the cost of housing and feeding the wife and family so that when a woman works, this cost is assumed to have already been paid – whatever the actual situation – so that she can be paid less. Thus women's work is seen as less important than men's and is paid at a lower rate.

Alongside the analysis of the oppression of women in the family, the Marxist concept of the reserve army of labour is also relevant. In the nineteenth century, Marx identified young people and agricultural workers who had been replaced by machinery, as well as the unemployed, as 'the industrial reserve army of surplus-population' (1876, cited in Beechey, 1987, p. 46). More recently feminists have located women, too, as a social group used in the same way (Bruegel, 1986, pp. 40–53; Beechey, 1987, pp. 45–50, 87–88). The use of women as part of the reserve army depends on existing, in this case sexual, divisions in the working class.

The reserve industrial army is necessary to capital in at least two ways:

> it provides a disposable and flexible population . . . labour power that can be absorbed in expanding branches of production when capital accumulation creates a demand for it, and repelled when the conditions of production no longer require it . . . It is also seen as a condition of competition among workers, the intensity of which depends on the pressure of the relative surplus population. This competitive pressure has two consequences. It depresses wage levels: Marx argues that the general movements of wages are regulated by the expansion and contraction of the industrial reserve army, which in turn corresponds to periodic changes in the industrial cycle. Competition also forces workers to submit to increases in the rate of exploitation through the pressure of unemployment.
>
> (Beechey, 1987, pp. 47–48)

The first point is best exemplified by the way in which women were drawn into engineering and munitions factories during the Second World War to replace the male population who were fighting. Nurseries were provided for children to facilitate this. With the return of soldiers into civilian life in 1945, women were encouraged to go back to their domestic roles, or into the caring and service sectors.

The second point, the ability of the reserve army to depress wages (and conditions), partly explains what took place during the 1980s and 1990s. These two decades saw a massive growth of women's jobs, alongside a loss of male ones, but it was not an equal swap. Male jobs in engineering, steel, mining, manufacturing, jobs that were unionised, with decent wages and security, were lost. Work normally associated with women and young people, in the service sector, in sales, and so on, jobs that are predominantly non-unionised, poorly paid, often part-time, sometimes on short-term, even zero-hours contracts – the infamous 'Mc Job'[18] – were created. In the process women and young people brought into the workforce were used to undermine the conditions and wages of traditional, male work and to introduce and normalise to the whole workforce such notions as part-time working and short-term contracts. This is the so-called 'flexible workforce'.

By the middle of the 1990s the composition of the labour force had changed. According to *Labour Market Trends* (March 1997), over 70 per cent of women between the ages of 16 and 59 were economically active at the start of 1996. Forty-four per cent were working part-time, compared to 8 per cent of men.

Of the 5.8 million people working part-time, 82 per cent were women (Sly, Price and Ridson, 1997). However, the 8 per cent of men working part-time doubled between 1986 and 1996, whereas the percentage of women working part-time had increased by only 1 per cent. The figures for temporary work are even more striking: the number of women in temporary jobs increased by 23 per cent, while for men the figure was 74 per cent.

It seems to be the case that the work of women, defined by their expected domestic roles, has been used to undermine both the level of wages and the conditions of work in the late twentieth century. While there have been a number of other factors in this process, including economic stagnation, de-industrialization, high levels of general unemployment and attacks on trade union rights, women's position as part of the reserve army of labour is at least one element in the process.

More recently the reserve army of labour has been augmented by a new group of workers – documented and undocumented migrant workers, including those from Eastern Europe, now part of the EU. Nobody knows how many undocumented migrant workers there are in Britain, but it is probably in the hundreds of thousands. They have come from all over the world, including Asia and Africa, and have little or no protection under law against their employers, landlords or others who control their lives. They are added to by the more numerous migrant workers with visas or work permits. But such legality does not guarantee dignity, decent wages, working conditions and lodgings. On the contrary, as recent events in Britain have exposed, legal and illegal workers can be equally exploited. Such migrant labour is used in food harvesting, food packaging, catering, construction and cleaning. In cities, especially in London, casual work in the building trade is increasingly carried out by migrant workers from Eastern Europe rather than from Ireland as was the tradition.[19]

With the new accession countries now part of the European Union (EU), two classes of migrant workers are emerging: those from the EU who may stay, and those from outside the EU who will only be allowed to stay for a short period, and without their families. This is creating a new 'reserve army of labour'.

Amongst these workers are many women; not working in agriculture or the building trade, but in the leisure and service industry, especially in the south east and in London. Cooking, serving and cleaning in the restaurants and bars, cleaning offices in the early morning and at night, and in the sex industry, in massage parlours, sex clubs, including lap-dancing clubs, and as prostitutes on the streets: women from Eastern Europe, from African countries and from Asia are doing the work that many women born here now refuse to do – at least for the minimum wages offered for these jobs, or in the conditions imposed in the sex industry.

Having used women born here to undermine wages and conditions in the 1980s and 1990s, this new reserve army, women and men forced to flee countries devastated by the neo-liberal economic policies imposed by the

International Monetary Fund and by the World Bank, and in some cases by the effects of climate change in their home countries, is being used to maintain and raise the profits of capitalism. Whilst racist attacks by politicians and the media on asylum seekers and economic migrants continue to try to divide and rule working people, anti-racists must argue for equal rights for these workers, including the right to join a trade union, so that their role as a reserve army is reduced as much as possible.[20]

Women and the recession

The impact of the recession and impending public sector cuts on women's employment is still unclear at the time of writing (February 2011). While women's employment has significantly increased over the last 30 years and men's has decreased, in the last recession the rate of female unemployment was much lower than for men. Over a similar period, while male part-time work has increased it is still much lower than for women – 16.1 per cent compared to 29 per cent. There is also a much greater contribution by women to the family income, especially as over one-quarter of all families are headed by a single parent, 90 per cent of whom are women.

However, a recent TUC report, *Women and the Recession*, published in 2009, revealed 600,000 women were facing involuntary part-time work, and 250,000 in involuntary temporary work: thus 10.3 per cent of women would prefer to be working full-time, the highest figure since March 1996.[21]

A very high proportion of women work in the public sector – 5,748,000 compared to 2,488,000 men – including in education, health and public administration. This represents 40 per cent of female employment compared to 15 per cent for men.[22] It is here in the next period where we will see much greater levels of redundancy that will hit women harder than men, not least because women are often in low-paid jobs and are unable to save for the difficult times ahead. The decision of the Tory/Liberal Democrat Coalition to prioritise paying back the deficit created by the near collapse of the banking sector will lead to swingeing public sector cuts, including a pay freeze, redundancies and cuts in pension provision over the next four years.

According to the Fawcett Society[23] the government failed to carry out an 'equality impact assessment' to show how their budget plans will affect women. Research by the House of Commons library, commissioned by shadow minister Yvette Cooper, claims women will suffer 72 per cent of the tax and benefit cuts. Four in 10 working women are in public sector jobs – which will be hit by a pay freeze and projected net losses of 600,000 posts. Women also make up 85.4 per cent of part-time jobs in the civil service, which makes them vulnerable to redundancy and job losses.

Among the long list of welfare benefits likely to be cut in the budget women will again suffer the most. Cutting back the Sure Start maternity grant will affect 262,000 women and no men; freezing child benefit, mostly paid direct to mothers, will affect a disproportionate number of women; housing benefit cuts will affect 2.9 million women against 1.9 million men; the tax credit reforms, and the removal of income support for lone parents when their children reach the age of five, instead of seven, will affect single parents, nine out of 10 of whom are women.

Although public sector pensions have been better than in the private sector, because women often have breaks in work owing to childcare, their pensions are still only 62 per cent of men's. Thus women are facing higher levels of unemployment and underemployment, have greater responsibilities for the family income, and will therefore suffer more than men in the coming period. Further, as users of public sector services, cuts in the welfare state will also affect women disproportionately.

The Coalition government's plan to replace lost public sector services by the vague notion of a 'big society' is riddled with flaws and contradiction. The idea that day centres for the elderly and disabled, legal advice centres, after-school clubs and the like can be run on unpaid voluntary labour is a nonsense. For any community or voluntary group to run effectively and efficiently there need to be experienced, paid workers at the heart of it – not least to organise the volunteers. Many such groups in existence for a number of years, such as the 60-year-old Refugee Council and the Citizen's Advice Bureau, are facing a huge loss of central or local government funding. The Refugee Council and other refugee services are facing a 60 per cent cut in April 2011 and a total cut in September 2011. It has already closed its day centre provision. There are increasing numbers of women and children using these and other asylum services as they flee war, famine and the effects of climate change in parts of Africa, Asia and elsewhere.

Just as the demand for legal advice on debt, cuts in benefits and homelessness is growing, local offices of the Citizen's Advice Bureau are closing their doors. The Tory mantra that 'We are all in this together' has never seemed so callous and cynical.

Conclusion

While formal equality may seem to have been achieved by equal pay laws and legislation outlawing sexual discrimination, capital works in devious ways to outwit and undermine such reforms. Formal legal equality within a capitalist society can never be real equality. Even though campaigning for such legislation is important in raising consciousness on these issues, we cannot depend on the legal process alone to achieve it. Underlying, structural reasons, the way in which capital operates, at both economic and ideological levels, make real equality more or less impossible to achieve under capitalism. However many women are in work, it is unlikely that we will be given equal pay, access to all levels and grades of work, adequately paid maternity leave (to say nothing of paternity leave), free childcare, equal rights in practice, without a complete change in the system. But fighting for changes now is not a waste of time. The achievements of the Women's Movements in the nineteenth and twentieth centuries put us in a better position than ever before to fight for equality with men. However, without realistically assessing our actual situation, that fight will take place with one hand tied behind our backs.

Forty years after the first Women's Liberation Conference in Oxford, women remain unequal – at work, in the home, in legal and social institutions. Achievements in some areas such as divorce, reproductive rights and legislation on equal pay and against sex discrimination are open to reversals and are often unenforceable. Capitalists and their supporters gain from social division and will always impede genuine equal rights for all, since capitalism is a system premised on inequality and the right of the rich to exploit the poor.

Notes

1 This should not be misunderstood as care for each child for 24 hours, but the availability of childcare for women at all times, thus allowing women to choose when to work and to have some leisure time without childcare responsibilities.

2 The largest difference in the average full-time hourly rate is in London where women earn only 76.4 per cent of the male rate. Furthermore if you look at weekly earnings, on average women work 3.5 hours less than men, so the figure drops to 75.4 per cent of male earnings. All figures from National Statistics at www.statistics. gov.uk unless otherwise stated.

3 According to the National Childcare Trust costs in 2010 are on average £88 for a 25-hour week, equal to more than half the gross average part-time pay of £153 a week. This is much higher in London with up to £11,050 a year being paid for a 25-hour week. Figures from www.daycaretrust.org.uk.

4 See Nina Power (2009) and Lindsey German (2007).

5 For a Marxist critique of poststructuralism and postmodernism, see Cole (2008, Chapters 4 and 5).

6 This was in response to fears of a decline of the 'race' in the face of the growing Empire, and more particularly the discovery of the poor health of working-class recruits in the Boer War 1899–1902 and the First World War in 1914. There was also a falling birth rate and rising infant mortality rates.

7 While it will not come as a surprise to anyone that in the nineteenth century education was oppressively gendered, it may come as more of a shock to discover that as late as 1963 the Newsom Committee Report, *Half Our Future*, published by the Central Advisory Council for Education, 1963, argued that for girls of average or less than average ability (whatever that is): 'their most important vocational concern [is] marriage', and therefore domestic science, as it became known, remained high on the curriculum agenda, with girls given the chance to run a flat for a week. Incidentally the mothers of these same girls were by this time almost certainly working outside the home (Open University, 1984; for a detailed discussion of gender and education, see Chapter 2 of this volume).

8 It is of course true that the appalling economic plight of the Soviet Union in the years following the revolution meant that, as Holt tellingly states, 'the collective was unable to do its duty towards women' (Holt, 1977, p. 120).

9 The percentages of women in work show an upward curve from around 30 per cent in 1918 to around 50 per cent today, but the sharpest increase is from the 1960s.

10 Seventy per cent of women are now part of the labour force in Britain, increased from 56 per cent in 1971. Comparable figures for men are 78 per cent in 2008 compared to 92 per cent in 1971.

11 'The gender pay gap – why it widened in 2002', Incomes Data Service, 20 January 2003, www.incomesdata.com.

12 Figures for men 4 per cent and 7 per cent respectively.

13 www.statistics.gov.uk.

14 www.carersuk.org/.

15 Income Data Services Ltd (1993) shows women as 49 per cent of the workforce, with a rise between 1973 and 1993 of two million women's jobs and a loss of 2.8 million male jobs. But this was not a straight swap, since at least 45 per cent of women in the 1990s were working part-time. In 1993 35 per cent of all workers were not in full-time, permanent jobs.

16 Engels (1978 [1984], p. 85).

17 The costs of rearing children, shopping for and cooking for a family, if paid at a going rate, would be astronomical.

18 This term comes from the employment practices of fast-food outlets, which include zero-hours contracts and employees clocking on and off dependent on the level of custom. Most of the employees are young.

19 I am indebted to Bill MacKeith's (2004) article for material in this section.

20 See Chapter 3 of this volume for a (neo-)Marxist analysis of migration and racism including that directed at Eastern European migrant workers; for comprehensive analyses of the multifaceted nature of racism in the UK, also written from a (neo-)Marxist perspective, see Cole (2011, Chapter 2).

21 Comparable figures for men are 24.9 per cent, the highest since February 1997. Involuntary temporary work numbers are 30.7 per cent for women and 38.9 per cent for men.

22 In the civil service these figures are even higher. The workforce is 67 per cent female and of part-time workers 87 per cent are women.

23 www.fawcettsociety.org.uk.

References

Barron, R.D. and Norris, E.R. (1976) 'Sexual Divisions and the Dual Labour Market', in D.L. Barker and S. Allen (eds), *Dependence and Exploitation in Work and Marriage*, London: Longman.

Beechey, V. (1987) *Unequal Work*, London: Verso.

Bolt, C. (1993) *The Women's Movements in the United States and Britain from the 1790s to the 1920s*, London: Harvester Wheatsheaf.

Bruegel, I. (1986) 'The Reserve Army of Labour, 1974–1979', in Feminist Review (ed.), *Waged Work: A Reader*, London: Virago.

Cole, M. (2008) *Marxism and Educational Theory: Origins and Issues*, London: Routledge.

Cole, M. (2011) *Racism and Education in the U.K. and the U.S.: Towards a Socialist Alternative,* New York: Palgrave Macmillan.

Engels, F. (1978 [1884]) *The Origin of the Family, Private Property and the State*, Peking: Foreign Language Press.

Fraser, N. and Nicholson, L.J. (1990) 'Social Criticism without Philosophy: An Encounter between Feminism and Postmodernism', in L.J. Nicholson (ed.), *Feminism/Postmodernism*, New York: Routledge.

German, L. (2007) *Material Girls: Women, Men and Work*, London: Bookmarks.

Holt. A. (1977) *Alexandra Kollontai: Selected Writings*, London: Allison and Busby.

Income Data Services Ltd (1993) *Management Pay Review*, May, London: IDS.

Kelly, J. (1992) 'Postmodernism and Feminism', *International Marxist Review*, 14 (Winter), Paris: Presse-Edition-Communication (PEC).

Kelly, J. (1999) 'Postmodernism and Feminism: The Road to Nowhere', in D. Hill, P. McLaren, M. Cole and G. Rikowski (eds), *Postmodernism in Educational Theory: Education and the Politics of Human Resistance*, London: Tufnell Press.

Liddington, J. and Norris, J. (1978) *One Hand Tied Behind Us: The Rise of the Women's Suffrage Movement*, London: Virago.

MacKeith, B. (2004) 'Migration: An Issue "for Britain" or for Workers' Rights?', *Socialist Outlook*, 3 (Spring), London: International Socialist Group.

Marx, K. (1876) *Capital: A Critique of Political Economy*, Vol. 1. London: Lawrence and Wishart (reprinted 1970).

Open University (1984) *Conflict and Change in Education: A Sociological Introduction*, Block 6: Gender, race and education; Unit 25: 'Women and Education', Milton Keynes: Open University Press.

Power, N. (2009) *One Dimensional Woman*, London: Zero Books.

Sly, F., Price, A. and Risdon, A. (1997) *Labour Market Trends*, London: Government Statistical Office, March.

TUC (2009) *Women and Recession: How will this recession affect women at work?*, www.tuc.org.uk/extras/womenandrecession.pdf (accessed 18 July 2011).

Chapter 2

Gender and education

Continuity and difference

Jane Martin

Mapping change in relation to gender equality in the late twentieth century, incoming president of the National Association of Schoolmasters and Union of Women Teachers, Pat Lerew, told the annual conference:

> I know we have come a long way from my grammar school days when the only career options seemed to be teaching or nursing and when, as a young married woman in the 1960s, my earnings could not be included in any mortgage application. I wasn't allowed to enter into any hire-purchase agreements and my life was not worth insuring. I suppose there was the small advantage of not being responsible for my own debts. Since then, equality laws have ensured that these situations no longer apply and on the face of it there is gender equality. We all know that the truth is very different.
>
> (*Guardian*, 13 April 2004)

Introduction

This chapter will focus on gender equity issues in education. The object is to provide a critical narrative of provision in England from the perspective of the twenty-first century, to show the impact of the past on the present. A storyline that begins in the 1960s is a useful starting point. An active women's movement coined the slogan 'the personal is political', which addressed the question of the power relations between men and women in the privacy of the family and provided a basis for drawing women to an understanding of feminist consciousness in relation to social processes and structures. Education constituted a core issue for women's activism, though it is important not to obscure how educational equality and achievements in school are related to issues of class, 'race', ethnicity, disability, sexuality, religion, citizenship and location, as well as gender, for a more holistic view of human experience.

The chapter is organised in four sections with the main aim of providing a historical overview of politics and policy-making in the field of gender and education, to illuminate the enduring patterns and preoccupations. The final sections use the history–sociology relationship to explore the ways in which those patterns permeate the workings of policy in the current context.

Historical perspectives on gender and education: 1800–1944

The education of children in the nineteenth century was organised along the lines of social class. Elementary education was associated with the working classes and secondary education, which was not confined to the three Rs, was associated with the middle classes. Girls rarely feature in general histories of the rise of mass schooling and orthodox accounts systemically ignored gender as an analytical category. Within the field of women's history, a sex/class binary manifested itself in a largely separate history of elite female education and of the institutions for girls and women created around the axis of class. The history of education for minority-group girls was largely overlooked.

This gendered reading of the growth of state provision in England draws our attention to patriarchy and emphasises perspectives on social life that encapsulate assumptions about normal or natural subordination of women. Because 'normal' policy-making has traditionally been so exclusively masculine in its assumptions, it follows that the 'masculinist' models embedded in the structure of provision fostered the maintenance of differentiation in local educational organisation. First, there were fewer school places for girls (Hurt, 1979). Second, girls were less likely to be sent to school (Martin, 1987). Third, the two sexes did not have access to a common curriculum. For example, needlework became compulsory for girls in 1862 when concern about value for money led the government to introduce payment by results for state schools. Each pupil earned the same amount for successful examination performance, but girls were permitted a lower standard of achievement in arithmetic because of the time they spent sewing (Weiner, 1994; Digby and Searby, 1981).

The 1870 Education Act was a watershed in English and Welsh education history. It put in place the development of a national state system of elementary schools for the working class run by directly elected local school boards (Simon, 1980). Gender differences were extended and increasingly formalised after the passage of the Act. Ostensibly co-educational, in urban areas the 'ideal' elementary or board school had different entrances for the sexes, as well as separate playgrounds and separate departments for older children (Turnbull, 1987).

This period also saw the promotion of a sex-differentiated curriculum. In 1878, for example, theoretical domestic economy became a compulsory specific subject for girls; four years later the government gave grants for the teaching of cookery. By the 1890s, a significant expansion in the curriculum prescriptions for working-class girls saw the inclusion of laundry work and housewifery. Despite the addition of male craft subjects like woodwork, Turnbull (1987, p. 86) concludes that working-class boys 'did not receive practical instruction equivalent to the girls' needlework, cookery, laundry work and so on'. Further, when national efficiency became a priority in the aftermath of military failures and deficiencies highlighted by the number of recruits declared unfit for call-up in the second Boer War (1899-1902), the Board of Education increased the quota of these lessons (Attar, 1990; Dyhouse, 1981; Turnbull, 1987). Hurt (1979) suggests military drill as the masculine equivalent to the housework and mothering lessons given to girls, but fails to acknowledge the proportion of time filled by domestic subjects instruction.

Here I use Anna Davin's (1979) suggestions that the purpose of mass schooling was to impose an ideal family form of a male breadwinner and an economically dependent, full-time wife and mother. As Gomersall has summed up:

> This was an ideal that came broadly to be shared by the bourgeoisie and men and women of the working classes alike, each for their own particular economic, political, cultural and social reasons. That it was unattainable for most outside the ranks of skilled and unionised labour was seen as unproblematic; it integrated the goals of the powerful men of the working classes with those of the dominant social and economic groups and served as an aspirational ideal to the unskilled, unorganised work-force.
>
> (Gomersall, 1994, p. 238)

Although texts like Mary Wollstonecraft's *Vindication of the Rights of Women* (1792 [1975]) applied liberal ideas of equality to women's/girls' education, her vision did not find favour at a time when British society was highly stratified by social class, and the educational needs of women and girls were perceived as largely inferior and subordinate to their male counterparts. The grounds for this injustice were cultural.

Family culture provided a rationale for the ways in which girls and women experienced schooling and education. Working-class girls often acted as surrogate 'wives' and 'little mothers' on washdays, or if their mother was ill or having a baby (Dyhouse, 1981; Davin, 1996). Middle-class girls were largely educated for the marriage market and Wollstonecraft argued that the frivolous education they received would simply reinforce already existing divisions and the maintenance of conservative social formations.

Emmeline Pankhurst (b. 1858), who led the British suffragette campaign for the vote, records that: 'My parents, especially my father, discussed the question of my brothers' education as a matter of real importance. My education and that of my sister were scarcely discussed at all' (1979, pp. 5–6). Where parents had to make choices about their children's education usually the precedence was determined by ideals of femininity and masculinity rather than by intellectual capacities. As Nora Lumb (b. 1912), the daughter of an English railway clerk, discovered she had to win one of the 10 scholarships awarded by her local education authority (Sunderland) to get to grammar school in 1923. Her parents would have paid for a boy, but not for a girl (cited in Burnett, 1994, p. 161).

For the daughters of the well-to-do (Pankhurst's father was a successful businessman), no paid work was thought suitable. Lady Violet Bonham-Carter (b. 1887) recalled having asked her governess how she was going to spend her life:

> Her answer came without a moment's hesitation. 'Until you are eighteen you will do lessons.' 'And afterwards?' 'And afterwards you will do *nothing*' . . . The deep river, the Rubicon which flowed between, was called 'Coming Out'. . . . One day one had a pigtail down one's back – short skirts, which barely cleared the knees. The next day, hair piled high on top of one's head . . . It used to be a sin to be vain – but now it became a sin to be plain . . . 'Lessons' were of course thrown to the winds . . . In fact, I remember being warned by a well-wisher to *conceal* any knowledge I *had* managed to acquire . . .'Men are afraid of clever girls'.
>
> (cited in Thompson, 1992, p. 60)

Likewise Emily Davies (b. 1830, who led campaigns for access to secondary and higher education for women) resented the fact that whereas her three brothers all attended private public schools for the ruling class followed by Trinity College, Cambridge she only received a limited education. This included a brief spell at a day-school supplemented by occasional paid lessons in languages and music (Caine, 1992).

Working people and women were the losers when the 1902 Education Act snuffed out the school boards (Simon, 1980; Martin, 1999). Working people because the division between elementary education for the working classes and secondary education for the middle classes became more firmly defined, women because they were disqualified by sex for election to the new education authorities. The Act made subcommittees of county councils responsible for the board schools, now called public elementary schools. For the first time the local education authorities were permitted to establish rate-aided secondary schools whose form and curricula were to follow those of the elitist, independent schools. Secondary school fees were set at £3 per annum, which excluded all save the high-ability working-class child who won a free place on the basis of an attainment test. Purvis (1995, p.14) has suggested that those who benefited were highly likely to be lower middle-class males.

Weiner (1994) notes the presence of four features of curriculum thinking – selection, differentiation, functionality and social advancement – within what Simon (1994, p. 42) calls 'the emergent system'. Increasingly a similar policy was pursued in elementary and secondary schools. Both the 1905 Code of Regulations for Public Elementary Schools and the Regulations for Secondary Schools imposed practical training in the female role. Policy guidelines incorporated a set of linked assumptions advocating separate but complementary adult roles for men and women. On the one hand, the female curriculum was discussed in terms of girls' biology and what this meant for their future after school. On the other, the principle of male-as-norm meant the teaching of other subjects was informed by the assumption that boys were breadwinners and secondarily fathers (Hunt, 1991). This was approved school practice by the 1920s and a report on the differentiation of the curriculum in secondary schools concluded that there were two main aims for education: first, to prepare children to both earn their own livings; and second, to be useful citizens. However, ideologies of femininity dictated that girls also needed to be prepared for family life and motherhood, since their primary vocation was to be 'makers of homes' (HMSO, 1923, cited in Hunt, 1991, p. 119). This one role was seen to supersede all other social principles, both inside and outside school.

State policy endorsed the view that women were different from men; not only biologically but socially, intellectually and psychologically as well. Within classrooms, girls were more likely to be taught by women. Male teachers tended to teach the boys, especially older boys (Purvis, 1995). This was crucial to the National Association of Schoolmasters (NAS), formed in 1923, who deplored the influence of female teachers on male students (Littlejohn, 1995). Only male teachers could reinforce 'normal' masculinity. As a writer in the union journal, the *New Schoolmaster* put it:

> in the matter of managing and instructing young children the sex of a person may matter but little [. . .] in the great task of educating children the sex of the teacher is of paramount importance. The character of children is the essential consideration, and the essentials of character lie in the sex of the person,
> (*New Schoolmaster*, November 1936, cited in Littlejohn, 1995, p. 50)

By the 1920s, approximately three-quarters of elementary school teachers were women. In these circumstances, the NAS continued to press their demands for male teachers for all boys over seven, and headmasters in mixed schools. Indeed, they did not relinquish the first objective until 1976. Clearly, this insistence on the importance of gender in teaching has implications for the construction of patriarchal relations in teachers' work. Indeed Littlejohn claims 'the most volatile and explosive issue of all was the appointment of women to the inspectorate with special responsibility for handicraft and physical education' (1995, pp. 53–54). To subject male teachers to the authority of women passing judgement on the teaching of technical crafts and sports was more than they could bear. It was emasculating.

Overall education policies remained tailored to processes of class formation in the inter-war years. Beyond that, there was evidence of gender-based asymmetries in terms of access to schooling; curriculum content and years of education attained.

Historical perspectives on gender and education II: 1944–75

The 1944 Education Act established the principle of universal and free secondary education for all children over 11. Many saw the reform as primarily about the realisation of class equality and the production of a new type of society. Nevertheless, this did not mean 'that all children now received what had before the Act been described as secondary education' (Thom, 1987, p. 131). Typically, 11-plus attainment testing became the principle of allocation of students to different types of post-primary school.

However, the envisaged tripartite system of grammar, technical and modern schools was largely implemented as a bipartite system with technical schools not set up in the numbers envisaged. In the general discussion of education:

> Gender was raised, but it was raised as a general social question, that is, the issue of whether girls and boys should receive a separate sort of education as a whole, not whether one girl should receive a different sort of education from another. No one asked what the implications were for equality in this; rather, whether boys and girls required a fundamentally different organisation of education.
>
> (Thom, 1987, p. 125)

The official ideology for female education still assumed homogeneity of female interests. Thus, for example, while the Norwood Report (1943) interspersed the word 'child' with 'boy', criteria particular to girls' schooling featured in a lengthy chapter on domestic subjects.

Throughout the 1940s and 1950s (when selection through the 11-plus examination predominated), girls had to outperform boys to get a place at a grammar or technical school (Deem, 1981; Thom, 1987). This was justified because girls' academic superiority in the early stages made it necessary 'to tilt the balance in the favour of those late-developing boys' (Grant, 1994, p. 37). The accepted theory was that boys would catch up by the age of 14. Medical practitioners who warned female students of the risks evoked by too much intellectual work reinforced gender stereotypes about male superiority (Dyhouse, 1981). As late as the 1930s, it was professed that a girl who worked hard might get brain fever (Rendel, 1997, p. 56).

Unsurprisingly, when it came to male–female 11-plus result patterns, common sense and social observation suggested the difference 'is not real because it does not last, it is not a phenomenon produced by the test, it is a phenomenon produced by "nature"'(Thom, 1987, p. 141). The fact that girls frequently scored better marks than boys prompted some local authorities to set up different norms; others added new tests to level up the sexes. Technical adjustment was necessary to balance the numbers of successful girls and boys; there was also a historic shortage of girls' grammar school places. It has to be accepted 'that there is no such thing as a fair test' (Gipps and Murphy, 1994, p. 273) but the special problems of girls were lost in the general problems of the tripartite system.

During the years of Clement Attlee's Labour governments (1945–51), politicians saw the domestic role of women as crucial for the construction and rehabilitation of social harmony and cohesiveness (Dean, 1991). When it came to policy and practice in education, planners and ideologues still placed their faith in that special curriculum for girls, organised around familial concerns. In the 1940s, influential school inspector John Newsom published a book, *The Education of Girls*, in which he cast doubt on the value of an academic education for girls. As time passed, Newsom's views on domestic education 'for the average girl (or rather the working-class girl), whose vocation was still seen as marriage and family, were not only still widely accepted, but even became more popular as sex education was introduced into schools after 1956' (Wilson, 1980, p. 36).

In the secondary modern schools (virtually synonymous with working-class schooling), the Crowther Report (1959), which dealt with the education of 15- to 18-year-olds, expressed sympathy with the idea that marriage and courtship should influence the education of the adolescent girl (Riley, 1994, p. 37). However, there is evidence of female disaffection with schooling in this period. Early leaving generated attention in the Gurney-Dixon Report of 1954 and Crowther commented on the fact that grammar school girls were more likely to leave school at the statutory age (Deem, 1981). Imputing motivation is difficult, but it is conceivable that fear of failure prompted early leaving. Challenging normative concepts that underpin constructions of meanings and interpretations, Spender and Sarah (1980) argue that in education women have learnt *how* to lose even though they may have had the ability to succeed academically. The educational biography of the American Pulitzer prize-winning novelist, Carol Shields (b. 1935), is revealing. A college graduate and trained teacher, as a young woman her expectations were simple: 'a baby, a TV, a fridge-freezer and a car' (*Guardian*, 23 May 1998).

During the late 1950s and early 1960s, government reports and academic research pointed to the 'wasted talent' the divided educational system produced and the inefficacy of intelligence testing as a device for meritocratic selection was highlighted. Secondary modern schools were regarded as second best and this strengthened support for secondary school reorganization on 'comprehensive' lines. Faith in the logic of human capital theory and the central assumption of 'upskilling', where education is seen as crucial to economic growth, precipitated the expansion and restructuring of schooling (Schultz, 1970; see Simon, 1991, pp. 222, 229 and 291 for a discussion). Reassessments of the concept of equal access saw the gradual shift to a non-selective system of secondary schooling in England and Wales, a change that accelerated the number of children educated in mixed schools in the state sector. This meant a changing balance of power among women and men staff in senior and managerial positions as schools became mixed, larger and more complex.

A cultural atmosphere had developed that assumed boys and girls should be educated together, rather than separately, on academic and social grounds. The feeling being that the presence of female pupils would have a 'civilising' influence on their male peers. As Arnot (1984, p. 50) has noted, 'never it would seem has the argument been reversed'. Overall, the removal of barriers to female success in the 11-plus examination inevitably benefited some, predominantly middle-class girls; discussion of who benefits academically from mixed or single-sex schooling runs on and will be returned to later.

In theory, Deem (1981) maintains the expansion of the curriculum in state-maintained secondary schools should have been 'helpful' to girls. In practice, Benn and Simon (1972) found that very few schools offered a common curriculum to all their pupils in the early days of the comprehensive reform. Divergence in the content of education was clearly seen in the provision of gender-specific courses in subjects like domestic science, typing and childcare, which were not open to boys; and woodwork, metalwork and technical drawing, which were not open to girls. Links between the distribution of educational knowledge and patterns of women's work remained in evidence despite the rise of a new feminist movement and the greater participation of women in the labour force.

The effects were carried forward into further study and employment at precisely the point when, for the first time since the Second World War, there was a growing problem of youth unemployment. Education was to take the blame for at least some of the nation's ills resulting from the economic and industrial problems of the early 1970s, as a worldwide oil crisis put increased pressure on public expenditure. Working-class boys and men were particularly affected by the decline of vocational apprenticeships and industrial jobs with release for college training. On the other hand, cutbacks in teacher training and fierce competition for university places in arts courses reduced opportunities for some young women.

Breaking boundaries I: equal opportunities?

When the Labour government under Harold Wilson passed the Sex Discrimination Act of 1975, it made direct and indirect discrimination on the grounds of gender illegal in a number of spheres of public life, including education (Carter, 1988). Previous attempts[1] to get sex included within the scope of the Race Relations Act had failed but on this occasion, the support of the minister Roy Jenkins helped overcome the opposition of some Home Office officials (Rendel, 1997, pp. 3, 12). Although the then Department of Education and Science was unenthusiastic, the Act outlawed discrimination in the provision of curricular and non-curricular facilities, and extra-curricular activities. Additionally, it covered standards of behaviour, rules regarding pupils' dress and appearance, school discipline and careers guidance, but did not apply to private schools.

It is in the context of an increasing entry of women into higher education, the establishment of women's studies courses and departments, and the performance of girls in examinations, that we have to consider the transformative powers of feminisms in educational thinking and practice. That is, the women's movement within the educational system. For optimistic feminist educators, equality legislation, making it illegal to discriminate against women in work, education and training, was a spur to groundbreaking work exposing the resilience of a patriarchal order. In so doing, they 'uncovered ideas and practices inimical to the full development of potential, not only girls but often of boys, too, and those disadvantaged by social or ethnic origin' (Watts, 2002, p. 146).

Feminists levelled criticism at schools across a diversity of areas. The interplay of gender and leadership was embedded within the work of schools, government and teacher unions. Generally, men ran the schools, dominating the administrative and policy-making side of education. Occupying teaching positions that required instructional expertise and nurturing, women mostly operated within female spaces. Hence, female heads of department in secondary schools were generally in low-status subject areas like home economics and girls' physical education. Women, who often find themselves made responsible for the failure of boys, dominate primary school classrooms.

Research at the time revealed that primary school teachers readily clustered behaviour into two categories, one for boys and another for girls, drawing on oppositional constructions of masculinity and femininity (Clarricoates, 1980). Boys were lively, adventurous, boisterous, self-confident, independent, energetic, couldn't-care-less, loyal and aggressive. Girls were obedient, tidy, neat, conscientious, orderly, fussy, catty, bitchy and gossipy. Stanworth drew a similar picture in her account of lack of space and attention in a mixed further education college. Higher teacher expectations towards boys had implications for the self-image of one young woman:

> I think he thinks I'm pretty mediocre. I think I'm pretty mediocre. He never points me out of the group or talks to me, or looks at me in particular when he's talking about things. I'm just a sort of wallpaper person.
>
> (Stanworth, 1986, p. 37)

Of course, such a description may reflect the use of discipline and control in teaching styles. This raises the point that the control of working-class boys, understood in terms of the problems of violence and truancy, also received a good deal of attention in research and public discussion.

Early texts dealing with the production of masculinity through resistance to schooling show how anti-school working-class 'lads' block teaching (Willis, 1983). Similarly, in *Schooling the Smash Street Kids*, Corrigan (1979) used the analogy of a 'guerrilla struggle' to represent the ability of white, working-class, heterosexual boys in the north east of England to monopolise space in the classroom, despite the 'occupying army' of teachers. Examples of disruptive behaviour included 'running about in classrooms', 'running under chairs' and 'tossing chairs about' (Corrigan, 1979, p. 58). By contrast, the resistance of anti-school girls was individual and personalised or 'invisible' – they 'skived off' school (Llewellyn, 1980). Although some rebellious girls used a feminine preoccupation with appearance in order to position themselves in opposition to school (Payne, 1980; Riddell, 1989).

In relation to subject choice by gender, the 1975 report on curricular differentiation highlighted the areas in which sexism flourished (DES, 1975). There were high levels of sex stereotyping in fields of study selection and teachers were criticised for influencing pupil preferences. Beyond that, Her Majesty's Inspectorate (HMI) found evidence of illegal segregation of craft subjects in 19 per cent of the schools studied in the years 1975 to 1978 (cited in Pascall, 1997, p. 119). Research on subject choice showed significant patterns of gender segregation informed by expectations of future employment. Prior to the introduction of a 'National Curriculum' in 1988, it seemed that if any group benefited from moves to promote equal access to curricular options it was the boys:

> Male students who took 'girls subjects' were assumed to be learning a skill for future use in the labour market. They were taken more seriously than their female peers in the same classes, to whom such skills were supposed to come naturally for use in their future roles as wives and mothers [. . .] Female students who took 'boys' subjects' were either presumed to be interested solely in flirting with the boys or discounted as unique exceptions.
> (Griffin, 1985, pp. 78–79)

Despite the achievement of equal rights legislation, most girls were still sitting examinations in a narrow cluster of subjects seen as supporting 'natural' female interests, needs and choices with respect to personal/domestic life.

In educational spaces, individual feminist teachers and groups of feminists (such as organisations like Girls/Gender and Mathematics Association – GAMMA) tried to act as change agents, by consciousness raising and encouraging small-scale school-based initiatives. Despite the lack of top-down reform of schooling to help girls, issues tackled ranged from staffing, classroom interaction, sexual harassment and the division of girls/boys in both administration and curriculum, besides extra-curricular activities (see Stantonbury Sexism in Education Group, 1984). One of the best-known projects, the Girls into Science and Technology initiative, was set up in Manchester (Kelly, 1985). Here researchers worked alongside and with teachers in 10 schools to encourage girls to take traditionally 'male' subjects, even after they became optional (then at age 14). To this end, the project team brought adult women scientists to act as role models, tried to raise awareness about the gender dynamics of classrooms, and experimented with single-sex classes.

Although the ambivalence of girls' responses to science changed little, early speculation about the impact of the equality legislation show a closing of the gender gap in terms of access to GCE O-level and CSE examinations and male–female success rates (Deem, 1981). However, fewer girls than boys achieved the three good A-levels which would have given them access to higher education, and there were prevailing inequities in curriculum and attitudes (Arnot, David and Weiner, 1999). Thus Arnot (1983, p. 71) argues that the development of co-educational state comprehensive secondary schools 'did not represent [. . .] a challenge to the reproduction of dominant gender relations but rather a modifi-cation of the *form* of its transmission.' The ubiquity of the discourse of women and caring is borne out by a homily recorded in a comprehensive secondary school in 1978:

> In assembly the lower school is addressed by the Senior Mistress, Mrs Marks. Pupils are told they will soon be given a form to take home – school wants the phone number of where mother works. Mrs Marks says that if they are ill or have an accident, school tries to get mother. The school try not to bother father, because he is the head of the family, his wage keeps the family while mother's is only for luxuries [. . .] If there is no-one at home – mum, granny or auntie – they will be put to bed at school.
>
> (Delamont, 1983, p. 93)

By the 1980s, it was observed that the New Right agenda, with its commitment to 'family values', might conflict with moves that could improve career prospects for girls (David, 1983).

Breaking boundaries II: social justice?

Arguments about social justice were shunned when the then Secretary of State for Education and Science, Kenneth Baker, proposed a radical restructuring of the school system. Introducing the Education Reform Bill at the 1987 Conservative Party Conference he declared 'the pursuit of egalitarianism is over' (quoted in Arnot, 1989/90, p. 21). The national goal was quality. The tool was a National Curriculum reflecting divisions of subject status. Feminist educators supported the notion of a common curriculum experience, albeit one that encompassed the hidden curriculum of schooling and *not* one posited on a male educational paradigm (Benn, Parris, Riley and Weiner, 1982). Knowledge is not a neutral commodity, but the emphasis on equal opportunities serves to rein-force the illusion of neutrality (Arnot, 1989/90). On the one hand, the 'National Curriculum' gave equal entitlement to all pupils (within the state sector) to develop the same learning skills and experience the same subjects. On the other, the privileging of maths, science and technology reinforced gender hierarchies. The status accorded male-centred forms of knowledge did little to challenge the values and practices of patriarchy/androcentricity:

In short, while girls must be educated in the skills and attitudes to achieve an academic equality with boys – and to challenge inequalities within the labour market – the education of boys in the skills and attitudes to address their equal responsibilities within the family are of equal if not greater importance. And this is where the formal equality accorded by the National Curriculum is most lacking, in the 'masculinisation' of the schooling of girls with no corresponding 'feminisation' of the schooling of boys.

(Gomersall, 1994, p. 246)

What this position represents is a concern to restructure boys' education in such a way as to break the circulation of stereotypical sex-role expectations. The views expressed emphasise that the majority of schooling operates for a particular form of hegemonic masculinity.

Arnot's (1994) review of gender research in British sociology of education highlights two theoretical traditions. The first is that of the cultural perspective, wherein cultural analyses concentrate on different socialisation processes. The second tradition that Arnot explores is political–economy theories. Key thematic influences and concerns that stand out in such approaches are the concept of *social reproduction*, suggesting that schools reproduce the values and ideologies of the dominant social groupings, as well as the status rankings of the existing class structure.[2]

Building on this work, Arnot adjusts the theory to enable her to combine a class and gender analysis. Here she develops the now well-established concept of gender codes, to refer to 'the principles which govern the production, reproduction and transmission of gender relations and gender hierarchies' (Arnot, 2002, p. 176). *Hegemony* plays a considerable theoretical role, showing the structural constraints or limits that shape a prevailing context in which individuals and groups act.[3] Sociological analysis can provide insight into how powerful groups within society maintain control, while showing how teachers, students and other human agents can and do play a crucial role in moderating or changing existing social norms. Within this spirit, it is accepted that individuals and groups may hold within them different ways of seeing and thereby offer routes to change in the name of, for example, women's rights.

Research undertaken for the Equal Opportunities Commission revealed how English and Welsh education reforms of the late 1980s influenced gender equality. Studying the figures on assessment performance for 1985–94, Arnot, David and Weiner (1996) used a statistical construct of a 'gender gap' to consider comparative achievement figures. The period covered the introduction of a new common examination, the General Certificate of Secondary Education (GCSE), plus coursework assessment, seen to have improved the performance of girls noticeably, as they have the performance of boys, though less dramatically. In the compulsory sector, the statistics showed the increasing dominance of boys in chemistry, computer studies and economics. On the other hand, a more balanced entry pattern was found in English, mathematics and history.

Overall more girls than boys were entered for GCSE examinations and girls were more successful in terms of the proportion of A–C grades gained, though the elite minority of girls in private single-sex schools seemed to be at a substantial advantage.

In the post-compulsory sector, the data showed sex segregation in subject choice was still marked. Far more young men completed A-levels (used for university entrance) in mathematics, physics and technology (Arnot *et al.*, 1996, p. 64). Similarly in vocational examinations and the various training schemes, women mostly took the less prestigious types like business and commerce, hairdressing and beauty and service courses. Gender patterns in post-school education show how being male or female impacts on career ambition. They also suggest that:

> a girl's experience of gender cannot be abstracted so neatly from any other aspect of her life. Girls from different social backgrounds will not experience patriarchal culture in identical ways, and the adult lives they anticipate will promise different kinds of opportunity, responsibility and experience. Their priorities as girls will reflect these disparities.
>
> (Miles and Middleton, 1995, p. 133)

Murphy and Elwood (1998) who observe that children's learning out of school has important consequences for what they choose to do within school corroborate this. It has an effect on performance, views of relevance, expectations, styles of expression and achievement.

In her research, Lees (1993) found that whereas academic girls expect careers, non-academic girls anticipate the need to combine unskilled and part-time employment with the responsibilities of housework and childcare. Pro-school and academically or work-oriented girls were typically white females from middle-class homes with strong parental support. Mirza (1992) comments that the Irish girls in her study saw their futures as homemakers, child carers and part-time workers, whereas the black girls she interviewed anticipated a career. Clearly, the way in which women perform relative to men varies according to class and ethnicity, as does the value of having or not having educational qualifications. Significantly, the mature women students interviewed by Pascall and Cox (1993) saw education as an escape route from a lifetime of domesticity and low-paid work. However, the gradual abolition of mandatory grants, the introduction of loans and the prospect of incurring high levels of debt had a major impact on this group of students.

The neo-liberal social policy and marketisation of education instigated by the Conservative governments of the 1980s and 1990s was developed with enthusiasm by the 'New Labour' administrations of Tony Blair and Gordon Brown (1997 to 2010) as a key way of improving institutional, group and individual standards and effectiveness in schooling. Within this policy movement, pupils and students become educational clients, with parents the consumers of education systems. Performance league tables, a more stringent school inspection process (set up in 1992) all serve as mechanisms to 'measure' standards, with an unprecedented emphasis on the phenomenon of the failing school.

These new regimes had a dramatic impact on equity discourses that sit alongside dominant educational narratives about school effectiveness. The concept of 'excellence' promoted plays through the dynamic of 'success' and 'failure', and Ball and Gewirtz (1997) pointed to the accretive value of 'successful' girls. Girls are positioned as 'a valuable and sought after resource' by strategies to increase school effectiveness through pupil achievement, because 'their presence in school normally conveys positive impressions to parents about ethos and discipline' (Ball and Gewirtz, 1997, p. 214).

In their study *Growing Up Girl* published in 2001, Walkerdine, Lucey and Melody offer longitudinal data on UK girls from working-class and middle-class backgrounds, showing how achievement is always a 'class related phenomenon'. Therefore, the meaning of the 'good' girl is constructed across class lines. None of the working-class girls who succeeded in education trod a straightforward academic path, whereas only one middle-class girl did not go on to university entrance. The educational trajectories of two girls, Patsy (working class) and Julie (middle class), who went to the same nursery, infant and junior schools, and whose parents did all the 'right things', may help to explain why. At 10, both girls were doing equally badly at junior school but whereas the teacher read Patsy's performance as lack of ability, Julie's performance was viewed as a problem of motivation. At 16, both girls got poor GCSE results and Patsy left school while Julie went on to university: 'at 21 Julie was back on track and was likely to become a graduate professional, while Patsy, painfully aware of her lack of qualifications, was equally likely to remain in relatively poorly paid, low-status work' (2001, pp. 125–26).

Analysing postwar education and social change, Arnot, David and Weiner (1999) make the argument that feminist campaigners were able to manipulate the concerns of the Conservative governments of the 1980s and 1990s by integrating equal opportunities work into debates about educational standards and performance and good schools. Sixteen-year-old girls were already improving their results in the 1970s but 20 years on, the alarm at girls' successes in statutory assessments would bring different aspects of the patterns that form the kaleidoscope of gender, education and equality to the fore. The underachievement of boys was what made hearts race, *not* the extraordinary success of schools and teachers in improving girls' academic performance.

In the 1990s, the rise in female performance roused media reports obsessed with threats to male breadwinning, the collapse of family life and the crisis of fatherhood, and a spill over into an increase in problematic and antisocial behaviours, crime and deviance. On the face of it, gendered reactions to the annual publication of the GCSE results developed a generalised narrative of female academic success and male failure. This received official legitimation in 1996, when Chris Woodhead, then Chief Inspector of Schools for England, wrote a column in *The Times* entitled 'Boys who learn to be losers: on the white male culture of failure'. In it he said that the apparent failure of white working-class boys was 'one of the most disturbing problems we face within the whole education system' (quoted in the *TES*, 26 April 1996). Two years later, when the publication of new official statistics showed girls outperforming boys in terms of the proportion of pupils obtaining five A–C grades at GCSE in all but one local authority (Kensington and Chelsea), concern for boys' under-achievement led then Schools Standards Minister Stephen Byers to intervene. In a speech at the 11th International Conference for School Effectiveness and Improvement, he argued that the 'laddish, anti-learning culture' was impeding boys' achievement (*Guardian*, 6 January 1998). Henceforth each local authority was required to address the issue of male disadvantage in drawing up its Education Development Plan. The new policy imperatives support the argument that framing debate in terms of male disadvantage makes gender equality a main-stream issue.

Others added their own recipes for change. Among them a recommendation that teachers appeal to boys' interests (humour, adventure and sport) and a drive to recruit male primary school teachers that harked back to the NAS backlash in the 1920s and 1930s (*TES*, 23 May 1997; *Daily Mail*, 5 January 1998). In this gendered terrain, researchers found evidence that newly qualified teachers had greater sympathy for class and ethnic equality than gender equality (Arnot, 1996). Others speculated whether rhetoric about a generation of male losers and the object of the failing boy might lead to a further masculinisation of class-room environments (Raphael Reed, 1998).

Anti-sexist work to raise achievement for all pupils might go further. Boys/ men negotiate and take up a variety of masculinities and some of these confer power and prestige, while others are stigmatised and subordinate. We can relate this to inequalities of social class and special need. Young boys positioned as slow learners, poor at sport and lacking physical strength and skill may resort to overtly challenging behaviour making them vulnerable to being classified as having special needs (Benjamin, 2003). Indeed, working-class boys are found in greater numbers in 'less acceptable' categories of emotional and behavioural difficulties and moderate learning difficulties and middle-class boys dominate the non-stigmatised category of specific learning difficulties.

Remapping the terrain of gender and education illuminates the need for con-tinual revision of understanding when the representational politics around gender equity tend to simplify and distort issues involved with school achieve-ment. Escalating hysteria about the educational phenomenon of the 'growing gender gap' glossed several things, notably that it may not actually *exist* (see Gorard, Rees and Salisbury (1999) for discussion of confusion over a tendency to confuse percentages and percentage points that may conflate the figures). Because statistical patterns of female performance at GCSE contradicted earlier assumptions about girls' underperformance, particularly in maths and sciences, the results proved shocking and provoked a media furore. However, the media-driven perception masks a number of things.

For example, when it came to literacy rates, there was panic about boys' apparent underachievement, even though girls have traditionally excelled at language-based subjects and despite empirical evidence to suggest boys' greater show of interest in film, computer and CD-ROMs may be a better preparation for changing world literacy than may often be the case for girls (Marsh, 2003). Longitudinal data from the Leverhulme Numeracy Research Programme, a study of teaching and learning in English primary schools between 1997 and 2002, shows girls do not match boys' performance in mathematics (Lucey *et al.*, 2003). At GCSE level, the tendency to play safe with examination entries of girls in mathematics means more girls than boys obtained grade C from the intermediate tier.

Often, only those who achieved a grade B or C from the higher tier are eligible to continue their studies. In August 2009, more boys were awarded A★ to C grades in GCSE mathematics, which prompted media speculation that a 20-year trend of girls 'increasingly outperforming boys could begin to reverse because coursework is now due to be scrapped for nearly all subjects following the move with maths this year' (*Daily Mail*, 28 August 2009).

It would seem that a perception of boys as innately clever continues. So does a tendency to imply that girls' academic attainment is the result of compliant hard work. Lamenting gendered perceptions of the differential abilities of boys and girls, Mahony (1998, p. 39) notes: 'it took a good deal of persuasion by (mainly) feminists before policy makers would look beyond the innate capacities of girls themselves for explanations.' Indeed, it is arguable that female school performance has improved *despite* the continuing male dominance in the classroom, the playground, regarding curriculum content and greater demands on teacher time and energy (Francis and Skelton, 2005).

Crucially, boys and girls are both much more successful at school than they were 50 years ago. However, when it comes to the life chances of all those who pass through the educational system, we should not lose sight of the fact that young people from the poorest homes (as measured by eligibility for free meals) still have fewer qualifications at GCSE and A-level (*Guardian*, 20 April 2010).

Conclusion

A historical perspective shows that girls have continued to do better in education when offered more opportunities. Nonetheless, UNISON President Angela Lynne offered a devastating critique of the ConDem public service cuts to the 2011 UNISON Women's Conference, 'which mean that some young women have even more obstacles to climb just to reach glass ceiling, even if they ever get off the sticky floor' (http://unisonactive.blogspot.com/2011/02/no-to-public-service-cuts-which-harm.html, accessed 5 July 2011). Hegemonic masculinities and social class continue to dominate the state education system much as they do British public life. To come full circle and return to the quote with which we started, yes, we do all know the reality is very different. While the male victors of Election 2010 talked up the dawn of a 'new kind of politics', their majority female audience (51 per cent of the British population) could be forgiven for thinking *plus ca change*!

In 2008, David Cameron promised he would give one-third of his jobs in his first government to women. Two years on, we find only four women seated around the cabinet table – 14 per cent of the total number (*Guardian*, 12, 14 May 2010). Women will be hardest by early public spending cuts to be adopted by the ConDem coalition. Whether it is through welfare cuts for middle-income families, reduced education spending or public sector 'downsizing', whether independent, wives/partners, mothers and/or workers, women are disproportionately affected. A TUC report *Women and the Recession – One Year On* (2010) shows that around four in 10 women work in public sector occupations compared to less than two in 10 men. Female unemployment has increased faster than men's since the start of the current recession. This is likely to escalate. So are poverty levels among the female 'baby boomers', since women are being forced to work longer for poorer pensions, which will increase the gender divide in retirement income.

Inequalities of gender still have consequences in relation to educational systems, practices and institutions. Albeit that, in a context of restructured schools and broader social change, the form of its transmission is more likely to be found in the micro-world of classroom interaction and the more subtle differentiated curriculum tracks (Arnot, 2002). To take but one example, might conforming to stereotype and choosing to study the arts, humanities and social sciences see female students being more heavily affected by the government's decision to withdraw the teaching grant from all but science, technology, engineering and mathematics (STEM) subjects? Post-1992 universities with higher proportions of disadvantaged students are being more heavily affected by this decision so we need to understand how gender interrelates as a category with social class and ethnicity. Will 2011 government-funding cuts trigger the same fierce competition for university places among current female 19-year olds, as for their mother's generation in the 1970s?

Writing of the teaching workforce, Jane Miller (1996) equates 'more' with women as she traces the acceptance of state responsibility for mass education provision. Demolishing a simple idea of history as progress, we need to think in terms of constant movement. If more does mean women when it comes to contraction of welfare state provision, will women form the majority of the unpaid volunteers in the making of David Cameron's 'Big Society'? Might female voices be more prominent in a different coalition: the Million Voices coalition that Lynes called for, as women pick up the pieces and withstand the worst of the ConDem public service cuts? Will a new generation resist what some Conservatives consider might be a useful nudge to changing the role of women in society, going back to the future with a woman's place in the home?

Notes

1   This was by the backbench MPs and campaigners Joan Vickers (Conservative) and Lena Jeger (Labour).
2   Louis Althusser (1918–90) illustrated this point through an analysis of the role played by the repressive state apparatus and the ideological state apparatus. In this framework of ideas, schools form part of the ideological apparatus of the state, functioning in part to mould individuals into subjects that fit the requirements of capitalism. Besides particular knowledge and skills imparted through the content of education, students learn submission, deference and respect for the established organisation of work and their place in it. The structuralist Marxism of Althusser takes social structure as its central focus. Here the emphasis is on institutional domination through the institutions created by dominant groups to ensure the continuance of their domination.
3   The term hegemony was used by the Italian Marxist Antonio Gramsci (1891–1937), founder and briefly leader of the Italian Communist Party. Gramsci was imprisoned by Mussolini and his writings in captivity were later published as *The Prison Notebooks*. Gramsci defines hegemony as the organising principle or world view diffused through agencies of ideological control and socialisation into every area of social life. In this context the key conceptual tool is what Gramsci calls cultural hegemony. Central to this idea is the notion that the dominant class lays down the terms and parameters of discussion in society; it tries to define and contain all taste, morality, and customs, religious and political principles. However, hegemonic control has to be won and maintained. Subordinate classes can always produce a counter hegemony in an attempt to modify, negotiate, resist or even overthrow the dominant culture. In humanist Marxism as articulated by Gramsci, humankind and the question of agency becomes the central focus.

References

Arnot, M. (1983) 'A cloud over co-education: an analysis of the forms of transmission of class and gender relations', in Walker, S. and Barton, L. (eds) *Gender, Class & Education*, Lewes: Falmer, pp. 69–91.

Arnot, M. (1984) 'How shall we educate our sons?', in Deem, R. (ed.) *Co-education Reconsidered*, Milton Keynes: Open University Press, pp. 37–56.

Arnot, M. (1989/90) 'Consultation or legitimation? Race and gender politics and the making of the national curriculum', *Critical Social Policy*, 29, pp. 20–38.

Arnot, M. (1994) 'Male hegemony, social class and women's education', in Stone, L. (ed.) *The Education Feminism Reader*, London: Routledge, pp. 84–104.

Arnot, M. (1996) 'The return of the egalitarian agenda? The paradoxical effects of recent educational reforms', *NUT Education Review*, 10 (1), pp. 9–14.

Arnot, M. (2002) *Reproducing Gender*, London: Routledge.

Arnot, M., David, M. and Weiner, G. (1996) *Educational Reforms and Gender Equality*, Manchester: Equal Opportunities Commission.

Arnot, M., David, M. and Weiner, G. (1999) *Closing the Gender Gap: Postwar Education and Social Change*, Cambridge: Polity Press.

Attar, D. (1990) *Wasting Girls' Time. The History and Politics of Home Economics*, London: Virago.

Ball, S.J. and Gewirtz, S. (1997) 'Girls in the education market: choice, competition and complexity', *Gender and Education*, 9 (2), pp. 207–22.

Benjamin, S. (2003) 'Gender and special educational needs', in Skelton, C. and Francis, B. (eds) *Boys and Girls in the Primary Classroom*, Maidenhead: Open University Press, pp. 98–112.

Benn, C. and Simon, B. (1972) *Half Way There. Report on the British Comprehensive-School Reform*, Harmondsworth: Penguin.

Benn, C., Parris, J., Riley, K.A. and Weiner, G. (1982) 'Education and women: the new agenda', *Socialism and Education*, 9 (2), pp. 10–13.

Burnett, J. (ed.) (1994 edition) *Destiny Obscure: autobiographies of childhood, education and family from the 1820s to the 1920s*. London: Routledge.

Caine, B. (1992) *Victorian Feminists*, Oxford: Oxford University Press.

Carter, A. (1988) *The Politics of Women's Rights*, London: Longman.

Clarricoates, C. (1980) 'The importance of being Ernest, Emma, Tom, Jane. The perception and categorization of gender conformity and gender deviation in primary schools', in R. Deem (ed.) *Schooling for Women's Work*. London: Routledge, pp. 26–41.

Corrigan, P. (1979) *Schooling the Smash Street Kids*, London: Macmillan.

David, M. (1983) 'Thatcherism is anti-feminism', *Trouble and Strife*, 1 (Winter), pp. 44–48.

Davin, A. (1979) 'Mind that you do as you are told', *Feminist Review*, 3, pp. 80–98.

Davin, A. (1996) *Growing Up Poor. Home, School and Street in London 1870–1914*, London: Rivers Oram Press.

Dean, D.W. (1991) 'Education for moral improvement, domesticity and social cohesion: the Labour government, 1945–1951', *Oxford Review of Education*, 17 (3), pp. 269–86.

Deem, R. (1981) 'State policy and ideology in the education of women, 1944–1980', *British Journal of Sociology of Education*, 2 (2), pp. 131–43.

Delamont, S. (1983) 'The Conservative School? Sex roles at home, at work and at school', in Walker, S. and Barton, L. (eds) *Gender, Class & Education*, Lewes: Falmer, pp. 93–105.

Department of Education and Science (DES) (1975) Curricular Differences for Boys and Girls, Education Survey 21, London: HMSO.

Digby, A. and Searby, P. (1981) *Children, School and Society in Nineteenth Century England*, London: Macmillan.

Dyhouse, C. (1981) *Girls Growing Up In Victorian and Edwardian England*, London: Routledge, Kegan and Paul.

Francis, B. and Skelton, C. (2005) *Reassessing Gender and Achievement: Questioning Contemporary Key Debates*, London: Routledge.

Gipps, C. and Murphy, P. (1994) *A Fair Test? Assessment, Achievement and Equity*, Milton Keynes: Open University Press.

Gomersall, M. (1994) 'Education for domesticity? A nineteenth century perspective on girls' schooling and domesticity', *Gender and Education*, 6 (3), pp 235–47.

Gorard, S., Rees, G. and Salisbury, J. (1999) 'Reappraising the apparent under-achievement of boys at school', *Gender and Education*, 11 (4), pp. 441–54.

Grant, L. (1994) 'First among equals', *Guardian Weekend*, 22 October, pp. 37–46.

Griffin, C. (1985) *Typical Girls? Young Women From School to the Job Market*, London: Routledge, Kegan and Paul.

Hunt, F. (1991) *Gender & Policy in English Education 1902–1944*, London: Harvester Wheatsheaf.

Hurt, J. (1979) *Elementary Schooling and the Working Classes 1860–1918*, London: Routledge, Kegan and Paul.

Kelly, A. (1985) 'The construction of masculine science', *British Journal of Sociology of Education*, 6, no. 2, pp. 133–154.

Lees, S. (1993) *Sugar and Spice: Sexuality and Adolescent Girls*, London: Routledge.

Littlejohn, M. (1995) 'Makers of men', in Dawtrey, L., Holland, J. and Hammer, M. with Sheldon, S. (eds) *Equality and Inequality in Education Policy*, Clevedon: Multilingual Matters in association with The Open University, pp. 46–55.

Llewellyn, M. (1980) 'Studying girls at school: the implications of confusion', in Deem, R. (ed.) *Schooling for Women's Work*, London: Routledge, Kegan and Paul, pp. 42–51.

Lucey, H., Brown, M., Denvir, H. Askew, M. and Rhodes, V. (2003) 'Girls and boys in the primary maths classroom', in Skelton, C. and Francis, B. (eds) *Boys and Girls in the Primary Classroom*, Maidenhead: Open University Press, pp. 43–58.

Marsh, J. (2003) 'Superhero stories', in Skelton, C. and Francis, B. (eds) *Boys and Girls in the Primary Classroom*, Maidenhead: Open University Press, pp. 59–79.

Martin, J. (1987) 'The origins and development of gendered schooling', unpublished MA dissertation, University of Warwick.

Martin, J. (1999) *Women and the Politics of Schooling in Victorian and Edwardian England*, Leicester: Leicester University Press.

Miles, S. and Middleton, C. (1995) 'Girls' education in the balance: the ERA and inequality', in Dawtrey, L., Holland, J. and Hammer, M. with Sheldon, S. (eds) *Equality and Inequality in Education Policy*, Clevedon: Multilingual Matters in association with The Open University, pp. 123–39.

Miller, J. (1996) *School for Women*, London: Virago.

Mirza, H. (1992) *Young, Female and Black*, London: Routledge.

Murphy, P. and Elwood, J. (1998) 'Gendered experiences, choices, and achievement – exploring the links', *The International Journal of Inclusive Education*, 2 (2), pp. 95–118.

Pankhurst, E. (1979) *My Own Story*, London: Virago.

Pascall, G. (1997) *Social Policy. A New Feminist Analysis*, London: Routledge.

Pascall, G. and Cox, R. (1993) 'Education and domesticity', *Gender and Education*, 5 (1), pp. 17–35.

Payne, I. (1980) 'Sexist ideology and education', in Spender, D. and Sarah, E. (eds) *Learning to Lose*, London: The Women's Press, pp. 32–8.

Purvis, J. (1995) 'Women and education 1800–1914', in Dawtrey, L., Holland, J. and Hammer, M. with Sheldon, S. (eds) *Equality and Inequality in Education Policy*, Clevedon: Multilingual Matters in association with The Open University, pp. 3–17.

Raphael Reed, L. (1998) '"Zero tolerance": gender performance and school failure' in Epstein, D. *et al.* (eds) *Failing Boys? Issues in Gender and Achievement*, Buckingham: Open University Press, pp. 56–76.

Rendel, M. (1997) *Whose Human Rights?*, London: Trentham.

Riddell, S. (1989) 'Pupils, resistance and gender codes: a study of classroom encounters', *Gender and Education*, 1 (2), pp. 183–98.

Riley, K.A. (1994) *Quality and Equality. Promoting Opportunities in Schools*, London: Cassell.

Schultz, T.W. (1970) 'The reckoning of education as human capital', in Hansen, W.L. (ed.) *Education, Income and Human Capital*, New York: National Bureau of Economic Research, pp. 295–306.

Simon, B. (1980) *Education and the Labour Movement 1870–1920*, London: Lawrence and Wishart.

Simon, B. (1994) *The State and Educational Change: Essays in the History of Education and Pedagogy*. London: Lawrence and Wishart.

Simon, B. (1991) *Education and the Social Order, 1940–1990*. London: Lawrence and Wishart.

Spender, D. and Sarah, E. (eds) (1980) *Learning to Lose*, London: The Women's Press.

Stantonbury Campus Sexism in Education Group, Bridgewater Hall School (1984) 'The realities of mixed schooling', in Deem, R. (ed.) *Co-Education Reconsidered*, Milton Keynes: Open University Press, pp. 57–73.

Stanworth, M. (1986) *Gender and Schooling. A Study of Sexual Divisions in the Classroom*, London: Hutchinson.

Thom, D. (1987) 'Better a teacher than a hairdresser? "A mad passion for equality" or, keeping Molly and Betty down', in Hunt, F. (ed.) *Lessons for Life. The Schooling of Girls and Women 1850–1950,* Oxford: Basil Blackwell, pp. 124–46.

Thompson. P. (1992) *The Edwardians*, London: Routledge.

TUC (2010) *Women and the Recession – One Year On,* TUC publications.

Turnbull, A. (1987) 'Learning her womanly work: the elementary school curriculum, 1870–1914', in Hunt, F. (ed.) *Lessons for Life. The Schooling of Girls and Women 1850–1950,* Oxford: Basil Blackwell, pp. 83–100.

Walkerdine, V., Lucey, H. and Melody J. (2001) *Growing Up Girl*, Basingstoke: Palgrave.

Watts, R. (2002) 'Pupils and students', in Aldrich, R. (ed.) *A Century of Education*, London: Routledge/Falmer.

Weiner, G. (1994) *Feminisms in Education,* Buckingham: Open University Press.

Willis, P. (1983) *Learning to Labour. How Working Class Kids Get Working Class Jobs*, Aldershot: Gower.

Wilson, E. (1980) *Only Halfway to Paradise Women in Postwar Britain: 1945–1968*, London: Tavistock Publications.

Wollstonecraft, M. (1792 [1975]) *A Vindication of the Rights of Woman*, Harmondsworth: Penguin.

Chapter 3

Racism in the UK

Change and continuity

Mike Cole

Introduction

In this chapter I begin by arguing that 'race' is an invalid scientific concept. I go on to identify nine features of contemporary racism. I then look at the neo-Marxist concept of racialization and at the nature of institutional racism, before asking the question: 'Why is it necessary to categorize racism?' I then consider older forms of British racism (colonial racism, antisemitism, and anti-Gypsy Roma and Traveller racism), before addressing some newer forms (xeno-racism, anti-asylum seeker racism, and Islamophobia). I argue that in contemporary Britain, there are a plethora of forms of racism. Given that contemporary British racism is multifaceted, and in order to set the scene for newer forms of racism, I begin by contextualizing them alongside older forms of racism, while also demonstrating that these older forms continue to flourish. For conceptual clarity I deal with colour-coded racism, non-colour-coded racism, and what I call hybridist racism separately. I make use of the neo-Marxist concept of racialization, and a newer concept of xeno-racialization to understand these multifarious forms of racism. I use the Gramscian concept of 'common sense' to assess how racialization interpellates[1] popular consciousness. Central to these processes of racialization and xeno-racialization are the roles of the Ideological State Apparatuses (ISAs) and the Repressive State Apparatuses (RSAs).[2] I conclude with a consideration of contemporary counter-hegemonic resistance to racism.[3]

'Race'

'Race' is a social construct. That this is the case is explained succinctly by Marxist geneticists Steven Rose and Hilary Rose (2005; see also Darder and Torres, 2004, pp. 1–12, 25–34). As they note, in 1972, the evolutionary geneticist Richard Lewontin pointed out that 85 per cent of human genetic diversity occurred *within* rather than *between* populations, and only 6 per cent to 10 per cent of diversity is associated with the broadly defined 'races' (Rose and Rose, 2005). As Rose and Rose explain, most of this difference is accounted for by the readily visible genetic variation of skin colour, hair form, and so on. The every-day business of seeing and acknowledging such difference is not the same as the project of genetics. For genetics and, more importantly, for the prospect of treating genetic diseases, the difference is important, since humans differ in their susceptibility to particular diseases, and genetics can have something to say about this. However, beyond medicine, the use of the invocation of 'race' is increasingly suspect. There has been a growing debate among geneticists about the utility of the term, and an entire issue of the influential journal *Nature Reviews Genetics* (Autumn 2004) was devoted to it. The geneticists agreed with most biological anthropologists that for human biology the term 'race' was an unhelpful leftover.

Rose and Rose conclude that '[w]hatever arbitrary boundaries one places on any population group for the purposes of genetic research, they do not match those of conventionally defined races'. For example, the DNA of native Britons contains traces of multiple waves of occupiers and migrants. 'Race', as a scientific concept, Rose and Rose conclude, 'is well past its sell-by date'. For these reasons, I would argue that 'race' should be put in quotation marks whenever one needs to refer to it.

Racism

I would like to identify nine features of modern-day racism, both in its ideological forms and its material practices. First, contemporary racism might best be thought of as a matrix of biological and cultural racism. I would argue that, in that matrix, racism can be based on biology or genetics. This is the case in erroneous beliefs that white people having higher IQs than black people (e.g. Frank Ellis—see Gair, 2006). Racism can also be based on culture and/or religion (as in contemporary manifestations of Islamophobia—see later in this chapter). Sometimes, however, it is not easily identifiable as either (e.g. 'Britain jobs for British workers'; see Cole, 2011a, Chapter 2), or is a combination of both. A good example of the latter is when Margaret Thatcher, at the time of the 1982 Falklands/Malvinas war, referred to the people of that island as 'an island race' whose 'way of life is British' (Short and Carrington, 1996, p. 66). Here we have a conflation of notions of 'an island race' like the British 'race' who, Baroness Thatcher believes, built an empire and ruled a quarter of the world through its sterling qualities (Thatcher, 1982) and, in addition, a 'race', which is culturally like 'us': 'their way of life is British'.

Second, there are also forms of racism that can be quite unintentional, which demonstrates that you do not have to be *a* racist (i.e. have allegiance to far-right ideologies) to be racist, or to be implicated in generating racism consequences. The use by some people in the UK, *out of ignorance,* of the term 'Pakistani' to refer to everyone whose mode of dress or accent, for example, signifies that they might be of Asian origin, might be an example of unintentional racism. The use of the nomenclature 'Paki', on the other hand, I would suggest, is generally used in an intentionally racist way because of the generally known negative connotations attached to the word in the UK. Another example from the UK is the now outmoded term 'coloured'—as in the usage 'coloured people', still used to describe black people. This may or may not be used in an intentionally racist way. There are, of course, terms used to describe black people that are intentionally offensive.

Third, racism can be direct or indirect. Direct racism is where a person is treated less favourably than another on 'racial' grounds. Indirect racism occurs when people from a specific 'racial' group cannot meet a rule, condition, or practice that should apply equally to everyone. For example, if school rules require a form of dress to which certain groups cannot comply for religious reasons—it could be because they are Muslims or Sikhs—this would be a form of indirect racism.

Fourth, racism, as practices, can be overt, as in racist name-calling in schools, or it can be covert, as in racist mutterings in school corridors, as a racialized (see the next section of this chapter) person walks by.

Fifth, whereas for neo-Marxist Robert Miles (1989, p. 79), racism relates to social collectivities identified as 'races' being 'attributed with negatively evaluated characteristics and/or represented as inducing negative consequences for any other', I would want to inflate Miles's definition to include 'seemingly positive attributes'.[4] Ascribing such attributes to an 'ethnic group' will probably ultimately have racist implications. For example, the subtext of describing a particular group as having a strong culture might be that 'they are swamping *our* culture'. This form of racism is often directed at people of South Asian origin in the UK who are assumed to have close-knit families and to be hard-working, and therefore in a position to 'take over' *our* neighbourhoods.[5] In addition, attributing something seemingly positive—'*they* are good rappers' or '*they* are good at sports'—might have implications that 'they are not good' at other things. In education this is something that facilitates the underachievement of working-class UK African Caribbean boys who are thought to be (by some teachers) less academically able, and 'problems'. Stereotypes and stratifications of ethnic groups are invariably problematic and, at least potentially, racist.

Sixth, racism can be dominative (in the form of direct and oppressive state policy) as in the apartheid era in South Africa or slavery in the US (see Cole, 2011a, Chapter 3), or it can be aversive, where people are segregated, excluded, or cold-shouldered on the grounds of racism (Kovel, 1988), or where they are routinely treated less favourably in day-to-day interactions.

Seventh, in certain situations, racism may well become (more) apparent given specific stimuli. For example, the media can generate racism (see Cole, 2011a). Similarly, racist sentiments or responses from a number of people who might be collectively present (physically or hooked up cybernetically) at a given moment or moments can facilitate further racist sentiments or responses. In addition, racism can increase with racist advances in the realm of the political ideological state apparatus. Racist attacks tend to increase when the fascist[6] British National Party (BNP) gains seats in local elections (e.g. Booth, 2010) or in European elections. Thus, following the election of BNP leader Nick Griffin to the European Parliament in June 2009, a string of racist attacks took place in the northwest of England, the area from which Griffin was elected (Choonara, 2009, p. 1).

Eighth, it should be noted that when somebody starts a sentence with the phrase 'I'm not racist but . . .', the undertone means that the next utterance will invariably be racist.

Ninth, racism is often colour-coded, but it can be non-colour-coded, or it can be hybridist, where it is not clear whether it is colour-coded or non-colour-coded. It can also be a combination of colour-coded and non-colour-coded racism (see Chapter 2 of Cole (2011a) for a discussion).

Racism defined

I would argue, therefore, that in order to encompass the multifaceted nature of contemporary racism, it is important to adopt a broad concept of racism rather than a narrow one, based as it was in the days of the British Empire, for example, on notions of overt biological inferiority. To reiterate our arguments, racism can be based on cultural and/or religious factors as well as biological ones, or it can be based on a combination of both biological and cultural and/or religious factors; racism can also be not easily identifiable as either biological or cultural. Racism can be unintentional as well as intentional; it can be direct or indirect; it can be overt as well as covert. Moreover, 'seemingly positive' attributes will probably ultimately have racist implications. Racism can be dominative (direct and oppressive) as well as aversive (exclusion and cold-shouldering). Racism can also become (more) apparent given certain stimuli. It should also be borne in mind that sentences that begin, 'I'm not racist but . . .' should be regarded as introducing a racist feeling or thought. Finally, racism is often colour-coded, but it can be non-colour-coded, or it can be hybridist, where it is not clear whether it is colour-coded or non-colour-coded. It can also be a combination of colour-coded and non-colour-coded racism. There can, of course, be permutations among these various forms of racism.

For these reasons, to underline my arguments, I would maintain that, in order to encompass the multifaceted nature of contemporary racism, it is important to adopt a broad concept and definition of racism, rather than a narrow one based on biological inferiority. Such a biological conception of racism was, of course, the norm in the days of the British Empire in India, Africa, and elsewhere. In this historical scenario, no doubt notions of cultural inferiority coexisted with perceptions of biological inferiority.

The neo-Marxist concept of racialization

Racialization refers to the categorization of people (falsely) into distinct 'races'. The neo-Marxist concept of racialization is distinct from other interpretations of racialization in that it purports that, in order to understand and combat racism, we must relate racism and racialization to historical, economic, and political factors. Specifically, the neo-Marxist concept of racialization makes the connection between racism and capitalist modes of production as well as making links to patterns of migration that are in themselves determined by economic and political dynamics. Thus the concept is able to relate to these factors; namely the real material contexts of struggle.

Miles (1993, pp. 50–52) has defined racialization as an ideological process, where people are categorized falsely into the scientifically defunct notion of distinct 'races'. Racialization, like racism, is socially constructed. In Miles's (1989, p. 75) words, racialization refers to 'those instances where social relations between people have been structured by the signification of human biological characteristics'. Elsewhere in the same book, Miles (p. 79) has added '[cultural characteristics] in such a way as to define and *construct* [my emphasis] differentiated social collectivities'. '[T]he process of racialization,' Miles states, 'cannot be adequately understood without a conception of, and explanation for, the complex interplay of different modes of production and, in particular, of the social relations necessarily established in the course of material production' (Miles, 1989, p. 7). It is this articulation with modes of production and with the ideological and the cultural that makes Miles's concept of racialization and my concept of xeno-racialization (Cole, 2004a)—see later in this chapter—inherently Marxist.

Racialization and 'common sense'

For Marxists, any discourse is a product of the society in which it is formulated. In other words: 'our thoughts are the reflection of political, social and economic conflicts and racist discourses are no exception' (Camara, 2002, p. 88). Dominant discourses tend to directly reflect the interests of the ruling class, rather than 'the general public'. The way in which popular consciousness is interpellated or hailed by spectres of racialized 'others' is via 'common sense'. 'Common sense' is generally used to denote a down-to-earth 'good sense' and is thought to represent the distilled truths of centuries of practical experience, so that to say an idea or practice is 'only common sense' is to claim precedence over the arguments of left intellectuals and, in effect, to foreclose discussion (Lawrence, 1982, p. 48). As Diana Coben (2002, p. 285) has noted, Gramsci's distinction between good sense and common sense 'has been revealed as multifaceted and complex'. For common sense:

> is not a single unique conception, identical in time and space. It is the "folklore" of philosophy, and, like folklore, it takes countless different forms. Its most fundamental characteristic is that it is . . . fragmentary, incoherent and inconsequential.
>
> (Gramsci, 1978, p. 419)

Good sense, on the other hand, for Gramsci is exemplified by Marxism. As Coben (1999, p. 206) has argued, good sense, for Gramsci, 'may be created out of common sense through an educative Marxist politics'. Gramsci believed that '"everyone" is a philosopher, and that it is not a question of introducing from scratch a scientific form of thought into everyone's individual life, but of renovating and making "critical" an already existing activity' (Gramsci, 1978, pp. 330–31). Gramsci also believed that '[a]ll men are intellectuals . . . but not all men have in society the function of intellectuals' (ibid., p. 9). Extending these insights to the whole of humankind (not just men!) forms the basis of the values that inform this book.

Institutional racism

The UK is an institutional racist society, and was recognized as such by the Stephen Lawrence Inquiry Report (Macpherson, 1999).[7] This definition was given a formal seal of approval by its having been read in the House of Commons on 24 February 1999 by the then Home Secretary, Jack Straw. It is interesting to note, however, that in repeating the definition verbatim in his speech to the House, Straw stresses the word 'unwitting'(http://news.bbc.co.uk/1/hi/uk/285553. stm, audio link available, accessed 5 July 2011). Institutional racism is defined in the report as:

> The collective failure of an organisation to provide an appropriate and professional service to people because of their colour, culture, or ethnic origin. It can be seen or detected in processes, attitudes and behaviour which amount to discrimination through unwitting prejudice, ignorance, thoughtlessness and racist stereotyping which disadvantage minority ethnic people.
>
> (Macpherson, 1999, 6.34)

From a neo-Marxist perspective, there is a need to situate the concept historically, economically, and politically. The Marxist concept of racialization thus also needs to be included to move away from the nebulous and ahistorical definition of institutional racism provided by Macpherson. I believe such a definition also needs to include 'common sense', which I argued in the last section of the Introduction connects racialization with popular consciousness.

Finally, in line with our definition of racism formulated earlier in this chapter, I would also want to add *intentional* as well as unintentional or unwitting racism. Institutional racism is thus reformulated as:

> Collective acts and/or procedures in an institution or institutions (locally, nationwide, continent-wide, or globally) that intentionally or unintention-ally have the effect of racializing, via "common sense," certain populations

or groups of people. This racialization process cannot be understood without reference to economic and political factors related to developments and changes in national, continent-wide, and global capitalism.

Why categorize racism?

Why then is it necessary to categorize racism? For those at the receiving end, it might well be argued that there may be less concern as to the origins of the racism experienced, and more concern about the effects such racism has. Racism is of course racism, irrespective of its origins. I would suggest, however, that there are three reasons for attempting to categorize contemporary British racism.

First, in the public perception, racism is assumed to be solely related to skin colour. This is a legacy of the British colonial era and its continuing significance. It is useful to the racist state in that it serves to mask other forms of racism. However, I will attempt to demonstrate that, while colour-coded racism remains highly significant, in fact, non-colour-coded racism also has a long history in Britain, and continues in newer forms, and also that we are witnessing a newer form of hybridist racism.

Robert Miles recognized the salience of non-colour-coded racism. Writing in 1993, he identified individuals and communities without skin colour markers from Ireland, Italy, Cyprus, Malta, Poland, and Jews from Russia and Germany.

The experiences of these communities highlighted, for Miles, that racism does not have to be based on skin colour. Miles (1993, p. 149) states that:

> it is not only "black" people that are the object of racism. Such an interpretation constitutes a strange perversion of European history, a history in which the concept of racism was generated to comprehend the use of "race" theory by the Nazis in the course of formulating a "final solution" to the "Jewish question".

Second, and allied to this, is the recent explosion of interest in Critical Race Theory (CRT) in the UK (e.g. Preston, 2007; Gillborn, 2008, 2009, 2010)[8] and, in particular, CRT's advocacy of the concept of 'white supremacy'. Critical Race Theorists argue that 'white supremacy' should be used to describe everyday racism in Britain, and not just the racism of fascist and other far-right groups. This provides another important reason to stress that both historically and contemporaneously not all racism is colour-coded, a fact that de facto limits the usefulness of 'white supremacy' as a descriptor.[9]

Third, in order to effectively combat racism, it is important to understand its multiple origins and forms. For the racist state in general, in the struggle to maintain hegemony, while it is important to divide the working class, it is equally important that named racism is restricted to as few scenarios as possible; ideally, merely to describe openly racist political parties and individuals. This can be useful for mainstream political parties to disguise their own racist policies and practices.

Older colour-coded racism

The colonial schema[10]

In the British colonial era, when Britain ruled vast territories in Africa, India, the Caribbean, and elsewhere, implicit in the rhetoric of imperialism was a racialized concept of 'nation'. Racism was institutionalized in popular culture in the British Imperial era in many ways: in popular fiction (Miles, 1982, pp. 110 and 119); in missionary work; in music halls; in popular art (Cole, 1992; Cole and Virdee, 2006); and in education. British capitalism had to be regenerated in the context of competition from other countries, and amid fears that sparsely settled British colonies might be overrun by other European 'races' (see Cole, 2009a, pp. 42–43).

The empire came home to roost after the Second World War. The demands of an expanding post-war economy meant that Britain, like most other European countries, was faced with a major shortage of labour. The overwhelming majority of migrants who came to Britain were from the Indian subcontinent, the Caribbean, and the Republic of Ireland (itself subject to British colonization in parts in the sixteenth and seventeenth centuries). Those industries where the demand for labour was greatest actively recruited Asian, black, and other minority ethnic workers in their home countries (Fryer, 1984; Ramdin, 1987). Despite the heterogeneous class structure of the migrating populations (see Heath and Ridge, 1983), migrant workers came to occupy, overwhelmingly, the semiskilled and unskilled positions in the English labour market (Daniel, 1968: Smith, 1977). Furthermore, they found themselves disproportionately concentrated in certain types of manual work characterized by a shortage of labour, shift working, unsocial hours, low pay, and an unpleasant working environment (Smith, 1977). The consequences of this process of racialization were clear. According to Miles (1982, p. 165), these different racialized groups came to occupy a structurally distinct position in the economic, political, and ideological relations of British capitalism, but within the boundary of the working class. They therefore constituted a fraction of the working class, one that can be identified as a racialized fraction.[11]

Today, while some descendants of migrant workers have moved up the social class ladder, racialization continues unabated. A couple of examples will suffice. As far as poverty is concerned, for example, there are stark differences with respect to ethnic group. Lucinda Platt (2007) summarizes this:

> Risks of poverty are highest for Bangladeshis, Pakistanis and Black Africans, but are also above average for Caribbean, Indian and Chinese people. Muslims face much higher poverty risks than other religious groups.

Two years later, Platt (2009, p. 26) noted that white British people had the lowest poverty rates, followed by Indians, black Caribbeans, black Africans, and Pakistanis, with Bangladeshis having the highest risks of poverty. Another example of the continued racialization of black and Asian people relates to institutional racism in the repressive state apparatus. Ministry of Justice statistics released in April 2009 revealed that black males are now eight times more likely to be stopped and searched by police than their white counterparts (cited in Ryder, 2009). Increasingly, these stops are being performed under section 44 of the Terrorism Act 2000 or under Section 60 of the Criminal Justice and Public Order Act 1994 (ibid.). As Matthew Ryder (2009) explains, unlike traditional measures, these powers do not require a police officer to have 'reasonable grounds for suspicion in making a stop' (ibid.).

This means that 'curiosity, dubious "hunches," even conscious or unconscious racial stereotyping, can go unchecked' (ibid.). The statistics reveal stop and search of African Caribbeans under counterterrorism legislation increased by 325 per cent in 2008 (ibid.). In London, half of all Section 60 stops were of black males (ibid.). Ryder (2009) points out that 'only a small percentage of stops glean meaningful information'. The Asian communities are also harassed. Ministry of Justice statistics also revealed that the number of Asian people stopped under the same laws rose by 277 per cent (Ministry of Justice, 2009, p. 29).[12] While anti-Asian racism (directed at those from the Indian subcontinent), as outlined above with respect to poverty, is a structural feature of UK society, police stoppages relate to Islamophobia, which I discuss under the heading of 'Newer hybridist racism' (see below).

Older non-colour-coded racism[13]

The schema of antisemitism[14]

While the biological 'inferiority' of Britain's imperial subjects was perceived mainly second-hand in the British colonial era,[15] the indigenous racism of the period was anti-Irish and anti-Semitic (e.g. Kirk, 1985; Miles, 1982). From the 1880s, there was a sizeable immigration of destitute Jewish people from Eastern Europe, and this fuelled the preoccupation of politicians and commentators about the health of the nation, the fear of the degeneration of 'the race', and the subsequent threat to imperial and economic hegemony (Holmes, 1979; Thane, 1982). Jewish people were routinely referred to in the same contemptuous way as the people in Britain's vast colonial empire (Cole, 2004b), described by the communications ISA as 'semi-barbarous', unable or unwilling to 'use the latrine', depositing 'their filth' on 'the floor of their rooms' (Holmes, 1979, p. 17) and involved in world conspiracy (thus directly threatening British Imperial hegemony): 'whenever there is trouble in Europe,' the ILP paper, *Labour Leader*, put it, '. . . you may be sure a hook-nosed Rothschild is at his games' (Cohen, 1985, p. 75). With respect to antisemitism today, while such racism is not generally acceptable in the public domain, it comes readily to the surface in certain contexts. As Soeren Kern (2009) argues, following the Israeli bombardment of the Gaza Strip in 2008–09, antisemitism increased dramatically across Europe. In Britain, the Community Security Trust (CST) reported a sharp increase in anti-Semitic attacks, including arson attacks on synagogues, physical assaults of Jews in London, and anti-Semitic graffiti scrawled in towns and cities across the country (Kern, 2009). British police also advised prominent British Jews to redouble their security arrangements after some of their names appeared on a 'Jewish hit list'.[16] As Mark Townsend (2009) explains, with anti-Semitic incidents running at around seven a day as of February 2009, safety fears were so acute that members of Britain's Jewish community were leaving the UK. He states that around 270 such incidents were reported up until then, whereas attacks recorded during the first Palestinian intifada of the late 1980s averaged 16 a month (ibid.). Scotland Yard, he goes on, is understood to have put prominent Jewish communities on heightened alert, and the Association of Chief Police Officers' national 'community tension team' was issuing weekly patrol directives to chief constables instructing them of threats to Jewish communities in their areas (ibid.). Townsend describes the nature of incidents:

> [They] include violent assaults in the street, hate emails and graffiti threatening "jihad" against British Jews. One disturbing aspect involves the targeting of Jewish children. A Birmingham school is investigating reports that 20 children chased a 12-year-old girl, its only Jewish pupil, chanting "Kill all Jews" and "Death to Jews."
>
> (Ibid.)[17]

In February 2009, the CST published its annual report on anti-Semitic incidents for 2008, which revealed that around 550 were recorded in the UK that year (cited in ibid.). Mark Frazer, spokesperson for the Board of Deputies of British Jews, said:

> We are seeing an unprecedented level of attacks directed at the Jewish community, both physical and verbal. It is incumbent upon us all to isolate and marginalise those who would derail the legitimate political debate with an extremist and hateful ideology.
>
> (Cited in ibid.)

One year later, CST (2010) recorded 924 anti-Semitic incidents in 2009, the highest annual total since it began recording anti-Semitic incidents in 1984, and 55 per cent higher than the previous record of 598 incidents in 2006. There were 124 violent anti-Semitic assaults in 2009, the highest number ever recorded by CST. Sixty-eight anti-Semitic incidents involved Jewish schools, school children, or teachers as targets. Another source, the Stephen Roth Institute for the Study of Contemporary Antisemitism and Racism (cited in

Lemberg, 2010), cited the UK as having the largest increase in the number of 'violent antisemitic incidents and vandalism' in the world in 2009—374— compared with 112 in 2008. Contemporary antisemitism in the UK, like Islamophobia (discussed below), needs to be seen in the context of hegemonic global US capitalism and imperialism, in which Israel is a key player. It is also crucial, of course, to be vigilant against 'world conspiracy theory', briefly referred to above, and 'holocaust denial', which have for so long been part of the rhetoric of fascists and other racists, the former reaching its apotheosis in that exceptional form of the capitalist state (Poulantzas, 1978, p. 123) and associated mode of production in Nazi Germany,[18] the latter mouthed by neo-fascists in various countries whose aim presumably is to reinstall similar exceptional forms of the capitalist state, and related modes of production. It is also vital to make a distinction between antisemitism on the one hand, and anti-Zionism and the State of Israel's close relationship with the US on the other. This is particularly important for Marxists and other left factions whose brief must be total and unremitting opposition to all forms of racism.[19]

Anti-Gypsy Roma and Traveller racism[20]

Gypsy Roma and Traveller communities include English Romani Gypsies, Welsh Gypsies, Irish Travellers, Scottish Gypsy/Travellers, Travelling Showpeople, Circus People, Boat-Dwellers, Fairground Travellers, New Travellers and Romanis from Central and Eastern Europe who have arrived as refugees or asylum seekers (Clark, 2006b, p. 8, Clark, 2006c, p. 12) (with respect to this last constituency, we have a possible conflation with xeno-racism and anti-asylum seeker racism—see below).

By the late nineteenth century, despite increased statutory controls, such as the 1822 General Turnpike Road Act that charged a 40-shilling fine for camping on the side of a turnpike road (Greenfields, 2006, pp. 60–61) (a law that was still in place until 1980 [Diverse Herts, 2009]), traditional stopping places were reasonably freely available (Greenfields, 2006, p. 62), and, as Duffy and Tomlinson (2009, p. 2) argue, always surviving on the margins of society, Gypsy people became a useful source of cheap labour seasonally in the fields, as blacksmiths and as entertainers.

A pattern of travelling on specific circuits continued until the Second World War, when with the need for intensive labour, members of the Gypsy Roma and Traveller communities were recruited into semi-permanent work on the land, in the mining industries, in the army, and in factory and munitions work (Greenfields, 2006, p. 63).

After the Second World War, with the mechanization of farming, the lifestyle of Gypsies changed drastically (Duffy and Tomlinson, 2009, p. 2). This mechanization of the traditional rural work started in the 1950s, and previous sources of livelihood in the rural areas were no longer sufficient. With industrialization began the migration from rural areas. The changes in society were also reflected in the Romany Gypsy population. No longer wanted for hop or strawberry picking and other traditional trades, they found that they had to adapt. Work was difficult to find for some families and the motorization of families also changed the travel patterns. Many Gypsies moved from the rural areas to the cities and towns (ibid.), often meeting hostile reactions from the local population and from the authorities (Greenfields, 2006, p. 65). Where caravans were visible to non-Gypsy Roma and Traveller people, for example, next to a roadside, this attracted the attention of the authorities, and thus began a cycle of rapid repeat eviction (ibid., p. 66). Many families reluctantly sought to be rehoused into local authority (Council) accommodation (ibid., p . 71). However, in 2006, some 3,500 to 4,000 Gypsy and Traveller families continued to live 'illegally' on the roadside (Clark, 2006a, p. 286).

It has been estimated that one-third of the total Gypsy Roma and Traveller population lives in 'unauthorised roadside encampments' (Greenfields, 2006, p. 57). As Rachel Morris (2006) has argued, Gypsy Roma and Traveller peoples are in many ways an 'invisible' minority. Although 'visible' in the literal sense, as Colin Clark explains, while English Romani Gypsies since 1988 and Irish Travellers since 2000 have been regarded in law as 'minority ethnic groups', in general terms, this legal status has largely been unrecognized by the majority of the settled population, and those working for local authorities and other agencies that deal with Gypsy Roma and Traveller communities (Clark, 2006a, p. 283). Far from being regarded as a 'real' minority ethnic group, they are regarded as an 'eyesore' or a 'nuisance' (ibid., p. 286). As such, racist acts may not be viewed as such. Clark (2006b, pp. 3–4) gives the example of the torching of an effigy of a caravan with a Gypsy family painted on the side, the registration plate of which was 'P1 KEY', the perpetrators of which were not prosecuted for incitement to racial hatred (Clark, 2006a, pp. 3–4). He also cites the racist murder of a 15-year-old Irish Traveller, who was kicked, stamped, and beaten to death. This was also judged not to be motivated by racist hatred, the defendants receiving four and a half years for manslaughter (ibid., pp. 5–6). Given that the barrister in this case argued that the attack was motivated by racist hatred of Irish Travellers (ibid., p. 5), and that the murdered young man had 'an identifiable Irish accent', we see here the conflation of anti-Gypsy Roma and Traveller racism and anti-Irish racism. Duffy and Tomlinson (2009, p. 1) reveal the extent of institutional racism that affects Gypsy and Traveller communities who have the poorest life chances of any ethnic group. There is a greater incidence of ill health among Gypsies and Travellers, and 18 per cent of Gypsy and Traveller mothers have experienced the death of a child, as compared to 1 per cent of the settled community.[21] With respect to education, in a survey of exam results in the UK's 30,000 secondary schools, children of 'Travellers of Irish Heritage' and those of 'Gypsy Roma' origin were the worst-performing minority ethnic group at GCSEs (General Certificate of Secondary Education) (Department for Education, Statistical First Release, 2010). At the same time, the proportion of pupils in the 'Gypsy/Romany' category reaching the expected level in both English and maths fell from 28.9 per cent in 2008 to 24.8 per cent in 2009 (Department for Children, Schools and Families, 2009). Families with young children, Duffy and Tomlinson point out, are evicted on a daily basis, under Section 62a of the Criminal Justice Act of 1994, which is used to hound homeless families from one district to another (ibid., p. 3), a clear example of the repressive state apparatus in practice. Duffy and Tomlinson (2009, p. 1) list many other issues faced daily by the community, such as the effects of the communications ISA; in particular, in the form of racist media reporting. As Clark (2006b, pp. 1–2) has argued, there has been a collective assumption that tabloid racism against Gypsy Roma and Traveller peoples is seen as 'safe ground', since there would be little response to this form of racism. As the then Commission for Racial Equality (now subsumed under the Equality and Human Rights Commission) put it in 2004, discrimination against Gypsies and Travellers is the last 'respectable' form of racism (CRE, 2004, cited in Gypsy Roma Traveller Leeds, 2007). The *Sun* both captures and creates working-class racism and racialization. In its 24 March 2008 edition, for example, the front page headlines declared: 'Gypsy Hell for Tessa.' The article was referring to the fact that 64 Travellers had 'set up camp just yards from the country home of the then Government Minister Tessa Jowell' (p. 1). Above the headline was the caption, 'Easter Holiday Invasion'. Other descriptors included '30 caravans swarmed on to the . . . field' (p. 1); 'Gypsy Nightmare'; 'crafty gypsies' (p. 4); 'these families' (p. 8). More recently, a columnist of the Murdoch Sunday paper, *The News of the World*, Carole Malone, referred to 'gypsies and travellers' in the following terms: '[n]one of these people have jobs or pay tax and most of them contribute little or nothing to society'; 'travellers are constantly moving and don't live ordered lives like the rest of us'; '[a]nd why do these armies of people who descend on peaceful villages all over Britain bringing chaos and distress get special treatment?'; '[i]t's not our fault they choose not to live in a house—although they seem fairly adept at knocking up jerry-built dwellings on land that doesn't belong to them'; '[a]nd how come they're allowed to break the law, particularly planning laws, with impunity, yet the minute one of us does 35mph in a 30 limit we get clobbered?' The interpellation concludes: '[i]t's not fair. It's not right' (*The News of the World*, 21 June 2009). A final example of the ongoing tirade against the Gypsy Roma and Traveller communities occurred at the time of writing. Andy Crick claimed in *The Sun* (27 August 2010, p. 34) that Irish Travellers wishing to see the Pope had 'thrown [his visit] into turmoil amid fears hordes of gipsies will gatecrash a mass'. He went to point out that '[w]aves' had already arrived. Duffy and Tomlinson (2009, p. 1) also note a lack of understanding by service providers. This is either through lack of cultural awareness, racism, or by just failing to understand the needs of the communities. Families cite racist bullying as a major issue for removing children from schools (ibid., 2009, p. 7). Under the ConDem government, Gypsy Roma and Traveller communities are already faring worse. The Regional Strategies plan that set targets for councils to provide land has been scrapped, and £30 million of funding for Gypsy and Traveller sites has been withdrawn (Robinson, 2010, p. 4). The coalition is drafting new laws that will allow police more powers to evict and arrest people for trespass on public land (*The Observer*, 2010). In addition, planning laws are also being altered to stop applications for retrospective permission to put caravans on private land; regional planning bodies that were to oversee provision of registered sites are being abolished; and grants for councils to provide sites have been slashed. At the same time, an estimated £18m a year is being spent on evictions (ibid.). Founding member of the Gypsy Council, Gratton Puxon, commented: 'Gypsies are being squeezed on all sides in this wave of intolerance and racism which is unlike anything I've ever seen before' (cited in ibid.).

Newer forms of racism

Liz Fekete (2009) has written at length about newer forms of racism. Her specific focus is on anti-asylum seeker racism, xeno-racism, and Islamophobia. Explaining the underlying economic dimension of these newer forms, Fekete explains how the combination of anti-immigration movements and an onslaught from the communications ISA in the form of the press became too much for mainstream parties. From the perspective of the political ISA: politicians knew full well that, because of Europe's declining birth rates, an ageing population and shortage of skilled workers in some areas, and semi-skilled and unskilled workers in others, Europe was in desperate need of migrant workers. But they also knew that to openly acknowledge this would be to antagonize the electorate. At the same time, governments feared that the globalization-inspired irregular movements of people, resulting in migratory flows of labour surplus to Europe's economic needs, would derail a political strategy based on micro-managing the migration process quietly and behind the scenes (Fekete, 2009, p. 6).[22]

Gareth Dale (1999, p. 308) notes how migrant workers are a perfect solution in times of intensified labour market flexibility, but also recognizes the contradiction between capital's need for (cheap) flexible labour and the need for hegemonic control of the workforce by racializing potential foreign workers:

> On the one hand, intensified competition spurs employers' requirements for enhanced labour market flexibility—for which immigrant labour is ideal. On the other, in such periods questions of social control tend to become more pressing. Governments strive to uphold the ideology of 'social contract' even as its content is eroded through unemployment and austerity. The logic, commonly, is for less political capital to be derived from the [social contract's] content, while greater emphasis is placed upon its exclusivity, on demarcation from those who enter from or lie outside— immigrants and foreigners.

Exemplifying institutional racism in the political ISA in the UK, and as a precursor to Gordon Brown's infamous racist interpellation in September 2007,

'British jobs for British workers', Fekete notes how, in the run-up to the 2001 General Election, Conservative leader William Hague, in a speech to the Conservative Party conference, used the phrase 'We will give you back your country' eight times (Fekete, 2009, p. 7). Current institutional racism of this form might be seen as the zenith of England's historic interconnection between racism and nationalism. As Robert Miles (1989) put it: 'English nationalism is particularly dependent on and constructed by an idea of "race," with the result that English nationalism encapsulates racism' and that 'the ideas of "race" and "nation," as in a kaleidoscope merge into one another in varying patterns, each simultaneously highlighting and obscuring the other.' 'British jobs for British workers' and 'getting our country back' can be perceived in Gramscian terminology as 'common sense'—'it's only common sense that we should put jobs for British workers first and keep the immigrants out; this will make sure we get our country back and keep our nationality in the face of this immigrant threat.'

Newer non-colour-coded racism

Xeno-racism

On 1 May 2004, 10 more countries joined the European Union (EU): Cyprus, the Czech Republic, Estonia, Hungary, Latvia, Lithuania, Malta, Poland, Slovakia, and Slovenia, bringing the total from 15 to 25 member states. On 1 January 2007, two more countries, Bulgaria and Romania, joined the EU. This fact has given rise to a new form of non-colour-coded racism, directed primarily at Eastern European workers: xeno-racism. Sivanandan (2001, p. 2) has defined xeno-racism as:

> a racism that is not just directed at those with darker skins, from the former colonial countries, but at the newer categories of the displaced and dispossessed whites, who are beating at western Europe's doors, the Europe that displaced them in the first place. It is racism in substance but xeno in form—a racism that is meted out to impoverished strangers even if they are white. It is xeno-racism.

Fekete's interpretation of xeno-racism is a wide one that incorporates not just racism directed at European migrant workers, but also Islamophobia (e.g. Fekete, 2009, pp. 43–44, p. 69) and anti-asylum seeker racism (e.g. ibid., p. 15, p. 19, pp. 41–42). While Sivanandan (2001) does refer to asylum seekers under this definition of xeno-racism, and indeed to those with darker skins from the former colonies as in the quote above, it is my view that conceptually it is better to restrict xeno-racism to that form of racism directed at Eastern European migrant workers. Indeed, in the Foreword to Fekete's book, Sivanandan writes of non-colour-coded racism directed at East European workers as follows: 'the treatment meted out to (white) East European immigrants [stems] from a compelling economics of discrimination, effectively racism under a different colour, xeno-racism' (Sivanandan, 2009, p. viii).

There are two reasons for my preference for restricting xeno-racism to (white) Eastern European migrant workers (and their families). First, those Eastern European migrant workers who are inhabitants of an EU country have the right, unlike other migrant workers, to work anywhere in the UK. Second, xeno-racism thus defined is region-specific, or even country-specific (unlike anti-asylum seeker racism and Islamophobia, which is not region-specific). Moreover, 'xeno-racism' is, of course, derived from 'xenophobia', and, if the Online Etymology Dictionary (2001) is correct, the latter was first used just before the First World War, in 1912, and itself had early Eastern European connections—between 1914 and 1917, in response to xenophobia aimed at citizens of the Austro-Hungarian Empire arising out of the First World War, 8,579 Eastern Europeans were interned (Berryhill and Sturgeon Ltd, undated).

There is abundant evidence of xeno-racism in this restricted definition of the term. Eastern European workers are also xeno-racialized and pathologized by the communications ISA; and certain tabloids (in particular, *The Sun*) have unleashed anti-Polish and other anti-Eastern European racist rhetoric on a regular basis, alleging a drain on resources, whereas in fact, Eastern European workers make positive contributions to the society on a number of levels (Ruddick, 2009, p. 8). Nevertheless, such workers are on the receiving end of institutional racism on a number of levels—having fewer rights than British workers, being subjected to immigration raids, having a higher rate of un-employment and lower wages (ibid.). Jane Hardy (2009, p. 137) notes how legally employed migrant workers 'face huge problems at work'. She describes the abuse of such workers over employment contracts and wages, and lists com-plaints of 'excessive working hours with inadequate breaks and no enhanced overtime' (ibid.). She cites evidence (Fitzgerald, 2007; Hardy and Clark, 2007; Anderson, Ruhs, Rogaly and Spencer, 2006) of 'recruitment and temporary labour agencies' imposing 'high charges for finding employment, lower payment than promised and the withholding of wages' (Hardy, 2009). In East Anglia, workers from the new EU countries, she states, are widely used in agriculture, food processing, distribution, and supermarkets, where 'there is evidence of terrible working conditions and bullying' (ibid.), and of 'gangmasters running some small towns' (ibid., pp. 137–138). Truck drivers from the new EU countries working in supermarket distribution centres, she concludes, are often on zero-hour contracts (contracts that do not guarantee work and pay only for work actually done), and Polish workers she interviewed in a fruit-packing factory were continually told to work faster to meet supermarket demands (ibid., p. 138).

Following Jordan and Düvell (2002) Hardy also notes complaints from migrant workers concerning overpriced, overcrowded, and shoddy housing (2009). There is well-documented evidence of contemporary racist attacks on Polish workers in the UK (see BBC News, 2008a, b, c, d, e, f, g, 2009a, b, c, d, e).

Like the migrant workers from the former British colonies in the immediate post-war period, the structurally distinct position in British capitalism of racialized Eastern European workers (Cole, 2009a, pp. 44–45) means that they also constitute, adapting Miles (1982, p. 165), a xeno-racialized fraction of the working class. I will thus restrict the usage of the term xeno-racism, and deal with anti-asylum seeker racism and Islamophobia separately, under the heading of what I will call hybridist racism.[23]

Newer hybridist racism

Under this heading I am including anti-asylum seeker racism and Islamophobia. My reason for using the term 'newer hybridist racism' is because, unlike the forms of racism described above that are on the one hand essentially colour-coded, and, on the other, essentially non-colour-coded, anti-asylum seeker racism and Islamophobia can be either colour-coded or non-colour-coded. These forms of racism can also encompass a combination of colour-coded and non-colour-coded racism. For example, most asylum seekers come from Iraq, Zimbabwe, Somalia, and Afghanistan (Refugee Action, 2009).[24] This means that, while the racism directed at most Zimbabwean asylum seekers is colour-coded, that meted out to Somalis, given that Somalia is in 'sub-Saharan Africa' (itself a term with colour-coded racist implications), will be colour-coded, but may also be Islamophobic, which is not necessarily colour-coded (see below), or it may be a combination of colour-coded (anti-black) racism and non-colour-coded racism (Islamophobia). That form of racism experienced by Afghans and Iraqis is also ambiguous, and may or may not be more Islamophobic than colour-coded.

Anti-asylum seeker racism[25]

We are interpellated that it is 'common sense' to keep out asylum seekers, just as we are interpellated that it is 'common sense' to have 'British jobs for British workers' and 'get our country back' and keep our nationality. This is dealt with both by the political ISA and the communications ISA; in particular, the right-wing tabloids. From the 1990s, political and legal ISAs laid the groundwork for the rendering of asylum seekers illegal. Fekete describes how 'both center-Right and center-Left parties began to implement laws that criminalized asylum seekers' (Fekete, 2009, p. 8). She provides painstaking documentation of the multifaceted horrors of anti-asylum seeker racism in contemporary Europe. While no one can deny the exploitative nature of the smuggling networks that bring asylum seekers to Europe, she reminds us that it is the blocking of legal routes that 'throw them into the arms of smugglers and traffickers' (ibid., p. 23). Institutional racism directed at asylum seekers by government RSAs is apparent throughout the continent. It is now an offence all over Europe, she notes, to assist anyone trying to cross an 'illegal' border, whether they are in need of protection or not (ibid.).

'Dealing' with asylum seekers also entails the brute force of the RSA—in the form of detention. Institutional racism exists also in the form of a separate prison complex for asylum seekers, where the 'use of measures more germane to serious criminal investigation, such as the compulsory finger printing of all asylum seekers . . . has become routine' (ibid., p. 39). Moreover, asylum seekers can be detained indefinitely under the Immigration Acts, as long as they are being detained 'with a view to removal' (ibid., p. 40). The aim of detention is 'to break down the will of detainees, so as to make them compliant to their own removal' (ibid., p. 15). Thus, Fekete concludes, those 'who challenge their proposed deportation may be asked to choose between lengthy detention in the host country or return to torture in their country of origin' (ibid.). Fekete quite rightly describes this as 'psychological torture' (ibid.).

Although the detention of children has now ended, families with all legal rights exhausted are given two weeks to leave the UK voluntarily. If they do not, children and parents are forcibly removed from their homes and taken directly to the airport to board a plane. In the event of parents of affected families resisting on the day, the family could be separated, with children possibly taken into care, while police/immigration officials deal with parents.

Fekete (2009, p. 137) explains that the motor that sets 'the brutal deportation machine' in motion is 'targets', initiated throughout Europe by respective government RSAs. For example, in 2004, Tony Blair established a deportation formula based on the 'monthly rate of removals' exceeding 'the number of unfounded applications' (ibid., p. 137). As Fekete argues, the imposition of such targets 'necessarily undermines the whole humanitarian principle of refugee policy—'need not numbers'—and becomes its obverse, 'numbers not need' (ibid.), with failed asylum seekers being reduced to 'a statistic for removal, even when they have strong claims to remain on humanitarian grounds' (ibid.). Forced removal involves 'officially sanctioned state violence' (ibid.) on both routine passenger flights and on chartered special flights and military jets (ibid.). The latter are increasingly favoured, since passengers, pilots, and crew on commercial flights object to the violence, which can include:

> crying children frogmarched on to planes . . . violent control and restraint methods against adult deportees, who may be bound head and foot, gagged (with special adhesive tape) or have their heads forced into the special deportation helmet (a chin strap prevents the deportee from moving [the] lower jaw, an additional strap covers the detainee's mouth).
>
> (Ibid.)

The tabloids are not the only element of the communications ISA brought into play to justify and effect asylum seeking. Sometimes, for example, the depor-tations are filmed to discourage attempts at seeking asylum. For example, the UK government sent a film crew to film the deportation of about 24 Afghans from Gatwick airport, to be broadcast in Afghanistan as a warning to those considering coming to Britain (ibid., p. 138). With respect to health, free National Health Service (NHS) treatment was removed from failed asylum seekers in 2004, except in the case of emergency, adversely affecting cancer sufferers, newly diagnosed HIV/AIDS patients, and pregnant women (Fekete, 2009, p. 37). The Department of Health in the UK even tried (unsuccessfully) in 2007 to ban failed asylum seekers from primary care at doctors' surgeries (ibid.).

In 2009, the Borders, Citizenship and Immigration Act came into force, designed to simplify immigration law, strengthen borders and extend the time it takes to gain citizenship.

According to a report published by the Institute of Race Relations (IRR) in October 2010 (IRR, 2010), racist-asylum seeker and immigration policies in the UK have led to the deaths of 77 asylum seekers and migrants over the past four years. Of these, seven are reported as dying after being denied health care for 'preventable medical problems'; more than one-third are suspected or known suicides after asylum claims have been turned down; seven are said to have died in prison custody; and 15 to have died during 'highly risky' attempts to leave the country (ibid.).

Islamophobia[26]

The first recorded use of the term 'Islamophobia' in English was in 1991 (Richardson, 2009, p. 11), which coincided with the first Gulf War (1990–91) and the upsurge of anti-Muslim racism and hate crime that accompanied it (Poynting and Mason, 2001). Islamophobia is a major form of racism in the modern world. It is important to stress that, while Islamophobia may be sparked by skin colour, like the forms of non-colour-coded racism described above, Islamophobia is not necessarily triggered by skin colour—it can also be set off by one or more (perceived) symbols of the Muslim faith. As Sivanandan (2009, p. ix) puts it, referring to British Muslims—'the terrorist within'—'the victims are marked out not so much by their colour as by their beards and headscarves' (ibid.).

As far as the communications ISA is concerned, Fekete points out how Muslim cultures are presented 'through the grossest of stereotypes and simplification' (ibid., p. 48), whereas in fact, such cultures are no more of a monolith than Christian ones (ibid., p. 85). Nevertheless they are treated as all the same, both in terms of the racism directed at them and in terms of being a threat— the 'repressive force [of] global Islam' (ibid., p. 125). The 'repressive force of global Islam' is met by the RSAs of the British state. Fekete (2009, p. 55) discusses the growing trend whereby arrests and prosecutions are based not on material evidence but on 'crimes of association'; that is, 'association with terrorists or with the associates of terrorists'. Thus the trustees of mosques fall under suspicion if they have been fundraising for international causes, such as humanitarian relief for Palestinian refugees in the occupied territories on the spurious ground that 'even though the emergency relief was not destined for terrorist organisations, some of it may have ended up in their hands' (ibid., p. 50).

The UK Terrorism Act of 2000 further cemented institutional racism aimed at Muslims by creating new offences based on the circulation of information useful for terrorism (Fekete, 2009, p. 109). The possession of certain books, for example, is an offence. Even accessing the internet, perhaps merely out of interest, for information on political or radical Islam can lead to imprisonment (ibid.). Finally, measures introduced throughout Europe make it possible to deprive citizenship of those with dual nationality who display symptoms of 'unacceptable behaviour' such as the glorification of terrorism (ibid., p. 119).

Unlike anti-asylum seeker racism and xeno-racism, Islamophobia has less to do with immigration and more, in its contemporary form, to do with the aftermath of the 9/11 attack on the Twin Towers in New York in 2001, and the suicide bombings of 7 July 2005 (7/7) in Britain, when a coordinated attack was made on London's public transport system during the morning rush-hour. Islamophobia is closely related to both old UK and new US imperialisms (e.g. in Iraq and Afghanistan) to hegemony and oil. The fact that 'Bin Laden' became a playground form of abuse for children perceived to be of Asian origin bears witness to this.

Contemporary counter-hegemonic resistance to racism

If we assess the 1950s and 1960s, it is clear that apart from isolated cases, there is little evidence of collective counter-hegemonic resistance to racism per se (Cole and Virdee, 2006). However, from the mid-1960s, such resistance intensified (for extensive analyses of resistance see, for example, Sivanandan, 1982, 1990; Virdee, 1999a, b; Virdee and Grint, 1994). Key 'single issue' organizations are active today such as the Board of Deputies of British Jews, which dates back to 1760; JCOR, the Jewish Council for Racial Equality, founded in 1976; the Palestine Solidarity Campaign, founded in 1972; the Muslim Association of Britain, formed in 1997; and the National Coalition of Anti-Deportation Campaigns (NCADC), open 24 hours a day, seven days a week, 365 days a year since it was founded in 1995. While centralizing their particular concerns, all take a general antiracist stance against institutional racism, and the various racist interpellation processes of the ISAs and the brute force of the RSAs.

Prominent in generalized antiracist activity in the twenty-first century are Unite Against Fascism, Searchlight, HOPE Not Hate, the Stop the War Coalition, and Love Music Hate Racism. The first three organizations focus on defeating the BNP, although campaign against racism generally, while the Stop the War Coalition coordinates campaigns against modern imperialist wars. Combining antiracist counter-hegemony with cultural resistance is Love Music Hate Racism.

Unite Against Fascism is a campaigning group that has the aim as 'a matter of the greatest urgency' of 'calling for the broadest unity against the alarming rise in racism and fascism in Britain today . . . in particular the British National Party (BNP)' (Unite Against Fascism [UAF], 2010). Formed in 2003, UAF aims to unite the broadest possible spectrum of society to counter the threat of the BNP, and more recently the English Defence League (EDL), Scottish Defence League (SDL), and the Welsh Defence League (WDL) (see Cole, 2011a, Chapter 1). Its members include a number of Members of Parliament of all political persuasions, as well as the Socialist Workers Party (SWP), trade union leaders, and some music bands.

The remit of Searchlight, a British anti-fascist magazine founded in 1975, is to publish exposés of fascism, antisemitism, and racism in the UK. Searchlight disaffiliated from the UAF in 2005, partly because of tactical issues (Searchlight favours a local rather than a national strategy).

HOPE Not Hate, an offshoot of Searchlight, mobilizes everyone opposed to the BNP's politics of hate. It was formed in 2005 as a positive antidote to the BNP and has the support of *The Daily Mirror*, trade unions, celebrities, and community groups across the country. It is involved in localized campaigning, working within the communities where the BNP is attracting its support.

The Stop the War Coalition was formed in 2001 at a public meeting of over 2,000 people in London. Its aims are to create a mass movement to stop the war currently declared by the US and its allies against 'terrorism', and to oppose any racist backlash generated by the war against terrorism (Stop the War Coalition, 2009). While Stop the War condemns the attacks on New York and feels the greatest compassion for those who lost their lives on 11 September 2001, it argues that 'any war will simply add to the numbers of innocent dead, cause untold suffering, political and economic instability on a global scale, increase racism and result in attacks on civil liberties' (ibid.).

In its own words, 'Love Music Hate Racism uses the positive energy of the music scene to fight back against the racism being pushed by Nazi organisations like the BNP' (Love Music Hate Racism, 2009). As the organization puts it:

> Our music is living testimony to the fact that cultures can and do mix. It unites us and gives us strength, and offers a vibrant celebration of our multi-cultural and multiracial society. Racism seeks only to divide and weaken us. Love Music Hate Racism was inaugurated in 2002 in response to rising levels of racism and electoral successes for the BNP. Its aim is to use the energy of music 'to celebrate diversity and involve people in anti-racist and antifascist activity—as well as to urge people to vote against fascist candidates in elections . . . in the tradition of the Rock Against Racism (RAR) movement of the late 1970s' in order 'to create a national movement against racism and fascism through music'.
>
> (Love Music Hate Racism, 2009)

Conclusion

In this chapter I began by arguing that 'race' is an invalid scientific concept. I then identified nine features of contemporary racism, before defining the neo-Marxist concept of racialization. Making the case that it is essential to categorize racism, I have attempted to outline some of its main forms in contemporary Britain. In the 1970s and 1980s, it was fashionable to draw a distinction between 'white' and 'black' with all racialized constituencies falling under the latter category. If that was inadequate terminology then, it is most certainly lacking in twenty-first-century Britain. From a Marxist perspective, the real enemy is not, of course, the various racialized minorities discussed in this chapter, but the very system that profits (literally and ideologically) from the exploitation of these minorities. In diverse ways, racism and (xeno-)racialization serve the 'divide and rule' tactics of capitalism and direct workers' attentions away from that real enemy and toward their racialized sisters and brothers. This was recognized by Marx some 140 years ago:

> In all the big industrial centres in England there is profound antagonism between the Irish proletariat and the English proletariat. The average English worker hates the Irish worker as a competitor who lowers wages and the standard of life. He feels national and religious antipathies for him. He regards him somewhat like the poor whites of the Southern states regard their black slaves.
>
> This antagonism among the proletarians of England is artificially nourished and supported by the bourgeoisie. It knows that this scission is the true secret of maintaining its power.
>
> (Marx, 1870 [1978]), p. 254)

Racism is a fluid process. It is unlikely that before the demise of Stalinism anyone would have predicted the xeno-racialization of Eastern European workers in the UK. In the current crisis in capitalism, as many of these workers return home, future trends in (xeno-)racialization are uncertain. What is clear from a Marxist perspective is that past, present, and future trends can be best understood with references to ongoing changes and developments in the economic and ideological manifestations of the capitalist mode of production, related patterns of migration, and the onward march of imperialism. From a neo-Marxist perspective, these changes and developments will be reflected in ongoing changes in state interpellative and hegemonic strategies. For (neo) Marxist counter-hegemonic resistance to be effective, these changes and developments merit close monitoring.

Notes

1 Interpellation is the concept Althusser (1971, p. 174) used to describe the way in which ruling class ideology is upheld and the class consciousness of the working class—that class's awareness of its structural location in capitalist society—undermined. 'Ideological' when used by Marxists means ideas that act in the interests of the capitalist class. Interpellation makes us think that ruling class capitalist values are actually congruent with our values as *individuals*. Althusser stressed that it is individuals rather than classes or groups that are interpellated or hailed, thereby bypassing any actual or potential social class allegiances.

2 Althusser (1971) identified two state apparatuses—the repressive state apparatuses (RSAs) and the ideological state apparatuses (ISAs). Each function both by violence and by ideology. As Althusser (1971, pp. 144–145) explains, while the repressive state apparatus 'functions massively and predominantly by repression (including physical repression)', it functions 'secondarily by ideology'. He gives the example of the army and the police, which while they form part of the RSAs, also 'function by ideology both to ensure their own cohesion and reproduction, and in the "values" they propound externally'. As far as the ISAs are concerned, Althusser notes that while they 'function massively and predominantly by ideology', they 'function secondarily by repression, even if ultimately, but only ultimately, this is very attenuated and concealed, even symbolic'. He instances schools, churches, the family, and the cultural ISAs that are not *only* ideological but use methods of punishment such as expulsion and censorship.

3 This chapter draws heavily on the Introduction and especially Chapter 2 of Cole (2011a).

4 Miles's discussions of racism, as an exemplar of neo-Marxist analysis, are probably the most widely cited in the UK. I should point out that my definition of racism is different from that favoured by Miles and his associates who are totally against inflating the concept of racism (see the Appendix to the Introduction of Cole (2011a) for a discussion).

5 Steve Fenton (2003, p. 164) has used the term 'ethnic majoritarian thinking' to describe the process of making a distinction between the (ethnic) majority, an almost unspoken 'us', and members of minority ethnic communities. This distinction is underlined by the fact that in Britain, for example, British Muslims have to substantiate their allegiance to Britain. After the Forest Gate terror raid (where the police raided the home of two innocent Muslim brothers, one of whom was shot, though not fatally; see Cole and Maisuria, 2010), the media highlighted the fact that the brothers stated they were 'born and bred' East Londoners and they 'loved Britain' (Getty, 2006, p. 5).

6 Fascism is a political philosophy based on racism and a strong patriotic belief in the nation. Once in power fascists centralize authority under a dictatorship, and promote belligerent nationalism. Workers and their organizations are smashed, as is any form of opposition through terror and censorship. Fascism tends to arise when capitalist democracy becomes unable to sustain capitalism. As Leon Trotsky put it: '[t]he historic function of fascism is to smash the working class, destroy its organizations, and stifle political liberties when the capitalists find themselves unable to govern and dominate with the help of democratic machinery' (Trotsky, 1944). The BNP do not self-describe as 'fascist', but there is considerable evidence (e.g. Copsey, 1994; Richardson and Wodak, 2009; Goodwin, 2010) that their core beliefs are such, and a wide spectrum of political opinion that concurs, including the right-wing Conservative prime minister, David Cameron (*The Telegraph,* 27 May 2009) (for an analysis of fascism, see Cole, 2011b).

7 The Stephen Lawrence Inquiry Report (Macpherson, 1999) followed a lengthy public campaign initiated by the parents of black teenager Stephen Lawrence,

murdered by racists in 1993. A bungled police investigation means that there have been no convictions. The report looked at racism in the Metropolitan Police and other British institutions, and acknowledged the existence of institutional racism in the police, the education system, and other institutions in the society. In subsequent years, the concept of institutional racism has been under sustained political attack in the UK (see Cole (2011a, Chapter 4) for a discussion).

8 In June 2009, a conference titled 'Critical Race Theory in the U.K. What is to be learnt? What is to be done?' was held at the Institute of Education, University of London. Over 30 papers were presented, and the conference included contributions from leading UK Critical Race Theorists David Gillborn, Namita Chakrabarty, and John Preston. There was a significant undercurrent of 'black exceptionalism' (see the beginning of Chapter 3 in Cole, 2011a). One of the main conference organizers, Kevin Hylton, heralded the birth of 'BritCrit'.

9 For a critique of the concept of 'white supremacy' as deployed by Critical Race Theorists, see Cole, 2009a, pp. 23–33; see also Cole, 2009b, pp. 247–255. For a CRT response, see Mills, 2009. The importance of differentiating the traditional use of the term 'white supremacy' to describe the ideology of fascists and other far-right racists from 'everyday racism' was underlined for me in the 2009 elections to the European Parliament (see Cole (2011b) for a discussion).

10 The concept of 'the colonial schema' is Etienne Balibar's (see Balibar, 1991, p. 12).

11 I recall seeing ads in shop windows for accommodation in Hammersmith, West London in the 1960s that (before it was made illegal) ended with 'No coloureds. No Irish.' Such racialization was typical and rampant at that time.

12 In 2010, a report by the Equality and Human Rights Commission found black people were at least six times more likely and Asian people about twice as likely to be stopped and searched than white people. The Commission said it could not rule out legal action against some forces (BBC News, 2010). The evidence suggested that racial stereotyping and discrimination were significant factors behind these higher rates of stops and searches (ibid.). Black and ethnic minority youths were also overrepresented in the criminal justice system (ibid.). Additionally, the police were more likely to give white young people more lenient reprimands or fines, while black young people were more likely to be charged. Along with the continued racialization of black and Asian constituencies, the racialization of the Irish also continues (see Delaney, 2007; Mac An Ghaill, 2000; see also the discussion in this chapter of anti-Gypsy and Roma Traveller racism).

13 Not all forms of racism discussed in this chapter under the heading of 'non-colour-coded racism' are necessarily definitively non-colour-coded. There are, for example, dark-skinned Jewish people who may experience colour-coded racism rather than or alongside antisemitism. The point is that the forms of racism discussed under this heading are not *necessarily* colour-coded.

14 This concept is also Etienne Balibar's (see Balibar, 1991, p. 12). However, whereas Balibar puts a hyphen between 'anti' and 'Semitism', I have omitted it, on the grounds that Jewish communal organizations in the UK—such as the Community Security Trust—use the unhyphenated 'antisemitism'. This more closely reflects Wilhelm Marr's use of the word that he and others advocate to describe a policy toward Jews based on 'racism' (Langmuir, 1990, p. 311, cited in Iganski and Kosmin, 2003, pp. 6–7). Not using a hyphen or a capital 'S' denotes that anti-semitism is a form of racism directed at Jewish people per se, and not at those who speak a Semitic language per se. Semitic languages are spoken by nearly 500 million people across large parts of the Middle East, North Africa, and Northeast Africa. The most widely spoken Semitic language is Arabic.

15 I use the adverb 'mainly' because there were settlements of colonial citizens in various parts of the UK during the colonial era (Fryer, 1984).

16 The rest of Kern's (2009) article takes an anti-left, pro-Israel stance.

17 While the reference to 'jihad' *could* imply the involvement of antisemitic radical Islamists, there is no evidence that contemporary antisemitic attacks are predominantly the work of 'extremist groups'. Indeed such attacks, including the daubing of swastikas on synagogues and graves, are prompted not 'by a particular ideological conviction or volition but instead unthinkingly manifest a common-sense antisemitism' (Iganski, 2009, p. 138).

18 The mode of production in Nazi Germany involved the state exercising ultimate control of the economy, with the seizure of the property of Jewish people. Selected corporations, which supported the state in its programme, operated with monopoly power. This mode of production also involved the slave labour of Jewish people and others deemed by the fascist state to be subhuman.

19 David Latchman (2010, cited in Reisz, 2010) has expressed concerns about antisemitism among some parts of the Muslim population in the UK, and what he describes as 'far Left' 'antisemitism'. It is my view that those who claim to be anti-imperialist and anti-Zionist and on the left, but also express antisemitism in any form, are not truly on the left and certainly not modern-day Marxists.

20 I deal with anti-Gypsy Roma and Traveller racism under the main heading of 'Non-colour-coded racism' because my focus is the UK. I am aware, of course, that many European Roma people have darker skins, and that this will be a component in the racism directed at them. An example of anti-Roma racism occurred in Belfast in June 2009, when there were violent attacks on a Roma community from Romania (Shilton, 2009). One of those affected stated: '[t]hey made signs like they wanted to cut my brother's baby's throat. They said they wanted to kill us.' Reports claimed that there was graffiti in the area containing the slogans of the neo-Nazi Combat 18 group. It was also reported that extracts from Hitler's *Mein Kampf* had been put through letter-boxes (ibid.). Attacks were also directed against those seeking to help the Roma people (ibid.). The fascists also wrote texts connecting racism against the Roma with xeno-racism, thanking 'all true loyalists for forcing Romanian Muslims out of Belfast and also Polish in mid Ulster out of their homes! These foreign nationals are a threat to Britain's Britishness' (see later in this chapter for a discussion of xeno-racism).

21 As Thomas Acton has pointed out, 'if official statistics about "Gypsies'" health relate only to poor caravan-dwelling people who have come to the notice of the authorities, they omit those Romani people who are living in houses or who use private caravan sites' (his comments on Cole (2011a, Chapter 2)).

22 Fekete's centralizing of 'the economic' accords with the neo-Marxist formulation of racialization.

23 Of course, there may be overlap between xeno-racism, anti-asylum seeker racism, and Islamophobia. For example, some Eastern European workers are Muslim, as are many asylum seekers (see the next section of this chapter).

24 My focus here on *current* anti-asylum seeker racism under the heading 'Newer hybridist racism' is not of course to underestimate the fact that this form of racism has a long history in the UK and elsewhere (for an analysis, see, for example, Schuster, 2002).

25 I recognize the problematic nature of the term 'asylum seeker'. It forms part of a 'discourse of derision' (Ball, 1990, p. 18) in the communications ISA, and in the political ISA in the pronouncements of certain politicians. 'Forced migrants' (Rutter, 2006) might be a more appropriate term.

26 Islamophobia as a concept is not without its problems, with some commentators making the case for different terms. For example, the Commission on the Future of Multi-ethnic Britain (2000) and Arun Kundnani (2007) prefer 'anti-Muslim racism', while others (e.g. Etienne Balibar, cited in Modood, 2005) favour Muslimophobia.

However, as Robin Richardson (2009, p. 11) points out, Islamophobia is widely used in the UK and in the deliberations and publications of international organizations, and '[d]espite its disadvantages, the term Islamophobia looks as if it is here to stay' (for a thorough analysis of Islamophobia and related concepts and terms, see Richardson, 2009).

References

Althusser, L. (1971) 'Ideology and Ideological State Apparatuses', in *Lenin and Philosophy and Other Essays,* London: New Left Books, http://www.marx2mao. com/Other/LPOE70NB.html (accessed 16 July 2011).

Anderson, B., M. Ruhs, B. Rogaly, and S. Spencer (2006) *Fair Enough? Central and East European Migrants in Low-Wage Employment in the UK,* York: Joseph Rowntree Foundation.

Balibar, E. (1991) 'Racism and Politics in Europe Today', *New Left Review,* 186, pp. 5–19.

Ball, S. (1990) *Politics and Policymaking in Education,* London: Routledge.

BBC News (2008a) 'Attack on House Treated as Racist', http://news.bbc.co.uk/1/hi/ northern_ireland/foyle_and_west/7452233.stm (accessed 27 July 2008).

—— (2008b) 'Cash Raised after Racist Attack', http://news.bbc.co.uk/1/hi/england/ shropshire/7304198.stm (accessed 27 July 2008).

—— (2008c) 'Gang Attack Polish Man with Knife', http://news.bbc.co.uk/1/hi/ england/lincolnshire/7299238.stm (accessed 18 December 2008).

—— (2008d) 'Man in Unprovoked Racist Assault', http://news.bbc.co.uk/1/hi/ scotland/edinburgh_and_east/7350036.stm (accessed 27 July 2008).

—— (2008e) 'Pole Subjected to "Racist Attack"', http://news.bbc.co.uk/1/hi/ scotland/north_east/7358197.stm (accessed 27 July 27 2008).

—— (2008f) 'Prison for Racist Polish Attack', http://news.bbc.co.uk/1/hi/scotland/ edinburgh_and_east/7433720.stm (accessed 27 July 2008).

—— (2008g) 'Rise in Racist Attacks Reported', http://news.bbc.co.uk/1/hi/ northern_ireland/7266249.stm (accessed 27 July 2008).

—— (2009a) '"More Needed" to Tackle NI Racism', http://news.bbc.co.uk/1/hi/ northern_ireland/8129460.stm (accessed 23 March 2010).

—— (2009b) 'Plea after "Brutal" Racist Attack', http://news.bbc.co.uk/1/hi/ scotland/north_east/8147157.stm (accessed 4 December 2009).

—— (2009c) 'Polish Man Attack "Was a One Off"', http://news.bbc.co.uk/1/hi/ scotland/north_east/8152527.stm (accessed 23 March 2010).

—— (2009d) 'Prison for Racist Polish Attack', http://news.bbc.co.uk/1/hi/scotland/ edinburgh_and_east/7433720.stm (accessed 23 March 2010).

—— (2009e) 'Racist Link to Town Gang Attack', http://news.bbc.co.uk/1/hi/ northern_ireland/7838319.stm (accessed 23 March 2010).

—— (2010) 'Police Stop and Search "Target Minorities"', http://news.bbc.co.uk/1/ hi/uk/8567528.stm (accessed 17 April 2010).

Berryhill and Sturgeon Ltd (undated) '1912 Canada Prime Minister Robert Borden Signed Letter', http://berryhillsturgeon.com/Archives/Canada/Borden/Borden 1912.htm (accessed 16 July 2011).

Booth, R. (2010) 'Rise in Hate Crime Follows BNP Council Election Victories', *The Guardian,* 15 January, www.guardian.co.uk/politics/2010/jan/15/hate-crime-bnp-local-council-elections (accessed 30 January 2010).

Camara, B. (2002) 'Ideologies of Race and Racism', in P. Zarembka (ed.), *Confronting 9–11, Ideologies of Race, and Eminent Economists*, Oxford: Elsevier Science.

Choonara, E. (2009) 'BNP Gains Led to This Racist Attack', *Socialist Worker*, 4 July.

Clark, C. (2006a) 'Conclusion', in C. Clark and M. Greenfields, *Here to Stay: The Gypsies and Travellers of Britain*, Hatfield: University of Hertfordshire Press.

—— (2006b) 'Introduction', in C. Clark and M. Greenfields, *Here to Stay: The Gypsies and Travellers of Britain*, Hatfield: University of Hertfordshire Press.

—— (2006c) 'Who Are the Gypsies and Travellers of Britain?', in C. Clark and M. Greenfields, *Here to Stay: The Gypsies and Travellers of Britain*, Hatfield: University of Hertfordshire Press.

Coben, D. (1999) 'Common Sense or Good Sense: Ethnomathematics and the Prospects for a Gramscian Politics of Adults' Mathematics Education', in M. van Groenestijn and D. Coben (eds), *Mathematics as Part of Lifelong Learning. The Fifth International Conference of Adults Learning Maths—A Research Forum, ALM-5* (pp. 204–209), London: Goldsmiths College, University of London, in Association with ALM, www.alm-online.net/images/ALM/conferences/ALM05/proceedings/ ALM05-proceedings-p204-209.pdf?7c979684e0c0237f91974aa8acb4dc29=36f0 is6pst9523pt8acs48p337 (accessed 7 June 2010).

—— (2002) 'Metaphors for an Educative Politics: "Common Sense," "Good Sense" and Educating Adults', in C. Borg, J. Buttigieg and P. Mayo (eds), *Gramsci and Education*, Lanham, MD: Rowman and Littlefield.

Cohen, S. (1985) 'Anti-Semitism, Immigration Controls and the Welfare State', *Critical Social Policy*, 13, Summer.

Cole, M. (1992) *Racism, History and Educational Policy: From the Origins of the Welfare State to the Rise of the Radical Right*, Unpublished PhD thesis, University of Essex.

—— (2004a) 'F★★★ You—Human Sewage: Contemporary Global Capitalism and the Xeno-racialization of Asylum Seekers', *Contemporary Politics*, 10 (2), pp. 159–165.

—— (2004b) '"Brutal and Stinking" and "Difficult to Handle": The Historical and Contemporary Manifestations of Racialisation, Institutional Racism, and Schooling in Britain', *Race Ethnicity and Education*, 7 (1), March, pp. 35–56.

—— (2009a) *Critical Race Theory and Education: A Marxist Response*, New York: Palgrave Macmillan.

—— (2009b) 'Critical Race Theory Comes to the UK: A Marxist Response', *Ethnicities*, 9 (2), pp. 246–269.

—— (2011a) *Racism and Education in the U.K. and the U.S.: Towards a Socialist Alternative*, New York: Palgrave Macmillan.

—— (2011b) 'Capitalist Crisis and Fascism: Issues For Educational Practice', in D. R. Cole (ed.), *Surviving Economic Crises Through Education*, New York: Peter Lang.

Cole, M. and A. Maisuria (2010) 'Racism and Islamophobia in Post-7/7 Britain: Critical Race Theory, (Xeno-)racialization, Empire and Education – A Marxist Analysis', in D. Kelsh, D. Hill and S. Macrine (eds), *Class in Education: Knowledge, Pedagogy, Subjectivity*, New York: Routledge.

Cole, M. and S. Virdee (2006) 'Racism and Resistance: From Empire to New Labour', in M. Cole (ed.), *Education, Equality and Human Rights: Issues of Gender, 'Race,' Sexuality, Disability and Social Class* (3rd edition), London: Routledge.

Commission on the Future of Multi-ethnic Britain (2000) London: Runnymede Trust.

Community Security Trust (CST) (2010) 'Antisemitic Incidents Report 2009', www. thecst.org.uk/docs/CST-incidents-report-09-for-web.pdf (accessed 16 July 2011).

Copsey, N. (1994) 'Fascism: The Ideology of the British National Party', *Politics*, 14, pp. 101–108.

Dale, G. (1999) 'Capitalism and Migrant Labour', in G. Dale and M. Cole (eds), *The European Union and Migrant Labour*, Oxford: Berg.

Daniel, W. W. (1968) *Racial Discrimination in England*, Harmondsworth: Penguin.

Darder, A. and R. D. Torres (2004) *After Race: Racism after Multiculturalism*, New York: New York University Press.

Delaney, E. (2007) *The Irish in Post-War Britain*, Oxford: Oxford University Press.

Department for Children, Schools and Families (DCSF) (2009) 'Statistical First Release', www.dcsf.gov.uk/rsgateway/DB/SFR/s000889/SFR312009KS2Attainment byPupilCharacteristics.pdf (accessed 19 December 2009).

Department for Education, Statistical First Release (2010) 'GCSE and Equivalent Attainment by Pupil Characteristics in England, 2009/10', www.education.gov. uk/rsgateway/DB/SFR/s000977/SFR37_2010.pdf (accessed 6 April 2011).

Diverse Herts (2009) 'Travellers Community History', www.diverseherts.org.uk/ community.php?CID=80&Title=Travellers (accessed 24 July 2009).

Duffy, R. and A. Tomlinson (2009) 'Education on the Hoof', Paper presented to the first Centre for Education for Social Justice Seminar at Bishop Grosseteste University College Lincoln, 19 January, www.bishopg.ac.uk/docs/C4E4SJ/Education%20on %20the%20Hoof.pdf (accessed 10 February 2011).

Fekete, L. (2009) *A Suitable Enemy: Racism, Migration and Islamophobia in Europe*, London: Pluto Press.

Fenton, S. (2003) *Ethnicity*, Cambridge: Polity Press.

Fitzgerald, I. (2007) *Working in the UK: Polish Migrant Worker Routes into Employment in the North East and North West Construction and Food Processing Sectors*, London: TUC.

Fryer, P. (1984) *Staying Power: The History of Black People in Britain*, London: Pluto Press.

Gair, R. (2006) 'Ellis Faces Disciplinary Charges', http://campus.leeds.ac.uk/news includes/newsitem3675.htm (accessed 2 September 2009).

Getty, S. (2006) 'East Enders Say They Love London', *The Metro*.

Gillborn, D. (2008) *Racism and Education: Coincidence or Conspiracy?*, London: Routledge.

—— (2009) 'Who's Afraid of Critical Race Theory in Education? A Reply to Mike Cole's "The Color-Line and the Class Struggle"', *Power and Education*, 1 (1), pp. 125–131.

—— (2010) 'The White Working Class, Racism and Respectability: Victims, Degenerates and Interest-Convergence', *British Journal of Educational Studies*, 58 (1), pp. 3–25.

Goodwin, M. J. (2010) *The New British Fascism: Rise of the British National Party*, Abingdon: Routledge.

Gramsci, A. (1978) *Selections from Prison Notebooks*, London: Lawrence and Wishart.

Greenfields, M. (2006) 'Stopping Places', in C. Clark and M. Greenfields (eds), *Here to Stay: The Gypsies and Travellers of Britain*, Hatfield: University of Hertfordshire Press.

Gypsy Roma Traveller Leeds (2007) 'Strategy on Gypsies and Travellers', www.grt leeds.co.uk/information/CRE.html (accessed 22 March 2010).

Hardy, J. (2009) 'Migration, Migrant Workers and Capitalism', *International Socialism*, 122, pp. 133–153.

Hardy, J. and N. Clark (2007) 'EU Enlargement, Workers and Migration: Implications for Trade Unions in the UK', Geneva: International Labour Organisation.

Heath, A. and J. Ridge (1983) 'Social Mobility of Ethnic Minorities', *Journal of Biosocial Science*, Supplement, 8, pp. 169–184.

Holmes, C. (1979) *Anti- Semitism in British Society 1876–1939*, London: Edward Arnold.

Iganski, P. (2009) 'The Banality of Anti-Jewish "Hate Crime"', in R. Blazak (ed.), *Hate Crime Offenders*, Westport, CT: Praeger.

Iganski, P. and B. Kosmin (2003) 'The New Antisemitism Debate: Background and Context', in P. Iganski and B. Kosmin (eds), *A New Antisemitism? Debating Judeophobia in 21st Century Britain*, London: Profile Books.

Institute of Race Relations (IRR) (2010) *Driven to Desperate Measures*, London: IRR.

Jordan, B. and F. Düvell (2002) *Irregular Migration, the Dilemmas of Transnational Mobility*, Cheltenham: Edward Elgar.

Kern, S. (2009) 'Anti-Semitism Sweeps Europe in Wake of Gaza Operation', *The Brussels Journal*, www.brusselsjournal.com/node/3745# (accessed 4 May 2009).

Kirk, N. (1985) *The Growth of Working Class Reformism in Mid-Victorian England*, London: Croom Helm.

Kovel, J. (1988) *White Racism: A Psychohistory*, London: Free Association Books.

Kundnani, A. (2007) *The End of Tolerance: Racism in 21st Century Britain*, London: Pluto Press.

Lawrence, E. (1982) 'Just Plain Common Sense: The "Roots" of Racism', in Centre for Contemporary Cultural Studies (ed.), *The Empire Strikes Back: Race and Racism in 70s Britain*, London: Hutchinson.

Lemberg, I. (2010) 'Anti-Semitic Incidents Rise Sharply in 2009, Study Says', CNN, http://edition.cnn.com/2010/WORLD/meast/04/12/anti.semitic.study/index.ht ml (accessed 26 April 2010).

Love Music Hate Racism (2009) www.lovemusichateracism.com/ (accessed 15 October 2009).

Mac An Ghaill, M. (2000) 'The Irish in Britain: The Invisibility of Ethnicity and Anti-Irish Racism', *Journal of Ethnic and Migration Studies*, 26 (1), pp. 137–147.

Macpherson, W. (1999) *The Stephen Lawrence Enquiry, Report of an Enquiry by Sir William Macpherson*, London: HMSO, www.archive.official- documents.co.uk/document/cm42/4262/4262.htm (accessed 30 January 2011).

Marx, K. (1870 [1978]) *Ireland and the Irish Question*, Moscow: Progress.

Memarian, O. (2009) 'Islamophobia Alive and Well in the U.S.', *IPS News*. http://ipsnews.net/news.asp?idnews=46620 (accessed July 3, 2010).

Miles, R. (1982) *Racism and Migrant Labour*, London: Routledge and Kegan Paul.

—— (1989) *Racism*, London: Routledge.

—— (1993) *Racism after 'Race Relations'*, London: Routledge.

Mills, C. W. (2009) 'Critical Race Theory: A Reply to Mike Cole', *Ethnicities*, 9 (2), pp. 270–281.

Ministry of Justice (2009) *Statistics on Race and the Criminal Justice System 2007/8: A Ministry of Justice Publication under Section 95 of the Criminal Justice Act 1991*, April, www.justice.gov.uk/publications/docs/stats-race-criminal-justicesystem-07-08-revised.pdf (accessed 16 July 2011).

Modood, T. (2005) *Multicultural Politics: Racism, Ethnicity and Muslims in Britain*, Edinburgh: Edinburgh University Press.

Morris, R. (2006) 'Nomads and Newspapers', in C. Clark and M. Greenfields, *Here to Stay: The Gypsies and Travellers of Britain,* Hatfield: University of Hertfordshire Press.

Observer, *The* (2010) 'New Wave of Evictions Threatens Gypsies', 1 August, www.guardian.co.uk/society/2010/aug/01/gypsies-evictions-planning (accessed 6 July 2011).

Online Etymology Dictionary (2001) /www.etymonline.com/index.php? (accessed 16 July 2011).

Platt, L. (2007) 'Poverty and Ethnicity in the UK', www.jrf.org.uk/publications/poverty-and-ethnicity-uk (accessed 16 May 2009).

—— (2009) *Ethnicity and Child Poverty: Department for Work and Pensions Research Report No 576,* London: Department of Work and Pensions.

Poulantzas, N. (1978) *State, Power, Socialism,* London: Verso.

Poynting, S. and V. Mason (2001) 'The Resistible Rise of Islamophobia: Anti-Muslim Racism in the UK and Australia before 11 September 2001', *Journal of Sociology,* 43 (1), pp. 61–86.

Preston, J. (2007) *Whiteness and Class in Education,* Dordrecht: Springer.

Ramdin, R. (1987) *The Making of the Black Working Class in Britain,* London: Gower.

Refugee Action (2009) 'The Global Perspective', http://www.refugee-action.org.uk/information/challengingthemyths1.aspx (accessed 23 May 2009).

Refugee and Migrant Justice (2010) *Safe at Last? Children on the Front Line of UK Border Control,* London: Refugee and Migrant Justice, http://refugeemigrantjustice.org.uk/downloads/RMJ%20Safe%20at%20Last%20WEB.pdf (accessed 23 March 2010).

Reisz, M. (2010) 'Library that Helped Bring Nazis to Justice to Relocate', *Times Higher Education,* 14 January, www.timeshighereducation.co.uk/story.as p?storyCode=409956&sectioncode=26 (accessed 4 February 2011).

Richardson, J. E. and Wodak, R. (2009) 'Recontextualising fascist ideologies of the past: right-wing discourses on employment and nativism in Austria and the United Kingdom', *Critical Discourse Studies,* 6 (4), pp. 251–267.

Richardson, R. (2009) 'Islamophobia and Anti-Muslim Racism—Concepts and Terms, and Implications for Education', *Race Equality Teaching,* 27 (1), pp. 11–16.

Robinson, S. (2010) 'Travellers Resist Tory Assault on Their Rights', *Socialist Worker,* 11 September.

Rose, S. and H. Rose (2005) 'Why We Should Give Up on Race: As Geneticists and Biologists Know, the Term No Longer Has Meaning', *The Guardian,* 9 April, www.guardian.co.uk/comment/story/0,,1455685,00.Html (accessed 2 November 2009).

Ruddick, S. (2009) 'Myths and Migrants', *Socialist Worker,* 8 August, p. 8.

Rutter, J. (2006) *Refugee Children in the UK,* Buckingham: Open University Press.

Ryder, M. (2009) 'The Police Need to Stop and Think about Stop and Search', *The Observer,* 3 May, www.guardian.co.uk/commentisfree/2009/may/03/matthew-ryder-police-stop-and-search (accessed 10 May 2009).

Schuster, L. (2002) 'Asylum and the Lessons of History', *Race and Class,* 44 (2), pp. 40–56.

Shilton, J. (2009) 'Northern Ireland: Racist Attacks Force 100 Roma Out of Belfast', *World Socialist Web Site (WSWS),* 4 July, www.wsws.org/articles/2009/jul2009/roma-j04.shtml (accessed 1 August 2010).

Short, G. and B. Carrington (1996) 'Anti-Racist Education, Multiculturalism and the New Racism', *Educational Review,* 48 (1), pp. 65–77.

Sivanandan, A. (1982) *A Different Hunger: Writings on Black Resistance*, London: Pluto Press.

—— (1990) *Communities of Resistance: Writings on Black Struggles for Socialism*, London: Verso.

—— (2000) 'UK: Reclaiming the Struggle', *Race and Class*, 42 (2), pp. 67–73.

—— (2001) 'Poverty Is the New Black', *Race and Class*, 43 (2), pp. 1–5.

—— (2009) 'Foreword' to L. Fekete, *A Suitable Enemy: Racism, Migration and Islamophobia in Europe,* London: Pluto Press.

Smith, D. J. (1977) *Racial Disadvantage in Britain,* Harmondsworth: Penguin.

Stop the War Coalition (2009) http://stopwar.org.u k/content/blogcategory/24/41/ (accessed 16 July 2011).

Thane, P. (1982) *Foundations of the Welfare State,* London: Longman.

Thatcher, M. (1982) 'Speech to Conservative Rally at Cheltenham', The Thatcher Foundation, www.margaretthatcher.org/document/104989 (accessed 16 July 2011).

Townsend, M. (2009) 'Rise in Antisemitic Attacks "the Worst Recorded in Britain in Decades"', *The Guardian,* www.guardian.co.uk/world/2009/feb/08/police-patrols-antisemitism-jewish-community (accessed 27 August 2009).

—— (2010) 'English Defence League Forges Links with America's Tea Party', *The Observer,* 10 October, www.guardian.co.uk/uk/2010/oct/10/english-defence-league- tea-party (accessed 16 July 2011).

Unite Against Fascism (UAF) (2010) http://uaf.org.uk/about/ (accessed 4 February 2011).

Virdee, S. (1999a) 'England: Racism, Anti-racism and the Changing Position of Racialised Groups in Economic Relations', in G. Dale and M. Cole (eds), *The European Union and Migrant Labour,* Oxford: Berg.

—— (1999b) 'Racism and Resistance in British Trade Unions: 1948–79', in P. Alexander and R. Halpern (eds), *Labour and Difference in the USA, Africa and Britain,* London: Macmillan.

Virdee, S. and K. Grint (1994) 'Black Self-organisation in Trade Unions', *Sociological Review,* 42 (2), pp. 202–226.

Chapter 4

Racism and education

From Empire to ConDem

Mike Cole

Introduction

In this chapter, I begin by stressing that Britain has always been a multicultural society. I go on to examine Britain's historical legacy of 'race',[1] class, gender and Empire, and look at the way this was represented in the school curriculum of the early twentieth century. I argue that the attitudes and images projected by school texts at this time and reinforced in government statements and policies served in part to racialize[2] the children of colonial and post-colonial immigrants as 'a problem', after mass immigration in the post-Second World War period. I then look at the educational experiences of Asian and black pupils/students,[3] before looking at some ways that were adopted to address 'the problems', which I argue lay in the education system itself and *not* in the pupils/students. In so doing I look at superficial multicultural education and antiracist education. In the chapter I also address some historical and contemporary threats to antiracism and to multiculturalism. My suggestion for ways in which racism can be undermined within education is through a radical and critical multicultural antiracist education along with anti-imperialist education.

Multicultural Britain

At the outset, I would stress that the social, cultural and religious diversity of British society is not a new phenomenon. Britain is a multicultural society and always has been. This is witnessed by the separate existences of England, Scotland and Wales. It is also evidenced by settlement from Ireland and elsewhere in Europe, both in the past and more recently.

Britain's links with Africa and Asia are particularly long-standing. For example, there were Africans in Britain – slaves and 'soldiers in the Roman imperial army that occupied the southern part of our island for three and a half centuries' (Fryer, 1984, p. 1) before the Anglo-Saxons ('the English') arrived.[4] There has been a long history of contact between Britain and India, with Indian links with Europe going back 10,000 years (Visram, 1986). Africans and Asians have been born in Britain from about the year 1505 (Fryer, 1984; see also Walvin, 1973), and their presence has been notable from that time on.

Empire, 'race', class and mass schooling

My concern in this chapter, however, is with the era of imperialism and its immediate and longer term aftermath. The origins of the Welfare State cannot be understood without reference to imperialism, nationalism and the racialization of the peoples of the (ex) colonies. The role assigned to mass schooling in maintaining the Empire was well expressed by Lord Rosebery, leader of the Liberal Imperialists:

> An Empire such as ours requires as its first condition an imperial race, a race vigorous and industrious and intrepid, in the rookeries and slums which still survive, an imperial race cannot be reared.
>
> (Simon, 1974, p. 169)

Here we see the links between the British 'race' and social class. Schooling was seen as a way of creating workers who could compete efficiently with other capitalist nations (epitomized in the slogan, 'national efficiency'). In the 1860s, British capitalists were particularly worried about competition with Germany, and the poor British showing at the Paris Exhibition in 1867 was seen as exemplifying British backwardness in technological education (Shannon, 1976, p. 86). The dual themes of nationalism and imperialism can be gleaned in the major landmark in mass schooling in the Victorian age:

> Upon this speedy provision of education depends . . . our national power. Civilized communities throughout the world are massing themselves together . . . and if we are to hold our position among men of our own race or among the nations of the world we must make up the smallness of our numbers by increasing the intellectual force of the individual.
>
> (Forster, 1870, cited in Maclure, 1979, p. 105)

This is how W.E. Forster, Vice-President in charge of the Education Department in Prime Minister Gladstone's first administration, introduced the Elementary Education Bill in the House of Commons in February 1870. Although the 1870 Education Act, passed three years after the humiliation in Paris, made education neither compulsory nor free, it laid the foundations for a system that was soon to begin to abolish fees and make attendance compulsory.

The quest for 'national efficiency' continued in the Samuelson Report of 1882–84, whose terms of reference were:

> to inquire into the instruction of the industrial classes of certain foreign countries in technical and other subjects for the purpose of comparison with that of the corresponding classes in this country; and into the influence of such instruction on manufacturing and other industries at home and abroad.
>
> (cited in Maclure, 1979, p. 122)

'National efficiency' served as a convenient label under which a complex set of beliefs, assumptions and demands could be grouped – it completed the imperial chain of social class, nation and 'race'. The survival and hegemony of the imperial 'race' were of course mutually reinforcing, as evidenced in the lead-up to the 1902 (Balfour) Education Act, which established an integrated system of elementary, secondary and technical education under the general direction of the Education Department (Shannon, 1976, p. 303). There was a fear that the 'race' might be dying. For example, the Reverend Mr Usher (quoting Darwin's forecast that, if artificial limitation of families came into general use, Britain would degenerate into one of 'those arreous societies in the Pacific') in his book *New Malthusianism* was sure about this: 'yes we cannot deny it, we are a decaying race' (cited in Armytage, 1981, p. 183). Gladstone held similar views.

It was not just the ruling class that held such views. The Webbs, Sydney and Beatrice, were most interested in education. Somewhat confusedly, the former once remarked that the role of London University in the new (twentieth) century should be to combine 'a sane and patriotic imperialism with the largest minded internationalism' (cited in ibid., p. 190). Elsewhere, Sydney was less ambiguous. He once declared that he felt that at every moment he was 'acting as a Member of a Committee . . . in some affairs a committee of my own family members, in others a committee *as wide as the Ayrian race*' (Webb, 1896, p. 6) (my emphasis). Like most Fabians, Webb was an avid supporter of imperialism (Hobsbawm 1964), and, with Liberal front-bencher Richard Haldane, set up Imperial College in 1903. At one stage, Sydney, like Lord Rosebery, called for the formation of a new party to plan the aims and methods of Imperial Policy (Simon, 1974, p. 174), a party of 'National Efficiency' – a party that would advocate sanitary reform, at least 'the minimum necessary for breeding an even moderately Imperial race' (Semmel, 1960, p. 73). Since it was 'in the classrooms . . . that the future battles for the Empire for commercial prosperity are being lost', the working class wanted to know, argued Webb, 'what steps' the followers of Rosebery would 'take to insure the rearing of an Imperial race' (ibid.). The general mood of the times was that the 'inferior races' of the colonies were a direct threat to the 'superior white races' (Armytage, cited in Maclure, 1979, p. 171).

The background of the 1918 Education Act was, of course, the First World War. The higher level of German education was seen as a threat, and the Act's most important clauses concerned continuation schools, and followed the German example (Simon 1974, p. 343). What this meant was that, with certain exceptions, every young person not undergoing full-time instruction was to be liberated from industrial toil for the equivalent of three half-days a week during 40 weeks of the year – two half-days to be spent in school, and one half-day holiday (H.A.L. Fisher, MP, President of the Board of Education and architect of the 1918 Act, introducing the Bill, cited in Maclure, 1979, p. 174). However, the Act was also directly related to social control. As Fisher put it, 'Education dispels the hideous clouds of class suspicion and softens the asperities of faction' (cited in Simon, 1974, p. 344). It is encouraging to observe, he went on, that 'the sense of the value in education as an end in itself, as one of the constituent elements in human happiness, is now widely spread among the manual workers of the country' (ibid.). Note that he stresses, 'end in itself'. Fisher is most definitely not advocating a meritocracy or social class mobility. He registered his disgust at any such notions when introducing the Bill:

> I notice . . . that a new way of thinking about education has sprung up among many of the more reflecting members of our industrial army. They do not want education only in order that they may become better technical workmen [sic] and earn higher wages. *They do not want it in order that they may rise out of their own class, always a vulgar ambition,* they want it because they know that in the treasures of the mind they can find an aid to good citizenship, a source of pure enjoyment and a refuge from the necessary hardships of a life spent in the midst of clanging machinery in our hideous cities of toil.
>
> (cited in Maclure, 1979, pp. 173–74, emphasis added)

The 1918 Act, then, was intended to increase 'national efficiency' – the imperial chain of social class, nation and 'race' – by promoting education. It was also intended as a means of social control, which of course also related to improved efficiency. As it turned out, by 1921, the continuation school sections of the Act had been abandoned for financial reasons (Simon, 1974, p. 30).

The imperial curriculum[5]

The curriculum of the early twentieth century was overtly racist. The primacy of the Bible and religion was replaced by the growing influence of imperialism, which was very central in shaping the changing school syllabus, especially from the 1900s onwards. Thus many English readers, for example, contained passages glorifying the monarchy and celebrating Britain's commercial wealth and progress, and English teachers were increasingly encouraged to give instruction in the duties of citizenship.

The addition of subjects like history, domestic science and games to the elementary school curriculum was conceived and justified by reference to their contribution to national strength, efficiency and, of course, the Empire. Thus, history texts, for example, told their readers that the British Empire was 'gained by the valour of our soldiers, or by the patient toil and steady enterprise of colonists from the mother country', and that Britain's imperial subjects in the colonies, 'of almost every race, colour and religion' were 'all living peacefully and prospering under the British flag, and content with the knowledge that the strong arm and brave spirit that gained freedom for them will always be ready to defend the precious gift' (Pitman's *King Edward History Readers – for Juniors* [1901] cited in Chancellor, 1970, pp. 127–28). The propagation of the British 'race' depended on the continued subordination of women in the home. Thus while boys were encouraged to think that 'the only safe thing for all of us who love our country is to learn soldiering at once and be prepared to fight at any moment' (Fletcher and Kipling's *A School History of England – for Juniors* [1911] cited in ibid., p. 130) and were told not to 'forget the man in the labourer . . . he is the autocrat of the home, the father of the family, and as a voter, one of the rulers of the Empire' (Bray's *Boy Labour and Apprenticeship* (1911) – cited in Hendrick, 1980, p. 166), working-class girls were being taught how to manage their homes efficiently. As Humphries (1981, p. 40) explains, the introduction of domestic science subjects was directly related to the fear of 'race' degeneracy. As he puts it, following Dyhouse and Davin:

> Subjects such as home economics, laundrywork, cookery and needlework aimed to instruct working-class girls in the correct performance of their future duties of motherhood, housework and domestic service, thereby promoting the reinvigoration of the nation and Empire through a sexist division of labour.

Geography texts were the prime conveyors of racialization. Each text laid out the conventional progression from hunting to pastoral to agricultural and finally to industrial societies (MacKenzie, 1984, p. 184). Thus, in Nelson's *The World and its Peoples* (c. 1907), the African was described as 'an overgrown child, vain, self-indulgent, and fond of idleness', while the 'wretched bushmen [were] the lowest and most debased human beings on the face of the globe' (ibid.). Asia was similarly demeaned by Nelson as a continent of dying nations rapidly falling back in civilization (ibid.) and Australian Aboriginals were 'among the most miserable of men [*sic*]' whose 'great poverty led them to practise vices like cannibalism and the murder of the sick and helpless' (A. J. Herbertson, *Man and his Work* (1902), cited in MacKenzie, 1984, p. 185). The 'English', by way of contrast, were portrayed as morally irreproachable. As one history text put it, '[t]hey all show the bold, frank, sturdy character which so strongly marks out the Anglo-Saxon race' (T. J. Livesey, *Granville History Reader* [1902], cited in Chancellor, 1970, p. 118). In another (Cassell's *Class History of England*, cited in Chancellor, 1970, p. 122), references were made to 'the barbaric peoples of Asia' and the most frequent impression conveyed about Indians and Afghans was that they were cruel and totally unfit to rule themselves. Imperialist texts could still be found in school libraries well into the 1980s.[6]

Humphries argues that the inclusion of games and sports in the school curriculum was to encourage a corporate spirit and develop the physical strength and moral fibre of [male] working-class youth – a direct transplant of elements of the public school ethos to state elementary schools, to foster the development of imperial warriors. The founding of cadet corps and rifle-shooting clubs for older children gave the fostering of imperialism a specifically militaristic form (ibid., p. 41).

Particularly influential in schools were the Empire Day Movement, the Lads' Drills Association and the Duty of Discipline Movement, all especially associated with the Earl of Meath, who particularly relished the idea of 'hardness' and believed that the 'British race . . . have ruled in the past because they were a virile race' (Lord Meath, 1910, cited in Mangan, 1986, p. 129). Meath was greatly concerned with the moral deterioration of the 'Anglo-Saxon' woman who should be prepared to face the obligations of the marriage tie (subordination to husband and state) and the sufferings and dangers of childbirth 'with as much coolness and courage as was expected of the man on the field of battle' (Lord Meath, 1910, cited in ibid.). He was also concerned with the 'Anglo-Saxon' man's increasing tendency to watch sport, rather than take part in it (ibid.). His solution was thus to train youth, via his various organizations, to build an imperial 'race', 'worthy of responsibility, alive to duty, filled with sympathy towards mankind and not afraid of self-sacrifice in the promotion of lofty ideals' (Lord Meath, 1910, cited in ibid., p. 130). Empire Day was said to have been celebrated in 1905, in 6,000 schools throughout the Empire and, by 1922, in 80,000 (ibid., p. 132)

Thus racialization ensured that the institutionalized racism (and indeed sexism) promulgated by the ruling class filtered down to the school and became part of popular culture.

Racializing the children through schooling

The demands of an expanding post-war economy meant that Britain was faced with a major shortage of labour, and how part of this vacuum was met by mass immigration from Britain's colonies and former colonies. In this section of the chapter, I consider the effects of the arrival in the British education system of the daughters and sons of these racialized migrant workers, and look at how they, in turn, became racialized through schooling, and were thereby constructed as a problem.[7]

In the 1960s, Sir Edward Boyle, the Minister for Education, heard complaints from white parents, in Southall in London, that there were too many immigrant children in the schools. These parents demanded separate classes for fear that their children would be retarded by the newcomers from the Indian subcontinent – an aversive reaction. The policy that ensued was to disperse children from minority ethnic groups to different schools in order to ensure that there were no more than 30 per cent in any one school (Hiro, 1971). The idea was both to prevent 'a lowering of standards in the schools' and to ensure rapid assimilation of the children into the 'British culture'.

In the following years it became clear from investigations carried out in London schools that another image – that of black people as threatening and needing to be firmly controlled – was also being transferred from the colonies to the 'mother country'. Bernard Coard exposed the iniquitous system of placing children into disciplinary units or 'sin-bins'. Black children, he discovered, were disproportionately represented amongst those in the units (Coard, 1971). What these actions against black children underscored was the deep-rooted nature of the racialized assumptions and stereotypes held of black people and which formed part of the 'common-sense' and 'taken-for-granted' ways in which white British made sense of 'non-white' British (Lawrence, 1982). Examples of the kinds of assumptions that underpinned suspensions of black children in British schools can be found in community and local authority journals and newsletters. A copy of *Issues* (Inner London Education Authority, 1981, p. 11) states:

> A study of disruptive units in a West Midlands local authority included a range of explanations from teachers for the disproportionate numbers of ethnic minority children in the units. One teacher referred to the children of West Indian origin as being physically larger than their white counterparts, and therefore 'more difficult to handle'; another that, 'West Indian children are lively and their liveliness gets them into trouble because teachers fear liveliness and schools like silence'.

While the belief that black children were disruptive was having an effect during the 1970s, this image was particularly strong during the 1980s when, through a series of urban disturbances, the first substantial number of black young people born in Britain began to assert their rights and rejected the assimilationist tendencies imposed on them. The manner in which these disturbances were projected via media and official sources such as the Scarman Report (Scarman, 1981) seemed to fix in the minds of white society the image of young black people (especially males) as representing trouble (see, for example, Cole, 1986, pp. 139–41). The view which carried into the classroom was that black children were not only disruptive (Wright, 1992a; Connolly, 1995), but also violent (Gillborn, 1990; Sewell 1997) – a clear extension of the racialization of their forbears.[8]

Asian school pupils/students, by contrast, were presented in seemingly benign terms as passive and studious and not presenting a disciplinary problem for teachers – a seemingly positive attribute. This notion of the 'passive Asian' student was juxtaposed against the 'aggressive' student of Caribbean origin and became, as Sally Tomlinson (1984) declared, 'a stick to beat the West Indian pupil with'.

This image of passivity applied in particular to Asian girls, but while, on the one hand, it presented them as 'ideal' pupils/students, on the other hand, this same 'passivity' was said to reflect their supposed cultural subordination (Brah and Minhas, 1985) and so was itself a 'stick to beat the Asian man with', as well as 'proof' of the 'cultural inferiority' of these groups. Here we see a form of institutional racism that exhibits seemingly positive attributes in addition to cultural manifestations. Moreover, despite this image of the 'ideal Asian pupil', this has not prevented widespread low expectations of the abilities of these pupils/students, or the inherent contradiction of the class-based view that Asian pupils/students are studious yet have no ambitions other than to be restaurateurs.

Underachievement

There were different kinds of representation for school pupils/students from different minority ethnic groups. Those of Asian background (namely Indian, Pakistani and Bangladeshi) were generally defined by the languages they spoke, and were therefore seen as an academic (and social) threat to white children (see Hiro, 1971), or as religious 'aliens' whose 'specific needs' posed a threat to the autonomy of schools (Blair, 1994) – a form of cultural racism.

By the early 1970s it had become clear that Asian and black children were not gaining the opportunities and advantages from the British education system that their parents had hoped for (Bryan *et al.*, 1985). Black pupils/students in particular were over-represented in suspensions and expulsions from school, and in units for pupils/students with emotional and behavioural difficulties, and were clearly not performing to the same level as their white peers in public examinations. Theories about the assumed disruptive, aggressive and violent natures of black children informed a number of strategies intended to contain such behaviour.

Writers have pointed, for example, to the disproportionate levels of reprimands and criticisms of, and disciplinary measures taken against, black pupils/students by teachers (see Tizzard *et al.*, 1988; Mortimore *et al.*, 1988; Gillborn, 1990; Wright 1992a, 1992b; Connolly, 1995). Besides removing (male) black pupils/students from conventional education and placing them disproportionately in alternative educational centres and schools or units for children with 'educational and behavioural difficulties' (EBD) (Cooper *et al.*, 1991), or suspending and expelling them, more 'liberal' strategies of control were used. There were attempts, for example, to channel the supposed excess energy of black pupils/students into more physical activities such as sport. The notion that black children were 'naturally' physically well coordinated worked hand in hand with the idea that academically they were not able – a seemingly positive attribute coupled with a negative one (see the discussion on racism in Chapter 3).

The issues for pupils/students of Asian origin have differed in some ways to those of black pupils/students. The 'seemingly positive' stereotype as 'ideal pupils/ students' that they have acquired masks some of the negative experiences that they have. Researchers have documented some of the overt as well as unintentional racism of teachers against pupils/students of Asian origin (Bagley, 1992; Wright, 1992b; Blair *et al.*, 1998), while others have revealed the extent of racial harassment to which they are often subjected by their peers (Kelly and Cohn, 1988).

The racializing of Asian pupils/students as 'language problems' has had a deleterious effect on their academic progress. In 1996 Gillborn and Gipps carried out an overview of the literature on the academic achievement of minority ethnic group pupils/students and reported that pupils/students of Pakistani and Bangladeshi, as well as of African-Caribbean origin were underperforming in relation to their white peers. Indian pupils/students, on the other

hand, appear to perform well in relation to all their peers, pointing to the interactions of class and ethnicity in the academic performance of Asian pupils/
students. Although most schools now adopt bilingual policies, which ensure that
the child uses his or her first language in the acquisition of English, Blair *et al.*
(1998) found that teachers were largely ill equipped to incorporate bilingual
issues in their everyday classroom practice.

Discipline

Researchers have obtained evidence of some of the unfair ways in which black
pupils/students have been treated. From his observations, Gillborn, for example,
reported that:

> Perhaps even more significant than the frequency of criticism and con-
> trolling statements which Afro-Caribbean [*sic*] pupils/students received was
> the fact that they were often singled out for criticism even though several
> pupils/students of different ethnic origins were engaged in the same behavi-
> our . . . In sum, Afro-Caribbean pupils/students were not only criticised
> more often than their white peers, but the same behaviour in a white pupil
> might not bring about criticism at all.
>
> (Gillborn, 1990, p. 30)

The result of these kinds of interactions has been widespread antagonism
between white teachers and black pupils/students because, as Wright (1987, p.
111) reported, 'pupils/students were inevitably forced into highly significant
face-winning, face-retaining and face-losing contests between themselves and
the teachers'. This tendency to over-discipline black pupils/students has resulted
over the years in high percentages of black pupils/students facing exclusion.

Addressing the problems[9]

The momentum for changing the situation of minority ethnic group pupils/
students came from minority groups themselves. Parents organized 'mother-
tongue' teaching for children in addition to instruction in the faith that they
received at the mosque. Black parents started their own supplementary or
Saturday schools. This reflected a growing frustration in black communities over
the failure of the education system to produce positive results for their children.
Supplementary schools were intended to counteract some of the distortions of
history, the misinformation and the inadequate academic instruction that
parents believed their children were receiving (Chevannes and Reeves, 1987).
Through Asian and black parent and teacher associations and through community action, the disadvantaged position of black pupils/students in schools was
placed on the public and educational agenda. In 1979, the government commissioned an inquiry into 'the education of West Indian children'. The Rampton

Report (1981) was made available in 1981 and confirmed what black parents had been saying all along – that racism against black children was indeed a major factor in their experience of school. However, the Report was not received wholeheartedly by the government, which commissioned another study, whose brief this time was extended to cover other minority ethnic groups. The Swann Report, *Education for All* (1985), confirmed some of the findings of the Rampton Report but also made some of the most wide-ranging suggestions for education in an ethnically diverse society. Amongst these was the suggestion that children in all schools should be educated for life in a multicultural society. One of the underlying principles of this suggestion was that if children were taught about each other and each other's cultures, this would help to reduce prejudice, especially amongst white children.

Superficial multicultural education

The Swann Report's predominant focus on culture set the trajectory of multicultural education along a superficial line in which children were taught about the food, the clothes, and the music of different countries usually by white teachers, without also understanding the structural and institutional inequalities that had been at the core of community campaigns (Sarup, 1986; Troyna, 1993). This approach is more to do with *schooling* rather than education, that is to say with the processes by which young people are attuned to the requirements of capitalism both in the form and the content of schooling. *Education*, on the other hand (*educare* in Latin means to 'bring out') describes a more liberatory process of education from birth to death, a process of human emancipation and socialism (see Chapter 5 in Cole (2011) for the example of the Bolivarian Republic of Venezuela). However, given the long history of the term 'multi-cultural *education*', I will retain it here. The exoticization of minority ethnic group cultures and customs served to reinforce the notion that these cultures were indeed 'other' and drew the boundary more firmly between 'them', the 'immigrants' or 'foreigners', and 'us', the 'real' British people (Cole and Blair, 2006, p. 80).

Nearly 30 years after Rampton, the colonial legacy remains. For example, while a higher percentage of Indian and mixed white and Asian students reach the expected level in English and mathematics than their peers (probably related to socioeconomic factors), a lower percentage of Black African, Black Caribbean and Pakistani students reach this level (Department for Children, Schools and Families (DCSF) 'Statistical First Release', 2009).

Antiracist Education[10]

Antiracist education has a long history in the UK, and has traditionally been associated with Marxism and other radical left thinking. Antiracist educators are critical of both monocultural and multicultural education. The antiracist critique of monocultural education is that in denying the existence of, or marginalizing the cultures of, minority ethnic communities, it was and is profoundly racist. The antiracist critique of multicultural education is that it was and is patronizing and superficial. It was often characterized as the three Ss: 'saris, samosas, and steel drums' (for a discussion, see Troyna and Carrington, 1990).

Antiracist education starts from the premise that UK society is institutionally racist, and that, in the area of 'race' and culture, the purpose of education is to challenge and undermine that racism. Over 10 years ago (Cole, 1998, p. 45), by way of example, I suggested the way in which an antiracist version of the Australian bicentennial of 1988 might have been taught in primary (elementary) schools in Britain. Here, in order to illustrate the fundamental differences between monocultural, multicultural and antiracist education, I will update this analysis, and extend it to incorporate how traditional monocultural and traditional multicultural approaches might manifest themselves today (my description of these three approaches applies to Britain, but could easily be extrapolated to other contexts).

In the monocultural classroom, children would be taught that Australia was discovered about 240 years ago by Captain Cook, a British man, and that, although Australia is on the other side of the world from Britain, the people there are like us, eat the same food, and have the same customs and way of life. The climate is much hotter and people can swim on Christmas day, and at many beaches Santa Claus arrives on a surfboard, or even on a surf lifesaving boat. There are still some Aborigines[11] in Australia and the government has enacted laws that safeguard their communities against drunkenness and other forms of antisocial behaviour.

With the multicultural approach, children would learn that Australia is a multicultural society, just like ours, with lots of different cultures and religions making the country an exciting place in which to live. As well as 'the British', other people have immigrated to Australia from most of the rest of Europe, and indeed the world. The multicultural nature of Australian society means lots of different foods, music, dance and national costumes. The Aboriginal people – the original inhabitants – have a thriving culture, and produce very original music and art.

The antiracist approach would focus on the fact that the indigenous peoples of Australia and their supporters view what happened two centuries ago as an imperialist colonial invasion. Given access to a comprehensive range of resources pertaining to life in Australia, children would discover that in reality, multicultural Australia is a racialized capitalist society stratified on lines of ethnicity, class and gender, with Australian-born and English-speaking white male immigrants at the top of the hierarchy and Aboriginal women at the bottom. They would learn about 'land rights' and other counter-hegemonic struggles, and the economic and ecological arguments pertaining to these rights. They would discover that Aboriginal communities have faced ongoing exploitation and oppression since the invasion, and how this has intensified in recent years. They would relate Australian indigenous struggles against injustice to other struggles for social justice in Australia, and to struggles worldwide.[12] The children would be encouraged to resist racist stereotypes from the media that attempt to distort and mask realities.

This example of antiracist education is provided to schematically emphasize the basic differences between the three approaches. It is not intended in any way of course to deny the importance and salience of indigenous cultures. Indeed later in this chapter, given advances in technology, I advocate multicultural antiracist education.

The anti-antiracist backlash

Up until the late 1990s, with their prognosis that Britain is an institutionally racist society, antiracists were branded by many as 'loony Lefties' and ostracized by national and local government.[13] In her memoirs, for example, Margaret Thatcher (Thatcher, 1993, p. 598) expressed extreme concern that I was teaching antiracist education in the late 1980s at what was then Brighton Polytechnic. At the time (1987), she also opined, with particular respect to primary mathematics:

> In the inner cities where youngsters must have a decent education if they are to have a better future, that opportunity is all too often snatched from them by hard-left education authorities and extremist teachers. Children who need to be able to count and multiply are learning anti-racist mathematics—whatever that is.
>
> (Cited in Lavalette *et al.*, 2001)

Similarly, her successor, John Major, declared at the 1992 Conservative Party annual conference speech:

> I also want a reform of teacher training. Let us return to basic subject teaching, not courses in the theory of education. Primary teachers should teach children to read, not waste their time on the politics of gender, race and class.
>
> (Cited in ibid.)[14]

The Stephen Lawrence Inquiry Report

It took the Stephen Lawrence Inquiry Report (Macpherson, 1999) to change all this. The report followed a lengthy public campaign initiated by the parents of Stephen Lawrence following the murder in 1993 by racists of black teenager Stephen Lawrence. The report looked at racism in the Metropolitan Police and other British institutions.

While it could have gone further in its castigation of the inherent racism in British society, for antiracists (Macpherson, 1999) it is nevertheless a milestone in being the first acknowledgement by the British State of the existence of widespread institutional racism in the police, in the education system and in other institutions in the society. Leading UK antiracist campaigner and writer Sivanandan rightly describes the inquiry as 'not just a result but a learning process for the country at large' (2000, p. 1). He argues that through the course of the inquiry, 'the gravitational centre of race relations discourse was shifted from individual prejudice and ethnic need to systemic, institutional racial inequality and injustice' (ibid., p. 1). Gillborn (2008, p. 132) is also right to describe the Stephen Lawrence case as 'one of the single most important episodes in the history of British race relations'.

The report led directly to the very progressive Race Relations (Amendment) Act (2000), which places a general duty on specified public authorities to promote 'race' equality. The report, however, is less to do with any caring intentions on the part of the capitalist state and much more to do with public campaigning. As David Gillborn (2008, p. 135) has insisted, the Lawrence Inquiry was 'not granted by a benign state' that wanted to put right an injustice, but as a result of 'high profile protests and public demonstrations'.

Multicultural antiracist education

Given advances in technology, most notably the World Wide Web, to facilitate authentic voices, I believe that a form of radical and critical multicultural antiracist education is now possible. To show what I mean by *multicultural* antiracist education, I have added in italics how multiculturalism could be woven into the description given immediately above.

Multicultural antiracist education would focus on the fact that the indigenous peoples of Australia and their supporters view what happened two centuries ago as an imperialist colonial invasion. *The children would discover that, at the time of the invasion, there were up to 400 indigenous nations and over 200 languages, clearly indicating a plethora of cultural formations.* Given access to a comprehensive range of resources pertaining to life in Australia, children would discover that in reality, multicultural Australia is a racialized capitalist society stratified on lines of ethnicity, class and gender, with Australian-born and English-speaking white male immigrants at the top of the hierarchy and Aboriginal women at the bottom. *They would find out that the dominant culture is the culture of Anglo-Australians, and that Aboriginal art, for example, is used as a selling point for tourism, while indigenous communities continue to live in the most appalling conditions.* Children would learn about 'land rights' and other counter-hegemonic struggles, and the economic and ecological arguments pertaining to these rights. *They would be able to relate these arguments to traditional spiritual beliefs that have links with socialism and Marxism: the land belongs to the people and the people belong to the land.* They would discover that Aboriginal communities have faced ongoing exploitation and oppression since the invasion, and how this has intensified in recent years. *In 2009, an Aboriginal representative body in New South Wales complained of a failure to protect Aboriginal culture and heritage from ongoing destruction and stated that this will continue without fundamental reform.* Children would relate Australian indigenous struggles against injustice to other struggles for social justice in Australia, and to struggles worldwide. *The children would find out that struggles against imperialism worldwide have a strong cultural dimension in the sense of counter-hegemonic resistance to Americanization, that is, white corporate US hegemony.* The children would be encouraged to resist racist stereotypes from the media that attempt to distort and mask realities. *This would include refusing to accept ongoing attempts to denigrate specified racialized groups and their cultures.*

With respect to this example of indigenous Australians, there is now a wealth of cultural information about the various communities (see, for example, Cultural Survival: Australia, 2009).

Threats to multiculturalism and antiracist education from the ConDem government

So far, it is not totally clear what the UK ConDem government's schools policies will entail, except that we know there will be an increase in the number of academy schools, that is, state-maintained but free of local authority control and independently run and open to control by private companies. All English primary and secondary schools will be encouraged to become academies. As Gillborn (2011, pp. 13–14) has argued the extension of academy status carries a number of threats, the most immediate being that such schools 'known to be less diverse and more middle class than the average are set to benefit from enhanced funding' when state budgets are being reduced elsewhere. There will be a total real reduction in the Education Department's spending of 3 per cent by 2014 to 2015, and teachers are facing a pay freeze and cuts to pensions (Darke, 2010). As Gillborn (2011, p. 14) concludes, 'the government's own data show that Black students achieve *less* well in academies but are even *more* likely to be permanently excluded from them'.

At the same time the creation of 'free schools', 'all-ability, state-funded schools, set up in response to parental demand', will also be academies. Sally Tomlinson (2011, pp. 28–29) sums up the effect of the changes:

> The promised increase in the number of Academy Schools and the creation of Free Schools will intensify divisions by faith, a majority of existing Academies already being faith sponsored, and interest in Free Schools expressed by Muslim, Sikh, Jewish and other groups. In sum . . . [this is] likely to make it more difficult for black and many minority young people to achieve high levels of qualifications; more are likely to be placed in Alternative Provision, and community cohesion would not seem to be enhanced by the promise of more Free Schools or faith schools.

Pro-imperialist education?

As far as the curriculum is concerned, Conservative Education Secretary Michael Gove has drawn on the services of popular historian, TV presenter and Labour Party supporter Simon Schama to make UK history more central to the curriculum. Gove talks of 'shame' as well as 'pride' in relation to the history of the UK, and of 'our common story', 'full of contention, not self-congratulation' (cited in Vasagar, 2010). However, the fact that right-wing, pro-imperialist popular historian Niall Ferguson (a TV presenter, too) is also involved provides a taste of what schooling might begin to look like *ideologically* under the ConDem government.

Ferguson (cited in Higgins, 2010) states that children should be taught that the 'big story' of the last 500 years 'is the rise of western domination of the world'. He argues that the syllabus is 'bound to be Eurocentric' because the world is Eurocentric (Higgins, 2010). For Ferguson, the British Empire was relatively benevolent, and in 2004, he argued that the American Empire, which 'has the potential to do great good', needs to learn from the lessons of the British Empire. First, it needs to export capital and to invest in its colonies; second, people from the US need to settle permanently in its colonies; third, there must be a *commitment* to imperialism; fourth, there must be collaboration with local elites. Success can only come, he concluded, if the Americans are prepared to *stay* (Ferguson, 2004). Ferguson (2005) also offered the then President Bush the idea of thinking of the US Empire (Ferguson's words, not mine) 'as a kind of sequel to the British Empire'.

With respect to the teaching of Empire in the UK curriculum, Gove has praised Ferguson for his 'exciting and engaging' ideas for a 'campaign for real history', and has stated that he is 'a great fan of Ferguson' (Higgins, 2010).

Conclusion

I believe that, rather than racism existing in multiple unrelated forms racism is a discrete phenomenon, but one that takes different forms in different historical periods and geographical locations. None of these forms can or should be viewed in isolation from economic and political factors, nor can they be understood, and dealt with, without reference to these factors. Thus in the imperial era, in order to justify the continuance of 'the strong arm and brave spirit' of the British Empire (see above), and the ongoing and relentless pursuit of expanding capital accumulation, the African subjects of the colonies were racialized, in school textbooks, as 'fierce savages' and 'brutal and stinking' (Glendenning, 1973, p. 35), while freed West Indian slaves were described as 'lazy, vicious and incapable of any serious improvement or of work except under compulsion' (Chancellor, 1970, p. 240). When the British 'race' and therefore Empire was seen to be under threat at home, foreign Jews were described at the same time, by the media, as 'semi-barbarous', unable or unwilling to 'use the latrine', depositing 'their filth' on 'the floor of their rooms' (Holmes, 1979, p. 17) and involved in world conspiracy (thus directly threatening British Imperial hegemony): 'whenever, there is trouble in Europe', the ILP paper, *Labour Leader*, put it, you may be sure a hook-nosed Rothschild is at his games' (Cohen, 1985, p. 75).

In the post-Second World War period, not surprisingly given the afore-mentioned colonial history, the British Cabinet racialized many of the African-Caribbean community as 'accustomed to living in squalid conditions and have no desire to improve' (*The Observer*, 1 January 1989), while their children were described, by one local education authority, as 'physically robust and boisterous, yet mentally lethargic'. At the same time, the same LEA perceived there to be 'very real problems' with the 'domestic habits and personal hygiene of the Asiatics' as well as 'the problem of [their] eating habits' (Grosvenor, 1987, pp. 34–35). Children from minority ethnic groups (not a source of cheap labour, as were their parents) were racialized as problems to be dealt with in these post-war years.

Racialization continues to deform the educational institutions of the society. During the Conservative era, equality issues were not only placed on the back burner, but actively demonized. Groups who attempted to restore public attention to equity issues found themselves increasingly marginalized and derided for 'political correctness', a pernicious concept invented by the Radical Right, and which, to my dismay, has become common currency.[15]

In the era of the ConDems, where we are faced with a government more Thatcherite than Thatcher, multicultural antiracist education is under severe threat. Perhaps the greatest threat to multiculturalism and antiracism has come from the Prime Minister himself, David Cameron. Proclaiming a 'sea-change' in the fight against 'home-grown' terrorism in Britain, he claimed that the root cause was neither social deprivation nor hostility to 'western foreign policy', but the product of 'state multiculturalism' that had 'encouraged different cultures to live separate lives, apart from each other and apart from the mainstream' (Hyland, 2011). Cameron demanded that there be 'stronger identities at home . . . Frankly, we need a lot less of the passive tolerance of recent years and much more active, muscular liberalism' (ibid.). As Julie Hyland argues, it is 'not mere coincidence that Cameron's speech coincided with the first-ever national march by the English Defence League (EDL), which attracted 3,000'. As she explains, the EDL:

> styles itself as a 'grassroots' upsurge against the threat of Islamic extremism and its consequences for Britain's 'democratic values'. In truth, it consists for the most part of football hooligans and fascists with links to the far-right across Europe that have helped spearhead anti-Muslim propaganda.

Anti-imperialist education

So, what needs to be done? In addition to ensuring strict adherence to the progressive human rights and equalities legislation (outlined in the Introduction to this volume) and pressing continually for multicultural antiracist education, one major way of amending the National Curriculum would be to re-introduce an honest and critical analysis of imperialism, past and present. As the afore-mentioned pro-imperialist conservative historian Niall Ferguson (2003) has argued:

> Empire is as 'cutting edge' as you could wish . . . [It] has got everything: economic history, social history, cultural history, political history, military history and international history – not to mention contemporary politics (just turn on the latest news from Kabul).

The teaching of imperialism, past and present, in schools, I would argue, provides more than this. It informs us *most precisely* about the historical and contemporary nature of British society. As well as being involved in *anti*-imperialist education, Marxist and other radical educators must also be part of a much wider and concerted effort to encourage all educational (and other) institutions to view the undermining of racism, not as an irrelevance or as an encumbrance but as one of the key issues facing the world in the twenty-first century.

Referring to the US (but equally applicable to the UK and other countries implicated in US aggression), Eric Mann (2002) has succinctly identified the central role that education against racism and imperialism plays in the struggle against capitalism:

> Right now the U.S. is financing its war against the world by super-exploiting the entire world, subjecting more than three billion people to abject poverty. In that racism and imperialism are at the heart of the U.S. ideological framework, antiracism and anti-imperialism are the central ideological concepts of contestation, the essence of counterhegemonic political education work.
>
> (cited in San Juan Jr., 2003)

In the light of escalating racism in Britain (see Chapter 3 of this volume), mainland Europe and worldwide, not least the ConDem government's central role in the US imperialist project, currently in full swing under the presidency of Barack Obama, the mandatory implementation of measures to undermine institutional racism is more urgent than ever. Despite current realities, Marxist and other radical left educators will continue to make the case for multicultural antiracist socialist education and education against imperialism.

Notes

1 I put 'race' in inverted commas for the reasons discussed in Chapter 3 of this volume.
2 For an in-depth discussion of racism and racialization, see Chapter 3 of this volume.
3 In concentrating on the experiences of Asian and black pupils/students, I fully accept that those who do not fall into this category also experience racism.
4 Fryer cites evidence of a large percentage of skeletons of black Africans found among 350 skeletons excavated in 1951, dating back to Roman times (Fryer, 1984, cited in Brandt, 1986, p. 7).
5 For a more in-depth analysis of the Imperial curriculum, see Cole (2004a, pp. 526–30).
6 Maud Blair worked as an adviser for multicultural education, and as late as 1989 was helping schools identify books with outdated colonial theories and racist views and images. Not only were there history and geography books, but story-books and well-intentioned books by NGOs such as Oxfam, even published in the 1970s, which still presented images that were demeaning to Asian and black peoples (Cole and Blair, 2006, p. 85).
7 This section of the chapter draws heavily on Cole and Blair (2006, pp. 75–78), and predominantly reflects the input of Maud Blair.
8 Cashmore and Troyna (1982) went so far as to claim that 'there is a penchant for violence within the West Indian culture' (p. 32). For a critique, see Cole (1986, pp. 128–33). Ironically, Troyna went on to totally abandon such notions and to become one of Britain's leading antiracist educators.
9 The introduction to this section of the chapter draws heavily on Cole and Blair (2006, p. 79) and predominantly reflects Maud Blair's input.
10 The rest of this section of the chapter draws heavily on Cole (2011, pp. 119–25).
11 I have deliberately chosen this traditional nomenclature, given that I am describing the monocultural approach.
12 Antiracist education in the UK has shown awareness of equality issues other than 'race' for over 20 years (e.g. Cole, 1986; Troyna, 1987).
13 It should be recorded that there were local government exceptions. For example, the left-wing Inner London Education Authority (ILEA), eventually abolished, against the wishes of the parents/carers, by Thatcher in 1988, published a number of equality documents in the 1980s, including *Race, Sex and Class: 4. Anti-Racist Statement and Guidelines* (ILEA, 1983), and distributed the pamphlets to all of its schools. (For an analysis of the political climate in the years of the radical right, see, for example, Hill, 1989, 1997; see also Jones, 2003; Tomlinson, 2005.)
14 This was all part of a concerted radical right attack on teacher education that was assumed to be a hotbed of Marxism (see Hill, 1989, 1994, 2001; see also Cole, 2004b, pp. 150–63). This legacy continues to this day. For example, the term 'trainee' rather than 'student teacher' relates to the radical right notion that teacher *training* is not a theoretical enterprise, but a combination of love of subject and practical skills. For similar reasons it is the *Training and Development Agency for Schools (TDA)* that oversees teacher education. However, progressive equalities legislation (see the Introduction to this volume; see also Equality and Human Rights Commission Website, 2011) has required departments of education in universities, university colleges and colleges to verse their student teachers in equality issues (for suggestions on promoting equality in the primary/elementary school, see Hill and Robertson (2009), and for ideas for the secondary/high school, see Cole (2009).
15 'PC' or 'Political correctness' is a pernicious concept invented by the radical right, which, to my dismay, has become common currency in the UK and the US. The term was coined to imply that there exist (left) political demagogues who seek to

impose their views on equality issues, in particular, appropriate terminology, on the majority. In reality, nomenclature changes over time. Thus, in the twenty-first century, terms such as 'negress' or 'negro' or 'coloured', nomenclatures that at one time were considered quite acceptable, are now *generally* considered offensive. Egalitarians are concerned with *respect* for others and, therefore, are careful to acknowledge changes in nomenclature, changes that are decided by oppressed groups themselves, bearing in mind that there can be differences among such oppressed groups. Thus, for example, it has become common practice to use 'working class' rather than 'lower class'; 'lesbian, gay, bisexual, and transgender' rather than 'sexually deviant'; 'disability' rather than 'handicap'; 'gender equality' rather than 'a woman's place'. Using current and acceptable nomenclature is about the fostering of a caring and inclusive society, not about 'political correctness' (Cole, 2008, pp. 142–43).

References

Armytage, W.H.G. (1981) 'Issues at stake: the biosocial background of the 1902 Education Act', *History of Education*, 10, (3).

Bagley, C. (1992), 'In-service provision and teacher resistance to whole-school change', in D. Gill, D.B. Mayor and M. Blair (eds) *Racism and Education: Structures and Strategies*, London: Sage.

Blair, M. (1994) 'Black teachers, black pupils/students and education markets', *Cambridge Journal of Education*, 24, pp. 277–91.

Blair, M. and Bourne, J. with Coffin, C, Creese, A. and Kenner, C. (1998) *Making the Difference: Teaching and Learning Strategies in Successful Multi-ethnic Schools*, London: DfEE.

Brah, A. and Minhas, R. (1985) 'Structural racism or cultural differences: schooling for Asian girls', in G. Weiner (ed.) *Just a Bunch of Girls*, Milton Keynes: Open University Press.

Brandt, G. (1986) *The Realization of Anti-Racist Teaching*, Lewes: Falmer.

Bryan, B., Dadzie, S. and Scafe, S. (1985) *The Heart of the Race: Black Women's Lives in Britain*, London: Virago.

Cashmore, E. and Troyna, B. (eds) (1982) *Black Youth In Crisis*, London: George Allen and Unwin.

Chancellor, V. (1970) *History for their Masters*, Bath: Adams and Dart.

Chevannes, M. and Reeves, F. (1987) 'The black voluntary school movement: definition, context and prospects', in B. Troyna (ed.) *Racial Inequality in Education*, London: Tavistock.

Coard, B. (1971) *How the West Indian Child is Made Educationally Sub-Normal in the British School System*, London: New Beacon Books.

Cohen, S. (1985) 'Anti-semitism, immigration controls and the welfare state', *Critical Social Policy*, 13, Summer.

Cole, M. (1986) 'Teaching and learning about racism: a critique of multicultural education in Britain', in S. Modgil, G. Verma, K. Mallik and C. Modgil (eds) *Multicultural Education: the Interminable Debate*, Lewes: Falmer.

Cole, M. (1998) 'Racism, reconstructed multiculturalism and antiracist education', *Cambridge Journal of Education*, 28 (1), Spring, pp. 37–48.

Cole, M. (2004a) '"Rule Britannia" and the new American Empire: a Marxist analysis of the teaching of imperialism, actual and potential, in the English school curriculum', *Policy Futures in Education*, 2 (3), pp. 523–38.

Cole, M. (2004b) 'Rethinking the Future: The Commodification of Knowledge and the Grammar of Resistance', in M. Benn and C. Chitty (eds), *For Caroline Benn: Essays in Education and Democracy*, London: Continuum.

Cole, M. (2008) *Marxism and Educational Theory: Origins and Issues,* London: Routledge.

Cole, M. (ed.) (2009) *Equality in the Secondary School: Promoting Good Practice across the Curriculum,* London: Continuum.

Cole, M. (2011) *Racism and Education in the U.K. and the U.S.: Towards a Socialist Alternative,* New York: Palgrave Macmillan

Cole, M. and Blair, M. (2006) 'Racism and education: from Empire to New Labour', in M. Cole (ed.) *Education, Equality and Human Rights: Issues of Gender, 'Race', Sexuality, Disability and Social Class,* London: Routledge.

Connolly, P. (1995) 'Boys will be boys? Racism, sexuality and the construction of masculine identities amongst infant children', in M. Blair and J. Holland (eds) *Equality and Difference: Debates and Issues in Feminist Research and Pedagogy,* Clevedon: Multilingual Matters.

Cooper, P., Upton, G. and Smith, C. (1991) 'Ethnic minority and gender distribution among staff and pupils/students in facilities for pupils/students with emotional and behavioural difficulties in England and Wales', *British Journal of Sociology of Education,* 12, 1, pp. 77–94.

Cultural Survival: Australia (2009) www.culturalsurvival.org/australia?gclid=CL2ii OSD6aMCFVMB4wodjk6Z2A (accessed 18 July 2011).

Darke, M. (2010) 'Education', *The Argus,* 22 October.

Department for Children, Schools and Families (DCSF) (2009) 'Statistical First Release'.

Equality and Human Rights Commission Website (2011) www.equalityhumanrights.com/ (accessed 16 July 2011).

Ferguson, N. (2003) 'Prince and empire are the key to history', *The Sunday Times,* 6 July.

Ferguson, N. (2004) 'American Empire—who benefits?', *Empire and the Dilemmas of Liberal Imperialism,* CD accompanying *Prospect,* March.

Ferguson, N. (2005) 'Admit it, George Dubya's medicine is not all bad', *Times Higher Education Supplement,* 18 March, www.timeshighereducation.co.uk/story.asp?story Code=194801&sectioncode=26 (accessed 16 July 2011).

Fryer, P. (1984) *Staying Power: The History of Black People in Britain,* London: Pluto Press.

Gillborn, D. (1990) *"Race" Ethnicity and Education,* London: Unwin Hyman.

Gillborn, D. (2008) *Racism and Education: Coincidence or Conspiracy?,* London: Routledge.

Gillborn, D. (2011) 'Fine words and foul deeds: why coalition education policy will make things worse for Black students and the White working class', *Race Equality Teaching,* 29 (2), Spring, pp. 9–14.

Gillborn, D. and Gipps, C. (1996) *Recent Research on the Achievement of Ethnic Minority Pupils/Students,* London: HMSO.

Glendenning, F.J. (1973) 'History textbooks and racial attitudes: 1804–1969', *Journal of Educational Administration and History,* 5, pp. 35–44.

Grosvenor, I. (1987) 'A different reality: education and the racialisation of the black child', *History of Education,* 16 (4).

Grosvenor, I. (1989) 'Teacher racism and the construction of black underachievement', in R. Lowe (ed.) *The Changing Secondary School,* Lewes: Falmer.

Hendrick, H. (1980) 'A race of intelligent unskilled labourers: the adolescent worker and the debate on compulsory part-time day continuation schools, 1900–1922', *History of Education*, 9 (2), pp. 159–73.

Higgins, C. (2010) 'Rightwing historian Niall Ferguson given school curriculum role', *The Guardian,* 30 May, www.guardian.co.uk/politics/2010/may/30/niall-ferguson-school-curriculum-role (accessed 16 July 2011).

Hill, D. (1989) *Charge of the Right Brigade: The Radical Right's Attack on Teacher Education,* Brighton: Institute for Education Policy Studies, http://www.google.co.uk/#hl=en&xhr=t&q=Hill%2C+D.+(1989)+Charge+of+the+Right+Brigade%3A+The+Radical+Right%E2%80%99s+Attack+on+Teacher&cp=82&pf=p&sclient=psy&site=&source=hp&rlz=1W1DKUK_en-GB&aq=f&aqi=&aql=&oq=Hill,+D.+(1989)+Charge+of+the+Right+Brigade:+The+Radical+Right%E2%80%99s+Attack+on+Teacher&pbx=1&bav=on.2,or.r_gc.r_pw.&fp=e28a0a03c8b215fd&biw=1024&bih=531 (accessed 16 July 2011).

Hill, D. (1994) 'Initial teacher education and ethnic diversity', in G. Verma and P. Pumfrey (eds) *Cultural Diversity and the Curriculum, Vol 4: Cross-Curricular Contexts, Themes and Dimensions in Primary Schools,* London: Falmer.

Hill, D. (1997) 'Equality in primary schooling: the policy context, intentions and effects, of the Conservative "reforms"', in M. Cole, D. Hill and S. Shan (eds) *Promoting Equality in Primary Schools,* London: Cassell.

Hill, D. (2001) 'Equality, ideology and educational policy', in D. Hill and M. Cole (eds) *Schooling and Equality: Fact, Concept and Policy,* London: Kogan Page.

Hill, D. and Robertson, L. H. (eds) (2011) *Equality in the Primary School: Promoting Good Practice Across the Curriculum,* London: Routledge.

Hiro, D. (1971) *Black British White British,* London: Eyre & Spottiswoode.

Hobsbawm, E. (1964) *Labouring Men,* New York: Basic Books.

Holmes, C. (1979) *Anti-Semitism in British Society 1876–1939,* London: Edward Arnold.

Humphries, S. (1981) *Hooligans or Rebels? An Oral History of Working-Class Childhood and Youth 1889–1939,* Oxford: Basil Blackwell.

Hyland, J. (2011) 'Britain's prime minister whips up anti-Muslim sentiment', World Socialist Web Site (WSWS), 9 February, http://wsws.org/articles/2011/feb2011/pers-f09.shtml (accessed 7 July 2011).

Inner London Education Authority (ILEA) (1981) 'ISSUES in race and education', 34, Autumn, London: ILEA.

Inner London Education Authority (ILEA) (1983) *Race, Sex and Class: 4. Anti-Racist Statement and Guidelines,* London: ILEA.

Jones, K. (2003) *Education in Britain: 1944 to the Present,* Cambridge: Polity Press.

Kelly, E. and Cohn, T. (eds) (1988) *Racism in Schools – New Research Evidence,* Stoke-on-Trent: Trentham Books.

Lavalette, M., Mooney, G., Mynott, E., Evans, K. and Richardson, B. (2001) 'The woeful record of the House of Blair', *International Socialism,* 90, http://pubs.socialistreviewindex.org.uk/isj90/lavalette.htm (accessed 16 July 2011).

Lawrence, E. (1982) 'Just plain common sense: the "roots" of racism', in Centre for Contemporary Cultural Studies, *The Empire Strikes Back: Race and Racism in 70s Britain,* London: Hutchinson.

MacKenzie, J.M. (1984) *Propaganda and Empire: The Manipulation of British Public Opinion 1880–1960,* Manchester: Manchester University Press.

Maclure, J.S. (1979) *Educational Documents: England and Wales 1816 to the Present Day,* London: Methuen.

Macpherson, W. (1999) *The Stephen Lawrence Enquiry, Report of an Enquiry by S. William*, London: The Stationery Office.

Mangan, J.A. (1986) 'The grit of our forefathers: invented traditions, propaganda and imperialism', in J.M. Mackenzie (ed.) *Propaganda and Empire: The Manipulation of British Public Opinion, 1880–1960*, Manchester: Manchester University Press.

Mortimore, P., Sammons, P., Stoll, P., Lewis, D. and Ecob, R. (1988) *School Matters: The Junior Years*, Wells: Open Books.

Rampton Report (1981) *West Indian Children in Our Schools*, Cmnd 8723, London: HMSO.

San Juan Jr., E. (2003) 'Marxism and the race/class problematic: a re-articulation', *Cultural Logic*, 6, http://clogic.eserver.org/2003/sanjuan.html (accessed 16 July 2011).

Sarup, M. (1986) *The Politics Of Multicultural Education*, London: Routledge and Kegan Paul.

Scarman, Lord (1981) *The Brixton Disorders 10–12 April 1981, Report of an Inquiry by the Rt Hon Lord Scarman OBE*, London: HMSO.

Semmel, B. (1960) *Imperialism and Social Reform*, London: George Allen and Unwin.

Sewell, T. (1997) *Black Masculinity and Schooling*, Stoke-on-Trent: Trentham Books.

Shannon, R. (1976) *The Crisis of Imperialism 1865–1915*, London: Paladin.

Simon, B. (1974) *Education and the Labour Movement 1870–1920*, London: Lawrence and Wishart.

Sivanandan, A. (2000) 'UK: reclaiming the struggle', *Race and Class,* 42 (2), pp. 67–73.

Swann Report (1985) *Education for All: Report of the Committee of Inquiry into the Education of Children from Minority Ethnic Groups*, London: HMSO.

Thatcher, M. (1993) *The Downing Street Years,* London: HarperCollins.

Tizzard, B., Blatchford, P., Burke, J., Farquhar, C. and Plewis, I. (1988) *Young Children at School in the Inner City*, Hove: Lawrence Erlbaum Associates.

Tomlinson, S. (1984) *Home And School In Multicultural Britain*, London: Batsford.

Tomlinson, S. (2005) *Education in a Post-welfare Society* (2nd edition), Buckingham: Open University Press.

Tomlinson, S. (2011) 'More radical reform (but don't mention race) gaps and silences in the government's discourse', *Race Equality Teaching,* 29 (2), Spring, pp. 25–29.

Troyna, B. (1987) 'Antisexist/antiracist education—a false dilemma: a reply to Walkling and Brannigan', *Journal of Moral Education*, 16 (1), January, pp. 60–65.

Troyna, B. (1993) *Racism and Education*, Buckingham: Open University Press.

Vasagar, J. (2010) 'Historian Schama to bring story of UK back to classroom', *The Guardian*, 6 October.

Visram, R. (1986) *Ayahs, Lascars and Princes*, London: Pluto.

Walvin, J. (1973) *Black and White: The Negro and English Society 1555–1945*, London: Allen Lane.

Webb, S. (1896) *The Difficulties of Individualism*, Fabian Tract, 69, London.

Wright, C. (1987) 'Black pupils/students-white teachers', in B. Troyna (ed.) *Racial Inequality in Education*, London: Routledge.

Wright, C. (1992a) 'Early education: multiracial primary school classrooms', in D. Gill, B. Mayor and M. Blair (eds) *Racism in Education, Structures and Strategies*, London: Sage.

Wright, C. (1992b) *Race Relations in the Primary School*, London: David Fulton.

Chapter 5

The making of sexualities
Sexuality, identity and equality

Simon Forrest and Viv Ellis

Introduction

> The forces of inhumanity are overwhelming, but only one's continued
> opposition can make any other order possible, can give an added strength
> for all those who desire freedom and equality to break at last those fetters
> that seem now so unbreakable.
>
> (R. Duncan in Blasius and Phelan, 1997, p. 233)

This quotation, from an essay written in the 1940s by the American poet
Robert Duncan, is an apposite epigraph for this chapter. It is indicative, in a
number of ways, of the content of the chapter, and comes from an essay to
which we will return in our discussion of the key issue of sexuality and identity.
First, it identifies a struggle for human rights, equality and freedom on the part
of those oppressed because of their sexuality. Second, Duncan's speculation on
the possibility of 'any other order' draws attention to a definition of sexuality as
a cultural field that is subject to both construction and reconstruction as part
of a historical process. Third, decontextualized as it is, the quotation appears to
allow for diversity of sexual potential rather than delimiting categories such as
heterosexual, homosexual, bisexual or transgendered. Finally, the epigraph
actually comes from an essay by a homosexual male, which demonstrates that,
even with categories based on sexual behaviour, there is no single or simple
identity across the category, neither no one homosexuality nor heterosexuality.
Duncan was arguing against such separate identities. It is this reading that
provides the context for this chapter in which we aim to trace some of the
history of the oppression of sexualities other than heterosexuality and consider
the implications of recent events and campaigns for the progress of the struggle
for equality of lesbian, gay, bisexual and trangendered (LGBT) people. Within
this enterprise we will consider attempts to define and represent sexuality,
particularly in the modern era, moving towards a discussion in which we focus
on conceptions of sexuality *per se* rather than individual categories, these categories being relatively recent cultural effects. So although we may try in this
chapter to generalize about sexuality as a cultural field, yet self-consciously hang

our comments on a history of categories, especially (but not exclusively) the male homosexual, we will inevitably come back to the very problematic nature of the production of these separate (and multiple) identities (and communities) based on sexual behaviour.

Defining sexualities

Definitions of sexuality medical, legal and otherwise abound. Some, like Oscar Wilde's famously expedient misreading of Plato in the dock, 'It is that deep, spiritual affection that is as pure as it is perfect. It is intellectual' (Wilde, 1895, p. 111), have attempted to side-step the issue of difference in sexual practices. Wilde's 'love that dare not speak its name' also, of course, involved sexual acts, criminalized by the Victorians as 'gross indecency', a crime of which Wilde and his co-defendant, Alfred Taylor (the keeper of a male homosexual brothel), were eventually convicted. The conversion of sexuality to sexual acts subject initially to religious codification, then to the pathologies of medicine and the jurisdiction of the law, is one on which we will focus in our 'history'.[1]

One of the earliest and most detailed attempts at categorizing sexualities was made by the nineteenth-century German sexologist Karl Heinrich Ulrichs (1994, 1997). He was a legal official who took a campaigning position against what he saw as repressive laws against male homosexuals, exemplified by Paragraph 175 of the German Imperial Code: 'Unnatural vice committed between two persons of the male sex or by people with animals is to be punished by imprisonment; the verdict may also include the loss of civil rights' (Ulrichs cited in Blasius and Phelan, 1997, p. 63). From the early 1860s, Ulrichs produced many short publications designed to challenge such legislation, based on conversations and correspondence with individuals throughout Europe. Alluding to Plato's terminology in *The Symposium*, Ulrichs devised a series of categories and subcategories that set the boundaries for what he thought to be all the possibilities for sexual behaviour. These included: 'Men' and 'Women', whose sexual object-choice lay exclusively in the opposite sex; 'Urnings', or male homosexuals, who could be 'Mannlings' (virile), 'Weiblings' (effeminate) or 'Intermediaries' (a mixed subcategory); through to 'Urningins' (lesbians), 'Uranodionings' (male bisexuals), 'Uranodioningins' (female bisexuals) and 'Hermaphrodites' (sharing the physical characteristics of both sexes). Ulrichs (1994, p. 314) actually defined a range of 12 sexual types if we include all his subcategories.

Although his intentions were progressive, Ulrich's project laid the ground for the subsequent pathologizing of sexual behaviour in the discourses of medicine and psychiatry that is still powerful today. The tensions between this progressive intention and the pathologizing effect can be seen in this extract from an appeal to the regional governments of North Germany and Austria in 1870:

> That an actual man would feel sexual love for a man is impossible. The urning is not a true man. He is a mixture of man and woman. He is man

only in terms of bodily build. The urning too is a human being. He, too, therefore has natural human rights. The urning is also a citizen of the state. He, too, therefore has civil rights: and correspondingly, the state has duties to fulfil vis-à-vis him as well. The state is not entitled to treat the urning as a man without rights, as it has up to now.

(Ulrichs cited in Blasius and Phelan, 1997, p. 65)

The drive to pathologize sexual behaviour was intensified throughout the nineteenth century by, for example, Karoly Maria Benkert (said to be the person who invented the term 'homosexual'), Richard von Krafft-Ebing and, of course, Sigmund Freud. By the middle of the twentieth century, the proposition that sexual behaviour that had been diagnosed as deviant could be treated was commonplace. Aversion therapies based upon a malign behaviourist psychology became part of the medical/psychiatric repertoire and led to the institutional abuse of countless homosexuals, transvestites, transgendered and transsexual people and others. It was comparatively recently that homosexuality was removed from some catalogues of mental disorders, and only then after a considerable struggle. The anthropologist Gayle Rubin (1993) has shown how medicine and psychiatry multiplied these pathologies in a hierarchy of (deviant) sexual behaviour that continues to be pervasive but, talking of the relative successes of homosexuals in establishing some human rights in some places and in coming out of the medical textbook, notes that '[s]exualities keep marching out of the *Diagnostic and Statistical Manual* and on to the pages of social history' (Rubin, 1993, p. 416).

The work of Alfred Kinsey (Kinsey *et al.*, 1948, 1953) on human sexual behaviour represents a watershed in the modern understanding and definition of sexuality. Kinsey set out to describe and catalogue the sexual behaviour of human beings by interviewing American men and women about their sexual lives and experiences and by observing sexual behaviour in the laboratory. A major achievement of his studies was to show that contemporary preconceptions about the mutual exclusivity of sexual identities were erroneous. Many of the men and women participating in his study reported both heterosexual and homosexual contacts, leading Kinsey to develop an analytic scale on which sexual behaviour could be described in terms of one of six points, ranging from exclusively homosexual with no heterosexual contacts to exclusively heterosexual with no homosexual contacts, with grades reflecting more or less homosexual and heterosexual behaviour respectively in between. By looking over study participants' sexual histories Kinsey was able to assign them a place on the scale. Although he found that most of the men and women participating in the study reported exclusively heterosexual contacts, and a relatively small number (a few per cent) reported exclusively homosexual contacts, up to 37 per cent of the men in his sample had experienced a same-sex sexual experience to the point of orgasm in their lifetime. While the findings of Kinsey's work challenged previously held notions of the exclusivity of homosexual and heterosexual behaviour it did so from within the paradigm of existing essentialist beliefs about sex and, as such, was not as progressive as it might at first appear. The focus on sexual acts rather than any idea of sexual identities did nothing to challenge critical perceptions of homosexuality as a deviancy. The discovery that apparently heterosexual men reported homosexual contacts in their youth could be dismissed as either evidence of a periodic 'arrested development' (à la Freud), or of a mature heterosexuality overcoming immature homosexual tendencies.

The fallout of essentialist investigations of sexuality via studies of sexual behaviour is still being felt. Most recently, attention has focused on the search for a genetic basis for homosexuality (and presumably, therefore, heterosexuality). This search is hampered by the inability of genetic science to explain ideas of a sexual identity any more satisfactorily than Kinsey's studies. Consequently, evidence from essentialist studies tends to become hostage to the ideologies of its commentators. Homophobic commentators have latched onto the potential existence of a gay gene as offering the possibility of genetic correction of a perceived sexual deviancy. However, some gay lobbyists have welcomed the 'gay gene' as biological proof that they are essentially biologically different from heterosexuals and have not created a deviant social identity for themselves. Between these lines, factions cross sides and, illustrating the political utility of essentialist findings, some gay lobbyists have argued for the rejection of Kinsey's work because it seems to provide too small an account of exclusive homosexuality. Some 'libertarian' right-wing ideologues draw the conclusion that, if homosexuality is genetically determined, then it is a natural state and should be decriminalized. For Kinsey, the reading of his work by the McCarthy-influenced US government at the time was sufficiently negative that funding was withdrawn from his studies.

While sexological surveys continue, the chief development of thinking about definitions of sexuality comes from fields outside the laboratory. Gagnon and Simon (1973) make the significant contribution to the sociology of sexuality by describing sex as a socio-cultural phenomenon rather than a natural act. This means that if sex is a social construct, subject to various meanings and deemed to have different functions at different times and in different places, it can be reconstructed according to social, cultural and political trends, needs and pressures. This paved the way for the work of Foucault (1978, 1984) who developed an analysis of sexualities as products of cultures and defined by the interaction of the personal with social norms, scientific knowledge, religious and legal doctrine and authority. Subsequently, feminist thinkers and activists have sought to destabilize patriarchal values and practices by challenging the cultural, social and political hegemony of male heterosexuality. By questioning the orthodoxies of gender, its roles and meanings, feminist authors like MacKinnon (1989) have concluded that sexuality is a cultural effect dependent upon constructions of gender. From this analysis flows a critique of the essentialist paradigm that sets up heterosexuality, and all the associated baggage about gendered sexual roles, as the dominant discourse and other sexualities as subordinate varieties.

We might conclude by observing that in setting out a paradigm of particular sexualities through essentialist studies earlier in the century, academics and activists provided the framework and evidence that has made it possible latterly to deconstruct that paradigm. Definitions of sexuality have moved from previously fairly solid ground on which a simple mutual exclusivity of heterosexuality and homosexuality seemed adequate to describe human experience, to a shifting terrain on which sexuality appears as a fluid, discursive phenomenon. A contemporary definition would have to acknowledge the complex interplay of social, cultural and intrapersonal factors in the production of a changing identity. We might describe sexuality as the element of identity that contains a sense of a self in which sexual feelings, ideologies, desires and needs are integrated with one another and reconciled with modes of sexual expression and behaviour. Bringing together our feelings, values and desires may be difficult, as may reconciling these with modes of expression and behaviour acceptable to ourselves and others. Without some reconciliation between these aspects of our internal world and ways of acting and interacting, we are vulnerable to feelings of dislocation between who we are and how we live. Reconciling feelings and actions does not take place only at a psychological level but in the context of the social world in which expressions of sexuality are differently valued. The inevitable consequence of this differentiation is that people who cannot reconcile their sexuality with those who are most socially valued can feel they themselves are less valued.

While on the one hand the weakening of prescriptive definitions opens the field for powerful legal arguments for the equalization of treatment of different sexualities, it also has the potential to undermine the resources available to minorities who feel a strong impulse to congregate around one identity label. In short, what is to be the relationship between sexual acts and identity? Can a gay man be gay in thought and not deed (as the Anglican Episcopal Church would seem to allow)? Can a heterosexual woman have a homosexual relationship and still feel herself to be heterosexual or ought she now regard herself as bisexual? At one level, the invention of a sexual identity that depends heavily on representation of the self has reinvigorated the sexual act as a defining idea. As we shall see, history and the contemporary media have both striven to re-inject sexual acts into representations of sexuality in order to keep the lines of distinction clear and position us still on the fringes of either reaction or revolution.

Representations of sexuality

Representations of sexuality are a central feature of contemporary popular culture. However, the possibilities for representation have been contested in a number of areas by special interest groups, and by the state in the manipulation of obscenity laws by police 'vice' squads and, paradoxically, given its daily content in terms of features, photographs, advertising and readers' letters, the tabloid press has often seen one of its most important editorial functions to be upholding notional standards of sexual morality.

As Epstein and Johnson have pointed out, grasping the influence of the media, especially the tabloid press, is critical in the formulation of an understanding of how the wider sexual culture is constructed and what kinds of tools and resources we are supplied with to help us make sense of this environment (Epstein and Johnson, 1998). Part of their attempt to theorize about the links between politics, culture, schooling and sexuality charts a series of high-profile outbursts of outrage in the tabloid press in the mid-1990s at the way that sexuality and sexual diversity has been represented to children and young people in schools. As Epstein and Johnson demonstrate in their unpicking of a series of 'scandals' surrounding the provision of sex education, the self-appointment of the tabloid press as an arbitrator on matters of sex and sexuality relies primarily on two constructs. First, the envisaging of a hierarchical arrangement of sexualities that implies both the primacy of one over others (heterosexuality over other sexualities) and the need for vigilance, resistance and even active action to suppress shifts within the hierarchy which threaten that dominance. Second, the identification of schools as particularly important sites in this struggle because young, innocent and ignorant minds are vulnerable to subversion and even corruption by teaching which lacks an explicit endorsement of heterosexuality as normative or 'natural'. The tendency of the tabloid press both to pick up stories about youthful sexuality and sex education in schools and to cover them in the context of these con-structs has continued in the 2000s. For example, the announcement in 2009 that the (New Labour) government would propose legislation to make PSHE (the curriculum context for sex education) compulsory produced some egregiously misleading tabloid headlines including, in *The Daily Mail* of 29 April 2009, the announcement that, 'Lessons about gays will be compulsory from the age of 11' (Harris, 2009). The article comprised a list of the sex education topics that would be covered at each key stage followed by a series of comments condemning the inclusion of references to same-sex relationships from representatives of right-wing organizations, claiming to represent 'family' and 'moral' interests and implacably opposed to sex education in schools. So, Simon Calvert of the Christian Institute was reported as observing that:

> 'pressing the virtues of homosexuality could lead to more experimentation which could be harmful to children.' He added, ' If this guidance purports to force faith schools to teach things which go against their faith then it is profoundly illiberal and must be resisted at all costs.'

This one short comment captures the essential characteristics of the discursive position identified by Epstein and Johnson: it misrepresents the facts in pursuit of an agenda that 'others' same-sex relationships' reduces them to sexual acts, and implies that children are malleable and vulnerable to 'conversion' if not 'perversion' from normative and normal heterosexuality to homosexuality. Furthermore, by implying that schools would be forced to conform to government diktat (again an error in understanding), it engages with an underlying right-wing fear that a liberal-intelligentsia is engaged on a secretive mission to impose its morally corrosive views on a powerless population.

While it is no surprise that the printed tabloid press with its traditionally hyperbolic, partisan and overtly political coverage of issues around sex and sexuality might strongly present issues as a straightforward matter of maintaining prescribed morals and morality, identities and behaviours against the insurgencies and challenges of alternatives, it is, perhaps, more surprising to be able to discern similar discursive undercurrents in other aspects of mass media.

For instance, as recent research has shown, the BBC, which is legally required to adopt a non-partisan position and fulfil a public-service and educative role, has a marked tendency to reinforce rather than challenge the views propounded by the tabloid press (Cowan and Valentine, 2006). Cowan and Valentine's study, conducted on behalf of Stonewall, the UK organization that lobbies for equality for lesbian, gay, bisexual and transgendered people, sought to bring together a systematic analysis of a tranche of BBC programme content with qualitative research exploring a variety of viewers' assessments of the impact of television representations of sexualities on their attitudes and experiences.

The initial component of this study comprised an analysis of over 150 hours of prime-time evening output broadcast by the BBC over the period of one month during 2005. The researchers focused on the depiction of gay life and issues, passing references to homosexuality, the portrayal of gay characters and celebrities and the use of language including stereotyping and homophobia. Instances were categorized as positive, unbiased or negative. The latter including cases where gay sexuality was depicted as a problem, its portrayal relied on clichéd stereotypes or the programme content was openly homophobic. This content analysis identified only six minutes of positive coverage in 168 hours of scheduling spanning 15 different programmes. These instances included the appearance of a lesbian couple on a game show, a celebrity talking about his experiences of 'coming out' and a fictionalized account of two men falling in love. Negative coverage was also reasonably limited totalling 32 minutes of programming transmitted across the period of study. Examples cited by the researchers referred predominantly to game shows and comedies in which presenters, celebrity contestants and hosts made homophobic jokes. The most common tropes in these cases characterized gay men as either effeminate or sexually promiscuous. Some examples are used to illustrate Cowan and Valentine's analysis suggestive of both the routine, casual and yet aggressive way that homophobic insults may be traded in the name of entertainment. For instance, they point to the sustained use of innuendo to belittle a contestant on the hugely popular teatime programme 'The Weakest Link'. In one edition the host, Anne Robinson, repeatedly addressed a contestant, Reza Mahamad, asking, 'What do you do in your restaurant? Just mince around?' and, later, 'Is Reza more puff than pastry?' (Cowan and Valentine, 2006, p. 9).

The content analysis element of the study found that gay people and issues were rarely depicted in factual programming. Specifically, while the researchers categorized about half the programming in the period under scrutiny as factual, only 3 per cent of all references to gay people and issues occurred in the context of this broadcasting diet. The researchers suggest that much of this coverage was either sensational or focused on sexuality as a problem, stating that:

> There were only two examples totalling one minute and three seconds where lesbians and gay men were depicted in conventional scenarios – such as with a partner, expressing affection or with family – in which their sexual orientation is clear, but it is not the focal point or the cause of a crisis. Nor was it common to see homophobia challenged either as part of a fictional story-line or in response to the views of real people.
>
> (Cowan and Valentine, 2006, p. 9)

Importantly, this study also draws attention to the almost total absence of lesbian lifestyles and identities within BBC programming. What little coverage the researchers found tended to recourse to either one or other of two stereotypes: the lesbian woman as either masculinized (generally in the context of comedic programming) or as a glamorous, feminine woman. Bisexual people, transsexuals and LGBT people with disabilities or from ethnic minorities were not represented at all in the programming subjected to scrutiny.

The negative influence of this limited and narrow representation of gay identities and lifestyles on attitudes and responses to same-sex relationships was very evident in the focus groups conducted both with lesbian, gay and also heterosexual people that comprised the second component in this study. Many lesbian and gay participants described the importance of representations of sexualities in television programming with reference to how they were perceived and treated within their immediate heterosexual social networks. Many felt that the representation of gay male identities predominantly in the context of camp comedy contributed to an expectation that gay men are 'party animals' – that is, vibrant, funny but also, essentially, superficial – and, by relying on innuendo relating to sexual practices as its comedic base, contributed to the idea that gay male sexuality is open to public scrutiny, especially by straight women. The effects of the reduction of non-heterosexual identities to sexual acts that are subject to the public, heterosexual gaze and interrogation was also evident in relation to views about representations of lesbian women. In these cases, gay men and lesbian women felt that the sexualization of relationships between women was intended to be titillating and both reflected and played to heterosexual men's fantasies.

Despite the fact that the findings of focus groups with gay men and lesbian women make largely depressing reading, Cowan and Valentine also draw attention to a few instances in which representations of gay lives on the BBC were found to be positive or useful. For example, some participants in discussions suggested that coverage provided a means by which to raise the issue of sexuality casually and in everyday contexts with friends and colleagues, and thereby to test the waters in terms of their attitudes, perhaps as a prelude to or as the decisive factor in deciding to come out to them. Positive representations were also perceived to play a role in counteracting and diminishing prejudice, and television as a shared cultural experience (again to some extent independent of whether it is evaluated as good, bad or indifferent) could be contributory to community identity and solidarity.

Interestingly, the Stonewall study also involved consulting with groups of heterosexual people. The researchers found that some people in these groups felt challenged by aspects of the BBC's programming. In particular, there was reported discomfort with instances where it was felt that lesbian and gay people were promoting their sexualities and with programmes that contained representations of physical intimacy between men. In contrast, heterosexual viewers described camp comedic characters with affection. For some participants in these focus groups, portrayal of same-sex identities, lifestyles and issues contributed to a feeling of greater understanding and helped to undermine a reliance on stereotyping. Instances where the experiences of gay people in coming out were foregrounded in coverage were perceived to be particularly influential in this respect.

Despite some potential limitations – the pragmatic focus on only a limited period of broadcasting and the absence of any comparative analysis of the portrayal of heterosexual identities and lifestyles – the Stonewall study provides a rich picture of both the content and perceived influence of mass media on sexual attitudes, views, experiences and lifestyles. The research also hints at the sophistication of the viewing public as consumers of portrayals of human identities and sexualities. There are indications in some of the citations from participants' contributions to group discussions that they identify the media, including the BBC, as reliant on contrivance, and particularly sensationalism, to meet the demands of the increasing commercial enterprise that the media has become: television is television not real life.

However, despite this level of media literacy some forms of portrayal appear to be rather elusive in terms of meaning and hence problematic in the public mind. Stonewall draws particular attention to the character of Daffyd – 'the only gay in the village' – from the series 'Little Britain' as an example of the focus for this ambivalence. Although the programme was not screened during the period in which the study took place references to it seem to have abounded within participants' discussions about media representations, their significance and effects. The problems seem to be multi-layered. Participants in the study were unable to decide if 'Daffyd' represented an attack on, or collusion with, stereotypes of gay men. The fact that the actor playing the role is a gay man added another layer of complexity. Is 'Daffyd' an expression of internalized homophobia or the subversion of comedic camp tropes and an assault on innuendo that sexualizes gay men? Is it more permissible for an openly gay man to engage in insidious resistance to homophobia of this kind and in this way? The report goes some way to teasing out these questions noting that responses to 'Daffyd' did seem in important ways to be patterned by people's experiences and specifically the social context and local culture in which they lived. For instance, the 'only gay in the village' was seen to be more collusive with stereotyping and homophobia by people living in rural and working-class localities. Similar difficulties around meaning and interpretation have arisen in relation to other media portrayals, in particular the recent film *Bruno*, which had a polarizing effect on debate about the influence of engaging with stereotyping representations of gay identities and lifestyles (Rackoff, 2009; Hari, 2009).

Given the evident difficulties in resolving questions of this kind, is it possible to say anything conclusive about the meanings of some forms of representation of sexualities? We believe that it is. It would be, we suggest, hard to contest that same-sex lifestyles remain problematized and subject to strict constraint within media representations. They tend to be corralled into a number of overly neat and limiting identities that are held at edges of social life. There is, in fact, no paradox that someone like Stephen Fry can achieve the status of a 'national treasure' but Gareth Thomas (a gay rugby league footballer) can be subjected to homophobic chanting by 'fans'. In all cases, whether representations seem to be positive or negative, what is being focused on is the 'problem' of sexualities and identities that are not heterosexual. This deflects from the more important question, which is: What is the problem with heterosexuality and why does it rely on 'othering' to maintain its power?

This discussion of some of the media representations of sexuality and sexual identity highlights some of the particularly rich contradictions in modern Western culture's definitions of sexuality. In her influential book *Epistemology of the Closet*, Eve Kosofsky Sedgwick (1994, p. 1) describes these contradictions as extremely powerful 'nodes of thought and knowledge' across 'twentieth century Western culture as a whole'. In tabloid media coverage issues around sex, sexuality and sex education, we see what Sedgwick describes as the 'minoritising view'. The gay man or lesbian woman is identified as one of 'them', and the question of identity is only an issue for 'them'. Heterosexual sexualities are not subjected to such intense and sustained scrutiny and discussion. As the public, we share in both the prurient interest of the tabloid press in non-straight sexual identities within the context of fixed conceptions of gender, primarily and determinatively associated with particular sexual behaviours and desires. This is why 'coming out' is, in important ways, a wider and more general signifier that can be commonly used in everyday conversation produced in an enormous range of contexts. Sedgwick argues that:

> exactly the opposite is true. I think that a whole cluster of the most crucial sites for the contestation of meaning in twentieth century Western culture are consequentially and quite indelibly marked with the historical speci-ficity of homosocial/homosexual definition.
>
> (Sedgwick, 1994, p. 72)

In this context we understand the tensions between secrecy, disclosure and private and public that the media so often focus on as an effect of an attempt at sexual and individual definition. We are able to recognize that our efforts to understand our own identities take place in the realm of competing yet co-existing discourses.

Even for those women and men who acknowledge their sexual attraction to people of the same sex, the question of identity is not simple. 'Dykes' or 'queens', 'butch/femme', 'straight-acting' or 'scene' are just some of the possibilities for self-identification that are open to homosexuals. There is not one homosexual identity but many. However, they all establish their meaning in a relationship with the 'other', whether that be a generic heterosexual other or another homosexuality. To this extent, they are all products of a minoritizing discourse. In his essay 'The Homosexual in Society', Robert Duncan argued against minoritizing discourses that produce a 'ghetto' or 'cult' of homosexual 'superi-ority'. He criticized what he saw as the triviality and vapidity of a developing homosexual subculture that sought to keep itself separate, secret and in some ways superior to a notional general population. In doing so, he created a simple opposition between being 'human' and being 'homosexual', which could poten-tially, in some readers' eyes, assign him to the category of self-hating gay man: 'It is hard . . . to say that this cult plays any other than an evil role in society' (Duncan cited in Blasius and Phelan, 1997, p. 231).

Duncan was actually arguing for the as-yet-unnamed act of 'coming out' to the whole of society rather than seeking a 'sense of sanctuary such as the Medieval Jew must have found in the ghetto' (Duncan cited in Blasius and Phelan, 1997, p. 232). He was regretting his own experience of being silent on the political issues and using the 'group language' of the cult. In his final paragraph he does ameliorate his criticism of members of the cult, yet at times his own language, particularly in his comments on camp, tone and 'self-ridicule' foreshadows that of members of the 'anti-gay' movement in the 1990s (e.g. Simpson, 1996). Nevertheless, the final sentence of his argument (used as the epigraph to this chapter) encapsulates the sense of political responsibility every individual must recognize in the struggle for equality, and the importance of self-disclosure, that remains at the heart of radical campaigning organizations such as Outrage.

Sex has no history

In this section, we will attempt to give an overview of some key events in a history of sexuality and sexual identity. Like any history, it is inevitably partial and the narrative structured from one perspective. The context for our brief discussion is Western societies and cultures, particularly Britain: we will not attempt to consider sexuality in other cultures or anywhere else on the other side of this epistemological border.[2] The history from which we draw most heavily is largely one of legal prohibitions on same-sex activity, most often directed at male homosexuals, and the struggle by oppressed groups for some degree of equality in the eyes of the law. We have chosen to focus on three significant moments in this history, each separated from the preceding by nearly 1,000 years. The purpose is not to dismiss the intervening stretches of time but rather to illustrate vividly how mutable are the social conventions around homosexuality. Throughout, we will view sexuality not as some essential expression of biological drives but as a cultural effect produced and changed by different discourses. The subheading to this section, taken from David Halperin's work, draws attention to this difference between sex ('a natural fact, grounded in the functioning of the body') and sexuality ('the appropriation of the human body and of its physio-logical capacities by an ideological discourse') (Halperin, 1989, p. 416). By looking at the shifting position of homosexuality in the eyes of the Christian Church, government, science and the law it is clear the extent to which sexuality is solicited by capital in the establishment and maintenance of particular kinds of social relationships between citizens/subjects and of particular kinds of social/moral order. In general, this has meant differentiating homosexuality from heterosexuality and privileging the latter in certain ways. In fact, heterosexuality has become the central resource of the capitalist, nationalist order as conservative visions of the heterosexual, 'nuclear' family as the basic building block of society imply. It provides the means for managing rights of succession and the transfer of capital and power, and the foundation for creating a belief in a natural national family. What our history shows us, in part, is the struggle to control that capital.

Although authors like Taylor (1997) have recently begun to explore the prehistory of sex through the study of early representations of the human being and body on artefacts and in paintings, studies of sexuality in history usually start with a number of observations about the supposed predilection of men in ancient Greece to bugger adolescent boys and the apparent acceptance of these 'homosexual', cross-generational relationships. This is either meant to show that homosexuality is the choice of educated and civilized people (one reading of Plato's *Symposium*, where the context for such relationships is educational in intent) or that it is an unspeakable, foreign vice (another reading of the same text by translators and editors of various historical periods who expunged the offending passages in Plato's original). It is clear, however, that the sexual activities that appear to be described in some classical Greek texts were not seen as an expression of any kind of 'sexual identity' that could be defined as homo-sexual. They were simply acts that took place in a completely different kind of relationship altogether. David Halperin has said that '[s]ex is portrayed in Athenian documents not as a mutual enterprise in which two or more persons jointly engage but as an action performed by a social superior upon a social inferior' (Halperin, 1989, p. 418). Halperin presents the sexual dynamic of classi-cal Athens as a relationship between a citizen 'penetrator' (male) and 'penetrated' minors. These 'minors' included women, post-pubertal 'free' males not old enough to be citizens and slaves. The penetrator and the penetrated each had separate 'identities' and the participation in the sexual act did not in any way bring them together in any shared identity based upon an identifiable 'sexuality'. Their personal, physical desires were real but 'their very desires had already been shaped by the shared cultural definition of sex as an activity that generally occurred only between a citizen and a non-citizen' (ibid., p. 419).

In his definitive study of Greek homosexuality, Kenneth Dover (1978) describes how Greek society, particularly between 480 BCE and 146 BCE, revolved around presumptions of the authority of adult male citizens and that sexual relations between men became overt and acceptable. However, these relationships took on a peculiarly stylized form and emotional tone and were largely confined to men of the higher social classes who mixed in more or less segregated groups as part of military and educational training. The central focus was on the development of a bond between an older man, an *erastes* (lover), and a younger man or boy, an *eromenos* (the loved). The older man, it was expected, would feel strong sexual attraction to the younger man, admiring his beauty, agility and physical attributes, and courting him with gifts. The younger man, rather than experiencing any emotional reciprocity, was expected to admire the older man for his wisdom and experience and look upon him as a model of masculinity. Over time it was anticipated that the relationship would alter as the younger man grew up, all emotional and sexual overtones would dim and the relationship would become one of friends.

The conventions about the emotional nature of the connection between the men in these relationships percolated through to influence the nature of their sexual intimacies. Officially at least, buggery was taboo, and in theory attracted the penalty of being stripped of one's citizenship. Hence, the usual method of intercourse was intercrural, the *erastes* being the active sexual partner. Sexual relationships between men of equal ages were frowned on, as was penetration of the *erastes*. The strict ideals about the nature of the relationship between men and the nature of Greek masculinity would be violated by such actions. As it stands, masculinity was associated with adult male status and sexual licence to be the penetrative and active partner. Another crucial aspect of Greek attitudes to homosexuality is the emphasis placed on restraint. The Platonic stress on transcending the real world and entering the world of Forms, where the universal essence of objects and ideas is arrayed, canonized restraint and emotional control. So, while Plato, and Socrates before him, accept and venerate homosexual feelings and relationships, their consummation is condemned since it shows passion blinding reason. Towards the end of his life, Plato was driven by inexorable logic, profoundly influential on later thinkers, to describe homosexual behaviour as unnatural. In Dover's translation, he writes:

> Anyone, who, in conformity with nature proposes to re-establish the law as it was before Laios, declaring that it was right not to join with men and boys in sexual intercourse as with females, adducing as evidence the nature of animals could, I think, make a very strong case.
>
> (Plato, *Laws*, 836c–e, trans. in Dover, 1978, p. 166)

In the Roman Empire, as in the Greek, people were not categorized as heterosexual or homosexual. While prostitution, both male and female, flourished under official licence, emphasis was placed on the maintenance of culturally and socially sanctioned ideals of masculinity and femininity that resulted in a continuation of the Greek proscriptions of penetrative and penetrated sexual roles. The 'genderbending' antics of the imperial classes attracted particular opprobrium from the Roman chattering classes. The satirist Juvenal, in his vitriolic *Second Satire*, turns his anger several times on effeminacy among the ruling classes. He castigates the Emperor Domitian for reintroducing tough laws on sexual activity while indulging in incest and sodomy, reserving his harshest judgements for the soldier Emperor Otho, whom, he suggests, betrays ideals of Roman masculinity through his effeminacy:

> Another queen or queer, even nastier/holds a hand mirror his face to show/ the very spectre of the pathic Otho/in which he admired his uniform/ while sounding the charge at Bedriacum./Is this the lesson of Rome's recent story/ 'The path of beauty is the path to glory?'
> (Juvenal, *Satire II*, 98–103, trans. in Plumb, 1968, p. 36)

Clearly, while censorious attitudes towards certain types of sexuality emerge in Hellenistic cultures the focus falls on twisting and breaking gender roles and not on sexual identity as a separate entity. A new and peculiar moral sensibility is added to these attitudes by the construction of sexuality emerging with early Judaeo-Christian doctrine and finding full voice in the teaching of the Christian Church in medieval Europe (Richards, 1990). Sexual feeling and experience became synonymous with sin. As St Anselm, Archbishop of Canterbury at the end of the eleventh century, wrote:

> There is one evil, an evil above all other evils, that I am aware is always with me, that grievously and piteously lacerates and afflicts my soul. The evil is sexual desire, carnal delight, the storm of lust that has smashed and battered my unhappy soul, drained it of all strength and left it weak and empty.
> (cited in Richards, 1990)

As the teaching of St Paul stressed, celibacy was therefore the highest achievable ideal and reproductive sex in the context of marriage an acceptable second best. The Church's control of sexual behaviour was extended principally through the establishment of a legal, sacred marriage service that celebrated, sanctified and moralized about the complementary roles of men and women exemplified by the biblical story of Adam and Eve. For women, this resulted in typification as at once inferior, as the product of Adam's body, and evil, for succumbing to the serpent's temptation. This connection between female sexuality and sinfulness made it logical to sanction wife-beating, as a measure for instilling discipline and the forbidding of women from holding public office or undertaking any military service.

The Church's view of the role of sex inside and outside of marriage is illustrated by accounts of confessions and penances for sexual acts. Payer's (1984) work on the penitentials (books guiding priests in determining the gravity of various sins and the consequent scale of penance) shows a broadly consistent religious attitude towards sexual activity. Sexual matters formed the largest single category of offences in most penitentials. Although the details of penances varied, they were generally based on fasting on bread and water and avoiding sex for a number of consecutive days in multiples of 10. The Church pronounced the proper form of intercourse within marriage as penetrative vaginal sex with the man lying on top of the woman. Dorsal intercourse, with the woman on top, would earn three years' penance; anal intercourse seven years'. Sex was encouraged only at night and then partially clothed. Burchard of Worms (d. 1025) graded penitentials as follows: 10 days on bread and water for male masturbation by hand, 20 days if it involved a perforated piece of wood. Interestingly, sexual intercourse with a female servant attracted the same penalty, illustrating the indulgence extended to young men and the social position and relative (un)importance of women. Highest penalties were reserved for incest, sodomy and bestiality. Burchard also proscribed the telling of dirty jokes, mixed bathing and fondling.

Medieval theology has no definition of homosexuality as such, only of homosexual acts. In fact, the terms used by St Paul to condemn homosexual acts imply their occurrence only among heterosexual people. The line was very clear. Drawing on the Book of Leviticus (18:22 and 20:13), homosexual sex was ranked alongside incest, adultery and bestiality as the most serious sin. While the Church dealt in sexual acts, there is evidence to suggest that a homosexual subculture centred on male brothels in barbers' shops and bath-houses sprang up in some French and Italian cities in the twelfth century (Boswell, 1980). Along with the emergence of poetry and song extolling the virtues of erotic love between men, an argot is recorded that refers to young gay men as 'Ganymedes', sex as 'The Game' and cruising as 'Hunting'. Perhaps partially in reaction to this emergent subculture, theologians began to conceptualize homosexuality as an insidious inversion of 'natural', God-given laws. They opined that it was inconceivable that God should have been perverse enough to create sexual activities that undermined His own law, so homosexuality must be the product of a deviant, unnatural and ungodly mind. Consequently, consent to homosexual sex was no defence. By the end of the twelfth century, monarchies in England, France and Spain decreed death as a suitable punishment for those convicted of homosexual acts.

A state of illegality effectively lasted for a further 700 years. In the years following the trial, conviction and jailing of Oscar Wilde in 1895, although there was no concerted attempt to force a liberalization of the law in Great Britain, homosexuality became more visible at the fringes of artistic society. The repression seemed to have been irretrievably undermined by the world wars in which sexual liberalism spread among the ranks of civilians and the armed forces alike.

With the advent of peace in 1945, however, sexual morals were supposed to be restored. The prosecution of gay men rose to new heights. In a climate of political retrenchment, the numbers of men arrested by the police and convicted rose threefold. A series of high-profile cases reached a peak early in 1954 with the conviction of Lord Montagu of Beaulieu, Peter Wildeblood, the diplomatic correspondent of *The Daily Mail* and Michael Pitt-Rivers, a wealthy land-owner, for conspiring to incite two RAF men to 'commit unnatural offences'. The case achieved notoriety, not only because of the social status of the defendants but because the prosecution painted a lurid scene of debauchery in a beach hut on the Beaulieu estate. Regardless of the fact that all the men were consenting adults and the discovery that both Montagu's and Wildeblood's homes were burgled in suspicious circumstances during the course of the trial, the defendants were convicted and sentenced to custody. They found themselves at the centre of a public debate about homosexual rights. A popular limerick of the time ridiculed the law:

> An aircraftsman named McNally
> Was caught with a lord in a chalet,
> The judge said my dears,
> They're patently queers,
> Give them two years for being too pally.

Pressure built for a reassessment of the law fuelled by the Church of England's Moral Welfare Council's publication of *The Problem of Homosexuality: An Interim Report*, which stated that although sex between men was undoubtedly a sin, so too were adultery and fornication, neither of which attracted legal censure. A notable Tory MP, Sir Robert Boothby, lobbied the Home Secretary, Maxwell Fyfe, for a Royal Commission on the matter. Contemporaneously, the Hardwicke Society, a senior debating forum for barristers, carried the motion 'The penal laws relating to homosexual offences are outmoded and should be changed'.

Succumbing to the inevitable, the Home Secretary relented to mounting pressure and established the Departmental Committee on Homosexual Offences and Prostitution under the aegis of John Wolfenden, the Vice-Chancellor of Reading University. This committee sat for the first time on 4 August 1954 and heard evidence from over 200 individuals and groups in the course of more than 60 meetings before publishing its report in September 1957. The committee quickly reached the conclusion that while homosexuality might be morally unacceptable, it could not be stamped out by legislation and continued crimi-nalization was legally untenable since it exposed homosexual men to blackmail and represented an indefensible intrusion into personal privacy. Consequently, Wolfenden's report concluded with the recommendation that homosexual behaviour in private between consenting adults (over 21) should be decrimi-nalized. Wolfenden added that it was not the business of law to 'settle questions of morality, to interfere in the private lives of the citizens; it is only when public decency is offended that the law is entitled to step in and institute criminal proceedings'.

The report received blanket coverage in the press. Seven national newspapers with a combined readership of over 60 per cent of the public gave the report favourable coverage; only two condemned it. However, as Wilde observed of the Labouchere Act, it was not public opinion but politicians' fear for their seats that determines what passes to the statute book. As if to prove the veracity of Wilde's observation that 'It is not so much public opinion as public officials that need educating', H. Montgomery Hyde was the first, but not the last, MP to be deselected by his constituency committee in the run-up to the 1959 election for supporting the adoption of Wolfenden's recommendations into law. It was observed, 'We cannot have as our member one who condones unnatural vice.' It took seven parliamentary debates on the Wolfenden Report between 1958 and 1967 before the recommendations were adopted into law, and only then by passing initially through the House of Lords where members could vote freely without having to concern themselves with constituency committees.

It would be disingenuous to interpret these historical events as evidence of the forces of reaction carving out a homosexual identity rather than any gay identity emerging through the activities of people themselves. The process of the invention of sexuality *per se*, and of a stigmatized gay identity in particular, is a complex interaction of action and reaction. However, authority has managed successfully to corral sexual acts into an identity that contains implications of ungodliness, unnaturalness and even potential sedition. These themes reappear in near-contemporary inventions of HIV/AIDS as a 'gay plague', and, between 1997 and 1999, the British newspaper *The Sun* expressed fears about a gay cabal at the heart of the New Labour government. A result of the politicization of sexuality by the state, the Church and the law has been to harden political activism among those affected by such moralizing and sermonizing. The modern gay rights movement has come to focus its attention on deficits in human rights that can only be addressed by the state. In the penultimate section of this chapter we look at three particular instances of contestation about equality of sexualities which illustrate these contemporary concerns.

Sexuality and equality: some current issues

With the emergence of HIV in the United Kingdom in the early 1980s gay men were subjected to a backlash of stigmatization. Partly fuelled by perceptions that gay men were responsible for the spread of HIV, surveys of British social attitudes throughout the 1980s showed a rising disapproval of homosexuality among a large section of the public. The Conservative government saw an opportunity to capitalize on these negative attitudes and embarrass Labour-led local authorities (many of which supported lesbian, gay and bisexual organiza-tions) by introducing legislation that made it illegal for local authorities to 'intentionally promote homosexuality or publish material with the intention of promoting homosexuality', or to 'promote the teaching in any maintained school of the acceptability of homosexuality as a pretended family relationship'. The amendment to the Local Government Act (1988), widely known as Section 28, in reference to the number that denoted its location within the statute, was, despite vague wording and widespread lack of clarity about its legal standing, effective in signalling an intention to return to the position prior to 1967 in which gay men and lesbians were not to behave as if their relationships were valid or as if they merited equal rights with heterosexuals. As recent research by Viv Ellis (Ellis with High, 2004; Ellis, 2005) has demonstrated, Section 28 may have led directly to the increases in the proportion of students reporting problems in school associated with their sexuality, particularly in relation to isolation, verbal abuse, teasing, physical abuse, ostracization and pressure to conform. Section 28 may have contributed to the marginalization of lesbian, gay and bisexual young people and fuelled some teachers' sense of their authority to broadcast moral judgements about their pupils.

The Labour administration that came to power in 1997 was committed to repeal but cautious both about public opinion and entering into a protracted and bitter struggle with the House of Lords that might obstruct its attempts at constitutional reform. It was only in 2003 that the Act was finally repealed and then, as we shall see, not without the institution of other legislation that replaced some of the proscriptions of Section 28. Similarly, legislation to equalize the age of consent at 16 (previously young men could only consent to sex with another man once they were aged 18) was coupled with the establishment of proscriptive legislation elsewhere in the Statute book. The reform of the laws relating to age of consent was precipitated directly by the actions of Chris Morris, at the time a 16-year-old student, and Euan Sutherland who took their case for equal treatment under the law on sexual consent to the European Court of Human Rights. Earlier that year the Court had handed down a preliminary ruling in favour of Lisa Grant, an employee of South-West Trains who had sought equal access to travel and pension rights for her female partner to those extended to heterosexual employees' partners. While the European Court was clearly keen to support equalization of gay rights and public opinion seemed to be untroubled and even supportive, the British Parliament initially stalled on the important issue of forcing a Bill through the Lords.

Again deadlock seemed to be broken by shoring up the law of consent elsewhere. So, in 2003 a new Sexual Offences Act (Act of Parliament, 2003) came into force that forbids any sexual activity between under-16s, ranging from touching to sexual intercourse. Although the government maintained the Act was put in place to protect children from inappropriate sexual attention and that it would instruct the Crown Prosecution Service (the organization that decides whether cases presented to it by the police should go to court) not to prosecute under-16s for consensual sexual activity, was to send the net effect of a strong message about sex and sexuality remaining the preserve of adulthood.

The reaction to the bitter debates about the effect of the repeal of Section 28 on the education of young people was deflected by introducing a passage to an Education Act, which placed a responsibility on the Secretary of State for Education to ensure that pupils at state-maintained schools:

(a)   . . . learn the nature of marriage and its importance for family life and the bringing up of children, and,

(b)   . . . are protected from teaching and materials which are inappropriate having regard to the age and the religious and cultural background of the pupils concerned.

(Act of Parliament, 2000, Section 148)

This has ensured that despite the repeal of Section 28, there is still scope for parents or others to challenge activities in schools in the context of sex education that they deem offensive. While it is clearly not unreasonable to provide parents and carers with some power to act in matters relating to their children, in this context the institution of this Act was clearly, in part, intended to signal to teachers that their activities in relation to teaching about sexuality would still be subject to regulation.

Coalition government, sexuality and human rights

With the formation of a coalition government in the UK following the general election that took place in May 2010, sexuality and especially the status of same-sex relationships has come into renewed focus. This is primarily because of lack clarity about Conservative Party commitment to maintain existing and develop new legislation and guidance protecting LGBT people from homophobia and discrimination, as well as their human rights.

Both prior to and since the election, David Cameron as Conservative leader, and latterly prime minister, has seemingly sought to signal a shift in both his personal and party attitudes towards same-sex relationships and lifestyles. He made a public apology for his support of Section 28, speaking about the 'mistake' he made. In the context of a gay pride event, he announced, to widespread media coverage, that 'I am sorry for Section 28. We got it wrong. It was an emotional issue. I hope you can forgive us' (for example, Pierce, 2009). However, such attempts to deal with the past neither take into account the wider pattern of his personal views as they have been expressed through his voting pattern on a range of legislation, the weight of traditional conservative views manifest in his party, or the differences in the ideological inclinations, personal comfort and policy commitments of the Liberal Democrat coalition partners.

So, while Cameron might be striving towards reconstruction of himself and his party as liberal, tolerant, committed to equality and anti-homophobic, he rather underplays the challenge that his past voting record suggests. The highlight would seem to be in 2004 when Cameron voted in support of civil partnerships as an opposition MP. However, in 2002 he supported a bill that sought to allow unmarried heterosexual couples to adopt children but would specifically ban gay couples from adopting and in 2008 he opposed giving lesbians the right to *in vitro* fertilization treatment. His lack of clarity about his change of heart on LGBT issues and commitment to making policy to protect and move towards further equality was evidenced in a now (in)famous interview given to *Gay Times* in which he seemed to first back away from then agree that it was confusing given his apparent reaching out to the gay electorate that Conservative members of the European Parliament had not been instructed to support a motion condemning a homophobic law in Lithuania. He was evidently flustered, suggesting first that human rights were internal matters for nations and traditionally decided by free-vote within the Conservative Party, and then retreating and admitting that human rights were not negotiable, political issues and ultimately asking for the interview to be stopped while he gathered his thoughts (Reid-Smith, 2009).

That the wider Conservative Party remains unsure about same-sex relationships and contains individuals with extreme and prejudiced views is evident and also poses a challenge to any reconstructive endeavour. 'Tory troubles' with sex and sexuality are far from new, but some recent spectacular statements from Conservatives suggest that gains made in terms of equality in recent years could easily be rolled back. For example, it is still unclear whether Chris Grayling's pre-election announcement that he thought that bed-and-breakfast owners should be free to turn away guests who were gay couples was recanted to avoid electoral disadvantage rather than a statement of authentic contrition (*Pink News*, 2010). Similarly, although Phil Lardner, Scottish Conservative candidate in North Ayrshire and Arran, was forced to stand down over his observation that 'I will always support the rights of homosexuals to be treated within the concepts of (common-sense) equality and respect . . . I do not accept that their behaviour is "normal" or encourage children to indulge in it'; it is not clear if he altered his views or how widely they were supported outside the party hierarchy (*The Sun*, 2010). It is not clear whether these and other similar events, and especially the associated recantations where they have come, indicate cosmetic rather than substantive changes of heart and a real rather than politically expedient commitment to gay rights. Lardner's comments are particularly illuminating in that they suggest human rights may be vulnerable to dilution if perceived within a conservative ideology as merely a matter of personal conscience.

The Conservative Party's position and commitments may become more apparent not through the resistance of political opposition but through the stresses and strains of relations within the coalition government. There are numerous sources of tension which have been, for now, skated over. The Liberal Democrats made manifesto pledges to push forward equality legislation around civil partnerships and gay marriage and to support anti-homophobic policy and practice. Their partners in power have meanwhile made no such commitments and also formed working relationships with openly racist and homophobic parties within the right-wing groupings at European Parliamentary level.

Common bonds? LGBT equality, 'race', class and gender

The relationship between the history of the struggle for equality in terms of sexuality and the struggle for equality in terms of 'race', class and gender is, at times, contradictory and conflicting. There is insufficient space to enter into this debate fully here but we will make brief comments on some of the problematic areas. First, the possibilities for representations of sexuality have been challenged at times not only by reactionary self-appointed guardians of morality and the state, but by feminists committed to the anti-pornography and lesbian–feminism movements whose starting point has been the exploitation of female subjects by a 'phallocracy' (Frye, 1981; Rubin, 1993). Feminists have also criticized some male homosexuals for appropriating a stereotypical female gender identity that is bound up with notions of 'effeminacy' at one end of the spectrum and 'camp' at the other.[3] There have also been criticisms of the black community in Britain and North America (from within those communities) for a perceived, endemic homophobia that is, at times, celebrated publicly in popular cultural representations (Harper, 1991).[4] Often the emergence of the homosexual, and of homosexuality leading to an identity choice, is seen as a consequence of a process that began with the rise of capitalism and the formation of the working class. Some commentators have explicitly identified an association between the increasing influence of capitalism and the opening up of possibilities for diverse sexual expression. The historian John D'Emilio has said that:

> gay men and lesbians have not always existed. Their emergence is associated with the relations of capitalism; it has been the historical development of capitalism – more specifically the free labour system that has allowed large numbers of men and women in the late twentieth century to call themselves gay, to see themselves as part of a community of similar men and women, and to organise politically on the basis of that identity.
>
> (D'Emilio, 1983, p. 468)

D'Emilio argues that it was the changes in the nature and role of the family produced by the free-labour market under capitalism that created the possibilities for diversity of sexual expression and the formation of sexual identities. To oversimplify his argument, he believes that, as the family was no longer 'an independent unit of production' (ibid., p. 469), there was no need to produce many children to labour in this unit. It became possible for individuals to live outside the family unit and to realize erotic lives that did not need to find their expression in reproductive sex. Capitalism allows the possibility for individuals to be economically independent, whereas the former model of family-based units of production made this virtually impossible. However, D'Emilio also recognizes that while capitalism makes this independence a possibility, it also values the family highly as a social structure that can, to some extent, guarantee continuity of production and the maintenance of the status quo. Capitalism, he says, forces individuals into families 'at least long enough to reproduce the next generation of workers' and, simultaneously, into the discourses of heterosexism and homophobia (ibid., p. 474).

But it is not possible to say that these discourses are simply a product of capitalism or that the oppression of dissident sexualities is one of its functions. For example, Marxism itself has been appropriated in such a way as to become implicated in pathologizing sexual behaviour. The boast made by groups such as the Socialist Workers Party that Bolshevik Russia abolished anti-homosexual laws is, albeit to be understood to be made in the context of a critique of Stalinism, profoundly misleading: all Tsarist laws were abolished shortly after the revolution, effectively legalizing murder (Edge, 1995, pp. 37–39). Indeed, later Stalinist legislation and public health documents pathologed homosexuality and made it subject to 'treatment' in state hospitals (ibid., p. 41). Edge goes on to outline a relationship between homosexuals and revolutionary socialists in the latter half of the twentieth century in which issues of class equality are consistently put above those of equality in terms of sexuality to the extent that violent homophobia is put to one side.[5] The very problem with sexuality for the revolutionary left, according to Edge, is that it makes sexual identity inequality an issue in itself rather than assimilating it into the common struggle against capitalist social class inequalities. The notion of a 'gay "identity" or "community" [becomes] a separatist diversion' (ibid., p. 47) to the 'greater' fight against capitalism.

Edge argues instead for the continued development of an autonomous lesbian and gay community on the political left that is able to fight for equality on its own terms, cutting across other categories of social injustice. In doing so, he is echoing Gayle Rubin, who argued for a 'radical theory' of resistance to the discourses of oppression that was not solely based on feminism:

> Sex is a vector of oppression. The system of sexual oppression cuts across other codes of social inequality, sorting out individuals and groups according to its own intrinsic dynamics. It is not reducible to, or understandable in terms of, class, race, ethnicity, or gender . . . even the most privileged are not immune to sexual oppression.
>
> (Rubin, 1993, p. 22)

The difficulties with locating and assimilating the struggle for lesbian and gay equality within a wider political struggle for equality, focused on inequalities of distributions of wealth and power, are illustrated in the debate between Nancy Fraser and Judith Butler in the *New Left Review* (Fraser, 1997, 1998; Butler, 1998).

Both authors seek, in Fraser's words, to 'combine an egalitarian politics of redistribution with an emancipatory politics of recognition' with regard to lesbian and gay equality. Both identify the rise of so-called cultural politics as problematic in that it seems to position some issues, like lesbian and gay equality, as ones of 'cultural misrecognition' rather than the social politics of redistribution. But where Fraser identifies difficulties with (re)appropriating lesbian and gay equality within the redistributive struggle because it might mean some loss of the sense of solidarity and the power that lesbians and gays derive from a culturally differentiated identity, Butler is confident that there is no potential for a loss of this kind since the politics of distribution can only be understood in terms of the reproduction of gender relationships that lead to heteronormativity and feed homophobic prejudices and discrimination.

Some socialist activists seem to have made sense of the difficulties exposed in this debate by making a link between the establishment of political and social equality and an end to the misrecognition of all sexual minorities. Identifying Section 28 of the Local Government Act (see the following chapter for a fuller discussion) and the inequality in ages of consent for heterosexual and homosexual men, as particular targets, Vallee et al. (1992), in a *Militant* publication on gay rights, identified the Thatcherite legal and rhetorical bolstering of the 'family' as a tactic for scapegoating a whole raft of minorities and blaming them for the failings of capitalism.

In this chapter we have illustrated that, in our view, there are inextricable links between struggles for cultural recognition and wider struggles for fairer social and economic distribution. And where the struggle seems, at first, to be solely about cultural recognition, we are of the view that it is always potentially about a political and economic freedom too, because invisibility can and does impede equal gay and lesbian participation in social actions and institutions.

Conclusion

There is some evidence of a steady, if not inexorable shift in British political and social life in relation to equality for LGBT people. A recent survey of British social attitudes (National Centre for Social Research, 2000) shows a decreasing proportion of the population, particularly among the young, who think that 'two adults of the same sex having sexual relations' is 'always wrong' (a 12 per cent decrease among both men and women from 56 per cent to 44 per cent and 44 per cent to 32 per cent respectively). The Conservative Party leadership has recently convened a 'summit' with gay groups, dropped its support for the restoration of Section 28 and has promised to offer Tory MPs a free vote on proposals to allow civil partnerships for lesbian and gay couples. But, these changes are not uncontested from within the Right. Some Conservative MPs have condemned the 'summit' as a cynical attempt to attract the 'pink' vote and others see it as an attempt to marginalize the 'family'. Meantime, as Ellis's research has suggested (Ellis with High, 2004), the quality of the educational experience for young lesbian, gay and bisexual people shows no sign of improving and may, in fact, be worse than ever. They identify a need to shift the content of sex education from essentialist approaches to sexuality to those that acknowledge it as an aspect of culture and identity. They also point to 'issue-driven' curricula that contribute to the marginalization of homo-sexuality, its representation as a 'controversial' issue, the continued pathologiza-tion of homosexuality as either a mental illness or indication of vulnerability to HIV, and the explicitly homophobic remarks and discriminatory actions on the part of teachers, which they note 'as reported by our respondents – had no compunction about demonstrating a form of prejudice that could have led to disciplinary action in the case of gender or "race"' (ibid.: 222) as essential contextual components in redressing inequalities in ways that will concretely improve young people's lives.

The issue of the role of schools in educating young people about sexualities is one we will return to in the next chapter of this book, but what we have attempted here is to explore the ways in which homosexuality has been con-structed as a negative, subordinate collection of activities and identities in relation to heterosexuality. We have demonstrated how the contemporary inven-tion of sexualities has evolved, in part, through the struggles of the repressed, principally gay men and women, against reaction and social authority that has denied them equal rights with straight men. Ellis's research illustrates the extent to which an embittered and hostile heterosexuality still succeeds in driving to the periphery alternative sexual lifestyles and identities. The message is clear that sexuality represents a cultural field in which the personal and private have been made political. Sexuality has been commodified by the interest of the press and made a legitimate concern of the state. As citizens and subjects, we are all implicated in a struggle to make sexual identities for ourselves, and defend those of others. As teachers, it is inevitable that engagement with young people will mean engagement with the political reality of sexualities. To realize the legitimacy of that engagement is only to reflect an awareness that young people are particularly vulnerable to the play of negative constructions of sexualities. And to begin, we must, as Halperin (1989, p. 426) notes:

> train ourselves to recognise conventions of feeling as well as conventions of behaviour and to interpret the intricate texture of personal life as an artefact, as the determinate outcome, of a complex and arbitrary constellation of cultural processes. We must, in short, be willing to admit that what seem to be our most inward, authentic, and private experiences are actually, in Adrienne Rich's admirable phrase, 'shared, unnecessary/and political'.

Notes

1   This raises the question of how we define and distinguish sexuality and sexual orientation. For the purposes of this and the chapter that follows, we regard sexual orientation as a fairly narrow concept relating to where an individual's

sexual attraction lies, which is usually regarded as being in either the same, other or another gender. Our argument progresses by demonstrating that orientation is often that basis for categorizing individuals and discrimination against them. However, sexual orientation is but one part of sexuality that we regard as the totality of expression, experience, attitudes, values, beliefs and behaviour that go to make up identity as a sexual being.

2 The anthropologist Gilbert Herdt offers an interesting comparative study of sexualities in different cultural contexts in *Same Sex, Different Cultures* (Oxford: Westview, 1997).

3 These beliefs are reflected in the journalism of popular British feminists such as Julie Burchill.

4 See also the coverage in the black British weekly, *The Voice*, following the footballer Justin Fashanu's coming out as a gay man and also following his suicide in 1998.

5 Edge quotes the SWP writer Mark Brown: 'Homophobia divides working class people. Only the working class can destroy the homophobic capitalist system. There can be no gay liberation without socialism' ('Socialism or Separatism?', *Rouge*, 18, London, 1994; Edge, 1995, p. 11).

References

Act of Parliament (2000) Learning and Skills Act, London: HMSO.

Act of Parliament (2003) Sexual Offences Act, London: HMSO.

Blasius, M. and Phelan, S. (eds) (1997) *We Are Everywhere: A Historical Sourcebook of Gay and Lesbian Politics*, London: Routledge.

Boswell, J. (1980) *Christianity, Homosexuality and Social Tolerance*, Chicago, IL: Chicago University Press.

Butler, J. (1998) 'Merely Cultural', *New Left Review*, 227, 33–45.

Cowan, K. and Valentine, G. (2006) *Tuned Out: The BBC's Portrayal of Lesbian and Gay People*, London: Stonewall.

D'Emilio, J. (1983) 'Capitalism and Gay Identity', in Snitow, A., Stansell, C. and Thompson, S. (eds), *Powers of Desire: The Politics of Sexuality*, reprinted in Abelove, H., Barale, M.A. and Halperin, D.M. (eds) (1993), *The Lesbian and Gay Studies Reader*, London: Routledge, pp. 467–78.

Dover, K.J. (1978) *Greek Homosexuality*, Cambridge, MA: Harvard University Press.

Duncan, R. (1944) 'The Homosexual in Society', *Politics* (August), reprinted in Blasius, M. and Phelan, S. (eds), *We Are Everywhere: A Historical Sourcebook of Gay and Lesbian Politics*, London: Routledge, 1997, pp. 230–33.

Edge, S. (1995) *With Friends Like These, Marxism and Gay Politics*, London: Cassell.

Ellis, V. (2005) 'Sexuality, strategic essentialism and the high school curriculum; or, how to be a particular non-contradictory person within a consistent story line'; paper presented at the American Educational Research Association Annual Meeting, Montreal, 11–15 April.

Ellis, V. with High, S. (2004) 'Something to Tell You: Gay, Lesbian or Bisexual Young People's Experiences of Secondary Schooling', *British Educational Research Journal*, 30(2), pp. 213–25.

Epstein, D. and Johnson, R. (1998) *Schooling Sexualities*, Buckingham: Open University Press.

Foucault, M. (1978) *History of Sexuality*, Vol. 1, New York: Pantheon.

Foucault, M. (1984) *The Use of Pleasure: Volume Two of The History of Sexuality* (trans. R. Hurley), Harmondsworth: Penguin.

Fraser, N. (1997) 'Comment: A Rejoinder to Iris Young', *New Left Review*, 223, pp. 126–29.

Fraser, N. (1998) 'Comment: Heterosexism, Misrecognition and Capitalism: A Response to Judith Butler', *New Left Review*, 228, pp. 140–49.

Frye, M. (1981) 'Lesbian Feminism and the Gay Rights Movement', reprinted in Blasius, M. and Phelan, S. (eds) (1997), *We Are Everywhere: A Historical Sourcebook of Gay and Lesbian Politics*, London: Routledge.

Gagnon, J. and Simon, W. (1973) *Sexual Conduct: The Social Sources of Human Sexuality*, London: Hutchinson.

Halperin, D.M. (1989) 'Is There a History of Sexuality?', *History and Theory*, 28, pp. 257–74, reprinted in Abelove, H., Barale, M.A. and Halperin, D.M. (eds), *The Lesbian and Gay Studies Reader*, London: Routledge, 1993, pp. 416–31.

Hari, J. (2009) 'Stop all this Brüno-bashing', *The Independent*, 22 July.

Harper, P.B. (1991) 'Eloquence and Epitaph: Black Nationalism and the Homophobic Impulse in Responses to the Death of Max Robinson', *Social Text*, 28, 68–86, reprinted in Abelove, H., Barale, M.A. and Halperin, D.M. (eds) (1993), *The Lesbian and Gay Studies Reader*, London: Routledge, pp. 159–75.

Harris, S. (2009) 'Lessons About Gays Will Be Compulsory from Age 11', *The Daily Mail*, 28 April.

Herdt, G. (1997) *Same Sex, Different Cultures*, Oxford: Westview.

Kinsey, A.C., Pomeroy, W.B. and Martin, C.E. (1948) *Sexual Behavior in the Human Male*, Philadelphia, PA: W.B. Saunders.

Kinsey, A.C., Pomeroy, W.B., Martin, C.E. and Gebhard, P.H. (1953) *Sexual Behavior in the Human Female*, Philadelphia, PA: W.B. Saunders.

MacKinnon, C. (1989) *Towards a Feminist Theory of the State*, Cambridge, MA: Harvard University Press.

National Centre for Social Research (2000) *British Social Attitudes: Focusing on Diversity*, London: Sage.

Payer, P. (1984) *Sex and the Penitentials*, Toronto: Toronto University Press.

Pierce, A. (2009) 'David Cameron Says "Sorry" Over Section 28 Gay Law', *The Daily Telegraph*, 1 July.

Pink News (2010) 'Shadow Home Secretary Chris Grayling Says B&Bs Shouldn't Ban Gay Couples and He Supports Gay Adoption', 14 April.

Plumb, C. (1968) *Juvenal: The Satires*, London: Panther Books.

Rackoff, D. (2009) 'Why "Brüno" is Bad for the Gays', *Salon*, 9 July.

Reid-Smith, T. (2009) David Cameron Pre-election Interview, *Gay Times*, www.gay times.co.uk/Interact/Blogs-articleid-6599-sectionid-713.html (accessed 30 September 2010).

Richards, J. (1990) *Sex, Dissidence and Damnation: Minority Groups in the Middle Ages*, London: Routledge.

Rubin, G.S. (1993) 'Thinking Sex: Notes for a Radical Theory of the Politics of Sexuality', revised edition reprinted in Abelove, H., Barale, M.A. and Halperin, D.M. (eds) (1993), *The Lesbian and Gay Studies Reader*, London: Routledge, pp. 3–44.

Sedgwick, E.K. (1994) *Epistemology of the Closet*, London: Penguin.

Simpson, M. (ed.) (1996) *Anti-Gay*, London: Freedom Books.

Taylor, T. (1997) *The Prehistory of Sex: Four Million Years of Human Sexual Culture*, London: Fourth Estate.

The Sun (2010) 'Anti-gay Tory Gets the Chop', 28 April.

Ulrichs, K.H. (1994) *The Riddle of 'Man-manly' Love: The Pioneering Work on Male Homosexuality* (trans. Michael A. Lombardi-Nash), Buffalo, NY: Prometheus Books.

Ulrichs, K.H. (1997) *Araxe5: Appeal for the Liberation of the Urnings's Nature from Penal Law* (trans. James Steakley), new translation of extract in Blasius, M. and Phelan, S. (eds), *We Are Everywhere: A Historical Sourcebook of Gay and Lesbian Politics*, London: Routledge.

Vallee, M., Redwood, H. and Evenden, M. (1992) *Out, Proud and Militant: The Fight for Lesbian and Gay Rights and the Fight for Socialism*, London: Militant Publications.

Wilde, O. (1895) Extract from the trial transcript, reprinted in Blasius, M. and Phelan, S. (eds), *We Are Everywhere: A Historical Sourcebook of Gay and Lesbian Politics*, London: Routledge (1997), pp. 111–12.

Chapter 6

Straight talking

Challenges in teaching and learning about sexuality and homophobia in schools

Simon Forrest

Introduction

Do/Did you feel safe at school as an LGBT student?

Hell no, to put it nicely. Ever since the 'rumours' about me started about 6 months ago, the homophobics at school have been singling me out at least daily.

Have you experienced homophobic bullying at school?

Frequently. Nothing too physical yet though. Mostly name-calling, and being tripped or spat on. Seems like it's only a matter of time though. Some days, I can't go into a lesson without comments and jokes being made at my expense.

If you have experienced homophobic bullying at school; did the school do anything about it?

No. They pulled me out of lessons to make sure that I was 'OK' and that 'I could handle it', but they never took it any further, since the majority of my school year are homophobic, so there's 'little hope of stopping them'.

Has your school told you as students that homophobic bullying is wrong? Has that had any effect on the cases of homophobic bullying?

No. I started there in year 9, two years ago, and have never heard anyone; teacher or student, standing up for the few of us LGBTs in the school. It is generally seen as unacceptable to make any effort to stop homophobics, though any racism is treated extremely seriously, which there is less of a problem with.

(Posted by Singalongnow on www.queeryouth.org.uk
on 31 August 2008, 02:26 AM)

I'm in year 12 and i have never have had any sex ed classes and never herd anything about different sexualities let alone transgendered stuff or anything like that. i think it would be extremely beneficial for some tips for what to say to someone who is coming out- or gay people in general. some basic stuff like just cos there gay doesn't mean they fancy you etc!

(Posted by Flooooo on www.queeryouth.org.uk
on 13 January 2009, 08:21 PM)

To learn about homosexualities would be helpful. What is masturbation on the feminine side? To understand what it is like when going through (and having) sexual intercourse would be information. To explore female genitalia deeper would be interesting. What is a period? IN DETAIL.

(Anonymous questions in a 'suggestion box' on sex education from a boy in Year 9)

Why have schools failed to satisfy the needs of these young people? What has prevented teachers from affirming young lesbian, gay, bisexual and transgendered (LGBT) people's identities and taking effective steps to ensure that they feel and are safe? Why do teachers steer clear of answering questions like those on the boy's list? What is the effect of not dealing with these experiences and concerns? And, what issues of equality are at stake here? This chapter sets out to address these questions by exploring the phenomenon of homophobia and teaching and learning about sex and sexuality in English secondary schools. I have four aims: first, to sketch out some of the ways that young people's knowledge, understanding and experience of their sexualities is framed by schooling; second, to give a brief description of the statutory requirements and guidance to schools in relation to teaching young people about sex and sexuality; third, to suggest some practical strategies for dealing with questions and concerns like those raised above; and, fourth, to demonstrate how tackling homophobia within schools addresses a deficit in equal rights.

Young people, sex, sexuality and schools

Schools are often in the spotlight when we think about how and what young people learn about sexuality. The mass media plays an important role in shaping both perceptions of and debates about these issues (Kingori et al., 2004). Commonly, press coverage is stimulated by publication in a tabloid paper of a story about either young people's sexual behaviour or the content of a programme of sex education in a school. Subsequent comment tends to take a predictable trajectory in which writers engage in a polarised exchange and take up positions arguing that the specific story illustrates a state of affairs that demands either reactionary measures to restore sets of values and mores that are perceived to be under threat or greater liberalism.

So, for example, in 2009 The Sun newspaper ran a front-page story claiming (wrongly as it later emerged) that Alfie Patten was, at 13, the father of a child conceived after 'a single night of unprotected sex' (Hagan, 2009). The paper reported that Alfie, 'who is 13 but looks more like eight, became a father four days ago when his girlfriend Chantelle Steadman gave birth to 7lb 3oz Maisie Roxanne'. The story continued, 'Alfie, who is just 4ft tall, added: "When my mum found out, I thought I was going to get in trouble. We wanted to have the baby but were worried how people would react. I didn't know what it would be like to be a dad. I will be good, though, and care for it."' While, as these extracts from the headline story suggest, *The Sun* ostensibly focused on Alfie's desire to be involved in parenting the child, the accompanying comment piece quickly rushed to judge both Alfie and Chantelle. They were condemned for their naivety and held up as 'a damning indictment on Britain's hugely expensive sex education programme in schools' (Moore, 2009).

This linking of individual stories and events to wider debates about young people, sexuality and sex education is typical of the trajectory of coverage in the British press as is a polarisation of views about the causes, effects and appropriate means of response to the issues it throws up. This process was evident in days following *The Sun's* coverage as the story was picked up and its implications debated widely across first the tabloid and then the broadsheets press as well other media. On 16 February Melanie Phillips, writing in *The Daily Mail*, argued that the story of Alfie and Chantelle was not unique but illustrative of wider social malaise and indicative of collapse in collective and personal moral values (Phillips, 2009). Phillips suggested that a combination of the provision of sex education and contraception to young people was effectively endorsing and promoting promiscuity. This was coupled with a welfare-dependent culture that removed any requirement for self-restraint and militated against the taking of personal responsibility for the consequences of one's actions. Finally, Phillips noted that 'narcissistic' liberalism contributed by refusing to stigmatise and attach shame to youthful sexual activity.

Weighing in, by now as much in response to Phillips' opinions as the original story, more liberal commentators writing in the broadsheets posed a counter-argument. For instance, in *The Times* and *The Guardian* on 17 February, David Aaronovitch and Polly Toynbee, respectively, drew attention to errors in Phillips' piece (specifically its claims that rates of conceptions to teenagers had risen in the United Kingdom when they had been falling) and the complexity of the issues. Both came down broadly in support of more rather than less education and support for young people, arguing that cases such as Alfie's and Chantelle's reflected not too much sex education but too little and too late (Aaronovitch, 2009; Toynbee, 2009).

In some relatively recent work on the topic of unplanned and unwanted conceptions among young people in rich, Westernised countries, UNICEF have suggested that these positions can be seen as broadly reflective of different understandings of the 'problem' posed by youthful sexual activities that are linked to moral positions:

> If the underlying premise is . . . reducing teenage births because of the disadvantages they tend to bring . . . then the solutions proposed are likely to lean towards earlier and more comprehensive sex education, more liberal abortion laws, and freely available contraception . . . If . . . the underlying motive has a strong religious dimension, including perhaps the axioms that sex and childbearing before marriage are wrong and that abortion is unacceptable then the solutions are more likely to revolve around abstinence

campaigns, restrictive abortion laws, reform of benefits systems and ambiguity at best about sex education and contraception.

(UNICEF, 2001: 7)

Young people, sexual attitudes, lifestyles and behaviour

How does this kind of media reportage relate to what is known about young people's sexualities, sexual experiences, attitudes and lifestyles?

There is good empirical evidence to show that sexualities and associated ideas about gender and identities are developing early in a person's life. For example, children from age five can identify aspects of sexuality and how it relates to adult relationships and, furthermore, articulate how sexuality is gendered. For example, Janus and Bess (1976) found children from Grade 2 telling stories about how kissing is what girls and boys do together; by the fourth and fifth grade, the following themes were predominant: touching and its association with sex, bodily shapes and personal tastes, awareness of intimate sexual activity and privacy with the opposite sex. Similarly, Terry Brown's work with six/seven- and 10/11-year-olds has shown the formation of strong perceived connections between sexual behaviour, sexuality, gender and relationships, and, furthermore, demonstrated the degree to which heteronormativity has permeated children's worlds with all images and accounts of sexuality pairing women and men and showing men in dominant and women in submissive sexual roles (Brown, 1995). Ideas, views and expectations that partake of a narrowly heterosexist and heteronormative model of sexualities become evident in other realms of children's lives and have been elegantly and powerfully described in a range of research on playground games and social interaction between children in other settings (Epstein, 1995, 1997a, 1997b).

The development of ideas, attitudes and beliefs about sexuality is coupled with and supplemented by the accumulation of sexual experience. This too can begin prior to adolescence. The work of Larsson and Svedin (2002), for example, involving the gathering of retrospective accounts from teenagers of their experiences prior to 13 years old shows that massive majorities have explored their own bodies, kissed, cuddled and talked about sex with other children and a significant proportion of boys have looked at pornography. This work and others confirms high levels of sexual curiosity among primary school-aged children and tracks emergent gender differences reflecting socialisation processes that construct masculine and feminine sexuality as complementary parts of a dominant and normative heterosexuality (Haugaard, 1996; Greenwald and Leitenberg, 1989).

Some research that has focused on teenagers and young people in early adulthood provides robust data about developing patterns of sexual behaviour and interaction. In the United Kingdom, the National Surveys of Sexual Attitudes and Lifestyles undertaken on a Britain-wide basis in the early 1990s and again in 2000 and a variety of associated trials of educational interventions and qualitative research has established the following (Wellings *et al.*, 1994, 2001; Wight *et al.*, 2000, 2008; Stephenson *et al.*, 2003; Wight and Forrest, 2010):

- That the median age at which young people first report having sexual intercourse is around 16 years old for both girls and boys. There was no change in the median age at which boys report first sexual intercourse in the decade between 1990 and 2000. The median age for girls slightly decreased.
- In 2000, 11.7 per cent of women and 8.1 per cent of men reported having felt a sexual attraction towards the same sex at least once in their lives.
- In 2000, 6.3 per cent of young men and 12.6 per cent of young women aged between 20 and 24 years old reported ever having had a sexual experience with a same-sex partner.
- In 2000, 4.2 per cent of young men and 6.5 per cent of young women in this age group reported ever having had sexual intercourse or genital contact with a same-sex partner.
- Proportions of both young men and women reporting same-sex interaction rose steeply with age, particularly at 18 years old, and had increased from 1990.
- Most young people reported enjoying their early sexual relationships, indicated that they enjoyed their time spent together, enjoyed their physical contact, and did not find it difficult to show affection. The majority used protection.

Sex education

In important ways, sex education operates against the background of both the realities of young people's sexual lifestyles and experiences and the concomitant needs for information, skills and support and the competing discourses around sexuality and morality of the kind sketched out by UNICEF and illustrated by the examples of press coverage that I have described above. In this section of this chapter I provide a brief overview of what is known about the content, quality and quantity of sex education in the United Kingdom.

Lessons about sex and relationships provided through school represent an important source of information for young people. They are consistently rated as at least as important as, if not more important than, friends, family and the media (Selwyn and Powell, 2006; DfEE, 2000, Wellings *et al.*, 1994). There are a number of good sources of information and data about both the quality and quantity of sex education in Britain including two Ofsted inspections (2002, 2007) and large-scale population-based studies that have involved mapping provision in central southern England and central Scotland (Strange *et al.*, 2006; Buston *et al.*, 2002).

According to Ofsted, provision of SRE (sex and relationships education) is patchy. Specific problems include weakness in assessment processes with the result that it is difficult to judge what impact provision is having on knowledge, attitudes and behaviour and the emphasis within provision on factual information rather than supporting the development of the skills and confidence that young people need to negotiate their personal lives and relationships. Ofsted have also noted that the quality of SRE is impaired by structural and organisational problems. Specifically, the inspectorate is critical of a trend towards organising 'drop down' days that isolate PSHE topics from the mainstream timetable, militates against developing cross-curricula and undermines continuity and student progression in learning. Ofsted also suggest that there are problems with cross-phase transition and in terms of ensuring that learning spirals in a continuous, cumulative manner as children move from primary to secondary school.

Much of Ofsted's commentary is consistent with research that has gone further than the exploration of quality and sought to explore the quantity and content of programmes of SRE. For instance, in a study of provision in 13 English secondary schools, Strange *et al.* (2006) report detailed data from students and staff on the time dedicated to organisation and content of programmes of SRE provided to two cohorts of students who were in Years 9–11 between 1997 and 2000.

This research found that in terms of quantity the average number of sessions dedicated to SRE across Years 9, 10 and 11 was six or seven. In one school there were no sessions at all for at least one cohort during these years and the maximum number of sessions provided by any school was 12. SRE was generally taught by form teachers. In two schools dedicated staff ran all the SRE provision supported by form tutors and one school implemented the 'drop down' approach noted in the Ofsted reports. Around one-third of the schools participating in the study supplemented teacher-led activity with some intervention from external agencies. That SRE is located mostly in tutor time seemed to be confirmed by findings suggesting that other than some limited teaching of biological aspects of sex education within science, almost no schools had established SRE as a cross-curricula theme.

Strange *et al.* also gathered data on the topics that were being covered in SRE. Contraception was most frequently cited (10 of the 13 schools reported that this topic was covered in either Years 9, 10 or 11 of cohort two). Sexually transmitted diseases (STDs) and relationships were the next most frequently reported topics, in both cases being mentioned by nine and eight schools, respectively, as being covered in either Years 9, 10 or 11 of cohort one. Some topics received little or no attention. Sexual stereotyping, sex and the law, religious, cultural and moral views, and homosexuality were cited as being covered by no more than four schools in either cohort. Indeed, homosexuality was touched on by only one school. These findings were confirmed by data gathered from students.

Finally, Strange *et al.* looked at teachers' explanations for the focus and quantity of provision. Confidence and enthusiasm were frequently cited as factors that influenced provision alongside the presence or absence of senior management support. It was felt that this support was reflected in structural matters such as whether SRE was given time within the timetable and placed under the aegis of a coordinator. Under half of the teachers contributing to the study had received any training in SRE and they perceived this to be a serious weakness.

The importance of collegial support and confidence to teachers' practice is confirmed by the findings and results of Buston *et al.*'s (2002) research in Scotland. In this study, which involved an assessment of fidelity to an intervention programme as part of a trial of teacher-led sex education, the researchers found that high adherence to the prescribed session content was associated with high confidence. Where teachers felt least skilled and confident about employing an activity or tackling a topic there was a much greater likelihood that they would amend it in order to reduce the perceived risks. Confidence about discussing homosexuality in the classroom was rated higher only than demonstrating condom use, discussing sexual activities other than intercourse and discussing pleasure/orgasms, and lower than teaching about attitudes towards people with AIDS, contraception, STDs and sexual relationships.

This research evidence clearly suggests that school-based SRE is, in practice, rather more limited and modest than the right-wing commentators in the press would have their readers believe. Partly as a consequence of structural weaknesses and in response to perceived cultural norms, it tends to veer away from sensitive subjects such as same-sex relationships. This conclusion is further supported by research that has paid attention to students' evaluations of school-based SRE. Here the recurrent themes are dissatisfaction with both the quantity and quality of provision. Drawing attention to what they term the 'sterility' of SRE provision, Selwyn and Powell (2006: 224) argue that this is 'exacerbated by the predominantly, one-way, top-down, delivery of lesson content, as opposed to a more interactive or discursive environment'.

They also add some illustrative commentary from interviews with young people. For example:

> As one 14-year-old reflected: They just don't like to talk about it at school though do they?

> Instead students reported being often set passive and non-interactive tasks:

> They just give us web sites to look at (female, 16).

> Mostly worksheets . . . in PSE we have to go through answering questions (male, 14).

> Watch the videos, that's the lot (female, 14).

> Yeah, there's these massive textbooks, and you have to read through it for a test, all about sex education . . . boring (female, 14).
>
> (Selwyn and Powell, 2006: 224)

The issue of steering clear of 'sensitive' topics is also reported by Lynda Measor. To give just one example of young people's views cited by her:

Gary: OK, but it could be more personal.

Sam: My school is quite open, but it never discusses very intimate things. We discuss contraception and sex but not what to do when having sex. We don't know.

(Measor, 2004: 157)

Sex education, heterosexism and heteronormativity

One effect of this risk-averse approach to SRE is that it fails to challenge dominant cultural norms and values and colludes with, if not reinforces, heterosexism and heteronormativity. There is clear evidence that teachers often choose to be passive and hence occupy what has been termed the 'heterosexual presumption' rather than challenge homophobia among students in classrooms (Buston and Hart, 2001). In fact Buston and Hart go as far as to suggest that SRE is premised on a basis that privileges heterosexuality by placing human reproduction and pregnancy prevention centre stage. Through questionnaire surveys and interviews with teachers and classroom observations they conclude that a significant minority of teachers are overtly homophobic. This took the form of complicity in student homophobia such as laughing along at homophobic comments and jokes and the active problematisation of homosexuality through the dissemination of myths and stereotypes or categorical comments. These teachers tended to frame homosexuality as being solely about sexual behaviour and this colludes with its pathologisation and the stigmatism of LGBT sexualities. In an equal number of lessons LGBT sexualities were rendered 'invisible' through the discussion of sexual intercourse entirely in terms of vaginal penetration and reference to relationships as being solely between males and females.

When it came to exploring the constraints under which teachers felt they were operating in relation to delivering inclusive, non-heterosexist sex education Buston and Hart identified discomfort with teaching about homosexuality as a general principle or in relation to their own attitudes and beliefs, lack of support from within senior echelons of their schools and wider concerns about local, regional and governmental policy and fear of adverse media exposure as major factors. They conclude that the factors that militate against 'good practice' are various and operate at a number of levels including the personal, institutional and cultural. At the personal/practice level they identify a lack of positive language and discourses that teachers can access, so homosexuality is often referred to as 'it' or 'that issue'. In terms of squaring these findings with pupil responses, which indicated a fairly tolerant attitude towards sexual and relational diversity, they conclude that homophobic behaviour may be 'mobbing' in the classroom and that the attitudes and behaviour of a vocal few are distorting teacher perceptions of the views of the many. They also note that teachers suggest that pupils may be more tolerant of the principle of homosexuality than they are about the 'possibility of their peers being gay or lesbian' (Buston and Hart, 2001: 108). Similar findings emerged from a study by Ellis and High (Ellis and High,

2004), which identified the treatment of homosexuality as an 'issue', and that teachers' own views served both to pathologise and problematise the topic.

Looking more closely at the heteronormativity imposed by ways of talking about sex and sexuality it is apparent that the dominant imagery of heterosexual vaginal intercourse interacts with ideals about masculinity and femininity to inform and reinforce homophobia in a particularly pernicious way. Male sexuality is characterised as thrusting, active, urgent and penetrating; female, conversely, as passive, receptive and penetrated (Reiss, 1998). As a result young people can reach the conclusion that same-sex sexual relationships must be pseudo-heterosexual and involve penetration and the partners in roles that mimic heterosexual gender roles. This may reinforce the stereotyping of gay men as effeminate and lesbian women as butch.

The centrality of the vagina and penis as penetrated and penetrating sexual organs effectively delegitimises some sexual acts. As Jewitt (1996) has pointed out, some sex education material describing human sexual organs fails to label the anus at all, thus making anal sex invisible. An effect of the conflation of sexual acts with heterosexual gender and sex roles is that gender role behaviour is used by young people both to explain and understand sexuality. The body itself can become suspect. For example, bigger, heavier girls, who do not conform to masculine stereotypes of a feminine body shape, can often find themselves labelled lesbian. Finally, since same-sex sexual activity is characterised as a substitute for heterosexual sexual behaviour, it is often portrayed as though it were an arrested sexual development, an immature or displaced heterosexuality. This may lie at the root of preconceptions that LGBT young people are failed heterosexuals who have either never had proper heterosexual sex or else were turned away by bad heterosexual experiences.

The hidden curriculum: classroom and playground

While SRE remains central in processes of supporting and maintaining cultures that oppress LGBT young people it represents only one arena within school where heterosexism and heteronormativity are reproduced. Furthermore, as the work of Buston and Hart (2001) makes clear, the practices of teachers represent a reaction to as much as a promotion of strident heterosexist cultures among many pupils. These are particularly manifest through the ways that boys and young men patrol sexualities and gendered identities among young people's peer groups. As Holland et al. (1998) have demonstrated, there is a dominant cultural 'language' of gender that privileges a particular form of hegemonic heterosexual masculinity such that it requires young men to demonstrate their identity and to achieve status through reinforcing distinctions between masculinity and femininity. This takes the form of both objectifying women and splitting male and female interests in relationships into publicly oppositional camps around love and commitment on the one hand and sex and independence on the other and also strident assertions of homophobia. This may reflect the fact that sexualities that are not heterosexual represent attempts to subvert this neat gendering and thus threaten masculine hegemony.

Both the role of young heterosexual masculinities in maintaining and reproducing heterosexism and heteronormativity and the ways that the structures and practices of schooling collude with these is particularly evident in the hidden curriculum relating to the management of the body. For both girls and boys, being in step with the physical, emotional, attitudinal and experiential development of their peers, balancing their development with perceived social and parental expectations, and managing to stave off the risks of being perceived as embodying inappropriate gendering or sexual identities makes an important contribution to their feelings of normalcy and confidence. The ritual nature of school and the ritualisation of embodied experience are central to this (Epstein and Johnson, 1998).

For example, menarche, a defining element of feminine sexuality, can be a traumatic experience for many girls who experience difficulty in getting hold of sanitary towels or tampons, find there is no soap or hot water in school toilets or locks on the doors. They soon learn that menstruation is a 'secret' and a potentially unpleasant and shameful fact of life as a woman (Prendergast, 1994). In addition, through sports and school uniform, for example, boys and girls find their bodies subjected to forms of regulation that seek to confine them within strict stereotypes of gendered sexuality. These stereotypes effectively condemn alternative sexualities as inversions or deviance. School-based rituals often demonstrate both patterns of 'identity-work', which both collude with these regulations and subvert them. For boys, sport, particularly football, is a powerful medium for learning about male sexuality. At breaks and lunchtimes school playing fields are usually dominated by groups of boys playing football. These games can be rough, physical contests in which social status off the field can be enhanced by success on it. In observing games of football it is apparent that some of the ritualised encounters between boys are primarily about the body and not the football. Prendergast and Forrest (1998, p. 161), in their work on boys' experiences of school, describe a daily ritual:

> Every lunchtime a group of small boys played football on the school fields. They, like other groups of boys, had their particular patch, their place in the occupation of the school space. A group of bigger boys often joined in with their game and took pleasure in getting the ball and keeping it from the smaller boys, who were unable to push them off or catch them when they ran away. In the game the big boys slid into tackles on the smaller boys, knocking them over. Some of the smaller boys slid into the big boys in return. The big boys laughed and got up. But sometimes the big boys then tackled the smaller boys with real viciousness, intending to hurt them.

Through these encounters boys are learning that size matters. The bodily capital of the male depends on his size and strength, and display of immunity from physical pain. The big boys indulge their smaller peers, initially knocking them over playfully, showing restraint, saving their bodily capital, but when they have had enough of the smaller boys' playfulness they use their added weight and height to hurt them. The account shows how boys engage with each other in games that are about physical hierarchies in which bigger is better. These rituals and their significance do not grow up spontaneously. They are a product of schooling that celebrates sporting prowess as manly. By pitting bigger boys against smaller boys they endorse cultures of male physicality that demean the masculinity of smaller boys.

Uniform rules are another vector through which schooling impresses orthodoxies about gendered sexualities on young people. This account, from field notes collected by the author while researching gender in schools, illustrates how a head teacher responds to calls from the school council for girls to be allowed to wear trousers. The head teacher seems not to see that making girls wear skirts makes them constantly sexually vulnerable, placing an onus on them to think about how they sit, stand and play so that boys cannot tease them.

> The Head tells us that the School Council is always complaining about uniform rules. They want girls to have the right to wear trousers instead of skirts. He says he thinks it is rather a trivial point which the Council meetings always get bogged down by. Last year he suggested to the Council that if it was really a matter of equal rights then they ought to lobby for boys to wear skirts too.

A final example, which vividly illustrates how discourses and practices that bind the sexual and gendered body are inhabited and reworked by young people, is provided by this extract from *P'tang, Yang, Kipperbang and Other TV Plays* (Rosenthal, 1984, p. 21) where physical intimacy is shorn of its sexual meaning and the rules of heterosexual engagement inverted. Eunice is not the target of the boys' sexual interest, but performs as though she is, and the boys for their part go through a performance of conventional masculine sexuality.

> A couple of girls are stuffing homework into their satchels and making for the door. They completely ignore the end-of-day routine which is being carried out across the room by the windows.
>
> The routine is this: Eunice stands with her back to the wall, blowing bubble-gum, as the boys, their homework in their satchels, form a queue in front of her. Each boy, in turn, then presses his body against Eunice's for a moment with complete absence of passion, then wanders from the room to go home.
>
> As each boy presses against her, Eunice – automatically and unconvincingly – complains: 'Honestly, you're terrible. You boys really! A girl just isn't safe! You're horrible . . . it's every night, the same? I'm disgusted with you, I am truly.'

It is evident that the way the body is treated in school carries strong messages about sexuality and about gender. Even where young people inhabit discourses and take on cultural practices associated with 'doing' sexuality and gender in ways that superficially challenge the dogmas of female vs. male, gay vs. straight, they have to do so through engagement with them that always acknowledges their privileged position as the dominant discourse. This is the discourse that demands that human sexuality is patterned in line with two genders, circling each other in complementary roles and capacities, and that other sexualities and genders must therefore fall outside.

Homophobia

One of the combined effects of enforced invisibility, oppressive sexual cultures and teaching that fails to challenge heterosexism and heteronormativity is to clear the way for homophobic beliefs and practices. These have proved remarkably resistant to change despite some evidence that social attitudes towards same-sex relationships are becoming more tolerant (Park et al., 2004; Ross and Sacker, 2010).

Research conducted by Hunt and Jenson (2007) and Guasp (2009) for Stonewall examined young LGBT people's and primary and secondary sector teachers' experiences and views of homophobia in schools, respectively. Hunt and Jenson's research involved surveying around 1,100 LGBT students across Great Britain and showed that two-thirds experience homophobic bullying. Nearly all of the respondents have been verbally bullied, 41 per cent subject to physical attack and 17 per cent received death threats. Of profound concern is the finding that around 30 per cent of contributors to the study identified adults as responsible for homophobic incidents in their schools. These findings were disappointingly similar to those made by Stonewall in a similar survey undertaken in 1994 (Mason and Palmer, 1995) and Nicola Douglas et al.'s work from the late 1990s (Douglas et al., 1998).

These findings are borne out by the outcomes of Guasp's survey which involved around 2,000 teachers in Great Britain (2009). This study also identifies the endemic nature of homophobic language reporting that 95 per cent of secondary and 75 per cent of primary school teachers hear phrases such as 'you're so gay' or 'that's so gay' used in their schools. Eighty and 40 per cent, respectively, reported hearing other insulting homophobic remarks such as 'poof', 'dyke', 'queer' and 'faggot'. Teachers' awareness of physical bullying is lower than that reported among students, with only 8 per cent of staff reporting awareness of physical threats, and just 1 per cent awareness of sexual assault of threat with a weapon. Teachers seemed to be aware of the difference between students' experiences and reported incidents with around half noting that homophobic bullying went unreported. The reluctance on the part of young people to come forward, partly for fear of reprisals and partly because they have low expectations that teachers will be able to take effective action to ensure the bullying stops and their safety guaranteed. Indeed, this seems plausible given that Guasp also found that the vast majority of teachers (90 per cent) had no training in the prevention or response to homophobic bullying, more than a quarter lacked confidence in supporting a pupil who decided to 'come out' and nearly 40 per cent would not feel confident in providing pupils with information, advice and guidance on lesbian and gay issues.

Guasp's survey also complements the work of Hunt and Jensen by drawing attention to teachers' awareness that gay pupils are not the only targets for homophobic bullying although, as King *et al.* (2003) have noted, young LGBT people are disproportionately vulnerable to homophobic bullying. So, according to Guasp, 75 per cent of secondary and 60 per cent of primary school teacher respondents reported that boys who 'act or behave like girls' experience homophobic bullying. Sixty per cent and 40 per cent, respectively, reported that boys who are not into sports and boys who are academic experience homophobic bullying in their schools. Teachers in both phases said that girls who 'act or behave like boys' experience homophobic bullying (20 per cent of secondary and 15 per cent of primary phase staff) and 10 per cent of respondents in both sectors said that pupils whose parents or carers are gay or who have gay friends are bullied.

> 'People seem to be very definite in their ideas of what a "proper" boy or a "proper" girl should do or be interested in. It takes very little deviation from these so called norms for a person to be singled out and picked on.' Afshan, teacher, primary school (East Midlands)
>
> (Guasp, 2009: 9)

Through detailed qualitative research, Rivers (1995, 1996) has drawn four conclusions about homophobic bullying in school. First, that the majority of homophobic bullying takes the form of non-physical attacks, including being given nasty stares and looks, vandalism of personal property and being 'sent to Coventry'. Second, that some of the main environments in which bullying takes place are unavoidable, public areas of school including classrooms, corridors, school yards and playing fields. Third, only the minority of bullying attacks are reported and in even fewer cases (about 6 per cent) did the victimisation end as a result. Finally, Rivers identified the most frequent perpetrators of bullying as groups of boys, then boys and girls together, followed by groups of girls.

The overtly homophobic culture so evident in schools also makes it unsafe for LGBT teachers. Again, while surveys of social attitudes suggest a degree of tolerance with around 60 per cent of respondents to one survey suggesting that they would be comfortable if their teacher (or teacher of a close relative) was lesbian or gay, reports from LGBT teachers suggest a less enlightened and tolerant culture (Citizenship 21, 2003). This research, for instance, suggests that many teachers feared being 'outed' because it would attract homophobic comments from both staff and students, lead to problems in classroom management, harassment and contribute to poor workplace confidence, achievement and being overlooked for promotion (Irwin, 2002).

Effects of homophobia

Young LGBT people are at greatly enhanced likelihood of experiencing profound emotional and psychological tension and feelings of isolation within their peer groups as a consequence of the threat posed by homophobia. Some of the accounts reported in Simon Blake's little book record recent experiences of young gay men in Britain (Blake, 2003). In this account, a young gay man talks about being forced to adopt avoidance tactics to escape unwanted attention from homophobes.

> There was this group of them in the year above me and they called me names and stuff for about two years. It was queer, backs to the wall, all those sorts of things, sometimes they would whistle at me and blow me kisses. I would just dread seeing them in the corridor or at lunch times, so I learnt to go to places where they would not be. Looking back, I probably spent half my time looking for places to hide and the other half waiting for them to say something.
>
> (Cited in Blake, 2003: 21)

The sense of having to negotiate 'unsafe' places may be coupled with social isolation. Young people struggling to find appropriate and meaningful labels for their identity, feelings and experiences may be fearful of being cut off by friends, as illustrated by this letter sent to the problem pages of a teenage magazine:

> She Had Sex with a Girl
> I was at a party when I saw my best friend go upstairs with another girl. A little while later I went upstairs into the room where they were and caught them having sex with each other. I freaked out and ran downstairs. I haven't spoken to her since. Will she always be like this?
>
> Rachel, 15, East Anglia (in Forrest et al., 1997, p. 9)

Young people have given graphic accounts of the costs in terms of psychological and physical health and happiness:

> I just felt so low and I couldn't ever imagine feeling any different, any better, and so I planned it all out. I was going to take pills, but in the end I couldn't do it, that scared me more than being gay.
>
> (Cited in Blake, 2003: 47)

Where these strategies prove insufficient to deflect or make homophobic bullying tolerable, Remafedi (1991) shows that experience can be linked to drug use, self-harm and suicide among young LGBT people.

Other coping strategies include truanting, although young people may find it hard to avoid school without facing difficult questions at home. School-phobia may be substituted for immersion such that young people avoid confrontation by concentrating on academic school work with the hope that success will lead to opportunities to escape to safer, more tolerant learning and working environments (Rivers, 1995, 1996).

The causes of homophobia

Homophobia has no unitary cause; however, research reviewed by Stephen Clift (1988) has identified some association between holding negative attitudes towards homosexuality and having no homosexual experiences or feelings, little or no contact with gay people, and negative attitudes towards sexual relationships outside marriage. Homophobia also strongly correlated with adherence to religious convictions that disapprove of sex and/or homosexuality and lower social and educational class. Homophobia also seems to be more overtly, aggressively and frequently displayed by boys than girls and may be associated with rigidity of models of masculinity (Forrest, 1997).

Contemporary homophobia also revitalised long-standing beliefs that homosexuality is morally deviant and represents either a source or vector for disease. Modern beliefs that gay men are both more susceptible to and responsible for the HIV/Aids pandemic in the North-Western world simply reproduce, for example, admonishments handed down to boys for over a century. Baden-Powell, the founder of the worldwide scouting movement, mounted an attack on masturbation and homosexuality over 70 years ago, which linked them to sexual and moral dissipation and degeneracy and, ultimately, diminution of the national bloodstock (Baden-Powell, 1930).

The role of heteronormativity in providing a legitimation for homophobia is also clear, for example, in implying that boys who show their feelings or who are too intimate with other boys are either 'girls' or 'poofs'. Equally, girls who are deemed to be too tomboyish run the risk of being called 'dykes' or 'lesbians'. The threat of victimisation that arises from failure to conform to gender role stereotypes actually produces homophobia as a means of showing off one's heterosexual credentials.

Homophobia may also have structural roots and be engrained in institutions in ways that mean membership requires collusion with it. For example, Nathanael Miles (2010) has recently demonstrated that the practices of the UK Border Agency around processing and questioning asylum seekers militates against disclosure of sexuality among non-heterosexual claimants. Bernstein and Kostelac (2002) have shown that institutional homophobia among some US police forces has a negative impact on crime reporting by LGBT people and disclosure of sexuality among LGBT officers.

It may also be that the representation of sexuality and identities in the mass media has an impact in terms of setting a tone that is at best negative if not overtly hostile. For example, Stonewall's recent report on how lesbian and gay people are shown in television for young people found that representation was not great and tended towards the stereotypical and negative (Guaps and Ward, 2010). Importantly, gay people tended to be portrayed as figures of fun, predatory or promiscuous and in just five and three-quarter hours of programming (4.5 per cent of the total for the period sampled) only seven minutes involved any scenes where homophobia was challenged.

Ideological and political frameworks of school sex education

In the UK, the legislative context for sex education is complex and currently there is lack of clarity about its status with the incoming Coalition government yet to make it clear whether it will see through commitments made in the last days of previous administration to make PSHE a statutory subject, thus ensuring that SRE along with other health education topics is guaranteed status and time within the national curriculum.

Since 1986 there has been a steady stream of policy-level activity manifest in the handing down of several volumes of guidance to state-maintained schools (which make up 90 per cent of all education providers), a number of education Acts that have reorganised or oriented sex education in relation to a national curriculum, and a number of relevant policy developments and Acts of Parliament dealing with sexual health.

The increasing involvement of government since the 1980s in describing the aims, limits and content of school sex education has to be seen in the context of an evolving political interest in bringing under increased control the whole system of maintained education. The restructuring of the financial management of schools under, first, local management and, latterly, grant maintenance, and the imposition of a national curriculum represent the two main mechanisms through which the autonomy of teachers and schools has been brought under the dual authority of central government and parents in the form of school governing bodies. The establishment of the Office for Standards in Education (Ofsted) and the gearing up of the parental right to choose have placed increased pressure on schools to be seen to perform successfully in relation to one another.

One effect of these changes has been to encourage schools to concentrate on populist measures that are perceived to increase their appeal to parents of potential pupils. Alongside activity within the taught curriculum, schools have often resorted to clamping down on unruliness, suspected, real or imagined drug use, and the imposition of rigid rules in order to present an orderly face to the outside world, thus implying firm leadership and, through firm leadership, success.

Such reactionary educational attitudes are, for the most part, supported by parents. A subsidiary effect of the dual focus on academic standards (measured through student successes in public examinations) and orderliness has been to further squeeze the time available for aspects of social education within the taught curriculum and marginalise their importance. Not only is social education often perceived to have no bearing on a school's standing in the exam league tables (despite emergent evidence to the contrary, for example, Weare, 2000), but emphasising social education may be perceived by parents as a reaction to some neediness on the part of students or weakness on the part of schools to combat misbehaviour or unruliness. Providing social education, particularly on sex and drugs, can also attract negative press and parental attention, as a series of highly publicised scandals has illustrated (see, for example, the review of media coverage of sex education in schools in Epstein and Johnson, 1998). Consequently, schools may be reluctant to foreground curriculum activity in relation to social education and teachers may be nervous about tackling the subject and may adopt repressive positions, providing only the basic facts about sexual behaviour as part of science teaching.

Alongside the development of education policy the UK government Department of Health has also provided impetus to school-based sex education through a number of policy directives and strategic initiatives focusing on or referring to young people and sexual health. In 1992, the then Conservative administration launched a strategy for national health, *The Health of the Nation* (Department of Health (DoH), 1992) which set a target for a 50 per cent reduction in the rate of pregnancies in girls under 16 years old by 2000. A revised version of the target was latterly set by the New Labour administration that took office in 1997.

Although the target, albeit subject to some revision of detail rather than in substance, neatly passed from a government of one hue to a government of another, the motives behind deploying it, and the mechanisms for achieving it, diverged in ways that were predictable given the ideological leanings of the administrations. For Conservative administrations the driving concern was welfare spending associated with single parenthood. In a series of highly publicised speeches, a succession of Conservative government ministers characterised absent fathers as irresponsible for failing to provide for the maintenance of their female partners and children, and young single mothers as feckless scroungers who got pregnant in order to jump housing queues and whose intention was to live off benefits (for example, see *Independent on Sunday*, 10 October 1993). This moralistic ideological thrust found specific form and definition in the Thatcherite rallying call to the post-1987 election Conservative Party conference for a return to 'family values'. The sexual behaviour of young people was characterised as a threat to traditional moral values and their attitude towards state benefits and welfare was cited as evidence of the decline. Schools were positioned on the front line in the attempt to counter the creeping moral decay.

Consequently, guidance to schools on sex education formulated under this Conservative administration emphasised a framework of values that sought to 'encourage [pupils] to appreciate the value of stable family life, marriage and the responsibilities of parenthood' (DfE, 1994) within the wider aims of the then current Education Act, which articulated the aim of education as the 'promot[ion of] the spiritual, moral, cultural, mental and physical development of pupils at the school and of society; and . . . prepares such pupils for the opportunities, responsibilities and experiences of adult life' (DfE, 1993).

The New Labour administration that came into office in 1997 established an initiative under the auspices of the Home Office aiming to formulate responses to social exclusion, which quickly turned its attention to teenage pregnancy and developed an overarching teenage pregnancy strategy (SEU, 1999). This strategy forms the major plank underpinning subsequent policy development with regard to sex education. The SEU (Social Exclusion Unit) report reconfigured the 'problem' of teenage sexuality in accordance with New Labour ideological inclinations. Although the economic costs of young parenthood still figured in the analysis, a wider brief also drew attention to the costs and disbenefits of early parenthood to teenagers themselves and to their children. Early parenthood was equated with the loss of educational and hence employment opportunities and increased risk of adverse health and social outcomes for children. The strategy recommended so-called 'joined-up' activity across government departments and areas of the public sector to address primary prevention of unplanned and unwanted pregnancies through sex education and improved sexual health services, especially facilitating access to contraception, to establish or enhance care and support to young parents and their children through the provision of continuing education to young parents (mothers in particular) and childcare. Notably, the teenage pregnancy strategy also identified socio-cultural attitudes towards young people and sexuality and 'mixed' media messages as important influences on sexual behaviour. This more liberal understanding of the 'problem' and contingent measures were coupled with more coercive actions including hiking up the pressure on young people to enter training or employment and increasing the powers of the state to pursue absent fathers for financial contribution to the costs of caring for their children.

The values and policy implications of the teenage pregnancy strategy heavily influenced the new guidance to schools on what became known as 'sex and relationships education' (SRE) handed down in 2000. This has been accompanied by a raft of other guidance documentation on the provision of sexual health services for young people, confidentiality and the needs of specific groups of young people that has mainly flowed from the cross-Departmental Teenage Pregnancy Unit set up to implement, fund and monitor the strategy.

Despite this strategic reconfiguration and directing of significant public monies towards teenage pregnancy (and young people and sexual health in general), SRE still has a marginal status with schools. Even with the restructuring of the national curriculum to incorporate a new subject in the portfolio of social education in the form of 'citizenship', nothing beyond the requirements of the national curriculum for science, which include the biological aspects of sex education, is mandatory. The current legislative requirements on schools and the content of guidance documents relating to SRE are arguably, therefore, substantively unchanged over the course of 15 years.

The guidance to schools defines SRE as 'lifelong learning about physical, moral and emotional development. It is about the understanding of the importance of marriage for family life, stable and loving relationships, respect, love and care. It is also about the teaching of sex, sexuality, and sexual health.' In addition, on a point to which we return, it notes that 'It is not about the promotion of sexual orientation or sexual activity – this would be inappropriate teaching' (DfEE, 2000: 5).

SRE is to be delivered through science and also across the curriculum in personal, social, health and citizenship education (PSHCE) and bound by each school, in a clear policy statement that details what will be taught, by whom, to whom and when. In terms of specifying the content of SRE programmes the guidance states that by the end of the primary school years (aged 11), under science provision, children should know:

> that animals including humans, move, feed, grow, use their sense and repro-
> duce . . . recognise and compare the main external parts of the bodies of
> humans . . . that humans and animals can produce offspring and these grow
> into adults . . . recognise similarities and differences between themselves and
> others and treat others with sensitivity . . . that the life processes common
> to humans and other animals include nutrition, growth and reproduction
> . . . about the main stages of the human life cycle.
>
> (DfEE, 2000: 20)

In addition, provision through PSHE and citizenship will ensure that all children 'develop confidence in talking, listening and thinking about feelings and relationships; are able to name parts of the body and describe how their bodies work; can protect themselves and ask for help and support, and; are prepared for puberty' (DfEE, 2000: 19).

With regard to the secondary school years (by the age of 16) the guidance notes that provision through science should mean that children know:

> that fertilization in humans . . . is the fusion of a male and female cell . . .
> about the physical and emotional changes that take place during adolescence
> . . . about the human reproductive system, including the menstrual cycle and
> fertilization . . . how the foetus develops in the uterus . . . how the growth
> and reproduction of bacteria and the replication of viruses can affect health
> . . . the way in which hormonal control occurs, including the effects of sex
> hormones . . . some medical uses of hormones including the control and
> promotion of fertility . . . the defence mechanisms of the body . . . how sex
> is determined in humans.
>
> (DfEE, 2000: 21)

In addition, provision through PSHE and citizenship will ensure that all children are:

> prepared for an adult life in which they can: develop positive values and a moral framework that will guide their decisions, judgments and behaviour; be aware of their sexuality and understand human sexuality; understand the arguments for delaying sexual activity; understand the reasons for having protected sex; understand the consequences of their actions and behave responsibly within sexual and pastoral relationships; have the confidence and self-esteem to value themselves and others and respect for individual conscience and the skills to judge what kind of relationship they want; communicate effectively; have sufficient information and skills to protect themselves and, where they have one, their partner from unintended/ unwanted conceptions, and sexually transmitted infections including HIV; avoid being exploited or exploiting others; avoid being pressured into unwanted or unprotected sex; access confidential sexual health advice, support and if necessary treatment; and, know how the law applies to sexual relationships.
>
> (DfEE, 2000: 20–21)

The guidance goes on to suggest some appropriate teaching strategies including detailing how to set and maintain ground rules with a group of students, deal with difficult questions and use active, participatory and project-based learning to maximum effect. Moreover, the guidance dedicates several pages to outlining the way in which schools should approach and deal with several specific issues within policy and practice including puberty, menstruation, contraception, abortion, safer sex, HIV/Aids and sexually transmitted infections, being sensitive to and inclusive of the needs of boys and young men, young people from ethnic minorities and those with special educational needs and learning difficulties.

Although these detailed sections are a departure from previous guidance documents, as noted the substantive position of SRE within the curriculum, its aims and content have remained unchanged despite the change in political administration. However, it is with regard to the explicit references to homo-sexuality and sexual orientation that a difference in tenor is striking, suiting the more inclusive and liberal social agenda set out by the New Labour government.

Despite the resolutely negative reference to 'sexual orientation' in the opening definition of SRE provided by the guidance document, there are several other places where a more positive tone is evident, much more congruent with the rights-based statements by the WHO cited at the end of this chapter. For example, in the fifth paragraph of the introduction the guidance states: 'Pupils need also to be given accurate information and helped to develop skills to enable them to understand difference and respect themselves and others and for the purpose also of preventing and removing prejudice' (DfEE, 2000: 4). This veiled reference is followed by this, from the section of specific issues to be addressed by SRE policy: 'It is up to schools to make sure that the needs of all pupils are met in their programmes. Young people, whatever their developing sexuality, need to feel that sex and relationships education is relevant to them and sensitive to their needs', and becoming, finally, completely clear that what is being referred to is that the needs of young LGBT people, it reads: 'The Secretary of State for Education and Employment is clear that teachers should be able to deal honestly and sensitively with sexual orientation, answer appropriate questions and offer support' (DfEE, 2000: 13). The guidance goes on to acknowledge that parental concerns about what this comprises will need to be met through liaison and consultation but caps it by noting that schools have a duty to address homophobic bullying (thus offering teachers a ready argument for including these issues in their provision) because of the 'unacceptability of and emotional distress and harm caused by bullying in whatever form – be it racial, as result of a pupil's appearance, related to sexual orientation or for any other reason' (DfEE, 2000: 13).

Under both Conservative and New Labour policy-makers the debate about the specific form the legislation and guidance to schools on sex education should take was heated. Recurrent themes have been balancing the rights of the child to SRE and the right of their parents to withdraw them from any part that lies outside the national curriculum (in other words, the basic reproductive science), identifying (or often fudging) the teacher's position in relation to giving contraceptive advice to young people and at what age SRE should be provided.

Both administrations struggled, in similar ways, with the needs to act pragmatically and on the basis of the best available scientific evidence (which has always pointed towards the provision of early, comprehensive SRE and free, easily accessible sexual health services) to address disease epidemics and silence the siren voices of moralists arguing for retrenchment.

So for the Conservative administrations from the mid-1980s the advent of HIV, the virus that causes AIDS, demanded a response that included the provision of school-based sex education about HIV since all the available evidence, then as now, specified it (Wight, 1993; HEA, 1998; Collins et al., 2002). However, moralistic approaches to sex education are not congruent with effective educational interventions in HIV/AIDS prevention. They cannot accommodate, for example, the need to challenge the stigmatisation of gay men, which contributes to their vulnerability to infection, since any tacit acceptance of homosexuality undermines the prescriptions of sexuality involved in promoting a narrow heterosexual preconception of 'family values'.

To some extent, similar problems have haunted New Labour, which has seen STIs rise exponentially among young people and needed on the one hand to silence the voices of the right-wing press and advocates for 'family groups', which argue that this is evidence of a failed analysis and wrong-headed response (they predictably prefer moral retrenchment) and on the other, to implement ever more radical solutions including making emergency contraception more easily and widely available and bringing sexual health services into schools and colleges in line with the body of effectiveness research.

Similar pressures seem to be playing on the new Coalition administration albeit mediated by an overarching commitment to slash public finances and the resources available to support any development of SRE. Currently, on the substantive issue of the future status of SRE, confusion reigns. This is demonstrated in Hansard on 21 July 2010 in which debate on the relationship between new academies (free of local authority control and effectively self-governing) and the national curriculum is reported.

The record shows that Diana Johnson (Labour MP for Hull North) drew attention to the importance of making PSHE statutory in order to meet pupils' needs around a variety of health and welfare issues including sexual health. She said:

> Pupils are pupils whether they attend an academy or any other type of school, and they all need to develop the life skills to make choices on subjects such as nutrition, sex and relationship education, and personal finance. In many constituencies across the land, we are very concerned about levels of teenage pregnancy . . . We believe that making PSHE mandatory in academies and, indeed, in all schools is the way forward to ensure that young people have the information they need to make sensible and good life choices.
>
> (Hansard, 2010: Columns 490–98)

However, it is unclear from responses by Dan Rogerson (Liberal Democrat MP for North Cornwall and Co-Chair of the Liberal Democrat Parliamentary Education Committee) what the government's thinking is on either the specific point about PSHE in academies or the more general issue of the status of PSHE in all schools. Indeed the debate went on to get bogged down in procedural issues around the failure of the previous Labour government to ensure that its proposal for PSHE to become statutory entered the statute book during the weeks before the general election and whether any amendment (or equivalent means by which the commitment might be fulfilled) should be attached to a yet to be tabled Education Bill, worked up in the House of Lords, or subject to a review.

At around 9.30 p.m. the House adjourned to vote on an amendment put down by Diana Johnson that 'the school [academy] has a curriculum which includes personal, social and health education as a statutory entitlement for all pupils'. The amendment was voted down by 314 votes to 200. It is hard not to conclude that an opportunity to seal the status of PHSE and with it SRE in schools has been lost and not to be so cynical as to wonder whether entangling the issue so greatly with other educational reform and parliamentary procedure is an attempt to push reconsideration out into a future so distant as to be unspecified.

Section 28

In 1988, under the Local Government Act, Margaret Thatcher's government, responding both to tabloid claims that young people were at risk of being corrupted in SRE lessons, and seeing an opportunity to make political capital from hardening public attitudes towards homosexuality in the light of the emerging HIV epidemic (Jivani, 1997) by accusing Labour-led local authorities of sponsoring gay and lesbian groups, passed an amendment to the Local Government Act 1986 that stated:

> a local authority shall not:
> (a) intentionally promote homosexuality or publish material with the intention of promoting homosexuality
> (b) promote the teaching in any maintained school of the acceptability of homosexuality as a pretended family relationship.
>
> (Act of Parliament, 1988)

The deleterious effects on school-based SRE are evident. Confusion in the classroom and the deterrence of teachers from responding to the needs of young LGBT people (Forrest *et al.*, 1997) and, worse still, an active endorsement of their own homophobia (Buston and Hart, 2001) and the provision of a twisted legitimation for victimisation and assaults of young LGBT people (Mason and Palmer, 1995). New Labour, finally, fulfilled a commitment to the repeal of this statute first in Scotland in 2000 and then more recently in England and Wales in 2003.

Despite its repeal the effects are still felt through, for example, the phrase within the DfEE guidance on SRE that warns against 'direct promotion of sexual orientation' and the admonishment that sex education 'is not about the promotion of sexual orientation' (see above). In addition, there have been moves at the level of local government to reintroduce versions of Section 28. For example, in the case of Kent County Council (KCC), which agreed that it would not 'publish, purchase or distribute material with the intention of promoting homosexuality' (Gillan, 2003) and statements from within the Conservative Party that Section 28 should be expanded to include other areas of the public sector rather than repealed (Willetts and Streeter, 2002). As Peter Cumper, a human rights lawyer with an interest in SRE, has noted, it is important to examine why this provision is incompatible with Britain's domestic and international human rights obligations in case any future administration should seek to reintroduce it (Cumper, 2004: 129). He concludes that it is incompatible with the freedom of expression enshrined in the European Convention on Human Rights, Article 8, which provides that 'Everyone has the right to respect for his private and family life' since it stigmatises homosexuality breaching principles of non-discrimination and suppresses the 'pluralistic treatment of homosexuality with the use of the pejorative term "pretended family relationship"' (Cumper, 2004: 131).

Notwithstanding its repeal, Section 28 still seems to exercise some degree of hold over teachers' practice within SRE. As Buston and Hart (2001) note (post-repeal in Scotland), although few teachers in their study referred explicitly to Section 28, they did seek recourse to the language constructions within the Act that refer to 'promotion of homosexuality' in explicating their reluctance and difficulties with discussing lesbian, gay and bisexual issues in the classroom.

Similarly, Ellis and High (2004), in researching young lesbian, gay and bisexual people's experiences of coverage of homosexuality in schools, assert that contrary to some propositions that Section 28 silenced discussion of homosexuality in schools, it may actually have contributed to the marginalisation of LGBT young people and been interpreted by some teachers as a legitimation of their authority to broadcast moral judgements about their pupils. For Ellis and High, the repeal of the Act, while removing its symbolic authority, will have little impact on young people's lives, arguing that its deleterious effects will only be mitigated by shifting the pedagogical ground from essentialist approaches to sexuality to approaches that locate it as an 'aspect of culture and identity' (2004: 223).

It remains to be seen how much the uncertainty created by the mixed messages sent by the new Prime Minister about same-sex relationships contributes towards additional instability and further undermines confidence among teachers. David Cameron has striven, indeed sometimes struggled, to make his personal views clear. Although he apologised publicly for his support of Section 28 and appeared to take a more tolerant line on equality issues with regard to sexuality (going so far as to slap down Chris Grayling who incautiously announced prior to the general election that he agreed with a proposal that bed-and-breakfast owners should be able to refuse to accommodate same-sex couples) there is evidence that he has to mollify more traditional and prejudiced views as expressed by members of the Conservative Party and allies in Europe (Mulholland, 2010).

Addressing sexuality in school

Ways forward

It has been said that sexuality is 'everywhere and nowhere' in school (Redman, 1994). This combination of pervasiveness and elusiveness may seem, initially, a deterrent to teachers looking for somewhere to start addressing issues like homophobia and heterosexism. Teachers' priority will, rightly, always fall on what can be done directly in relation to young people. However, in addressing sexuality it may be better to begin at the level of staff training and policy-making. A first step is to achieve some agreement on the need and motives for raising awareness of sexuality within the school. These might include any of the following:

- Young people have a right to accurate information about sexuality. Since sexualities are diverse and not limited to concerns about disease or reproduction, sex education that does not address the diversity of sexualities is not accurate.

- Students frequently discuss and play about with sexuality among themselves. To exclude it from the formal curriculum is to collude with the inevitable perpetuation of misinformation that may cause some young people anxiety.
- Attempts to tackle bullying that exclude explicit reference to challenging homophobia and sexism are unlikely to succeed.
- Partly as a result of homophobic bullying, LGBT young people need extra support in school.
- The wider school community, including some parents and governors, may welcome attempts on the part of a school to alter sexist and homophobic attitudes among young people.
- The stigmatisation of young gay men and the exclusion of relevant information about safer sex from school sex education increases their vulnerability to HIV infection and may also decrease young heterosexual people's awareness of their vulnerability to sexually transmitted infections, including HIV.

A positive step is to assess these motives in relation to existing policy in a relevant area: for example, considering whether anti-bullying policy contains a sufficiently explicit commitment to challenging homophobic remarks; also, whether the way in which homophobic bullying is dealt with is likely to encourage disclosures from other victims. Within sex education and elsewhere in the curriculum opportunities exist for opening up sexuality for discussion. Teachers can establish sufficiently safe classroom environments for discussion of gender or attitudes towards sexuality in the course of drama, English and history lessons. Harris (1990) provides a detailed guide to suitable resources available to the English teacher. Accounts are readily to hand in the works of Jeanette Winterson (1985) and extracts from *The Diary of Anne Frank* (Frank, 1997) and among collections of gay and lesbian stories and histories (Jivani, 1997). Leaflets that contain accounts of the experiences of young gay men are available from such organisations as the AIDS Education and Research Trust (AVERT) and the Terrence Higgins Trust (THT).

A useful activity for staff may be to collect a selection of leaflets from local and national lesbian, gay and bisexual help and advice services and to use them as prompts to discussion about what information should be made available to students on notice boards in the school. These same materials can be used by students, along with other service information, within a sex education lesson in order to make a poster or flyer detailing local agencies available to young people. Most materials of this kind are available free in small quantities from the relevant agencies.

In their reports on homophobia in schools (Hunt and Jensen, 2007; Gausp, 2009), Stonewall also provides some useful tasters of what positive responses to homophobia and sexuality issues in schools might comprise. Policy and practice both figure prominently, including developing robust policies on homophobic bullying and implementing them alongside engaging in active, positive teaching about LGBT issues.

What stands out in teachers' accounts (which figure prominently in Stonewall's report) is their confidence about engaging with children and young people in an appropriate, clear and concise way in which their values are apparent, and the exploitation of cross-curricula contexts including English literature, film studies and geography as well as PSHE. Two examples give a flavour of teachers' endeavours in the secondary and primary sector, respectively:

'I teach English – in teaching texts such as *Two Weeks with the Queen* and *The Colour Purple* issues of sexuality frequently arise. I am confident in discussing these issues and have also discussed them in PSE lessons.'
(Kirsten, teacher, secondary school, Scotland) (Guasp 2009:18)

'Bearing in mind these children are six, one child was talking about his mum's new girlfriend and another child attempted to correct him (saying 'you mean boyfriend'). We had a very brief discussion about how families could consist of different makeups – e.g. mum, dad/partner of either sex, grandparents etc. This was appropriate for the children's level of under-standing and satisfied the child's interest.'
(Kiera, teacher, faith primary school, South East) (Guasp 2009:24)

Sexuality, education and equality

The previous chapter described the 'invention' of sexuality and showed how there has been a movement towards depathologising and politicising homo-sexuality in recent years. Sexual practices have become to a lesser extent the domain of the medical and legal establishment as people have demanded the right to their own sexual identity and to engage in whatever sexual practices they choose. The tendency to liberalisation has not, however, been uncontested. Reactionary political and moral forces have sought to champion institutions like 'the family', and to establish a strong link between homosexuality and disease, and homosexuality and moral decline. However, the increasing visibility of LGBT people, and the 'outing' of historical figures, makes these positions untenable.

Within education, however, as a result of the combined pressures to scale down social education (seen by the political right as a transgression on personal freedom and the role of the family), to avoid offending parents and making the school vulnerable in the educational marketplace and prurient media interest in sex education, the conservative tendency has not been fully reversed. A gulf has opened between young people's experience of the wider world, in which sexuality is seen as more fluid and pleasure-orientated, and schooling, where it remains fixed to traditional gender-role stereotypes and focused on policing reproductive sex. Currently, young people are being denied a right to an education that equips them for adult life. For young LBGT people, their enforced invisibility, the denial of equal access to basic relevant sex education and systemic and widespread failures to ensure that they are safe and free from homophobic bullying represent breaches of basic human rights as they have been expressed and interpreted by the World Health Organisation, which proposes that existing International Human Rights documents already include sexual rights. For the WHO, the right

> of all persons, free of coercion, discrimination and violence, to: the highest attainable standard of health in relation to sexuality, including access to sexual and reproductive health care services; seek, receive and impart information in relation to sexuality; sexuality education; respect for bodily integrity; choice of partner; decide to be sexually active or not; consensual sexual relations; consensual marriage; decide whether or not, and when to have children; and to pursue a satisfying, safe and pleasurable sexual life, is self-evidently part of their wider human rights.
>
> (WHO, 2003a)

If we adopt, as the United Kingdom has done, such commitments into law as principles guiding policy and legislative practice, then the 'problem' posed by sexuality lies not with people who choose to form relationships with people of the same sex, for this is their human right, but with those who would seek to stigmatise, discriminate or act against them for it. In this context, homophobia is assigned the same status as racial and sexist discrimination and, moreover, linked by WHO to poorer health outcomes. As the WHO submission to the fifty-ninth Session of the UN Commission on Human Rights stated (WHO, 2003b):

> Discrimination causes and magnifies poverty and ill health. In other words, overt or implicit discrimination can lie at the root of poor health status. The link between health and discrimination leads to the conclusion that the respect, protection, and fulfilment of human rights can reduce vulnerability to, and impact of, ill health. Societies that address racism, sexism, xeno-phobia, and homophobia also tend to provide for better health.

In a climate of uncertainty about the future direction of educational policy and the moral agenda that might be followed out by a new government, uncertainty about the commitment and leadership that the prime minister might show on equality if he comes under pressure from allies of more reactionary mien, and an uncertain fit between coalition partners' stance on equality issues, SRE and sexuality equality issues are vulnerable.

References

Aaronovitch, D. (2009) We must hate the kids to put them through this, *The Times*, 17 February.

Act of Parliament (1988) *Local Government Act 1988*, London: HMSO.

Baden-Powell, R.S.S. (1930) *Rovering to Success: A Book of Life-sport for Young Men* (fifteenth edition), London: Herbert Jenkins Ltd.

Bernstein, M. and Kostelac, C. (2002) Lavender and blue: attitudes about homosexuality and behavior toward lesbians and gay men among police officers, *Journal of Contemporary Criminal Justice* 18: 302–28.

Blake, S. (ed.) (2003) *Young Gay Men Talking: Key Issues and Ideas for Action*, London: Working With Men.

Brown, T. (1995) Girls have long hair, *Health Education* 2: 23–29.

Buston, K. and Hart, G. (2001) Heterosexism and homophobia in Scottish school sex education: exploring the nature of the problem, *Journal of Adolescence* 24: 95–109.

Buston, K., Wight, D., Hart, G. and Scott, S. (2002) Implementation of a teacher-delivered sex education programme: obstacles and facilitating factors, Health *Education Research* 17(1): 59–72.

Citizenship 21 (2003) *Profiles of Prejudice. The Nature of Prejudice in England: In-depth Analysis of Findings*, London: Stonewall/Citizenship 21.

Clift, S.M. (1988) Lesbian and gay issues in education: a study of first year students in a college of higher education, *British Educational Research* 14 (1): 31–50.

Collins, J., Robin, L., Wooley, S., Fenley, D., Hunt, P., Taylor, J., Haber, D. and Kolbe, L. (2002) Programs-that-work: CDC's guide to effective programs that reduce health-risk behaviour of youth, *Journal of School Health* 72 (3): 93–99.

Cumper, P. (2004) Sex education and human rights – a lawyer's perspective, *Sex Education* 4 (2): 125–36.

Department for Education (DfE) (1993) *Education Act 1993*, London: HMSO.

Department for Education (DfE) (1994) *Education Act 1993: Sex Education in Schools*, Circular 5194, London: HMSO.

Department for Education and Employment (DfEE) (2000) *Sex and Relationships Education Guidance*, London: HMSO.

Department of Health (1992) *The Health of the Nation*, London: HMSO.

Douglas, N., Warwick, I., Kemp, S. and Whitty, G. (1998) *Playing it Safe: Responses of Secondary School Teachers to Lesbian, Gay and Bisexual Pupils, Bullying, HIV and AIDS Education and Section 28*, London: Health and Education Research Unit, University of London.

Ellis, V. and High, S. (2004) Something to tell you: gay, lesbian or bisexual young people's experiences of secondary schooling, *British Educational Research Journal* 30 (2): 213–25.

Epstein, D. (1995) 'Girls don't do bricks': gender and sexuality in the primary classroom, in J. Siraj-Blatchford and I. Siraj-Blatchford (eds) *Educating the Whole Child: Cross-Curricular Skills, Themes and Dimensions*, Buckingham: Open University Press, pp. 56–69.

Epstein, D. (1997a) Cultures of schooling/cultures of sexuality, *Journal of Inclusive Education* 1 (1): 37–53.

Epstein, D. (1997b) Boyz' Own Stories: Masculinities and Sexualities in Schools, *Gender and Education* 9: 105–15.

Epstein, D. and Johnson, R. (1998) *Schooling Sexualities*, Buckingham: Open University Press.

Forrest, S. (1997) 'Confessions of a middle shelf shopper', *The Journal of Contemporary Health* 5: 10–14.

Forrest, S., Biddle, G. and Clift, S. (1997) *Talking about Homosexuality in the Secondary School*, Horsham: AVERT.

Frank, A. (1997) *The Diary of a Young Girl: The Definitive Edition* (trans. O. Frank and M. Pressler), London: Penguin.

Guasp, A. (2009) *The Teachers' Report: Homophobic Bullying in Britain's Schools*, London: Stonewall.

Guasp, A. and Ward, A. (2010) *Unseen on Screen: Gay People on Youth TV*, London: Stonewall.

Gillan, A. (2003) Section 28 gone . . . but not forgotten, *The Guardian*, 17 November.

Greenwald, E. and Leitenberg, H. (1989) Long-term effects of sexual experiences with siblings and non-siblings during childhood, *Archives of Sexual Behaviour* 18: 389–99.

Hagan, L. (2009) Baby-faced boy Alfie is father at 13, *The Sun*, 13 February.

Hansard (2010) House of Commons Debates, 21 July, Academies Bill, Vol. 512, Part No. 36.

Harris, S. (1990) *Lesbian and Gay Issues in the English Classroom*. Milton Keynes: Open University Press.

Haugaard, J.J. (1996) Sexual behaviours between children: professionals' opinions and undergraduates' recollections, *Families in Society: Journal of Contemporary Human Services* 77: 81–89.

Health Education Authority (HEA) (1998) *Reducing the Rate of Teenage Pregnancies: An Overview of the Effectiveness of Interventions and Programmes Aimed at Reducing Unintended Conceptions in Young People*, London: HEA.

Holland, J., Ramazanoglu, C., Sharpe, S. and Thomson, R. (1998) *The Male in the Head: Young People, Heterosexuality and Power*, London: Tufnell Press.

Hunt, R. and Jensen, J. (2007) *The School Report: The Experiences of Young Gay People in Britain's Schools*, London: Stonewall.

Irwin, J. (2002) Discrimination against gay men, lesbians and trangender people working in education, *Journal of Gay & Lesbian Studies* 14 (2): 65–77.

Janus, S.S. and Bess, B.E. (1976) Latency: fact or fiction, *The American Journal of Psychoanalysis* 36: 339–46.

Jewitt, C. (1996) *Forum Factsheet 11: Supporting the Needs of Boys and Young Men in Sex and Relationships Education*, London: Sex Education Forum.

Jivani, A. (1997) *It's Not Unusual: A History of Lesbian and Gay Britain in the Twentieth Century*, London: Michael O'Mara Books.

King, M., McKeown, E., Warner, J., Ramsay, A., Johnson, K., Cort, C., Wright, L., Blizard, R. and Davidson, O. (2003) Mental health and quality of life of gay men and lesbians in England and Wales, *British Journal of Psychiatry* 183: 552–58.

Kingori, P., Wellings, K., French, R., Kane, R., Gerrusu, M. and Stephenson, J. (2004) Sex and relationship education and the media: an analysis of national and regional newspaper coverage in England, *Sex Education* 4 (2) (July): 111–24.

Larsson, I. and Svedin, C. (2002) Sexual experiences in childhood; young adults' recollections, *Archives of Sexual Behaviour* 31: 263–73.

Mason, A. and Palmer, A. (1995) *Queerbashing: A National Survey of Hate Crimes against Lesbians and Gay Men*, London: Stonewall.

Measer, L. (2004) Young people's views of sex education: gender, information and knowledge, *Sex Education* 4 (2): 153–160.

Miles, N. (2010) *No Going Back: Lesbian and Gay People and the Asylum System*, London: Stonewall.

Moore, J. (2009) My view, *The Sun*, 13 February.

Mulholland, H. (2010) David Cameron stumbles through interview on gay rights: Tory leader appears less than confident when asked about attitude of Conservative MEPs and peers to homosexuality, *The Guardian*, 24 March.

Ofsted (2002) *Sex and Relationships Education in Schools*, London: Office for Standards in Education.

Ofsted (2007) *Time for Change? Personal, Social and Health Education*, London: Office for Standards in Education.

Park, A., Phillips, M. and Johnson, M. (2004) *Young People in Britain: The Attitudes and Experiences of 12 to 19 Year Olds*, DfES Research Report RR564, London: DfES.

Phillips, M. (2009) Alfie, Chantelle and the sheer madness of sex education that teaches nothing about morality, *The Daily Mail*, 16 February.

Prendergast, S. (1994) *This Is the Time to Grow Up: Girls' Experiences of Menstruation in School*, London:Family Planning Association.

Prendergast, S. and Forrest, S. (1998) 'Shorties, low-lifers, hardnuts and kings': boys, emotions and embodiment in school, in G. Bendelow and S. Williams (eds) *Emotions in Social Life: Criticial Themes and Contemporary Issues*, London: Routledge.

Redman, P. (1994) Shifting ground: rethinking sexuality education, in D. Epstein (ed.) *Challenging Lesbian and Gay Inequalities in Education*, Buckingham: Open University Press.

Reiss, M. (1998) The representation of human sexuality in some science textbooks for 14–16 year olds, *Research in Science and Technology Education* 16: 137–49.

Remafedi, G. (1991) Risk factors for attempted suicide in gay and bisexual youth, *Paediatrics* 87: 869–75.

Rivers, I. (1995) The victimisation of gay teenagers in schools: homophobia in education, *Pastoral Care* 3: 35–41.

Rivers, I. (1996) Young gay and bullied, *Young People Now*, 18–19 January.

Rosenthal, J. (1984) *P'tang, Yang, Kipperbang and Other TV Plays*, Harlow: Longman.

Ross, A. and Sacker, A. (2010) Understanding the dynamics of attitude change, in *British Social Attitudes: the 26th Report*, London: Sage for NatCen.

Selwyn, N. and Powell, E. (2006) Sex and relationships education in schools: the views and experiences of young people, *Health Education* 107 (2): 219–31.

Social Exclusion Unit (SEU) (1999) *Teenage Pregnancy*, London: HMSO.

Stephenson, J., Strange, V., Forrest, S., Oakley, A., Copas, A., Allen, E., Black, S., Ali, M., Monteiro, H., Johnson, A. and The RIPPLE Study Team (2004) Pupil-led sex education in England (RIPPLE study): cluster-randomised intervention trial, *The Lancet* 364: 338–46.

Strange, V., Forrest, S., Oakley, A., Stephenson, J, and the RIPPLE Study Team (2006) 'Sex and relationship education for 13–16 year olds: evidence from England', *Sex Education* 6(1): 31–46.

Toynbee, P. (2009) Alfie's story is characteristic of New Labour's failings, *The Guardian*, 17 February.

UNICEF (2001) *A League Table of Teenage Births in Rich Countries Innocenti Report Card No. 3*, July, Florence: UNICEF Innocenti Research Centre.

Weare, K. (2000) *Promoting Mental, Emotional and Social Health: A Whole School Approach*, London: Routledge.

Wellings, K., Field, J., Johnson, A.M. and Wadsworth, J. (1994) *Sexual Behaviour in Britain*, London: Penguin.

Wellings, K., Nanchahal, K., Macdowall, W., McManus, S., Erens, B., Mercer, CH., Johnson, A.M., Copas, A.J., Korovessis, C., Fenton, K.A. and Field, J. (2001) Sexual behaviour in Britain: early heterosexual experience, *The Lancet* 358: 1843–50.

Wight, D. (1993) A reassessment of health education on HIV/AIDS for young heterosexuals, *Health Education Research* 8 (4): 473–83.

Wight, D. and Forrest, S. (2010) *How Was it for You? The Quality of Young People's Sexual Relationships*, Briefing 50, Edinburgh: Centre for Research on Families and Relationships, University of Edinburgh.

Wight, D., Henderson, M., Raab, G., Abraham, C., Buston, K., Scott, S. and Hart. G. (2000) Extent of regretted sexual intercourse among young teenagers in Scotland: a cross sectional survey, *British Medical Journal* 320: 1243–44.

Wight. D., Parkes, A., Strange, V., Allen, E. and Bonell, C. (2008) The quality of young people's heterosexual relationships: a longitudinal analysis of factors shaping subjective experience, *Perspectives on Sexual and Reproductive Health* 40 (4): 226–37.

Willetts, D. and Streeter, G. (eds) (2002) *Renewing One Nation*, London: Politics Publishing.

Winterson, J. (1985) *Oranges Are Not the Only Fruit*, London: Pandora Press.

World Health Organisation (2003a) UN Commission on Human Rights Agenda item 6, Racism, Racial Discrimination, Xenophobia, and all Forms of Discrimination, Statement by the World Health Organisation, Geneva, 24 March, www.who.int/reproductive-health/gender/sexual_health.html (accessed 20 April 2005).

World Health Organisation (2003b) WHO statement to the fifty-ninth Session of the UN Commission on Human Rights, 17 March–24 April, http://66.102.9.104/u/who?q=cache:0NCN8HquTj8J:www.who.int/entity/hhr/information/en/item6_final.pdf+homophobia&hl=en&ie=UTF-8 (accessed 20 April 2005).

Chapter 7

The struggle for disability equality

Richard Rieser

Introduction

At least 15 per cent of the world's people have a significant, long-term, physical or mental impairment that can and usually does disable them from taking part in the usual educational, social and economic activity in their community. This is due to barriers in attitudes, in the built environment and in the way society is organized, which prevent us from participating on an equal level with others. The reason why most of these barriers exist is because societies have until very recently not recognized that the systematic way in which they discriminate against disabled people, when backed by discriminatory laws and practices of the state, often amounts to oppression. Barnes (1991) gives a full account of the discrimination disabled people encounter in all areas of life. This oppression has developed from our history, from myths and beliefs that attribute characteristics to disabled people that are unrelated to the reality of disabled people's lives. Such collections of attitudes often determine how non-disabled people respond to the 'different' in their midst; how they form stereotypes of the disabled person as saint, sinner, super-hero, freak, fi lo, victim, obsessive avenger, isolationist, the butt of jokes, just a burden, or someone to be pitied. The particular form of stereotyped thinking depends on the society's history, its explanation of how it has come to be and the resultant culture.

In December 2006 the United Nations adopted a groundbreaking new human rights treaty recognizing the above and requiring all States Parties who adopt and ratify this treaty to 'undertake to ensure and promote the full realization of all human rights and fundamental freedoms for all persons with disabilities without discrimination of any kind on the basis of disability'. Thus Article 1 of the United Nations Convention on the Rights of People with Disabilities (UNCRPD 2006) addresses the need for equality for disabled people throughout the world. To convince the United Nations of the need for the Convention it was necessary to demonstrate how disabled people were systematically denied the Human Rights others take for granted. In the United Kingdom, which ratified the Convention in June 2009, we have also passed into law the 2010 Single Equalities Act, which addresses disability and the other equalities issues addressed in this book. These two statutes can provide a new impetus for developing disability equality and developing inclusion.

The dimensions of inequality to do with gender, sexual orientation, 'race' and class all interact with disablement to create additional oppressions for those subjected to one or more of these oppressions. However, until very recently, the arguments for disability equality have often been ignored in the development of thinking about equal opportunities. In 2005 the Cabinet Office produced a far-reaching strategy to get disability equality for disabled people in the UK. Tony Blair, Prime Minister, writing the Foreword, had this to say.

> This report therefore sets out an ambitious vision for improving the life chances of disabled people so that by 2025 disabled people have full opportunities and choices to improve their quality of life and will be respected and included as equal members of society.
>
> (Cabinet Office 2005, p. 6)

Whether such commitments survive the change of UK government in 2010 and the harsh cutbacks brought about by the banking crisis remains increasingly unlikely with 14 separate attacks on disabled people's entitlements and benefits by March 2011, but at least it was an official recognition of the deep-seated inequalities associated with being a disabled person in British society.

In this chapter, therefore, I will begin by looking at how disablement is defined and modelled. I will then look at the extent of disability, worldwide and in the UK, and the impact and scope of the UNCRPD and the Equalities Act for developing disability equality. Next, I will give a brief history of disablement, including the growth of the Disabled People's Movement and our struggle for civil rights. I will conclude with an examination of the way that ideas of disability equality can be raised in the general school curriculum. This can help to counter prejudicial and discriminatory attitudes, which lead to harassment and bullying. In English schools 80 per cent of disabled pupils report bullying: two and a half times the level of non-disabled children (DCSF 2008; EHRC 2010). Outside school hate crime against disabled people has only recently been recognized as a largely hidden but serious human rights abuse. The United Kingdom Disabled People's Council report identifying media reports of 69 murders and 549 serious attacks on disabled people in the UK in the three and a half years to July 2010 (SCOPE 2008; UKDPC 2010).

Article 8 of the UNCRPD requires governments as part of awareness-raising to ensure '(b) Fostering at all levels of the education system, including in all children from an early age, an attitude of respect for the rights of persons with disabilities'.

Three ways of viewing disablement: the 'traditional model', the 'medical model' and the 'social model'

The 'traditional model' of disability

The 'traditional model' is a many-headed monstrosity that has helped human beings in all societies and cultures give an explanation to that which they did not understand. It relies on belief in the supernatural, religion, magic and fantasy. It is an 'othering' process that helps deal with fear, curiosity and pain caused by the occurrence of physical and mental impairment. Impairment is ever present and is seen as a threat to sense of well-being by non-disabled people (Rieser 2008a). Here are just a few such notions:

- Disabled people bring good luck or have supernatural powers, sixth sense or ability to tell the future.
- Disabled people are a punishment from God or bad karma.
- Disabled people are bad luck or evil.
- Disabled people are figures of fun, the butt of jokes or jesters/clowns that help us forget our troubles.
- Disabled people are possessed by demons.
- Disabled people are vengeful and have a chip on their shoulder. Disabled people are a burden on everyone else.
- Disabled people are asexual and perpetual children.
- Disabled people are contagious and have to be kept separate from everyone else, and many other false notions.

While we may think such ideas are long gone, a surprising number of people in many cultures are influenced by such ideas and they persist in the stereotypes promulgated in literature and the media (Rieser 2004). Many of these ideas arise from the way we have been perceived and treated in the past as will be seen from the section 'The history of disablement'.

The 'medical model' of disability

The 'medical model' sees the disabled person as the problem. We are to be adapted to fit into the world as it is. If this is not possible, then we are shut away in some specialized institution or isolated at home, where only our most basic needs are met. The emphasis is on dependence, backed up by the stereotypes of disability that call forth pity, fear and patronizing attitudes. Rather than on the needs of the person, the focus is usually on the impairment. With the medical and associated professions' discourse of cures, normalization and science, the power to change us lies within them. Often our lives are handed over to them.

Other people's (usually non-disabled professionals') assessments of us are used to determine where we go to school; what support we get; what type of education; where we live; whether or not we can work and what type of work we can do; and indeed whether we are even born at all, or are allowed to procreate. Similar control is exercised over us by the design of the built environment, presenting us with many barriers, thereby making it difficult or impossible for our needs to be met and curtailing our life chances. Whether it is in work, school, leisure and entertainment facilities, transport, training and higher education, housing or in personal, family and social life, practices and attitudes disable us.

Powerful and pervasive views of us are reinforced in language, and in the media, books, films, comics and art. Many disabled people internalize negative views of ourselves that create feelings of low self-esteem and achievement, further reinforcing non-disabled people's assessment of our worth. The 'medical model' view of us creates a cycle of dependency and exclusion that is difficult to break.

'Medical model' thinking about us predominates in schools where special educational needs are thought of as emanating from the individual who is seen as different, faulty and needing to be assessed and made as normal as possible (see Figure 7.1).

The 'social model' of disability

If, instead of focusing on differentness within the individual, the focus were on, for example, all children's right to belong and to be valued in their local school, then we would be asking 'what is wrong' with the school and looking at the strengths of the child. This second approach is based on the 'social model' of disability. This model views the barriers that prevent disabled people from participating in any situation as being what disables them. The social model makes a fundamental distinction between impairment and disability. *Impairment* is defined as 'the loss or limitation of physical, mental or sensory function on a long-term, or permanent basis', whereas *disability* is 'the loss or limitation of opportunities to take part in the normal life of the community on an equal level with others due to physical and social barriers' (Disabled People's International 1981, in Dreiger 1989). Article 1 of the UNCRPD demonstrates how this latter approach is at the heart of a human rights approach to disabled people:

> Persons with disabilities include those who have long term physical, mental, intellectual or sensory impairments which in interaction with various barriers may hinder their full and effective participation in society on an equal basis with others.

In recent years this social model approach to disability has been adopted by the World Health Organisation, UNESCO, UNICEF and the World Bank. In the UK it formed the basis of the Duty to Promote Disability Equality in the 2005 Disability Amendment Act.

The Disability Movement, which consists of organizations controlled by disabled people, comprises those disabled people and their supporters who

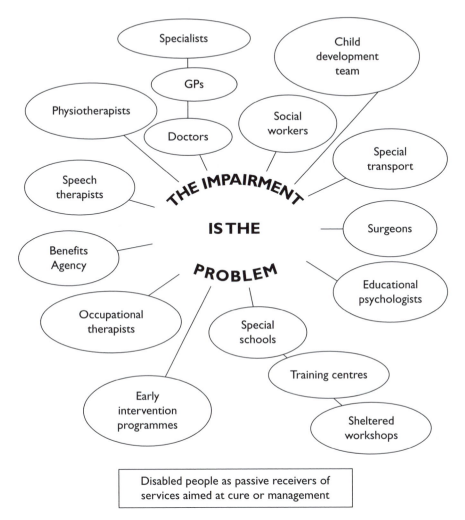

Figure 7.1 The medical model

understand that they are, regardless of their particular impairment, subjected to a common oppression by the non-disabled world. We are of the view that the position of disabled people and the discrimination against us are socially created. This has little to do with our impairments. As disabled people, we are often made to feel that it is our own fault that we are different. The difference is that some part, or parts, of our bodies or minds are limited in their functioning. This is an impairment. This does not make us any less human. But most people have not been brought up to accept us as we are. Through fear, ignorance and prejudice, barriers and discriminatory practices develop that disable us. This understanding of the process of disablement allows disabled people to feel good about ourselves and empowers us to fight for our human rights (Oliver 1990; Morris 1991; Mason and Rieser 1994) (see Figure 7.2).[1]

I will illustrate the two models of disability, with reference to my own history. I had polio in 1949, which led to the loss of muscle in my left leg, right arm and back. My impairment by the time I was six years old was not major – I could walk, swim, ride a bicycle and so on – but I walked with a limp. However, when I expressed the desire to attend the local primary school, which was all built on one level, the head teacher refused to have me, claiming that I was a fire risk. I was accordingly sent to a school for 'the physically handicapped'. This was my first experience of disablement. The school smelled like a hospital and I did not want to go there. So my parents kept me off school until the London County Council (LCC) agreed to pay for me to attend a private 'progressive' school that was not very good. There I was diagnosed as having 'learning difficulties' and 'behaviour problems'. Seven years later, I chose to leave and went to the local secondary modern, a year below my age group. Again I was disabled by not being allowed to use the lift in the six-storey building, by being bullied and being made to feel bad about myself in PE. Despite this, I did get the necessary O and A levels to enter university, though at some considerable cost to my self-esteem. In all of these situations people were disabling me by presenting barriers to my equal participation.

The Disabled People's Movement

The Disabled People's Movement represents the view that the 'cure' to the problem of disability lies in the restructuring of society. Unlike medically based 'cures', which focus on the individual and their impairment, this is an achievable goal and to the benefit of everyone. This approach, referred to as the 'social model', suggests that disabled people's individual and collective disadvantage is due to a complex form of institutional discrimination as fundamental to our society as social class exploitation, sexism, racism or heterosexism. This leads to discrimination and the internalized oppression we experience. This is not to deny or devalue the discomfort and pain we often experience as a result of having an impairment. Indeed a number of disabled writers (Morris 1993; Crow 1996; Shakespeare 1992; Oliver 1996; Shakespeare and Watson 1997) have argued that the 'social model' of impairment must include these experiences – for example, pain, discomfort and dying – and that the Disabled People's Movement will only attract larger numbers of disabled people if it takes these ideas and practices on board. There has been understandable resistance from those who experienced their lives as dominated by the 'medical model' and the real problem is that our current 'social model' has not been developed to encompass our experience of impairment and so to develop our own responses to it.

In addition to this, the obsession with finding medically based cures distracts us from looking at causes of either impairment or disablement. In a worldwide sense, most impairments are created by oppressive systems – hunger, lack of clean water, exploitation of labour, lack of safety, child abuse and wars (see below).

Clearly, the 'social model' has important implications for our education system, particularly with reference to primary and secondary schools. Prejudicial attitudes towards disabled people and indeed against all minority groups are not inherited. They are learned through contact with the prejudice and ignorance of others. Therefore, to challenge discrimination against disabled people, we must begin in our schools.

Our fight for the inclusion of all children, however 'severely' impaired, in one mainstream education system will not make sense unless the difference between

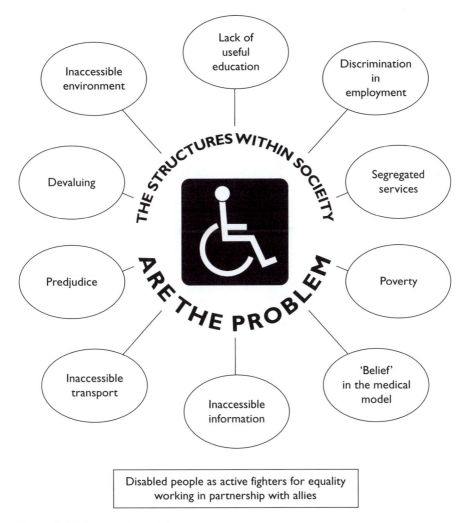

Figure 7.2 The social model

the 'social' and the 'medical' model of disability is understood (see Chapter 8 of this volume for a discussion of disability and education). I recently mapped the traditional, medical and social models of disability into the educational context (Rieser 2008a, p. 28) (see Table 7.1). What is clear from this analysis is that only a social model perspective in education leads to a dynamic school change process that leads to inclusive education.

The 'social model' has empowered many disabled people and been important in uniting previously disparate, often impairment-based organizations. The self-representation of disabled people has been important in a situation where

Table 7.1 Types of thinking about disabled people (DP) and forms of education

Thinking/ model	Characteristics	Form of education
Traditional	DP a shame on family, guilt, ignorance. DP seen as no value.	**Excluded** from education altogether.
Medical 1	Focus on what DP cannot do. Attempt to normalize or if cannot make to fit into things as they are keep them separate.	**Segregation** Institutions/hospitals Special schools (with 'expert' special educators)
Medical 2	Person can be supported by minor adjustment and support, to function normally and minimize their impairment. Continuum of provision based on severity and type of impairment.	**Integration** in mainstream: a) At same location – in separate class/units. b) Socially in some activities (e.g. meals, assembly or art). c) In the class with support, but teaching and learning remain the same. **What you cannot do determines which form of education you receive.**
Social model	Barriers identified – solutions found to minimize them. Barriers of attitude, environment and organization are seen as what disables and are removed to maximize potential of all. DP welcomed. Relations are intentionally built. DP achieve their potential. Person-centred approach.	**Inclusive education** – schools where all welcomed and staff, parents and pupils value diversity and support is provided so all can be successful academically and socially. This requires reorganizing teaching, learning and assessment. Peer support is encouraged. **Focus on what you can do.**

organizations 'for' disabled people, but run by non-disabled people, have sought to do things in our name, but without finding out what disabled people want. The British Council of Disabled People, made up of 129 organizations of disabled people that are run by disabled people, has had a long battle over the last 21 years to establish itself. This has now become the United Kingdom Disabled People's Council. This battle has been particularly hard when large charities 'for' disabled people such as the Royal National Institute for the Blind (RNIB), the Royal National Institute for the Deaf (RNID), the Royal Association for Disability and Rehabilitation (RADAR), SCOPE (for people with cerebral palsy) and MENCAP (Royal Society for Mentally Handicapped Children and Adults) get large amounts of government funding to provide services for disabled people, have influence, but do not represent disabled people and are not controlled by them. This was very apparent when the 1995 Disability Discrimination Act passed through Parliament and these organizations welcomed the new law in the face of opposition from disabled people's organizations.

The Disability Discrimination Act was seen by the Disabled People's Movement as weak and full of 'get-out' clauses, such as a 'reasonable' discrimination. In addition, the Act did not create a Commission to enforce it and support disabled complainants although a Disability Rights Commission was subsequently established in 2000. Transport and Education were largely left out of the Act's provisions, and the legislation only applied to employers with 20 or more employees – thus exempting 96 per cent of employers (after pressure, this was reduced to 15 or more employees and from October 2004 to all employers as a result of new European legislation). The split in the Rights Now Coalition (a group campaigning for civil rights legislation) between the factions 'of' and 'for' us was patched up, with the establishment of the Disability Rights Task Force.

The Labour government did not honour its manifesto commitment to introduce enforceable civil rights legislation for disabled people, but it did introduce, in 2001, the Special Educational Needs and Disability Act. This extended the DDA to cover the provision for the whole education system. In 2005 transport and other areas were brought under the legislation. Also a new duty to promote disability equality was introduced for all public bodies including schools. A weakened form of this duty has made its way into the 2010 Single Equalities Act with public bodies from April 2011 no longer needing to have a Disability Equality Scheme, the result of consultation, but only to set vague equality targets. The Single Equality Act has also consolidated and strengthened disability discrimination with a new category of indirect discrimination and disability-based discrimination. The Duty to Promoted Disability Equality followed the introduction of the Race Relations (Amendment) Act 2000, which followed the inquiry into the death of Stephen Lawrence and introduced a duty to promote race equality on all public bodies.

From April 2011 all previous duties are consolidated into a duty on public bodies not to discriminate against people in the seven protected characteristics: gender; race, ethnicity and nationality; disability; sexual orientation; gender age;

religious belief and no belief; transgender. None of these developments would have occurred without pressure from the trade unions, community groups and disabled people's organizations.

What is disablement?

World figures

Disablement, then, is a social process, but many of the attempts to enumerate disabled people do not take account of this; instead, they view it as a medical problem or personal tragedy. In 1996, the United Nations estimated there were at least 500 million disabled people in the world. This was made up of people with the following impairments: 55 million visually impaired (11 per cent), 70 million hearing impaired (14 per cent), 130 million with severe intellectual impairment (26 per cent), 20 million with epilepsy (4 per cent) and 160 million with some sort of mobility impairment (Disability Awareness in Action 1995, p. 7). Many poor countries do not have information on disability. In some, cultural taboos lead to disabled people being hidden away. In addition, major categories of impairment, such as mental distress, facial disfigurements and deformities, cancer, HIV/AIDS, hidden impairments like diabetes, sickle-cell anaemia, acute asthma and many other conditions that affect physical or mental functioning on a long-term basis, are not included in these figures.

If all these groups were to be added, the number would certainly increase sig-nifcantly to at least 850 million, or one in eight. The World Health Organisation in 2011 estimates more than one billion (World Report on Disability).

The UN figures also reveal the major causes of impairment. These include: malnutrition (100 million [20 per cent]); accident, war and trauma (including 20 million injured by land mines; 78 million [15.6 per cent]); infectious diseases, such as TB, polio and leprosy (all of which are preventable) (56 million [11.2 per cent]); non-infectious diseases (100 million [20 per cent]); and congenital diseases (100 million [20 per cent]). It has been estimated that 80 per cent of the impairments in the world are preventable as they are caused by poverty, war, hunger and disease. The report gives many examples of self-help projects from around the world, where disabled people have managed to dismantle barriers to their inclusion (Disability Awareness in Action 1995, p. 9).

It is also clear that the number of people counted as 'disabled' increases as the standard of living increases, showing it to be a social construct. The proportion of disabled people in Austria, for example, is 20 times higher than that in Peru (Coleridge 1993, p. 105). Local perception, barriers, survival rates and longevity vary considerably from rich to poor countries and will help to explain such variations. Recently the World Health Organisation (2011) has revised the number of disabled people in the world to 1 billion and presented a compre-hensive report on the challenges of implementing the UNCRPD.

The United Nations (2007) identify that disabled people are growing as a proportion of the population:

- ninety per cent of disabled pupils in the South do not attend school
- thirty per cent of street children have an impairment;
- up to 80 per cent of disabled adults are without work;
- disabled girls and women are much more likely to be beaten or raped.

UK figures

A DfEE Workforce Survey (Winter 2006) showed that only 50 per cent of disabled adults of working age (16 to 65 years old) were working or registered unemployed. This is an increase of 10 per cent from 1995 and the increase coincided with a 10-year period of economic growth and the implementation of the Disability Discrimination Act. The rest – 50 per cent or 3.4 million disabled people – were on benefit and not looking for work. Whether these improvements will be sustained in the new times of austerity is a real test of whether the principles of disability equality have been incorporated by the government and employers.

These figures follow on from a ground-breaking sample survey in the mid-1980s by the Office of Population Census (*6 Reports Survey of Disability in Great Britain*, cited in Martin *et al*. 1988) that sought to enumerate the number of disabled people in the United Kingdom. This showed that there were at least 6.5 million disabled people in Britain. Of these, 6.2 million were adults (14.2 per cent of the adult population); 41.8 per cent or 2.59 million of these were aged 16 to 65 and 360,000 were five to 16 years old. More recent surveys show increases in all categories. The survey did not include under-fives who, given the rise in the birth rate and improved medical techniques, would number at least another 300,000. This is borne out by the 1991 Census that recorded 6.9 million people who were disabled or long-term sick.

To be classed as disabled in this Office of Population Census (OPCS) survey, one had to have a significant impairment that 'restricted or led to a lack of ability to perform normal activities, which has resulted from the impairment of a structure or function of body or mind' (OPCS 1988, p. xi). Thresholds were set on 10 scales such as mobility, hearing, sight, incontinence, lifting and mental ability. Panels of judges developed the scales by examining the responses to narrowly based questions. People were interviewed and asked 'what they normally can do'. Anyone who is disabled has had to learn to do things in an environment and with objects that are not designed for us to use. Second, the questions asked were individualized rather than socialized and did not examine people's impairments against a background of the social and environmental contexts of disabled people's lives.

Criticizing the survey method and the ideology that lies behind it, Mike Oliver (1990) makes the different orientations clear. From the OPCS survey

(1986–88), he examines questions that were drawn from the face-to face interviews. The questions were:

1 Can you tell me what is wrong with you?
2 What complaint causes you difficulty in holding, gripping or turning things?
3 Do you have a scar, blemish or deformity that limits your daily activity?
4 Have you attended a special school because of a long-term health problem or disability?
5 Does your health problem/disability affect your work in any way at present?
6 Do your health problems/disability make it difficult for you to travel by bus?

These questions clearly see disability as individualized and are based on 'medical model' thinking. They could have been put in an alternative way that draws on a 'social model':

1 Can you tell me what is wrong with society?
2 What defects in design of everyday equipment like jars, bottles and lids cause you difficulty in holding, gripping or turning things?
3 Do other people's reactions to any scar, blemish or deformity you have limit your daily activity?
4 Have you attended a special school because of your education authority's policy of sending people with your long-term health problem or disability to such places?
5 Do you have problems at work as a result of the physical environment or the attitudes of others?
6 Do poorly designed buses make it difficult for someone with your health problem/disability to use them?

(Oliver 1990, pp. 7–8)

Abberley (1992, p. 154), in criticizing the surveys, has this to say:

It is a matter of political choice that OPCS surveys were designed in terms of an individualistic 'personal tragedy' approach to disability, rather than to devote significant resources to an exploration of the ways in which it is society that disables impaired people. Whilst there are ways in which we may utilise OPCS data, we must not in doing so lose sight of this most fundamental flaw. Information gathered on the basis of an oppressive theory, unless handled with circumspection, is itself one of the mechanisms of oppression.

Anyone who has followed the pronouncements of the New Labour government in the UK on disability benefits can see the dangers of this oppressive theory.

Despite announcing a task force to recommend full civil rights legislation for disabled people, the government allowed the Benefits Integrity Project to whip up pressure generally to cut back on the non-means-tested Disability Living Allowance (DLA) by producing false figures that one in five claimants was bogus. When this was shown to be false they claimed that if everyone who was entitled to claim Disability Living Allowance did, then 8.6 million people would be eligible on the current criteria, thus creating a climate for cutbacks. This time a huge outcry from disabled people and their allies prevented any threat to DLA. The allowance was the one positive thing that came out of the OPCS surveys, which showed definitively that disabled people lived in poverty and needed extra money to participate in society. *OPCS Report 2* (Morris and White 1988) established that disabled people were poorer than any other section of UK society. Now DLA is under threat because the government fails to understand that the barriers in society disable us and until they have been removed we need to be compensated for the extra cost of being disabled. These statistics are shifting sands. Using the DDA definition the 2001 Census identified 10.5 million adults who are long-term sick or disabled – that is, 22 per cent of the adult population. In addition, the DfES in 2004 identified 700,000 young people under 16 who are disabled. This is an underestimate as there are 1.6 million children with special educational needs, many of whom would come under the DDA definition.

> A person has a disability if he has a physical or mental impairment which has a substantial and long-term adverse effect on his ability to carry out normal day-to-day activities.
>
> (DDA 1995, Part 1)

This definition has recently been incorporated into the 2010 Equalities Act, though arguments that were put forward to have a more social model definition were not heeded by Parliament. In June 2009 the UK government ratified the UNCRPD with four reservations. The UK government now has international treaty obligations on the rights of people with disability as well as the Treaty entering into the law of the United Kingdom. So it would appear that the legal framework for disability equality and rights is firmly in place. However, implementation is another matter dependent on wider changes in attitude in society.

The duty to promote disability equality

In 2005 the UK government introduced a duty to promote disability equality for all public bodies and a specific duty for certain bodies such as NHS Trusts, schools, colleges, universities and local authorities to have a Disability Equality Scheme explaining how they would implement this duty (DRC 2005). When carrying out their function public bodies had to have due regard to the following:

- promote equality of opportunity between disabled persons and other persons;
- eliminate discrimination that is unlawful under the Act;
- eliminate harassment of disabled persons that is related to their disabilities;
- promote positive attitudes towards disabled persons;
- encourage participation by disabled persons in public life;
- take steps to take account of disabled persons' disabilities, even where that involves treating disabled persons more favourably than other persons.

Furthermore, implementation was based on an understanding of the 'social model' of disability:

> The poverty, disadvantage and social exclusion experienced by many disabled people is not the inevitable result of their impairments or medical conditions, but rather stems from attitudinal and environmental barriers. This is known as 'the social model of disability', and provides a basis for the successful implementation of the duty to promote disability equality.
>
> (DRC 2005, p. 172)

From December 2006 universities, colleges and secondary schools and other public bodies had to implement these duties. From December 2007 primary and special schools had to implement them. There was no comprehensive programme for training schools on these duties and most did not take them very seriously, as is evidenced by the scarcity of published schemes (Rieser 2008b). In 2009 the Lamb Inquiry into parental confidence in the Special Educational Needs system recommended, based on evidence of a low take-up of the duties by schools, that OFSTED should make compliance with equalities duties a limiting grade in inspections and that schools have to publish their Disability Equality Schemes on the internet. This was agreed by the Secretary of State (Lamb Inquiry 2009).

In 2008 I carried out an action research project for the Secretary of State to ascertain if the new duties were improving the experience of disabled children in English schools. Working with HEYA (Helping Empower Youth Activists) we identified 11 meetings of disabled children and young people.

We worked with 143 disabled pupils from 14 secondary schools, two academies, five special schools and five primary schools. We used a series of games and recorded views and filled in questionnaires. One activity was to get the young people's views on their schools on a number of dimensions by using symbol cards that they could either move to or show. This produced a mixed picture and there was considerable variation across schools. Those where there was a higher proportion not liking playgrounds and corridors reported higher levels of bullying (Rieser 2008b).

There was evidence of some improvement in schools identifying barriers and changing practice to accommodate disabled pupils, but in too many cases little

Table 7.2 What disabled pupils thought of their schools

Area of the school	Excellent	Good	Not so good	Bad
The school building	25%	40%	10%	25%
Playtime	33%	39%	16%	12%
School dinners	17 %	24.%	15%	44%
Assemblies	17%	31%	15%	37%
School trips	47%	21%	9%	23%
PE and games	29%	43%	12%	16%
Lessons	24%	36%	8 %	32%
Teachers	19%	46%	5%	30%
Teaching ass.	40%	39%	7%	14%
Other children	22%	28%	18%	32%
School council	37%	5%	29%	29%
School clubs	25%	25%	26%	24%
Corridors	8%	15%	17%	60%

had changed, with the disabled pupil being seen as the problem. In individual interviews it became clear that those pupils who disliked the corridors and playground were the same ones who experienced bullying on a daily or weekly basis. In English schools 70 per cent of disabled pupils report bullying; two times the level for non-disabled children (DCSF 2008). Recently the EHRC report on 'How Fair is Britain?' (2010b) increased this to 80 per cent.

The history of disablement

The continuing inequality we face will not be rectified by ramps, lifts and accessible communications, or the outlawing of discriminatory behaviour, welcome as these may be. The well-spring of our oppression comprises deeply held social attitudes that reflect generations of prejudice, fear and discrimination towards disabled people in education, work and social life. The main reasons are negative attitudes and stereotypes, which are based on untrue ideas that have been around for thousands of years, and which are amazingly persistent.

We can, at any time, all become disabled – develop a physical or mental impairment. Perhaps the need to distance ourselves from this reality makes it convenient to rely on negative attitudes and stereotypes of disability. They are less troubling than accepting the individuality, the joy, the pain, the appearance, the behaviour and the *rights* of disabled people.

Work by anthropologists (Hanks and Hanks 1948) has established that there is no one way that disabled people are viewed across a wide range of societies. Views ranged from high status to outcast. There appears to be an underlying economic basis, so in societies with more surplus produce, such as agricultural rather than nomadic or hunter-gatherer, there was more acceptance of disabled members of those societies. There was more chance of their being supported as there was surplus food. However, there were exceptions, and some evidence exists that hunter-gatherers have valued disabled members of their societies. A band of Northern Territory Aborigines carried a member of their band who could not walk with them on their wanderings for 60 years (Davis 1989). Where an impairment was more commonly occurring, such as blindness in a Mexican village (Gwaltney 1970), or on Martha's Vineyard, an island off the New England coast with an unusually high proportion of deaf people (Groce 1985), the whole culture changed to accommodate guiding and signing, respectively. Though no systematic cross-cultural study of the position of disabled people has yet been carried out, it is clear that the individualized tragic view of disability prevalent in modern Western society is not universal.

The ancient world

To understand the development of this particular view of disabled people, we must go back to ancient Greece, to the beginning of 'Western civilization'. In Greek mythology Zeus and Hera had a child, Hyphaistos, God of Fire, who was born with a 'club-foot'. He was thrown off Mount Olympus into the sea, but, being a god, he survived to return and become the butt of jokes of all the other gods (Garland 1995). He was a forger of metal and as he grew up his sexual relations with women were frequently fraught with difficulty because of the attitudes of the other gods. His wife, according to Homer, was the beautiful Aphrodite, who deceived him by having an affair with Ares. Here, we witness one of the most pernicious myths about disabled adults – that they are incapable of adult sexual relations.

The Greek and Roman attitude was to worship and adore the body beautiful. This is exemplified by the many perfectly proportioned sculptures of the human body, bodies with 'beautiful' symmetrical features. In representations on vases, tablets, sculptures and so on, there are very few disabled people. The Olympic ideal was to aspire to be like the gods in physique, intellect and morals. This is still often apparent in the Olympic Games, where the Para Olympics and Games for People with Learning Difficulties still segregate disabled athletes, although some sensory-impaired people have recently competed in the main Games.

The cult of the body beautiful was put into practice, particularly among the patrician or ruling classes in ancient Greece and Rome. Aristotle wrote 'that you should take your child off if they are imperfect and get rid of them' (Garland 1995, p. 15). The status of 'child' was not conferred until seven days after birth, so there was time to dispose of unwanted babies legally. In militaristic Sparta, children were the property of the state and inspected at birth. 'If the child be ill-born or ill-formed', the father was required to expose it at a chasm-like place called Apothetai or the Place of Exposure (ibid., p. 14). In Rome disabled infants were meant to be drowned in the Tiber and the games at the Coliseum put on to entertain and pacify the 'mob' included disabled children being thrown under horses' hooves, blind gladiators fighting each other and 'dwarves' fighting women. The rest of the ancient world was not as proscriptive, but nevertheless, exposure was widespread. Those with less significant impairments who survived generally led a half-life, disdained and ridiculed, often having to rely on begging. There were exceptions. Even in Sparta, King Agesilaos was afflicted with 'congenital lameness' but this acted as a spur to his ambition and he desired to be first in all things (ibid., p. 40). Clearly, then, exposure did not always occur, as parents do tend to love their children, and many disabled people survived infancy. In Rome, despite the dislike of and cruelty towards people with impairments, there is evidence that at least one emperor was disabled: Claudius may well have had cerebral palsy (*clauditas* in Latin means lameness). Claudius' mother, Antonia, described him 'as a monster of a man, not fin Lati by nature but only half done' (ibid., pp. 40–42). Echoed in Shakespeare's *Richard III*, this develops into an abiding stereotype as the evil and avenging man/monster.

The Judaeo-Christian tradition

Another seminal source of thinking about disabled people was the Judaeo-Christian tradition that fundamentally disability is a punishment for evil – 'if humans are immoral they will be blinded by God' (Deuteronomy, 27:27); in Exodus (20:5) God tells Moses that retribution for sin will be inflicted on the offspring of the sinners for many generations. In the books of Exodus, Numbers and Deuteronomy, the people of Israel are repeatedly punished for their sinful ways through physical impairment (Rose 1997).

The Jewish faith, however, has a more complex position, with some parts of the Talmud advocating disability as a holy state and a means of getting to heaven. Similar sentiments are expressed towards those who help disabled people. Some of this is reflected in the parables of the New Testament, but usually with Christ performing miracle cures. Rarely are disabled people accepted as themselves.

The Book of Leviticus (21:16–20) has a clear message that impairment is unclean and polluting, and prevents disabled people from receiving sacraments:

> And the Lord said to Moses none of your descendants throughout the generations who has a blemish shall draw near, a man blind or lame or one who has a mutilated face or a limb too long, or a man who has an injured foot or an injured hand or a hunchback or a dwarf, or a man with defective sight or itching disease or scabs or crushed testicles. He may eat the bread of his God, both of the most holy and of holy things, but he shall not come near the veil or approach the altar, because he has a blemish, that he has a blemish, that he may not profane my sanctuaries.

This message was taken seriously. Until the 1950s people with learning difficulties were not allowed to receive certain sacraments in the Roman Catholic Church.

The medieval period

Disabled people were treated in medieval Europe as both saints and sinners. On the one hand, they were 'innocents unstained by normal and sinful human characteristics' (Barnes 1991, p. 12) who should be offered asylum and alms; on the other, they were evil changelings – the work of the devil (Haffter 1968).

Martin Luther, the architect of the Reformation, believed that changelings had no soul and advocated that children so 'afflicted' should be taken to the river and drowned. Nevertheless, the bulk of disabled people born into feudal villages or acquiring impairments would have been accepted and did what they could, while those with more severe impairments may have been subject to infanticide.

Veterans of war were often treated better. The first record of a sheltered workshop in Europe was the Congregation of Three Hundred, established in France in 1254 for 300 crusaders who had had their eyes gouged out by Saracens (Ford 1981).

At times of crisis disabled people were likely to be scapegoated as superstition took over – for example, during the Plague or during the Great Witch Hunt of 1480–1680. The 'Malleus Maleficarum' – 'the Hammer of Witches', 1487, written by two priests – was a bestseller in Europe and went to 70 editions in 14 languages. It includes whole sections on how you can identify witches by their impairments or by their creation of impairments in others; or giving birth to a disabled child. Between eight million and 20 million people, mainly women, were put to death across Europe and a good proportion were disabled. Three witches were recorded as hanged after an Oxford trial in 1613, one of whom was put on trial because she was a disabled person using crutches (Rieser 1995, p. 6). Recent research on the treatment of people with learning difficulties, however, suggests that naturalistic accounts of learning difficulties and mental illness were accepted, rather than the disabled people being demonized (Neugebauer 1996).

The 'disabled witch' comes through in the folklore of Britain and Europe. The Brothers Grimm collected the oral stories of Northern Europe and made them into their fairy-tales. The witch in *Hansel and Gretel* is deformed, blind, ugly, disabled and carries a stick (this book has been adapted for use with children as young as two years old). There are also story-books that feature evil imps swapping healthy babies for disabled ones – changelings (Rieser 1995, p. 5).

There are many pictures and stories from medieval times of penitent sinners. Groups of penitent 'cripples' are depicted trying to get alms and, if they wandered around long enough, feeling humble enough, then maybe they would make it in the next life. A very strong message therefore came across. Disabled people were often scapegoated for the ills of society, as in Brueghel's painting *The Cripples*, where the fox tails denote wrongdoing. Outside any medieval church are the deformed ones, the gargoyles; and on the inside are the 'perfectly formed' pictures around the crypt.

Until the seventeenth century those disabled people rejected by their families relied upon the haphazard and often ineffectual tradition of Christian charity and alms – gifts for subsistence (Barnes 1991, Chapter 2). During the sixteenth century the wealth and power of the Church was greatly reduced due to the confrontation between Church and State in England. There was also a growth in those seeking alms due to a rise in population, poor harvests, the beginning of the commercialization of agriculture and immigration from Ireland and Scotland (Stone 1985). To secure the allegiance of local gentry and magistrates, the Tudor monarchs were forced to make economic provision for people dependent upon charity. The 1601 Poor Law marks the first recognition of the need for the state to intervene in the lives of disabled people. Some 200 years earlier, the Peasants' Revolt of 1381 had led to a mandate to local officials to distinguish the 'deserving poor' from the 'undeserving poor'. The bulk of relief went to the deserving poor in the form of 'household relief' to people in their homes. Segregation did not really emerge until the nineteenth century (Barnes 1991, pp. 14–19).

Close examination of Rembrandt's sketches reveals that the beggars are often wearing white headbands. This is because in seventeenth-century Holland the bacillus leprosy, brought inadvertently on the back of the 'spice trade' from colonies in the tropics, spread quickly around urban areas. An edict was passed by the state that all those who contracted it had to report to The Hague, and once their condition was confirmed they had all their worldly goods confiscated, had to wear a white headband, and they and their families had to rely on alms as penitent sinners. Those with leprosy had to live in segregated colonies and their only reward for penance was rehabilitation in heaven (Toth-Ubbens 1987).[2]

The eighteenth and nineteenth centuries

The development of industrial capitalism and its inherent requirement for workers to sell their labour power meant that those with significant impairments were excluded from the labour market. Those disabled people who were able to work were forced to the bottom rungs of the labour market ladder (Morris 1969, p. 9). As a result, disabled people came to be regarded as a social and educational problem, and were increasingly segregated out of the mainstream, in institutions of various kinds: workhouses, asylums, colonies and special schools (Oliver 1990, p. 28). According to Finkelstein (1980), this is Phase 2 of disabled people's development, the phase when we were separated from our class origins and became a special segregated group, with disability seen as an impairment, requiring segregation from the labour market as well as social restriction.[3]

Throughout the eighteenth and nineteenth centuries the policy of segregating severely impaired people into institutional settings slowly spread. The main impetus was the change from working as groups or families on the land, down the mines or as cottage industry to factory work. The latter required set rates of working on repetitive tasks for long hours; time was money. By 1834, Poor Law household relief was abolished for the 'non-deserving poor' – the unemployed. The deserving poor were categorized – children, the sick, the insane, defectives and the aged and infirm, the last four being categories of impairment – and provision was uniform across the country. Deterrence was built into relief as a principle of 'least eligibility' was introduced. This meant that those on relief would be less comfortable than an 'independent labourer of the lowest class' before benefits would be granted (Barnes 1991, p. 16). Charles Dickens and others have vividly described the horrors of the workhouse. Charities increasingly set up asylums for the insane and then special schools for blind and deaf children. This role was taken over by the state from the 1890s (Hurt 1988).

The 'insane', which included 'idiots', 'lunatics' and the mentally infirm, were, after the 1845 Lunacy Act, able to be detained on the certification of a doctor. This was based on a theory advanced by the medical profession that mental illness had physiological causes that were treatable. This marked the beginning of the medical profession's state-endorsed involvement in the lives of disabled people (Barnes 1991). This power is still exercised today; as a disabled person, if you want a Blue (parking privileges) Badge, Disability Living Allowance or Incapacity Benefit you have to be examined by a doctor. Now Atos has won a contract to prove by a computerized test that many claimants with established work-limiting impairments are fit for work. This is leading to many being wrongly put on lower benefits and some committing suicide (*The Guardian*, 14 February 2011). Interestingly the same article reported that 40 per cent of such decisions were overturned on appeal. Disabled people are not trusted in general and there is always a belief that people will pretend to be disabled to get benefits fraudulently, but this does not explain the continual checking of our impairments even when medical science has no solutions and our conditions are stable or deteriorating. In fact the same *Guardian* article reported a fraud rate of less than 1 per cent despite outrageous headlines to the contrary in *The Daily Mail*. Far more disabled people who are entitled to benefits don't claim them than the bogus claims from non-disabled people that are made; the latter, in reality, being rarities. This symbolic treatment of disabled people who are at the margins of the workforce very much defined who was part of the workforce and who was not (Oliver 1990).

In the last quarter of the nineteenth century, another strand of thought became highly influential – the eugenics movement. This had and continues to have a disastrous effect on the lives of disabled people. Drawn from the ideas of Aristotle, eugenics thinking first wrongly applied Darwin's theories of natural selection to ideas about racial degeneration and was then applied to disabled people. The birth of disabled children, it was claimed, would weaken the gene pool and outbreed non-disabled people. This, in turn, would weaken the European population in its task of colonizing and controlling the rest of the world (see Chapters 3 and 4 of this volume for a discussion of racism and imperialism).

The twentieth century

Traditional myths that there were genetic links between physical and mental impairments, crime, unemployment and other social evils were constantly proposed by the likes of Galton (1883, 1909), Dugdale (1895) and Goddard (1913), and many others. They wished to improve the British and American 'races' by preventing the reproduction of 'defectives' by means of sterilization and segregation. In the UK in the 1900s pressure from eugenicists for 'voluntary' sterilization increased (Ryan with Thomas 1987) (see the website www.eugenics archive.org for much more detail).

These ideas spread quickly to intellectuals of all political complexions as the century of science got under way: H.G. Wells, Sidney and Beatrice Webb, Bernard Shaw and D.H. Lawrence, W.B. Yeats, J.M. Keynes, Winston Churchill and Aldous Huxley to name but a few.

> If I had my way, I would build a lethal chamber as big as Crystal Palace, with a military band playing softly, and a Cinematograph working brightly; then I'd go out in the back streets and the main streets and bring them in, all the sick, the halt and the maimed; I would lead them gently, and they would smile me a weary thanks; and the band would softly bubble out the 'Hallelujah Chorus'.

So wrote D.H. Lawrence in 1908 in a letter to Blanche Jennings (Boulton 1979, p. 81). This was part of an elitist intellectual culture, which included a dislike for the industrial world and the social disorder it had spawned, and eugenicist views towards disabled people (Carey 1992).

The Mental Deficiency Act of 1913 was the result of eugenicist agitation and it led to the incarceration of 'idiots', 'imbeciles', 'the feeble-minded' and 'moral imbeciles', the last category usually referring to young people who had had illegitimate children. Many were incarcerated for life in sex-segregated institutions to prevent them from reproducing. At first it was argued that units or extra classes attached to ordinary schools were best, but soon the eugenicist view prevailed and the early part of the century saw large numbers of segregated schools for 'crippled children, epileptics, educable morons and feeble minded children' (Copeland 1997, p. 714; see also Hurt 1988).

A great wave of building ensued after the First World War with large institutions and colonies being erected on the outskirts of towns. Simon and Binet's false science of IQ testing, refined by supporters such as Cyril Burt (1977), was developed to distinguish the educable from the ineducable. An IQ of less than 50 meant you were destined for a mental deficiency institution as a child and probably for life. It is estimated that 50,000 children with no mental deficiency were sent to these institutions prior to 1950, on the false diagnosis of doctors who, at this time, subscribed to bogus theories, such as that someone's intelligence could be determined by their head shape and size (Humphries and Gordon 1992).

Children perceived to be ineducable, including many with cerebral palsy, Down's syndrome and speech impairments, went to junior training establishments right up until 1972. At that time, some 60,000 children joined the education system in severe learning difficulty schools. Today, many with the same conditions successfully attend ordinary schools.

In the US, compulsory sterilization was in wide use by the 1930s. Forty-one states had provision for the sterilization of the insane and feeble-minded, and 17 states prohibited people with epilepsy from marrying. In many states women born deaf were sterilized. Twenty-seven states still had these laws until very recently, though they were seldom enforced. In China, some 30 million people with 'mental incapacity' have been compulsorily sterilized under a law that was enacted in 1995. This is an abuse of their human rights and, as *The Guardian* reported in 1997, is a particular outrage since it is known that many of these women have developed their condition from iodine deficiency in their environment.

Recently it has been reported that in Scandinavia and France, mentally defective women were compulsorily sterilized up until the 1980s. This all took place despite the findings of a study carried out for the Wood Committee in 1929 which showed that only 7.6 per cent of patients of one particular asylum had defective parents.

Disabled people are seen as a burden, and at times of economic stress this view intensifies. The Nazis, when they came to power in Germany in 1933, introduced a law for the Prevention of Hereditary Diseases that led to the forced sterilization of more than 300,000 people. Under the Third Reich, propaganda films were made to show how we were a burden on the State. We were the 'useless eaters', and we should be got rid of. In the beginning, voluntary euthanasia was advocated to end the suffering of 'the incurable', but this ultimately evolved into mass murder. In November 2003 the German government acknowledged that 240,000 physically and mentally disabled people were murdered in 1939–40 at the hands of the doctors of the Third Reich in six so-called clinics, which were staffed by many of those who went on to run the concentration camps where six million Jews were exterminated (Burleigh 1994). More recently in *War Against the Weak* (Black 2003) the author estimates that more than one million disabled people died in this programme in the German Empire.

With cutbacks in the Welfare State, the eugenicist argument is currently undergoing a revival in Britain. A recent poll on GMTV revealed that 86 per cent of people who rang in thought that a doctor was right to abort two disabled children. In Holland and Tasmania laws have been introduced to allow voluntary euthanasia. This is indicative of the way in which, through history, people have been socialized to view disabled people. The medical ethics committees are allowing the Genome Project to map the seat of all genetic disorders. Soon science will have the capability to eradicate many forms of impairment. It remains to be seen if society wishes to cut off such a great source of leadership, innovation and hope. Do we want a Society without Beethovens (deaf) Einsteins (dyslexic/autistic), Hans Christian Andersons (autism), Stephen Frys (bipolar) or Tanni Greys (spina bifida)?

This brief excursus through the history of disabled people should cause us to ask if normality and uniformity are so important or is it difference that makes life interesting? The medicalization of impairment ignores the social context. In 1972 in the UK a child with Down's syndrome (an extra chromosome) would be deemed ineducable. Today, many such children who have attended main-stream schools are able to sit seven or eight GCSEs and are accepted by their peers. What would their lives be like if prejudice and discrimination were to be eradicated? Yet the medical profession insists on genetically screening all preg-nant women over 30 for Down's syndrome with a view to termination if it is identified. We would not have Pablo Pinedas – a Spanish actor and teacher completing his Masters Degree in Spain who has Down's syndrome (*Inclusion Now* 2010).

The struggle for human dignity

The oppression of disabled people, over the years, has not gone uncontested. On the contrary, many disabled people have consistently struggled for human dignity and for inclusion in mainstream society. The National League for the Blind and Disabled and the British Deaf Association, for example, were both run by disabled people and, from the 1890s, campaigned for rights. In the 1920s, when unions of disabled veterans were formed all over Britain, sit-ins and occupations were held in an attempt to force the introduction of legislation for disabled people's rights. In the 1920s and 1930s, there were hundreds of thou-sands of First World War veterans with no rights at all in the UK. Even those young people incarcerated in institutions for the blind or deaf had a culture of resistance; for example, when sign language was banned deaf pupils managed to develop their own pigeon sign language.[4]

In 1944 the Disabled Persons Act was passed. This included a quota system, whereby 3 per cent of the jobs in any given business had to be allotted to dis-abled people. This was to accommodate injured war veterans, and was abolished by the Disability Discrimination Act of 1995.

In the 1970s war veterans in the US started the disability movement there and successfully campaigned until they achieved full civil rights legislation in the Americans with Disabilities Act of 1991 (Dreiger 1989).[5] In the 1970s in the UK the Union of Physically Impaired Against Segregation was formed. This was initiated by Paul Hunt, who lived in a Cheshire home that he called the new workhouse. He wrote a letter to *The Guardian* (20 September 1972) calling on severely physically impaired people to form a new consumer group to put forward their views. This and a number of other organizations run by disabled people and formed in the 1970s amalgamated into the British Council of Organizations of Disabled People (BCODP). The Council, which supports the 'social model' of disability, now represents some 300,000 disabled people who all control their own organizations. The BCODP also linked a number of the local Centres for Independent Living and Local Coalitions of Disabled People (Campbell and Oliver 1996). These organizations campaigned for full civil rights legislation. Fifteen attempts were made from 1980 to 1995 to get a Civil Rights Bill through Parliament in the UK. Instead, all that was achieved was the 1995 Disability Discrimination Act. The Direct Action Network of disabled people expressed the frustration of millions of disabled people in a series of actions that brought London and other cities and towns to a standstill. As a result, the Labour government set up a ministerial task force to advise on the implementation of full anti-discrimination legislation based on the 'social model' of disability. Disabled people are still struggling for the rights to use public transport, to get into buildings, to go to school or college with their friends, to get a job and even to go to the cinema. In October 1998, the MP Glenda Jackson announced that £500 million would be spent on making London Transport buses accessible. In 2005 more was achieved with the introduction of the Public Service Duty to promote disability equality. In 2011 Disabled People Against the Cuts (DPAC) have taken on the mantle of DAN to challenge the human rights abuses of the Conservative–Liberal coalition against disabled people.

Recycling old ideas in the representation of disabled people

As disabled people, we often feel that the culture we are in characterizes us in a number of false ways that make us seem different to everyone else. Stereotypes of the disabled abound. Thus, there is the 'super-crip' or the disabled person who 'triumphs over tragedy'. Have you ever noticed how often perfectly ordinary things that disabled people do become newsworthy – the blind mountain climber, the boy with cerebral palsy who walked one mile, or the deaf man who was a chess champion? These things are only seen as newsworthy because journalists have a view that disabled people usually cannot or should not be doing ordinary things. The 1996 London Marathon was advertised by Nike showing a man with no legs or arms. The caption was: 'Peter is not like ordinary people. He's done the Marathon.' This plays on two ideas: first, that we are not able to do things; and second, that we are objects of curiosity – 'freaks' who are worthy of public attention.

We are often referred to as 'cripples'. This comes from an Old German word *kripple*, meaning to be without power. We do not like being called this. President F.D. Roosevelt, the only man to be elected President of the US four times, had physical impairment, having had polio in both legs, and was unable to walk unaided. Yet he perfected ways of disguising it, such as never being photographed in his wheelchair. He once observed that 'the American public would never vote for a president who was a cripple'. He may well have been right.

With the development of the printing press in 1480, at a time when most people in Europe could not read, cartoons and other graphic representations became popular ways of making political and moral comments to a mass audience. The old ideas of the Greeks became recycled: humankind was created by gods who were physically perfect. Since human beings were created in the gods' own image, the less physically perfect were less worthy. Evil, moral weakness and powerlessness were depicted by caricatured disabled people. For example, in an attempt to discredit Richard III, historians portrayed him as a disabled and vengeful mass murderer. However, when his portrait that hangs in the National Portrait Gallery was X-rayed, it was discovered that the King's hump had been added 60 years after his death. Modern film-makers often make their villains disabled. Little changes.

One need only look at pirates. From Lego to Stevenson's Long John Silver or Blind Pew, or Barrie's Captain Hook in *Peter Pan*; nearly all have eye-patches, hooks and wooden legs. All these disabled pirates do not accord with historical reality. Pirates had a system of simple social security long before anyone else. They had common shares in the common purse so, if they were injured during the course of their endeavours, they would retire to a tropical island with as much money as they needed. They were unlikely, therefore, to go on trying their luck as an impaired pirate (Greenwich Museum, private exhibition, 1994). Yet in the nineteenth century a number of writers became obsessed with disabled and evil pirates. In previous centuries pirates had been socially acceptable as they plundered and built up the British Empire. For example, Daniel Defoe wrote a bestseller about a certain Captain Singleton, pirate, popular hero and, on his return, thrice Lord Mayor of London. But pirates outlived their usefulness as privateers who expand the Empire, and after the Battle of Trafalgar the Royal Navy could do the job on its own (Rieser 1995).

Many charity adverts are designed to create fear. Take, for example, the one depicting a girl living 'under the shadow of diabetes'. She probably did not even know she was 'in a shadow' until she found herself up on the billboards of England for three years. She was simply injecting insulin every day and that was all right. Other charity advertisements use black and white imagery to make us look pitiful (for a detailed analysis of how charities use images of disabled people to disable us, see Hevey 1992).

There is, however, some cause for cautious optimism. The Invisible Children Conference, for example, jointly organized by Save the Children and The Alliance for Inclusive Education, was an exciting and thought-provoking day held in London on 1 March 1995 and attended by more than 150 key image-makers. The conference decided that 'disabled people should be shown as an ordinary part of life in all forms of representation, not as stereotypes or invisible'. The 1 in 8 Group, which grew out of this conference, issued the following useful guidelines to the media. There are ten main stereotypes of disabled people; the disabled person as:

- Pitiable and pathetic: e.g. charity advertisements and telethons, concepts like *Children in Need* and characters like Tiny Tim in *A Christmas Carol* or Porgy in Gershwin's *Porgy and Bess*.

- An object of violence: e.g. films such as *Whatever Happened to Baby Jane* or *Wait until Dark*, which set the style for countless TV films.
- Sinister or evil: e.g. Shakespeare's *Richard III*, Stevenson's *Treasure Island*, the films *Dr Strangelove, Dr No, Hook* or *Nightmare on Elm Street*.
- Curios or exotica: e.g. 'freak shows', images in comics, honour movies and science fiction, films such as *The Hunchback of Notre Dame* or *X-Men*.
- Super-crip or triumph over tragedy: e.g. films like *Reach for the Sky*, the last item on the television news – featuring a disabled person climbing a mountain, for example.
- Laughable: e.g. films like *Mr Magoo, Hear No Evil, See No Evil* and *Time Bandits*.
- Having a chip on their shoulder: e.g. Laura in the film *The Glass Menagerie*. This is often linked to a miracle cure as in *Heidi* and *The Secret Garden*.
- A burden/outcast: e.g. as in *Beauty and the Beast* set in subterranean New York, or the Morlocks in the *X-Men*.
- Non-sexual or incapable of having a worthwhile relationship: e.g. Clifford Chatterley in *Lady Chatterley's Lover, Born on the Fourth of July*, O'Casey's 'Silver Tassie' or the film *Life Flesh*.
- Incapable of fully participating in everyday life: our absence from everyday situations, not being shown as integral and productive members of society.

(Biklen and Bogdana 1977, amended by Rieser and Mason 1992)

Images: the way forward from and for disabled people

- Shun one-dimensional characterizations and portray disabled people as having complex personalities and being capable of a full range of emotions.
- Avoid depicting us as always receiving; show us as equals – giving as well as receiving.
- Avoid presenting physical and mental characteristics as determining personality.
- Refrain from depicting us as objects of curiosity. Make us ordinary.
- Our impairments should not be ridiculed or made the butt of jokes.
- Avoid sensationalizing us, especially as victims or perpetrators of violence.
- Refrain from endowing us with superhuman attributes.
- Avoid Pollyanna-ish plots that make our attitude the problem. Show the societal barriers we face that keep us from living full lives.
- Avoid showing disabled people as non-sexual. Show us in loving relationships and expressing the same range of sexual needs and desires as non-disabled people.
- Show us as an ordinary part of life in all forms of representation.
- Most importantly, cast us, train us and write us into your scripts, programmes and publications.

(Rieser 1995, p. 44)

Unfortunately, most children and young people still rarely meet disabled children in their schools and form their views of them mainly through the media. The inclusion of disabled people in producing and creating images, and the portrayal of disabled people as 'real people', is crucial. It was felt that now is the time to achieve this.

With a very few welcome exceptions – such as the children's television serial *Grange Hill*, the BBC drama *Skallagrigg* or the serial drama aired on Channel 4, *ER*, and the films *Four Weddings and a Funeral, Shine, Muriel's Wedding* and *The King's Speech* – disabled characters and images are largely absent, or when they do appear they are presented in a negative and stereotypical way. Change is slowly occurring. Twenty years ago Asian, black and other minority ethnic people were in a similar position. Now the necessity for their inclusion is taken for granted. Lack of portrayal of disability in our society is not accidental. Western culture from Greek and Roman times, reinforced in Renaissance Europe, has seen 'the body beautiful' as an ideal, and those with physical or mental imperfections have been seen as being in receipt of divine retribution. Such ideas are deeply embedded in myth, legend and classical literature. Today's digital entertainment culture reinforces the tendency to judge people by their appearance.[6]

More recently the British Broadcasting Corporation has commissioned a number of dramas – *Every Time You Look at Me* (April 2004), *The Egg* (2003) and *Flesh and Blood* (2002) – which include disabled characters as ordinary. As part of the European Year of Disabled People (2003), The British Film Institute and Disability Equality in Education collaborated to produce for teachers a website and a DVD examining how disabled people are shown in moving image media (www.bfi. org.uk/disablingimagery). The DVD and text containing an analysis and many activities for eight- to 18-year-olds are also available in a book (Rieser 2004). In 2009/10 World of Inclusion (2010) carried out work for the Qualification Curriculum Development Authority with 25 schools to identify ways to bring an understanding of the social model and discriminatory and stereotyped ways of thinking into the National Curriculum so that teachers and young people could develop their non-discriminatory thinking about disabled people. Teachers, schools and pupils were not only prepared to experiment, but also reported a high level of pupil satisfaction and a broadening of horizons. Material from this project and nine films of promising practice can be found on the web (World of Inclusion 2010).

In 2010 the first UK Disability History Month (22 November to 22 December and each subsequent year at this time) was held providing a focus for schools, colleges, communities, trade unions and workplaces to hold events to examine our struggle for rights, the oppression we have faced and the need to continue to achieve equality (www.ukdisabilityhistorymonth.com).

In the next chapter I will examine how both traditional thinking about disabled people and the 'social model' impact on the English education system, one which has grown out of the oppressive history of disabled people and 'medical model' thinking, are predominant in special needs education. I will argue that inclusive education, rooted in an understanding of these diverse processes, is the way forward in eliminating both disadvantage and prejudicial attitudes.

Notes

1   Mason and Rieser (1994) is for teachers and school governors.
2   This book is written in Dutch, with an English summary.
3   In Phase 1, disabled individuals were part of a greater feudal underclass. In Phase 3, which is just beginning, disability comes to be seen solely as *social restriction*. The surplus value generated in capitalist societies, combined with modern technology, means that we can be exploited as workers by capitalism in much the same way as non-disabled people. However, it also means that we can make the case *not* to be segregated either in the world of work, or more generally in the mainstream society.
4   The book *Out of Sight* contains first-hand oral histories and photographs of life in special schools and institutions in the first half of this century (Humphries and Gordon 1992).
5   This is a good account of the international development of the Disabled People's Movement.
6   Norden (1994) gives a fascinating account of how the image of disabled people has been developed through Hollywood, while Pointon (with Davies 1997) provides a very useful handbook on how the disability movement has developed a critique and a response to the way disabled people are shown in the media. These ideas could also be useful to educationalists in the way they reproduce and interpret images of disabled people in the classroom.

References

1 in 8 Group (1995) 'Disability in the Media Broadsheet', 78, www.worldofinclusion. com/res/disimg/disability_in_media.pdf (accessed 14 July 2011).
Abberley, P. (1992) 'Counting us Out: A Discussion of the OPCS Disability Surveys', *Disability, Handicap and Society*, 7 (2), pp. 139–56.
Barnes, C. (1991) *Disabled People in Britain and Discrimination*, London: Hurst.
Black, E. (2003) *War Against the Weak: Eugenics and America's Campaign to Create a Master Race*, Four Walls Eight Windows, London.
Biklen, D. and Bogdana, R. (1977) 'Media Portrayals of Disabled People: A Study of Stereotypes', *Inter-racial Book Bulletin*, 8 (6 and 7), pp. 4–9.
Boulton. J.T. (1979) *The Letters of D.H. Lawrence Vol. 1 1901–1913*, Cambridge: Cambridge University Press.
Burleigh, M. (1994) *Death and Deliverance: Euthanasia in Germany 1900–1945*, Cambridge: Cambridge University Press.
Burt, C. (1977) *The Subnormal Mind*, Oxford: Oxford University Press.
Cabinet Office (2005) 'Prime Ministers Strategy Unit Report on Improving the Life Chances of Disabled People', www.cabinetoffice.gov.uk/media/cabinetoffice/ strategy/assets/disability.pdf (accessed 14 July 2011).
Campbell, J. and Oliver, M. (1996) *Disability Politics: Understanding our Past, Changing our Future*, London: Routledge.

Carey, J. (1992) *The Intellectuals and the Masses: Pride and Prejudice amongst the Literary Intelligentsia, 1880–1939*, London: Faber & Faber.

Coleridge, P. (1993) *Disability, Liberation and Development*, Oxford: Oxfam.

Copeland, I. (1997) 'Pseudo-science and Dividing Practices: A Genealogy of the First Educational Provision for Pupils with Learning Difficulties', *Disability and Society*, 12 (5), pp. 709–22.

Crow, L. (1996) 'Including all our Lives: Renewing the Social Model of Disability', in Barnes, C. and Mercer, G. (eds), *Exploring the Divide: Illness and Disability*, Leeds: The Disability Press.

Davis, A. (1989) *From Where I Sit: Living with Disability in an Able Bodied World*, London: Triangle.

DCSF (2008) *2008 Secretary of State Report on progress towards disability equality across the children's and education sector*, www.dcsf.gov.uk/des/sosreport.shtml (accessed 14 July 2011).

Disability Awareness in Action (1995) 'Overcoming Obstacles to the Integration of Disabled People', UNESCO sponsored document for the World Summit on Social Development, Copenhagen, March.

Disability Discrimination Act (1995) London: TSO.

Disability Rights Commission (2005) 'The Duty to Promote Disability Equality', London: TSO, www.dotheduty.org/files/Code_of_practice_england_and_wales.pdf (accessed 18 July 2011).

Disability Rights Commission (2005) *The Duty to Promote Disability Equality Statutory Code of Practice Disability*, London: Rights Commission.

Dreiger, D. (1989) *The Last Civil Rights Movement*, London: Hurst.

Dugdale, R.L. (1895) *The Jukes: A Study in Crime, Pauperism, Disease and Heredity*, New York: G.P. Putnam's Sons.

Equality and Human Rights Commission (2010) *Equalities in the UK Triennial Review*, London: EHRC.

Equality and Human Rights Commission (2010b) Triennial Review: How Fair is Britain?, London: EHRC.

Finkelstein, V. (1980) *Attitudes and Disabled People: Issues for Discussion*, New York: World Rehabilitation Fund.

Ford, B. (1981) 'Attitudes towards Disabled Persons: An Historical Perspective', *Australian Rehabilitation Review*, 5, pp. 45–49.

Galton, F. (1883) *Inquiries into Human Faculty*, London: Macmillan.

Galton, F. (1909) *Essays in Eugenics*, London: London Eugenics Society.

Garland, R. (1995) *The Eye of the Beholder: Deformity and Disability in the Graeco-Roman World*, London: Duckworth.

Goddard, H.H. (1913) *The Kallikak Family: A Study in the Heredity of Feeble-mindedness*, New York: Macmillan.

Groce, N. (1985) *Everyone Here Spoke Sign*, London: Harvard University Press.

Gwaltney, J. (1970) *The Thrice Shy: Cultural Accommodation to Blindness and Other Disasters in a Mexican Community*, London: Columbia University Press.

Haffter, C. (1968) 'The Changeling: History and Psychodynamics of Attitude to Handicapped Children in European Folklore', *Journal of Behavioural Studies*, 4 (1) pp. 55–61.

Hanks, J. and Hanks, L. (1948) 'The Physically Handicapped in Non-Occidental Societies', *Journal of Social Issues* 4 (4) pp. 11–20.

Hevey, D. (1992) *The Creatures Time Forgot: Photography and Disability Imagery*, London: Routledge.

Humphries, S. and Gordon, P. (1992) *Out of Sight: The Experience of Disability 1900–1950*, Plymouth: Channel 4 Books.

Hurt, J. (1988) *Outside the Mainstream: A History of Special Education*, London: Batsford.

Inclusion Now (2010) 'Confronting Cameron', Interview with Jonathan Bartley, www.allfie.org.uk/pages/articles/vol26.html#bartley (accessed 18 July 2011).

Lamb Inquiry (2009) 'Special Educational Needs and Parental Confidence', London: DCSF, www.dcsf.gov.uk/lambinquiry/downloads/8553-lamb-inquiry.pdf (accessed 14 July 2011).

Martin, J., Metzler, H. and Elliot, D. (1988) *OPCS Report 1: The Prevalence of Disability among Adults*, London: HMSO.

Mason, M. and Rieser, R. (1994) *Altogether Better*, London: Comic Relief.

Morris, J. (1991) *Pride against Prejudice*, London: Women's Press.

Morris, J. (1993) *Independent Lives: Community Care and Disabled People*, London: Macmillan.

Morris, J. and White, A. (1988) *OPCS Surveys of Disability in Great Britain Report 2, The Financial Circumstances of Disabled Adults Living in Private Households*, London: HMSO.

Morris, P. (1969) *Put Away*, London: Routledge.

Neugebauer, R. (1996) 'Mental Handicap in Medieval and Early Modern England: Criteria, Measurement and Care', in Wright, D. and Digby, A. (eds), *From Idiocy to Mental Deficiency: Historical Perspectives on People with Learning Disabilities*, London: Routledge.

Norden, M.F. (1994) *The Cinema of Isolation: A History of Physical Disability in the Movies*, New Brunswick, NJ: Rutgers University Press.

OPCS (1988) *Surveys of Disability in Great Britain*, London: HMSO.

Oliver, M. (1990) *The Politics of Disablement*, London: Macmillan.

Oliver, M. (1996) *Understanding Disability from Theory to Practice*, London: Macmillan.

Pointon, A. with Davies, C. (1997) *Framed: Interrogating Disability in the Media*, London: British Film Institute Publishing.

Rieser, R. (ed.) (1995) *Invisible Children: Report of the Joint Conference on Children, Images and Disability*, London: Save the Children.

Rieser, R. (2004) *Disabling Imagery? A Teaching Guide to Disability and Moving Image Media*, London: Disability Equality in Education (www.diseed.org.uk).

Rieser, R. (2008a) *Implementing Inclusive Education: A Commonwealth Guide to Implementing Article 24 of the UN Convention on the Rights of People with Disabilities*, London: Commonwealth Secretariat, pp. 13–14.

Rieser, R. (2008b) 'The Impact of the Duty to Promote Disability Equality in Schools in England: A Report for the Department for Children, Schools and Families' (DCSF), www.worldofinclusion.com/res/impact/dpdes.doc (accessed 10 July 2011).

Rieser, R. and Mason, M. (1992) *Disability Equality in the Classroom: A Human Rights Issue*, London: DEE.

Rose, A. (1997) 'Who Causes the Blind to See?': Disability and Quality of Religious Life', *Disability and Society*, 12 (3), pp. 395–405.

Ryan, J. with Thomas, F. (1987) *The Politics of Mental Handicap*, London: Free Association Books.

SCOPE (2008) 'Getting Away with Murder: Disabled People's experience of hate

crime in the UK', www.scope.org.uk/sites/default/files/pdfs/Campaigns_policy/
Scope_Hate_Crime_Report.pdf (accessed 2 September 2011).

Shakespeare, T. (1992) 'Renewing the Social Model', *Coalition*, September, pp. 40–42.

Shakespeare, T. and Watson. N. (1997) 'Defending the Social Model', *Disability and Society*, 12 (2), pp. 293–300.

Stone, D. (1985) *The Disabled State*, London: Macmillan.

Toth-Ubbens, M. (1987) *Lost Image of Miserable Beggars: Lepers, Paupers, Guex*, Lochem-Gent: Uitg. Mij. De Tijdstroom.

United Kingdom Disabled People's Council (UKDPC) *The Bigger Picture Report to EHRC*, www.ukdpc.net/index.asp?getpage=true&sid=66&ssid=0&sssid=0&page=3 (accessed 14 July 2011).

United Nations Convention on the Rights of People with Disabilities (UNCRPD) (2006) www.un.org/disabilities (accessed 11 July 2011).

United Nations (2007) 'Handbook for Parliamentarians on the Convention on the Rights of Persons with Disabilities', Geneva, www.un.org/disabilities/default.asp?id=212 (accessed 10 July 2011).

World Health Organisation (2011) *World Report on Disability*, New York: WHO, http://whqlibdoc.who.int/publications/2011/9789240685215_eng.pdf (accessed 14 July 2011).

World of Inclusion (2010) 'Curriculum Guidance for Schools on Disability Equality', www.worldofinclusion.com/qcda.htm (accessed 10 July 2011).

Chapter 8

Inclusive education
A human right

Richard Rieser

Introduction

When I first had Kim he was my son.

A year later he was epileptic and developmentally delayed. At eighteen months he had special needs and he was a special child. He had a mild to moderate learning difficulty. He was mentally handicapped.

I was told not to think about his future.

I struggled with all this.

By the time he was four he had special educational needs. He was a statemented child.

He was dyspraxic, epileptic, developmentally delayed and had complex communication problems. Two years later, aged six, he was severely epileptic (EP), cerebral palsied (CP) and had complex learning difficulties. At eight he had severe intractable epilepsy with associated communication problems.

He was showing a marked developmental regression. He had severe learning difficulties. At nine he came out of segregated schooling and he slowly became my son again.

Never again will he be anything else but Kim – a son, a brother, a friend, a pupil, a teacher, a person.
>   (*Kim* by Pippa Murray, in Murray and Penman 1996)

The great majority of children with special educational needs (SEN) will, as adults, contribute economically; all will contribute as members of society. Schools have to prepare all children for these roles. That is a strong reason for educating children with SEN, as far as possible, with their peers. Where all children are included as equal partners in the school community, the benefits are felt by all. That is why we are committed to comprehensive and enforceable civil rights for disabled people. Our aspirations as a nation must be for all our people.

So wrote David Blunkett, Secretary of State for Education and Employment, in his Foreword to the government Green Paper *Excellence for All Children: Meeting Special Educational Needs* (DfEE 1997, p. 4). Blunkett is himself a disabled person who attended a special school for the blind and left without any formal qualifications. He had to attend evening classes, while working full time, to gain the necessary qualifications to go to university. The UK government's (1997–2010) commitment to developing inclusive education, in principle, is clear. However, the government lacks an understanding of how deeply 'medical model' thinking (see Chapter 7 of this volume) permeates the world of education. Unfortunately this commitment was already weakened by 1998 in the Action Plan (DfEE 1998). In addition, the government is easily deflected by those wishing to maintain the status quo of segregated provision. For example, in the Special Schools Working Group Report (DfES 2003), the government sees a continuing and important role for special schools – in other words, segregated provision.

These contradictions at the heart of the Labour government were brought to a head when they had to ratify the UN Convention on the Rights of People with Disabilities in 2009. Article 24 requires State Parties to develop an inclusive education system where disabled children have a right to attend their local school, and the support they need should be provided along with reasonable accommodations so they can thrive socially and academically. While the UK government had no problem with this formulation during the negotiations in New York that led to the Convention (2001–06), they did have when it came to ratifying the Convention. The concerns of the government were echoed by the Joint Parliamentary Committee on Human Rights Report on the UN Convention (2009).

Article 24 of UNCRPD provides that states recognise the right of persons with disabilities to education. Its provisions include that:

> With a view to realizing this right without discrimination and on the basis of equal opportunity, State Parties shall ensure an inclusive education system at all levels and lifelong learning [. . .]

> In realizing this right, State Parties shall ensure that:

> (a) Persons with disabilities are not excluded from the general education system on the basis of disability, and that children with disabilities are not excluded from free and compulsory primary education, or from secondary education, on the basis of disability;
> (b) Persons with disabilities can access an inclusive, quality and free primary education and secondary education on an equal basis with others in the communities in which they live;
> (c) Reasonable accommodation of the individual's requirements is provided;
> (d) Persons with disabilities receive the support required, within the general education system, to facilitate their effective education;

(e) Effective individualized support measures are provided in environments that maximize academic and social development, consistent with the goal of full inclusion.

(UNCRPD 2006)

Any economic and social rights in the Convention, including the right to education, are subject to the principle of progressive realization according to available State resources (Article 4, UNCRPD 2006).

Despite representations to the committee from over 30 parents and disability organisations not to have a reservation they took more notice of one parents organisation that argued for maintaining the status quo.

We have now seen three justifications for the reservations or interpretative declarations being considered by the Department of Schools Children and Families:

* the need to continue to maintain some specialised provision outside the mainstream;
* the need to recognise that not all disabled children can, or will, be able to secure appropriate education close to home; and
* the need to support parental choice.

(Para. 78)

In the event the UK government is the only country so far out of 105 who have ratified who felt the need to place such a reservation. The main reason the other countries have not is that education as an economic and social right is subject to progressive realisation. The only conclusion that can be drawn from this is that the UK government was not prepared to envisage a fully inclusive education system at any point in the future. The new government led by David Cameron is committed to removing 'the bias towards inclusive education' (Conservative Manifesto 2010, p. 53).

The Coalition government from May 2010 has had a policy of 'removing the bias to inclusive education'. This bias does not exist. The law has built in bias to those parents who want a special school. Under pressure from parents and inclusion organisations Michael Gove, the current Secretary of State, has admitted the policy is one of parental choice. They are likely to be more hostile to the continuing development of inclusive education, though it is worth noting that during the election campaign David Cameron, Prime Minister, was challenged by a parent who had had real difficulty getting his disabled son into the same primary school as his daughters. The confused thinking of the Conservatives is a reaction to bad integration rather than a response to good inclusive practice (see www.reversethebiascampaign.com).

The interpretive declaration the Labour government lodged at the UN does at least contain an ongoing commitment to inclusive education:

The United Kingdom Government is committed to continuing to develop an inclusive system where parents of disabled children have increasing access to mainstream schools and staff, which have the capacity to meet the needs of disabled children. The General Education System in the United Kingdom includes mainstream, and special schools, which the UK Government understands is allowed under the Convention.

(Education – Convention Article 24 Clause 2 (a) and (b))

Nevertheless, and despite the reservations to inclusion of the ruling Coalition in the UK, the expectation of the forthcoming period in education is that an increasingly wide diversity of pupils will be educated alongside their peers in mainstream classrooms as this is what the majority of parents of disabled children choose. This is certainly the case around the world as more countries begin to meet their obligation under Article 24 of the UNCRPD.

A forthcoming Green Paper will set out the Coalition's policy in more detail. However, two other threats to inclusive education are being promoted by the Coalition government. First, their wish to introduce more academies and free schools whose admission criteria and rigid curriculum are likely to exclude disabled pupils. Second, the major cuts in public expenditure brought about by the banking crisis which are already hitting children's services across the country and are bound to squeeze resources allocated for special educational needs.

If inclusive education is to be effective, teachers have to adopt 'social model' thinking about disabled people (see Chapter 7 of this volume). They must analyse the growing documentation of good practice, but they should also be aware of the barriers that prevent inclusion. These include physical barriers, communication barriers, social barriers, attitudinal barriers, educational barriers and institutional barriers. By physical barriers I mean the separate special school system and inaccessible school buildings and equipment; communication barriers are to do with lack of appropriate signing, lack of Braille and augmented communication, a lack of the use of plain jargon-free language, or of appropriate computers and other aids. Social barriers include separate classes or units, or 'discrete' courses within mainstream provision, which can lead to isolation and a lack of non-disabled friends. Attitudinal barriers include ignoring, bullying and devaluing us; denying the history, experience or culture of disabled people. Educational barriers consist of inadequate and inappropriate staffing levels, training or material resources within mainstream schools to address the real teaching and learning needs of all. Institutional barriers are the rules, regulations and procedures, including streaming, inappropriate testing, targets and examinations, which discriminate against disabled people. Finally, emotional barriers are to do with low self-esteem, lack of empowerment and the denial of the chance to develop worthwhile reciprocal relationships.

The term 'disabled' includes people with: physical impairments, sensory impairments (deaf people, blind people); chronic illness or health issues, including

HIV and AIDS; all degrees of learning difficulties, including specific learning difficulties such as dyslexia and speech and language impairments; and impairment based on emotional and behavioural difficulties. It also includes people with hidden impairments such as epilepsy, diabetes, sickle-cell anaemia; children labelled as 'delicate'; people who identify as 'disfigured'; people of diminutive stature; and people with mental distress. All are excluded by barriers, though not all have physical or mental impairments.

The fixed continuum of provision

In Chapter 7 I examined society's historical response to difference and how, in the early part of the twentieth century, as a result of eugenicist thinking, segregation and separation of adults and children with physical and mental impairments became the norm. I also argued that people became identified by their impairment and were thus the target of professional interventions under 'medical model' approaches, which, for the sake of efficiency, were provided in specialised settings. These processes have led to a geographically discrete and fixed continuum of provision in most local education authorities (LEAs). In many parts of the country a child is assessed independently of their local school and community. From this assessment they will be placed where their 'need' can best be met, often in a school for that type of need away from their peers, segregated with other children with that particular need or impairment (see Figure 8.1).

This continuum of provision is very often located in the schools and institutions that were expressly set up in the past to segregate young disabled people from their communities. A brief examination of the factors that led to a separate special school system will be useful to understand the social forces that led to the separation of children with more severe impairments (Mason and Rieser 1994; Cole 1989). Despite the good intentions of legislators, if one adds in Pupil Referral figures this has risen and then remained remarkably stable in the last 15 years (see Table 8.1). At the same time the numbers with any sort of special education need in mainstream schools have risen to 21.6 per cent of secondary and 19.9 per cent of primary school intake in 2010.

The origin of special schools

Following the Forster Education Act of 1870, School Boards were set up to provide elementary education for all. The Act did not specifically include provision for disabled children. For the next 15 to 20 years, most disabled children were in units attached to elementary schools, or not at school at all. Elementary classes were large and instruction was based on the 'Official Code' with rote learning and memory tests. Teachers were paid by results. Large numbers of children made little or no progress and the scale and complexity of learning difficulty and impairment in the population became apparent for the first time.

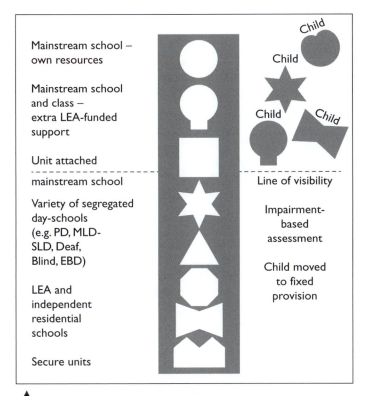

Mainstream school –
own resources

Mainstream school
and class –
extra LEA-funded
support

Unit attached
mainstream school

Variety of segregated
day-schools
(e.g. PD, MLD-
SLD, Deaf,
Blind, EBD)

LEA and
independent
residential
schools

Secure units

Child
Child
Child
Child

Line of visibility

Impairment-
based
assessment

Child moved
to fixed
provision

▲ In the fixed continuum the disabled child is slotted and moved
according to an impairment-based assessment

Figure 8.1 The fixed continuum of provision

Source: Mason and Rieser (1994).

Some progress was made in providing specialist tuition for blind and deaf children in the aforementioned units. For example, by 1890 in Scotland and by 1893 in England and Wales, all blind children aged between five and 16 and all deaf children between seven and 16 were sent to school as of right. Much of this provision was made by extending existing elementary schools. No such rights to education applied to the much larger group of 'physically and mentally defective' children. In 1913, the Mental Deficiency Act was passed. Consistent with eugenicist thinking, this required LEAs to ascertain and certify which children aged seven to 16 in their area were 'educable defectives' and which were 'ineducable defectives'. In 1914 and 1918, respectively, rights to education were provided for those considered 'educable mental and physical defectives'. However, prior to this, many LEAs had made some such provision. In 1921, under strong eugenicist pressure, five categories of disablement were identified: blind, deaf, mental

Table 8.1 Number of disabled children educated separately
in England

Date	Number of children
1897	4,739
1909	17,600
1914	28,511
1919	34,478
1929	49,487
1939	59,768
1947	40,252*
1955	51,558*
1965	70,334*
1967	78,256*
1977	135,261*+
1987	107,126*+
1994	104,431*+
2001	111,500**
2005	112,100**
2010	110,770

Note:
* hospital schools not included; + includes severe learning difficulty
** 10/30 DfES Special Education Statistical Bulletin includes maintained
and non-maintained special schools and pupils in pupil referral units
with a statement. England only.

Source: Cole (1989) based on Chief Medical Officer, Ministry of
Education, DfEE circular 9/13 1998 for England, only includes statemented children in maintained and non-maintained independent
schools and PRUs and special schools. DEE, DFES, DCSF Special
Education Statistics include pupils within pupil referral units those
with statements in independent schools.

defective, physical defective and epileptic. Children thus labelled were certified
and provided for only in separate schools or certified classes.

Following the increasing popularity of IQ testing in the 1920s and 1930s, the
Spens Report recommended a tripartite system. The 1944 Education Act
established secondary schools for all, but segregated into grammar, secondary
modern and technical. Entry at 11-plus was based in part on IQ tests. Selection
by ability prompted selection by 'disability' and the growth of special schools,
the number of children in which rose sharply when 11 categories of children
based on impairment were introduced. These were blind, partially sighted, deaf,
partially deaf, delicate, diabetic, educationally subnormal, epileptic, maladjusted,
physically handicapped and those with speech defects. Regulations prescribed
that blind, deaf, epileptic, physically handicapped and aphasic children were
seriously 'disabled' and *must* be educated in special schools.

It was hoped that the majority of other categories would receive their education in ordinary schools. However, as a result of overcrowding, prejudice,

misinterpretations of the legislation and teacher resistance this did not take place. In fact, it was not until the 1950s that large numbers of new special schools were opened. This continued throughout the 1960s and 1970s. Throughout this period, as new demands were made on teachers, nearly always without additional resources or training, the pressure to exclude more children became greater. In 1965, Circular 10/65 was introduced with the intention of abolishing selection at 11-plus and of instituting a system of comprehensive education, the aim being to cater for the needs of all children regardless of gender, 'race', class or ability. Ironically, this led to a further rise in the number of children in special schools, as a result of a fear over declining standards. In addition, economic cuts meant that the majority of comprehensives stuck to streaming rather than mixed-ability teaching and never catered for the full ability range. This is because effective mixed-ability teaching requires more preparation and planning time, and staffing cuts made this difficult. Even so, over the next 30 years, comprehensives proved to be the most effective way of educating the whole cohort, and where there was mixed ability there was overall the greatest exam success (Benn and Chitty 1997).

In 1970, in England and Wales, the last 60,000 children who had been considered ineducable under the terms of the 1913 Mental Deficiency Act secured the right to education, but with the label 'educationally subnormal (severe)' (later 'severe learning difficulty') attached to them. Some 400 new special schools were created largely out of the old junior training centres, which were where 'ineducable children' previously received training. Similar moves took place in Scotland in 1974.

The 1976 Education Act was intended to provide schooling for all categories of disabled children in mainstream schools. The then Secretary of State decided not to introduce it, however, owing to resistance from special schools and some LEAs, and the economic cost.

The 1981 Education Act, following the 1978 Warnock Report, again stressed the need for children with special educational needs to be educated in mainstream schools where possible, and introduced the principle of integration. However, no extra resources were made available, and despite some significant moves in some parts of the country, and some excellent examples of good practice, the proportion of the segregated school population has not declined significantly (1.41 per cent in 1977, 1.35 per cent in 1988, 1.29 per cent in 1997 and 1.27 per cent in 2003). In addition, owing to local variations in LEA policies, there is an eightfold difference in your chances of going to a mainstream school if you have a statement of special educational need depending on where you live (Norwich 1997). This increased to a 24-fold difference in 2003 with only 0.1 per cent of Newham pupils attending special schools and 2.4 per cent of children in Brighton and Hove attending special schools (DfES 2004a, p. 34).

The good practice in some areas has been matched by an increase in the percentage of pupils in special schools in other areas, particularly in the period from 1988 to 1991. There is little doubt that the 1988 Education Reform Act has increased the pressure in some schools to segregate disabled children, especially when schools have not already established good integration policies and allocated resources accordingly. Publication of test results is making many schools more selective about their intakes. Statemented children who have earmarked resources attached to them are a more attractive proposition to locally managed budgets, allocated by inflexible, cost-cutting formulae. In many areas the use of School Action Plus with an additional 485,250 pupils (2010) funded from beyond the school budget and delegated SEN budgets have helped to make things more flexible in recent years.

The Audit Commission (2002, p. 2) examined how the 1981 and 1996 Special Education Acts were working. It reported that schools were struggling They found it a struggle to balance pressures on schools to raise attainment and to become more inclusive; that national targets had not reflected the good work done with many pupils with special educational needs. There was still a major need to help all children fulfil their potential and these children's interests needed to be reflected in every part of the education system. The report was entitled 'Special Educational Needs: A Mainstream Issue'. The government's response was a new strategy 'Removing Barriers to Achievement', which laid great emphasis of improving the capacity of mainstream schools to effectively include a wider range of students. As the DfES put it: '[w]e are committed to removing the barriers to learning that many children encounter in school' (DfES 2004b, p. 28).

But the impact of discrimination in education goes much deeper. As Colin Barnes (1991, p. 28) put it after having completed a survey of government reports on education for the Disability Movement:

> Institutional discrimination against disabled people is ingrained throughout the present education system. The data shows that most of the educational provision for disabled children and students remains basically segregative, is dominated by traditionally medically influenced attitudes and commands a low priority as a whole. As a result, rather than equipping disabled children and young people with appropriate skills and opportunities to live a full and active life, it largely conditions them to accepting much devalued social roles and in so doing condemns them to a lifetime of dependence and subordination.

Unfortunately, both the 1993 and 1996 Education Acts kept the 'get-out' clauses of the 1981 Act with respect to special needs provision. These clauses, which have so often been used to compel disabled children, against their and their parents'/carers' wishes, to attend special schools (Mason 1998), stipulate

> that educating the child in a school which is not a special school is compatible with:

a   his [sic] receiving the special educational provision which his learning
     difficulty calls for,
b   the provision of efficient education for the children with whom he is
     educated, and
c   the efficient use of resources.

The SEN and Disability Act 2001 removed clauses (a) and (c) in general from
Section 316 of the 1996 Act, but left these get-out clauses intact in Schedule
27. So although the government's intention was to give more choice of mainstream school placement to disabled children and their parents this is not
proving to be the case. The SEN Disability Tribunal is still, in some cases,
upholding Local Education Authority views on placement in special schools
against the wishes of parents who want a mainstream place.

   It is clear that this has much more to do with attitudes and commitment than
anything else. It is also clear that where integration has been planned and
resourced, and where all staff have developed it as a whole school policy, it is
much more successful (Hegarty and Pocklington 1981; Booth et al. 1992; Booth
and Ainscow 1998; Sebba and Schadev 1997).

   The Special Educational Needs and Disability Act 2001 is in force following
a lengthy review process. However, the fundamental point is that this legislation
does not guarantee the right to an education in the mainstream, if you want it.
It is still concerned with assessing the individual, rather than assessing to what
extent schools have removed the barriers to inclusion, inherited from the past.
So long as these stipulations remain, disabled children will always be threatened
with being compelled to go to a special school when the political climate shifts,
when there are insufficient resources, or if the school has failed to meet their
needs. There is a wider symbolic problem. As long as there are institutions called
special schools, mainstream schools and teachers will not feel they have to
change their buildings, ethos or teaching and learning strategies to accommodate disabled children.

   All of us involved with education must engage in the ongoing task of
changing deep-seated attitudes and discriminatory behaviour if we are to create
an inclusive future in which all will benefit.

   Segregated education has not been good for disabled people. Hirst and
Baldwin (1994) carried out a major comparative survey of the lives of young
disabled and non-disabled people (aged 13 to 22), which showed stark differences in lifestyle. Most telling was an index of self-esteem that clearly showed
that those who attended special schools had a significantly lower score than
disabled people who attended mainstream schools, and their scores were also
significantly below those of non-disabled people.

   A recent Ofsted Report (2004) found that the legislative framework had had
little effect on the proportion of pupils with SEN in mainstream schools, or on
the range of needs for which mainstream schools cater. There has been an
increase in the number of pupils placed in pupil referral units and independent

Table 8.2 Unequal opportunities growing up disabled

	A Disabled	B Non-disabled
Living with parents	92%	86%
Gone on holiday with friends	25%	52%
Had a spare-time job	22%	32%
Looked after siblings	34%	57%
Had own key	51%	76%
Paid work	35%	67%
Had a boy/girlfriend	30%	40%
Difficulty making friends	35%	20%
Satisfactory network of friends	57%	74%
Self-esteem score	7.3+	8.5*
Internal locus	8.8	9.3*

Notes

Group A: 400 disabled people on OPCS category 1–10; Group B: 726 non-disabled people; all respondents aged 13–22.

+ Self-esteem score of those in special schools, 6.2; those in mainstream, 7.5.

* Response score to 12 questions – 6 agree and 6 disagree.

Source: Hirst and Baldwin (1994).

Table 8.3 Difference in GCSE and GNVQ results for year 11 students in state special and all schools for England 2001–04

Year	School type	Grade			
		5 A*–C	5 A*–G	1 A*–G	No passes
2001	All schools	50%	88.9%	94.5%	5.5%
	Special school	0.6%	6.5%	29.3%	70.7%
2002	All schools	51.5%	88.9%	94.6%	5.4%
	Special school	0.6%	5.0%	37.2%	62.8%
2003	All schools	52.6%	88.6%	94.6%	5.4%
	Special school	0.9%	5.4%	32%	68%
2004	All schools	53.4%	86.4%	95.8%	4.2%
	Special schools	0.4%	4.8%	59%**	41%
2008	All schools	65.3%	91.6%	98.6%	1.4%
	Special schools	5.7%	14.2%	68% **	32%

Note

** in 2004 and 2008 includes entry level qualification in 2004 which is at a significantly lower level.

Source: UK Education Statistics DfES (www.dfes.gov.uk/statisticsGCSE-GNVQ attempts+ achievement and Table 3 GCSE & Equivalent Exams 2007/08 SFR 02/2009) DCSF Special schools include community and foundation special schools, pupil referral units and hospital schools. Data from the Department for Education for 2009/10, provided by them from unpublished performance data, breaks results down by impairment type by type of school shows huge variations e.g. children with autism in mainstream do 22 times better at the end of KS2 in SATs than those in special schools and twice as well in KS4 tests (5A*-G) for those with autism in mainstream than special.

special schools. A minority of mainstream schools meet special needs very well with high expectations, effective whole school planning seen through by committed managers, close attention on the part of skilled teachers and support staff and rigorous evaluation remain the key to success. Over half the schools visited had no access plans despite being legally bound to have them from April 2003.

Yet, government statistics show at least 588,000 disabled pupils in primary (6.7 per cent of all pupils), secondary (6.2 per cent of all pupils) and special schools. But only 15.4 per cent of disabled pupils attended maintained and non-maintained special schools. So clearly a large majority of disabled pupils are attending mainstream schools, but are not receiving inclusion, but some inadequate form of integration.

However, disabled pupils attending mainstream schools still do much better than disabled pupils attending special schools and, for the first time using the national pupil database, it was possible to establish this. A government commissioned research 'Inclusion and Pupil Achievement' (Dyson et al. 2004, p. 39), shows that LEAs with high rates of inclusion in mainstream schools did no worse than low, including LEAs in national tests. As to the difference between individuals they also showed that: at KS4 in 2002 average point score was 38.55 (the average point score is the total of GCSE or GNVQ exams with eight for a single subject grade A$\star$ and one for a single subject grade G); for non-statemented pupils with special educational needs in mainstream the mean score was 21.85; for statemented pupils in mainstream the mean points score was 16.99 and for pupils in special schools the mean points score was 2.4 – or seven times below the score for statemented mainstream pupils.

In addition, Gary Thomas (1996) analysed GCSE results by type of school and found that 70 per cent of special schools did not enter any pupils for GCSE. He went on to show that 93 per cent of mainstream Year 11 students get at least one A$\star$–G grade, whereas only 16 per cent of Year 11 students in special schools get at least one A$\star$–G grade. This is particularly shocking if one considers the largest group of pupils in special schools are labelled as having 'Moderate Learning Difficulty' (nearly 55,000), and that in mainstream schools they would all be entered for GCSE. As Table 8.3 shows this has improved to 68 per cent of special school pupils getting some form of accreditation, though this is mainly entry grade. The reality in 2010 is that disabled people are still three times more likely than anyone else to not have any qualifications (EHRC 2010).

The language we use

The inheritance of the past conditions current attitudes, policies and practice towards disabled children and young people in society and within education. This is nowhere more clearly demonstrated and symbolised than in the language used. Take, for example, the negative connotations associated with 'cripple' (without power), 'sufferer', 'invalid' and 'handicapped' (commonly used as a noun to describe children, when it is actually a verb meaning imposed disadvantage from beyond the person).

We wish to be known as 'disabled people' in recognition of the common oppression we face regardless of our specific impairment. People with learning difficulties reject 'mental handicap', wishing to be known as the former. We reject the inhumanity and 'medical model' thinking involved in labelling and identifying people by their impairing condition. Calling someone a 'Down's' or 'spina bifida' child makes the child no more than their condition. Using 'the blind', 'the deaf' or 'the disabled' to describe us diminishes us. We wish to be known as blind people, deaf people or disabled people. If it is necessary to identify a particular impairment, one should say, for example, 'child [or person] with Down's syndrome'.

Within education, impairing condition labels such as 'epileptic' and 'diabetic' and evaluative labels such as 'educationally subnormal' or 'physically handicapped' have been replaced by labels based on bands of need and derived from Warnock, for example, 'MLD' ('mild learning difficulty') or 'SLD' ('severe learning difficulty'). Inevitably, since children are assessed to fit these categories of need, they become known by their label, and their destination, which tends to be specific separate provision.

In 1991 the Department for Education produced five categories of staffing provision, linked to impairment. These are now increasingly widely used and children are becoming labelled, for example, as 'PMLD' ('profound and multiple learning difficulties') – the most severe category of need with the best staffing ratio. This has reinforced the idea of a continuum of fixed provision in separate schools. We must reject the legacy of the past that has excluded us. We have to recognise that all children and adults have a right to be included in mainstream education and society as a fundamental human right (Mason and Rieser 1994; Rieser and Mason 1990/1992).

A constellation of services supporting inclusion

In the fixed continuum of provision, the disabled child is slotted in and moved around according to an impairment-based assessment (see Figure 8.1). In contrast, the constellation of services provides what the child and the class teacher need in mainstream schools. This includes a variety of services, resources and specialists who bring their expertise to the child rather than vice versa. This conception allows for the development of inclusive schools (see Figure 8.2). It also provides much greater flexibility but, because it is new and unknown, it is seen by many professionals as threatening. These two figures show the transition we wish to achieve from an education service structured on the 'medical model' to one based on the 'social model'.

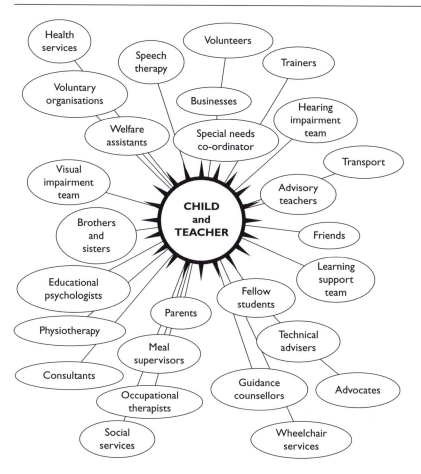

▲   The constellation of services provides what the child and the class teacher need in ordinary schools, from a variety of services, resources and specialists. This conception allows for the development of inclusive schools.

Figure 8.2 The constellation of services

Source: Mason and Rieser (1994).

Integration and inclusion

Integration

Integration is a matter of location and there are at least four variants:

- Periodic integration: children from special schools are bussed into a main-stream school at a regular time each week for 'integration', or an 'integration event' is organised.

- Geographical integration: disabled children may be educated in units or school on the same campus or site as their non-disabled peers, but do not mix, even socially.
- Social integration: disabled children may share meals, playtime and assemblies with non-disabled peers, but are not taught with them.
- Functional integration: disabled and non-disabled children are taught in the same class.

What all forms of integration have in common is the assumption of some form of assimilation of the disabled child into the mainstream school. The school remains largely unchanged and the focus is on the child fitting in. As we have seen, if the child is unable to do this, the law can be used to direct her/him to a special school or unit.

Inclusion

Inclusion, on the other hand, is about a child's right to belong to her/his local mainstream school, to be valued for who s/he is and to be provided with all support s/he needs to thrive. Since mainstream schools are generally not organised in this way, it requires planned restructuring of the whole school. This restructuring should be seen as an extension of the school's equal opportunities policy and practice. It requires a commitment from the whole staff, the governors, parents/carers and pupils/students. Inclusion is not a static state like integration. It is a continuing process involving a major change in school ethos and is about building a school community that accepts and values difference.

In order to become inclusive, schools should adopt a 'social model of disability'. They must identify the barriers within the school's environment, teaching and learning strategies, attitudes, organisation and management that prevent the full participation of disabled children and, as such, are part of the social oppression of disabled people. Functional integration is a precondition for the development of inclusion and disability equality. It does not, in itself, achieve it. The Index for Inclusion (Booth and Ainscow 2002) was sent by the government to every school in England, Wales and Scotland. There is now an early years and play version (Booth and Ainscow 2004) and it has been translated into 17 languages and is being used in more than 70 countries. The index enables schools to hold a mirror up to themselves, identify barriers and find out how inclusive they are in ethos and/or culture, in policies and practice. Ownership of the process of inclusion by the school is essential.

Inclusion depends on the extent to which all children get what they need to grow and develop, and how open the teacher and the children in the class are to learn and respect each and every child's experience. This sounds idealistic, but the alternative is to continue to reproduce the status quo, with its built-in discrimination against disabled children. Inclusion fundamentally challenges the traditional approach that regards impairment and disabled people as marginal, or an 'afterthought', instead of recognising that impairment and disablement are a common experience of humanity and should be a central issue in the planning and delivery of a human service such as education.

Mike Oliver (Oliver 1992), an educationalist and a leading member of the Disability Movement, drew out the differences between integration and inclusion in a paper he gave during National Integration Week in May 1992:

Old Integration is:	'New' Integration or Inclusion is:
a state	a process
non-problematic	problematic
a professional and administrative approach	politics
changes in school organisation	change in school ethos
teachers acquire skills	teachers acquire commitment
curriculum delivery must change	curriculum content must change
legal rights	moral and political rights
acceptance and tolerance of children with special education	valuation and celebration of disabled children and children with learning difficulty
normality	difference
integration can be delivered	inclusion must be struggled for

Inclusive education should be the guiding principle. We should be working towards a system and an ethos where mainstream schools should accommodate all children regardless of their physical, intellectual, social, emotional, linguistic or other conditions.

Central to inclusive education is the involvement of disabled people in its consultation, planning and implementation. Examples already exist of the successful inclusion of children with every type and severity of impairment in mainstream schools in the UK. Many changes in school organisation and practice have been necessary to make this happen, but from all such changes the non-disabled majority of children have benefited.

The best way to initiate whole school change is to have a training day delivered by disabled disability equality trainers with experience of the education system (see www.worldofinclusion.com for advice on such a highly valued network). The school should then set up a representative working group to either use the checklist below or use the index for inclusion and regularly report back to staff and the board of management or governors.

Pupils/students need to be involved in this process through whole class discussion, assemblies and pupil/student councils. Parents/carers of disabled children are often disempowered by professional interventions that have threatened or broken their relationship with their disabled child. Parents for Inclusion are developing training to address this issue. The LEA, Social Services and Health Service need to provide the support and additional resources to the school to help overcome the barriers to inclusion.

The inclusion process is part of school improvement and developing more effective comprehensive schooling for all. Goals need to be built into the School Development Plan to be met over a five- or 10-year time-scale and their achievement must be monitored.

The inclusion of profoundly deaf pupils and students requires particular thought and attention. The eugenicist origins of 'special education' and the ensuing impact on current-day segregation and integration had a particular impact on the education of deaf people, particularly those who use sign language. In Milan in 1880 educationalists from 21 countries met and decided to outlaw the education and instruction of deaf people through sign language and develop instruction through the oral method. It was feared that the thriving deaf culture and sign language, which had developed in the previous 90 years, now posed a threat to the gene-pool of hearing people (Facchini 1985). This led to enforced education of deaf children through the oral method, which led to them having a literacy level of half that of their hearing peers. The deaf community has rightly fought hard for deaf children to be educated in their first language – sign language.

Many deaf children are still forced to learn without sign language. This has often meant that recently schools for the deaf and deaf clubs are the only places where sign language is readily available (Ladd 2003). There are now models of inclusion where deaf children are included with simultaneous interpreting – English/BSL, sufficient number of deaf students to form a BSL using peer group, deaf BSL using adult instructors to develop their sign language and the hearing pupils learning sign language to communicate with their peers. This occurs successfully, for example, at Selwyn Primary, Lister Secondary School in Newham or Cottingley Primary School in Leeds and leads to deaf pupils having the best of the hearing and deaf worlds. At present this means resourcing some mainstream schools. However, given the educational history of most deaf people it is quite right that they insist on education through sign language. Oralism still seeks to educate deaf children through high-tech hearing aids and cochlear implants, but the deaf community argue that they miss out on both deaf language and culture, and still do not understand all that is being said. It is up to mainstream schools to meet the challenge of including deaf pupils by the means outlined above. In recent years this has been reinforced by medical advice not to use sign language for those with cochlear implants. However, all deaf students have a human right to access sign language, and a total communication environment benefits all deaf children. The recent UNCRPD has enshrined this right, yet much oralism still persists.

What follow are some of the necessary changes that schools, teachers, governors, non-teaching staff, parents/carers and pupils/students have to undertake to become inclusive.

A whole school policy on disability equality and inclusion

a) Access audit of the school environment. Carry out a full access audit of your building. Involve pupils/students. Cost and set targets of major and minor works to be included in the school development plan. Involve the governors in pressing the LEA for access works. Money is available through the school devolved capital budget and all refurbishments and rebuilds need not only to comply with Part M of the Building Regulations, but also the Disability Equality Duty (2005).

b) Audit access to the learning environment. Audit software and hardware suitable for supporting learning difficulties. Maintain up-to-date information on adaptations, for example, signing, Brailling, vocalising, voice recognition, touch screen, laptops, switching and ICT programs. Make lessons multimedia. Make sure visuals can be described or subtitled if necessary.

c) Ensure disability issues are in the curriculum. When planning a curriculum unit, topic or module think of including a disability dimension. Build up resources and literature that are non-discriminatory and include disabled people in a non-patronising way (see guidelines in Chapter 7 of this volume). Promote the 'social model' of disability. All Equal All Different (Rieser 2004) is one such resource pack for Early Years and KS1. See www.worldofinclusion/qcda.htm for many lesson ideas, filmed examples of good practice and resources.

d) Disabled people are positively portrayed. Ensure all children have access to positive images of disabled adults and children in non-stereotyped activities and roles. Make sure the school has a range of picture or reading books and posters that do this (see References at the end of this chapter). Involve disabled adults from the community in activities and lessons.

e) Diversify the curriculum. When planning the curriculum, use a wide variety of approaches to draw on different strengths, learning styles – auditory, visual or kinesthetic – and aptitudes of the pupils/students. Build up a resource bank of ideas and lessons allowing time for joint planning and review. Check that teaching and learning strategies and targets are appropriate for the needs of all children in the class.

f) Develop collaborative learning and peer tutoring. The pupils/students comprise the biggest learning resource in any school. Involve them in pairing with children of different abilities and groups. All children benefit from these approaches.

g) Effective team approach for learning support and curriculum planning. Ensure that learning support is effectively coordinated throughout the school and in each classroom. Allow time for joint planning in the school day, involving teachers and teaching assistants. Develop the skills and confidence of the learning support assistants to carry out different roles in the classroom with groups of children. Pay teaching assistants to attend staff meetings regularly.

h) British Sign Language. When a school includes deaf children, make use of British Sign Language translators and teachers. Offer deaf children the chance to work with native signers including those with cochlear implants. Offer hearing children the chance to study sign language as part of the curriculum. Give a positive value to different forms of communication. For deaf and partially hearing children, it is important to understand their need for induction loops, lip-reading and good room acoustics.

i) Accessible communication with parents/carers. Recognise that not everyone communicates by written or spoken English. Audit the communication needs within the school and of parents and provide notices, reports, information and directions in the relevant format, for example, large print, easy read, Braille, tape, videos in British Sign Language, computer disks and pictograms, and use symbols for people with learning disabilities.

j) Be critical of disablist language. Examine language used in teaching and by other pupils. Much of it is disablist and impairment derived. Develop a critical reappraisal through disability equality training, assemblies and in class. Monitor this and log it as harassment.

k) Challenge impairment-derived abuse, name-calling and bullying as part of the school behaviour policy. Introduce effective policy to prevent abuse, name-calling and bullying because of physical, mental or sensory differences. Make this part of your school anti-bullying policy and monitor it.

l) Involve all pupils in developing behaviour policy. Policies devised with pupil/student involvement and based on principles of self-regulation and mutual respect are the most effective. Cultivate developmental discipline. Sometimes it is necessary for adults to take a lead in setting up circles of friends and buddy systems. All children should remain on roll even if for some time they are out of class. Devise systems where distressed children can take 'time out' and talk to sympathetic adults. Have access to counselling and psychiatry. About 5 per cent of pupils have attachment issues and do not respond to positive discipline. You need a differentiated behaviour policy as a reasonable adjustment.

m) Develop a whole school ethos on accepting difference. Use events like assemblies, plays and sports days to demonstrate this, as well as in day-to-day functioning.

n) Develop empowerment and self-representation of disabled pupils/students. Set up structures through which disabled pupils/students can express their views, develop self-esteem, and have some influence on school policies. Involve disabled adults in this process. Develop training in self-advocacy.

Find ways of ensuring disabled students are represented on the School Council. You are allowed to use positive action if under-represented.

o) Physical Education. Ensure PE and sporting activities involve all pupils/ students, develop collaboration and encourage all pupils to improve their personal performance. Use adaptation and creative imagination to succeed in this.

p) Transport and school trips policy. Make sure this includes all. Ensure that transport to and from the school for disabled pupils fits in with the school day and cater for attendance at after-school activities. Allow the disabled child's friends and siblings to use transport to break down isolation. Ensure that no pupil is excluded from a trip or visit because their access or other needs are not met. This means careful advance planning and pre-visits. Ensure you don't use risk assessment to exclude pupils who think laterally to find solutions.

q) Have an increasing inclusion ethos in the school development plan. The school should examine every aspect of its activity for barriers to inclusion, identify temporary and longer term solutions, describe how these will be achieved, who will be responsible, how they will be funded, how their impact of student achievement will be measured, and incorporate these into the school development planning process.

r) Include outside specialist support. Plan the work of speech, physio- and occupational therapists in a coordinated way that best supports pupils'/students' curriculum needs and reduces disruption to their learning and social needs.

s) Policy on administering medication and personal assistance. Devise a policy on administering routine medication that is easy for pupils/students to use and develop systems that maintain their dignity on personal hygiene issues. Have a system for handling medical emergencies that is easy for everyone to use. Give training to the whole staff on these techniques and then ask who does not want to do it. New TAs (Teaching Assistants) should have it in their contract.

t) Maintain equipment. Ensure that specialist equipment is properly maintained, stored and replaced when necessary. Mobility aids, for example, wheelchairs and walking frames, should be regularly checked and staff trained in their proper use.

u) Increase the employment of disabled staff. The Single Equality Act applies to employment in all schools including disabled staff. Revise the equal opportunity employment policy to increase the employment of disabled teaching and non-teaching staff. There is Access to Work money available for disabled employees from DWP Job Centre Plus. All children need disabled adult role models.

v) Disability equality training and ongoing INSET for staff and governors. Organise a programme of in-service training for teachers, support staff and governors to help them move towards inclusion and disability equality. Ensure all staff are involved in and understand the process of inclusion.

w) Governing body representation. Appoint a governor to have a brief for special educational needs/disability equality, with the whole governing body involved in developing inclusion policy. Try to recruit disabled governors.

x) Consultation with and involvement of parents/carers. Ensure there are effective arrangements for involving parents/carers in all parts of their child's school life, including any decisions that have to be made. These arrangements should involve counselling and support in helping a child towards independence. With their permission, maintain information about parents/carers who are themselves disabled, so that their access and other needs can be met.

y) When planning lessons start with what you want all members of the class to learn. Then examine different styles of learning and access needs and type of grouping. Then provide the support and individual adjustments. Finally, assess what your students have learned (Bunch 2002). Remember the class teacher is legally responsible for the learning of all the students on their register. This cannot be delegated to TAs. They can be very useful but they must work with you as a teacher.

Moving towards inclusion

In many schools the largest barriers to including pupils/students with needs that have not previously been catered for at the school are the fears and attitudes of the staff. These can best be addressed by putting disablement into an equal opportunities framework and by having whole staff disability equality sessions that should be led by disabled disability equality trainers (World of Inclusion offers training – see References). This should be followed by an audit of the barriers in the school, the development of an action plan to minimise the barriers and incorporation of the plan into the school's SEN policy (CSIE 1996; Booth and Ainscow 2002).

Sometimes particular information about children's impairments is required and this can be most usefully obtained from the children themselves or their parents. They are experts on their impairments.

Sometimes medically based professionals such as occupational therapists, physiotherapists and speech therapists can be useful in providing certain procedures or specialist equipment and practices. But it should always be remembered that the child is at school to learn alongside his or her peers and wherever possible this support should be given in class and in the least disruptive way. Often these other adults can benefit groups of children in the class.

There will often be teaching assistants in the class, usually to support particular children. The more they can be involved in joint planning, the more able they are to make a positive contribution to the learning and teaching in the class, not just for their particular pupil. The disabled pupil also benefits by not being velcroed to the TA and having their learning planned by a qualified teacher. The class or subject teacher has to take a lead in coordinating the activities of all of these adults and making their activities part of the educational activity in the class. The SENCO (special educational needs coordinator) can play a vital role in developing such working partnerships.

For inclusion to work best requires a child-centred pedagogy in well structured mixed-ability classrooms. There are many pressures from Ofsted, the government and the league tables to set and stream. But these are moves that undermine an inclusive ethos and can often replicate segregative practices within one institution, leading in the longer term to a drop in overall standards. This is illustrated by the increasing gap in attainment between the top achieving 75 per cent and the bottom quartile that has developed in England in the last 10 years. A mixture of teaching styles can meet these competing pressures: whole class teaching with peer tutoring; collaborative groups; individual or paired work; and joint teaching with another class. The more flexible the teaching style, the more likely to include a wider variety of pupil/student needs.

Many teachers say they are in principle in favour of inclusion, but it requires a massive increase in resources to be possible. It must be remembered that one-seventh of all education budgets is spent on special educational needs. There is a need for increased capital investment in the school building stock to make it accessible, and, thanks to the Within Reach Campaign organised by SCOPE and the NUT, this happened from 1995 to 2010. The reduction in capital spending, loss of Building Schools for the Future and the deregulation of premises for Free Schools mean we will still not have any end date to when all schools will meet physical access standards in England. Another major problem is that a disproportionate amount of SEN spending is in the wrong place – some 1,200 special schools for 90,000 children. Co-location and school federations with mainstream schools in a planned way may enhance access and inclusion. The important point here is that LAs should agree to ring-fence all resources and posts to special educational needs as they transfer them to the mainstream. LAs must also set up adequate monitoring and advisory teacher posts to ensure that the resources put into mainstream schools including academies and foundation schools are being used to further inclusion and meet the needs of children with SEN.

The London Borough of Newham (Jordan and Goodey 1996) provides a useful indicator of how such moves towards inclusion can occur in a poor, multicultural, inner-city area. In 1984 a group of parents of disabled children ran for and were elected on to the council with the express wish of seeing the ending of segregated special education. They achieved their aim in a council policy that recognised the rights of children, whatever their needs, to learn together. The borough's latest policy has a goal of making it possible 'for every child, whatever special educational needs you may have, to attend their neighbourhood school'. Between 1984 and 1998 the number of special schools in the borough was reduced from eight to one and the number of children segregated in special education dropped from 913 to 206. Parents/carers are becoming increasingly confident in the ability of their neighbourhood school to meet diverse needs and teachers have signed an agreement on inclusive education.

This was achieved in an educational and political climate that was hostile to this process. Resourced schools were set up to meet certain needs in mainstream schools' response to parental/carer concerns. These are now planned to be phased out as Newham moves to inclusive neighbourhood schools. The process from the start envisaged radically changing mainstream schools rather than fitting children with SEN into the existing system. An independent report commented that having to cater for children with serious learning difficulties helped schools make better provision for all pupils (Rouse and Florian 1996). This was borne out between 1997 and 2003. Newham schools had the biggest improvement nationally in the GCSE results of all students in grades A–G. Many children labelled as having severe learning difficulties are now passing exams. In addition, the numbers of exclusions have been falling while they have been rising in most other parts of the country. The LEA has now appointed four monitoring officers proactively to address this process of developing inclusion from integration.

It will help to understand the inclusion process to give a thumbnail sketch of two inclusive schools.

The first is one of 17 resourced mainstream schools in Newham. It is a purpose-built inclusive school with funding for 36 statemented children with severe and profound learning difficulties. In addition, there are six other statemented children. Free meals are provided for 59.6 per cent of the children and the school has a multicultural intake. There are four wings: Nursery and Reception, with 120 pupils; Years 1 and 2, with 120; Years 3 and 4, with 120; and Years 5 and 6, with 96 pupils. The additional teaching staff are organised in teams with the class teachers to give six teachers in each wing. In Key Stage 1 there are also six support staff who work as part of the team. The children choose when and what they will do each day, though they must do reading, writing and maths. They keep their own diaries and these are used as the IEP (individual education plan) for statemented children. In each wing there is a practical room, a reading room, a writing room, a finding-out room for science, geography and history, and a quiet room. There are no breaks but all children do a PE activity every day, including various sports and physiotherapy. The lunchtime is a continuous sitting and there are many clubs then. The children all seem engaged in learning and are very pleasant to each other, while the support staff are deployed across the teams to meet particular needs. All staff 'change' children and administer medicines if parental permission is given. Each team has a team leader. In the wings one teacher is responsible for one part of the curriculum for the week for all 120 children. In Years 5 and 6, this is for half a term. The additional resourcing allows for shaping teams to meet the needs of all the children. The school has eight extra teachers and 14 extra support staff, giving a staff of 50. There is now an excellent account of school change with respect to teaching and learning for inclusion written by staff and pupils at the school (Alderson 1999). Unfortunately a change of head teacher in 2010 has put these gains into reverse. Inclusive practice is still very fragile and needs strong imbedding into the whole school. Much still needs to be done to develop an inclusive pedagogy to ensure that all children make educational progress within an inclusive environment.

The second school is a comprehensive high school with 1,100 Year 8 to Year 11 pupils, with 10 forms of entry. It is an additionally resourced mainstream school for 36 physically disabled students. They have a head of learning development, 8.4 full-time teachers, one part-time (two days a week) teacher, eight learning assistants and a clerical assistant. There is a learning development room where staff from the department work and it is open to any student to come to ask for help at lunchtime or after school. Next door is a physio/resource/changing/toilet/shower suite. In addition to the 36 students for the resourced provision, the learning development department leads on the identified learning needs of the 247 students on the special needs register. The building has been adapted so that all rooms are accessible. The school has developed collaborative/partnership teaching in which departments make bids to work with teachers from the learning development department for a term or a year. The purpose of this is to develop a shared understanding of all the arrangements and practice involved in working together, joint planning and evaluation. Time is essential for this process. This is achieved by timetabling learning development teachers and subject teachers to have non-contact periods at the same time, and these are ring-fenced so they are never asked to cover. The collaboration includes shared aims, the joint preparation and presentation of resources and shared responsibility for group discipline, marking and report writing. I visited a science, music and art class and saw the inclusive practice in process. Having disabled students in the class seemed natural to all the students. The teaching staff all seemed happy with the arrangements and talked of their benefit to everyone and how the department's flexibility gave them all the support they needed.

Thomas *et al.* (1998) have analysed the Somerset Inclusion Project, which drew its inspiration from a special school in Canada (Shaw 1990). The Somerset Project centred on the Princess Margaret School for Physically Disabled Pupils. In 1992 it was a day and boarding special school. However, on closing in 1997, it had managed to include the vast majority of its pupils successfully in mainstream schools. Ninety staff were retrained and relocated to support the children in the mainstream. The study gives many insights into the management of change, not least because one of its authors, Dave Walker, was the head teacher of Princess Margaret and effectively oversaw a process that was to leave him without a job.

In conclusion the authors state that:

> with vision and careful planning special schools can successfully change their work in such a way to enable their mainstream partners to include children even with serious disabilities. One of our clearest findings has been that while many mainstream staff were highly sceptical about the inclusion

project before it started, they had changed their views entirely after several months of seeing it in practice and were fulsome in their support of inclusion.

(Thomas *et al.* 1998, p. 198)

Conclusion

Inclusion is fundamentally a school-based process. Mel Ainscow (1994, 1995, 1998) has argued that inclusion is part of the process of developing school effectiveness. 'Moving' schools, those that are open to change, which are usually non-hierarchical, but with strong leadership, are much more able to develop inclusive practice. 'Stuck' schools, on the other hand, have hierarchical structures, poor leadership and lack of involvement of staff in change, and are much less likely to be able to undergo the restructuring that is necessary to become inclusive. Certainly the variance in inclusive practice between similar schools would support this. Teachers deciding what type of school they want to work in would do well to remember this distinction.

The thinking of the disability movement, the development of the 'social model' and the voice of disabled people who have experienced segregated and integrated education are essential in the development of inclusion. *The Salamanca Statement and Framework for Action on Special Needs Education* (UNESCO 1994) recognises this crucial role: 'encourage and facilitate the participation of parents, communities and organizations of disabled people in the planning and decision making processes concerning the provision for special educational needs.'

Inclusion is a process of school change that benefits not only disabled people but the entire school community. Eventually society will experience a reduction in prejudice and discrimination against disabled people as difference becomes part of everyone's experience and disabled people become part of the community in their own right. Article 24 of the United Nations Convention on the Rights of People with Disabilities makes inclusion a human right (Rieser 2008). In the coming period of school restructuring educationalists will need to maintain a principled stand in whatever type of school they work to ensure that all students are included and accorded equality and their human rights. In reclaiming control over teaching and the curriculum as promised by the Education Act 2011, teachers will need to remember that there are always conflicting pressures, but if we navigate by principles of equality and inclusion we can build strong links with the communities we serve to develop the basis of a progressive, more just and equal education system.

References

Ainscow, M. (1994) *Special Needs in the Classroom: A Teacher Education Guide*, London: Jessica Kingsley.
Ainscow, M. (1995) 'Education for All: Making it Happen', *Support for Learning*, 10 (4), pp. 147–57.

Ainscow, M. (1998) 'Reaching out to all Learners: Opportunities and Possibilities', keynote presentation at North of England Education Conference, Bradford.

Alderson, P. (1999) *Learning and Inclusion: The Cleeves School Experience*, London: David Fulton.

Audit Commission (2002) 'Special Educational Needs: A Mainstream Issue', London: Audit Commission LAR2894 www.audit commission.gov.uk.

Barnes, C. (1991) *Disabled People in Britain and Discrimination*, London: Hurst.

Benn, C. and Chitty, C. (1997) *Thirty Years on: Is Comprehensive Education Alive and Well or Struggling to Survive*, London: Penguin.

Booth, T. and Ainscow, M. (1998) *From Them to Us: An International Study on Inclusive Education*, London: Routledge.

Booth, T. and Ainscow, M. (2002) *Index for Inclusion: Developing Learning and Participation in Schools*, Bristol: Centre for Studies on Inclusion.

Booth, T. and Ainscow, M. (2004) *Index for Inclusion: Developing Learning, Participation and Play in Early Years and Childcare*, Bristol: CSIE, www.inclusion.org.uk.

Booth, T., Swann, W., Masterton, M. and Potts, P. (1992) 'Diversity in Education' and 'Curricular for Diversity in Education', in *Learning for All*, London: Routledge.

Bunch, G. (2002) *The Inclusion How To Book*, Toronto: Inclusion Press.

Centre for Studies of Inclusive Education (CSIE) (1996) *Developing an Inclusive Policy for Your School*, Bristol: CSIE.

Cole, T. (1989) *Apart or a Part?: Integration and the Growth of British Special Education*, Milton Keynes: Open University Press.

Conservative Manifesto (2010) London, http://media.conservative.s3.amazonaws.com/manifesto (accessed 14 July 2011).

DfEE (1997) *Excellence for all Children: Meeting Special Educational Needs*, London: HMSO.

DfEE (1998) *An Action Programme for Special Educational Needs*, London: HMSO.

DfES (2003) *The Report of the Special Schools Working Party*, London: HMSO.

DfES (2004a) *Removing Barriers to Achievement: The Government's Strategy for SEN*, DfES /0117/2004, London: HMSO.

DfES (2004b) *Statistics of Education: Schools in England*, London: HMSO.

Dyson, A., Farrell, P., Hutcheson, G. and Polat, F., (2004) *Inclusion and Pupil Achievement*, London: DfES RR578.

Equality and Human Rights Commission (2010) Triennial Review: How Fair is Britain?, London: EHRC.

Facchini, M. (1985) 'An Historical Reconstruction of Events Leading to the Congress of Milan in 1880', in W.C. Stokoe and V. Volterra (eds) *SLR '83: Proceedings of the Third International Symposium on Sign Language Research*, Rome, 22–26 June 1983, Rome/SiverSpring: CNR/Linstok Press, pp. 356–62.

Hegarty, S. and Pocklington, K. (1981) *Educating Pupils with Special Needs in Ordinary Schools*, Windsor: NFER.

Hirst, A. and Baldwin, S. (1994) *Unequal Opportunities Growing up Disabled*, London: HMSO.

Joint Human Rights Committee (2009) 'First Report The UN Convention on the Rights of Persons with Disabilities' London, http://www.publications.parliament.uk/pa/jt200809/jtselect/jtrights/9/0907.htm#a8

Jordan, L. and Goodey, C. (1996) *Human Rights and School Change: The Newham Story*, Bristol: CSIE.

Ladd, P. (2003) *Understanding Deaf Culture: In Search of Deafhood*, Bristol: Multilingual Matters.

Mason, M. (1998) *Forced Apart: The Case for Ending Compulsory Segregation in Education*, London: Alliance for Inclusive Education.

Mason, M. and Rieser, R. (1994) *Altogether Better*, London: Comic Relief.

Murray, P. and Penman, J. (1996) *Let Our Children Be: A Collective of Stories*, Sheffield: Parents with Attitude.

Norwich, B. (1997) *A Trend towards Inclusion: Statistics on Special School Placement and Pupils with Statements in Ordinary Schools England 1992–96*, Bristol: CSIE.

Ofsted (2004) *Special Educational Needs and Disability: Towards Inclusive Schools*, London: Ofsted.

Oliver, M. (1992) 'Talk given to Greater London Association of Disabled People', Integration Week, May 1992, Bristol: CSIE.

Rieser, R. (2004) *All Equal All Different: A Unique Resource to Develop Disability Equality in Early Years and Key Stage 1*, London: Disability Equality in Education, www.diseed.org.uk.

Rieser, R. (2008)*Implementing Inclusive Education: A Commonwealth Guide to Implementing Article 24 of the UN Convention on the Rights of People with Disabilities*, London: Commonwealth Secretariat.

Rieser, R. and Mason, M. (1990/1992) *Disability Equality in the Classroom: A Human Rights Issue*, London: Disability Equality in Education.

Rouse, M. and Florian, L. (1996) 'Effective Inclusive Schools: A Study in Two Countries', *Cambridge Journal of Education*, 26 (1), pp. 71–80.

Sebba, J. with Sachdev, D. (1997) *What Works in Inclusive Education?*, Essex: Barnardos.

Shaw, L. (1990) *Each Belongs: Integrated Education in Canada*, Bristol: CSIE.

Thomas, G. (1996) *Exam Performance in Special Schools*, Bristol: CSIE.

Thomas, G., Walker, D. and Webb, J. (1998) *The Making of the Inclusive School*, London: Routledge.

UNCRPD (2006) 'United Nations Convention on the Rights of People with Disabilities' New York, www.un.org/disabilities/.

UNESCO (1994) *The Salamanca Statement and Framework for Action on Special Needs Education*, Paris: UNESCO.

Selection of recommended inclusive children's books and resources can be found at http://www.worldofinclusion.com/res/qca/Resources.doc.

Many other useful resources to develop disability equality and develop inclusive education for staff and students can be found at http://www.worldofinclusion.com/resources.htm.

Chapter 9

Social class, Marxism and twenty-first-century socialism

Mike Cole

Introduction

It is possible, though difficult, to imagine a capitalist world rid of the inequalities of gender, 'race', sexuality and disability analysed in Chapters 1 to 8 of this volume. However, without social class exploitation, capitalism could not exist. This is because it is underpinned by and depends for its very existence on the exploitation of one class, the working class, by another, the capitalist class. In this chapter, I begin by addressing the unique strengths of Marxism, as both an analytical framework, and as a harbinger of a non-exploitative future world. In so doing, I look briefly at some historical challenges to it. I then outline two central tenets of scientific socialism (how Marx's co-writer Friedrich Engels described Marxism). The first is Marx's Labour Theory of Value, which provides an explanation of the pivotal position of social class as the basis of surplus value and profit under capitalism. The second is the materialist concept of history, which stresses how deeply the processes of production affect our lives. I then raise some common objections to Marxism and respond to them, concluding with a brief discussion of twenty-first-century socialist developments in the Bolivarian Republic of Venezuela.

The strengths of Marxism

The major strengths of Marxism are that it provides both a comprehensive and coherent analysis and explanation of the fundamental exploitative nature of capitalist society *and* a vision for the future. Moreover, this vision of the future is not static. Marxism is not, as some would have it, a moribund set of beliefs and practice. On the contrary, as Jean-Paul Sartre (1960) noted, Marxism is a 'living philosophy'. To Sartre's observation, Crystal Bartolovich (2002, p. 20) has added that Marxism is not 'simply a discourse nor a body of (academic) knowledge' but a living project. Challenges to Marxism perhaps began with the sociologist Max Weber. Although Albert Salomon's famous observation that Weber was involved in a debate 'with the ghost of Marx' (Salomon, 1935) may be somewhat overstated, ever since Weber (1915 [1947]) made a number of criticisms of Marx and Marxism, the intellectual struggle against Marxist ideas has been at the forefront of academic writing. Weber suggested that social class might not be solely related to the mode of production; that political power does not necessarily derive from economic power; and that status as well as class might form the basis of the formation of social groups. Subsequent attempts to challenge Marxist ideas have ranged from the post-structuralist writings of Michel Foucault who believed that power is diffuse rather than related to the means of production, and of Jacques Derrida who stressed the need for the deconstruction of all dominant discourses; through the postmodernism of Jean-François Lyotard who was incredulous of all grand narratives, of Jean Baudrillard who argued that binary oppositions (such as the ruling and working classes) had collapsed; to the scholarly endeavours of Critical Race Theorists. Elsewhere (Cole, 2008, 2009), I have defended Marxism against these various challenges, but have also acknowledged some of the insights of these diverse theories. None, however, have succeeded in surpassing Marx and Engels' exposition of scientific socialism. Crucially none provide a viable *vision* of a future free of exploitation and oppression.

From utopian socialism to scientific socialism

The common ownership, cooperation and collective activity that socialism entails predate contemporary socialism. In fact, in very early history, most, if not all, societies held common property in the soil and were grouped according to kindred. Modern socialism, however, was born in the nineteenth century, in Britain and France. The word was first used publicly in English in 1827 in connection with the movement associated with Robert Owen; and in French, in 1835, with respect to the supporters of Henri de Saint-Simon (Berki, 1975, p. 12). The other prominent French socialist theoretician was Charles Fourier.[1] For Engels (1892 [1977], pp. 398–404), Saint-Simon's major contribution to Marxism was his recognition of class struggle; Fourier's was dialectical thinking;[2] and Owen's bequest was communism[3] and his dedication to workers' welfare. What these utopian socialists all had in common was that, unlike Marxists who advocate the revolutionary emancipation of the working class in order to change society, the utopian socialists were concerned with liberating all humanity without such revolutionary changes. As Marx and Engels (1847 [1977], p. 60) point out, Saint-Simon, Fourier and Owen all recognised the class antagonisms in existing societies, but viewed the working class as 'a class without any historical initiative'. This is primarily because of the 'undeveloped state' of the proletariat[4] at the time (ibid.). For the utopian socialists, change was to come about by 'peaceful means,' by 'small experiments' and by 'force of example' (ibid.). Marx and Engels, on the other hand, 'openly declare that their ends can be attained only by the forcible overthrow of all existing social conditions' (ibid., p. 63).[5]

Although Marx denounced utopian socialism, he never actually referred to his own ideas as 'scientific socialism'. It was, in fact, Engels (1892 [1977], p. 404) who, believing utopian socialism to be 'a mish-mash' of 'absolute truth, reason, and justice' based on 'subjective understandings' associated with various schools of utopian socialist thought, argued that 'to make a science of socialism, it had first to be placed upon a real basis' (ibid., p. 405: his and Marx's conception of 'utopia' accords with its original meaning, 'a place that does not exist'). Engels (ibid., p. 428) explains the role of scientific socialists in capitalist society, when referring to the proletarian revolution, which:

> frees the means of production from the character of capital they have thus far borne, and gives their socialised character complete freedom to work itself out . . . To thoroughly comprehend the historical conditions and thus the very nature of this act, to impart to the now oppressed proletarian class a full knowledge of the conditions and of the meaning of the momentous act it is called upon to accomplish . . . is the task of the theoretical expression of the proletarian movement, scientific socialism.

The 'real basis' of Marxism is the *materialist conception of history* and the *labour theory of value* (LTV) (the basis of *surplus value*). As Engels (1877 [1962], p. 43) argues:

> [t]hese two great discoveries, the materialist conception of history and the revelation of the secret of capitalistic production through surplus value, we owe to Marx. With these discoveries socialism became a science.

The materialist conception of history

As Engels explains, the materialist conception of history 'starts from the proposition that the production of the means to support human life and, next to production, the exchange of things produced, is the basis of all social structure' (Engels, 1892 [1977], p. 411). The materialist conception of history is most clearly explained by Marx (1859) [1977] in the 'Preface' to *A Contribution to the Critique of Political Economy*. Marx argues that the way we think is fundamentally related to forces of production. As he puts it, in sexist language characteristic of his time:

> My inquiry led me to the conclusion that neither legal relations nor political forms could be comprehended whether by themselves or on the basis of a so called general development of the human mind, but that on the contrary they originate in the material conditions of life . . . In the social production of their existence, men inevitably enter into definite relations, which are independent of their will, namely relations of production appropriate to a given stage in the development of their material forces of production. The totality of these relations of production constitutes the economic structure of society, the real foundation, on which arises a legal

and political superstructure and to which correspond definite forms of social consciousness. The mode of production of material life conditions the general process of social, political and intellectual life. It is not the consciousness of men that determines their existence, but their social existence that determines their consciousness.

Marx argued that societies progress through various stages. Moreover, all past history, with the exception of its most early stage (primitive communism—the original hunter-gatherer society of humanity) is, according to Marx and Engels, the history of class struggles. These warring classes are always the products of the respective modes of production, of the *economic* conditions of their time. Thus slaves were in class struggle with their owners in the historical epoch of ancient slavery; feudal serfs with their lords in times of feudalism; and in the era of capitalism, workers are engaged in a class struggle with capitalists.

Like ancient slavery and feudalism, capitalism is viewed merely as a *stage* in human development. Marxists see such stages as containing a number of *contradictions*, which resolve themselves dialectically. Thus when these contradictions become too great, a given stage gives way to another. For example, just as the privileges that feudal lords held and the hereditary basis of subordinating serf to lord in the feudal societies contradicted the need for 'free' labour power in emerging capitalism ('free' in the sense that workers were not needed to be indentured to the capitalists; they were, of course, forced to sell their labour power in order to survive), present-day capitalism contains contradictions that Marxists believe, *given the right circumstances*, can eventually lead to its demise, and be replaced by socialism.

It is worth stressing here that socialism, as understood by Marx and Engels, is profoundly and genuinely democratic. Under socialism, wealth is shared equally, workers own and control the means of production distribution and exchange, and make decisions *democratically*. Democracy entails decisions being taken by workers, not just in the political realm, but in the schools, factories, shops, offices and everywhere else they work, workplaces that would be collectively owned by these workers. Socialism, thus understood, is far removed from many dictatorial regimes that have described themselves as 'socialist,' even though some, such as the Soviet Union, began with democratically socialist ideals (see the Appendix to this chapter for a fuller discussion of socialism).

The labour theory of value

Whereas sociological definitions of social class tend to focus on factors such as income, occupation, status, life chances and so on, a Marxist interpretation relates class to the mode of production and to exploitations. This is encapsulated in the labour theory of value. As Tom Hickey (2006) has explained, capitalism has an inbuilt tendency to generate conflict, and is thus *permanently* vulnerable to challenge from the working class. As he puts it:

The objective interests of the bourgeoisie and the proletariat are incompatible, and therefore generate not a tendency to permanent hostility and open warfare but a permanent tendency toward them. The system is thus prone to economic class conflict, and, given the cyclical instability of its economy, subject to periodic political and economic crises. It is at these moments that the possibility exists for social revolution.

(Ibid., p. 192)

An understanding of the source of this incompatibility and permanent tendency towards hostility can be facilitated by Marx's labour theory of value (LTV). The LTV explains most concisely why capitalism is objectively a system of exploitation, whether the exploited realise it or not, or indeed, whether they believe it to be an issue of importance for them or not. The LTV also provides a *solution* to this exploitation. It thus provides *dialectical* praxis—the authentic union of theory and practice.

According to the LTV, the interests of capitalists and workers are diametrically opposed, since a benefit to the former (profits) is a cost to the latter (Hickey, 2002, p. 168). Marx argued that workers' labour is embodied in the goods that they produce. The finished products are appropriated (taken away) by the capitalists and eventually sold at a profit. However, the worker is paid only a fraction of the value s/he creates in labour; the wage does not represent the *total* value s/he creates. We *appear* to be paid for every single second we work. However, underneath this appearance, this fetishism, the working day (like under serfdom) is split in two: into socially necessary labour (and the wage represents this); and surplus labour, labour that is not reflected in the wage.

Greatly oversimplifying matters, let us assume that a capitalist employs a worker to make a table. Let us say that the value of the basic materials is £100, and that after these basic materials have had labour embodied in them (i.e. have become a table), that table has a value of £500. Let us further assume that in the time it takes to make the table, £20 of overheads are used up. What happens to the £400 surplus value that the worker has created? The worker is paid, say, £100, and the remaining £300 is appropriated, taken away, by the capitalist. After overheads are paid, the capitalist still has £280 *surplus* that s/he can reinvest to create more surplus.

To continue the example, with this £280 surplus, the capitalist can buy £200 worth of basic materials, and employ two workers, and after these basic materials have had labour embodied in them (e.g. have become two tables), those tables have a value of £1,000. Assuming overheads increase to £30, and two workers are each paid £100, the capitalist is now left with £770 surplus that can be thrown back into production to create yet more surplus value, and so on and so on. If the capitalist continues to employ workers, say, seven, the surplus would be over £6,000. It is thus easy to see how surplus value multiplies and how capitalists' surplus (which is converted into profit) is, in truth, nothing more than accumulated surplus value, really the 'property' of the worker but appropriated from that worker.[6] While the value of the raw materials and of the depreciating machinery is simply passed on to the commodity in production, labour power is a peculiar, indeed unique commodity, in that it creates new value. 'The magical quality of labour-power's . . . value for . . . capital is therefore critical' (Rikowski, 2001, p. 11). 'Labour-power creates more value (profit) in its consumption than it possesses itself, and than it costs' (Marx, 1894 [1966], p. 351). Unlike, for example, the value of a given commodity, which can only be realised in the market as itself, labour creates a new value, a value greater than itself, a value that previously did not exist. It is for this reason that labour power is so important for the capitalist in the quest for capital accumulation.

It is in the interest of the capitalist or capitalists (nowadays, capitalists may, of course, consist of a number of shareholders, for example, rather than outright owners of businesses) to maximise profits, and this entails (in order to create the greatest amount of new value) keeping workers' wages as low as is 'acceptable' or tolerated in any given country or historical period, without provoking effective strikes or other forms of resistance. Therefore the capitalist mode of production is, in essence, a system of exploitation of one class (the working class) by another (the capitalist class).

Whereas class conflict is endemic to, and ineradicable and perpetual within, the capitalist system, it does not always, or even typically, take the form of open conflict or expressed hostility (Hickey, 2002, p. 168). This is, in large part, due to the successes of the state apparatuses and of ruling class hegemonic power. Fortunately for the working class, however, capitalism is prone to cyclical instability and subject to periodic political and economic crises. At these moments, the possibility exists for social revolution. Revolution can only come about when the working class, in addition to being a 'class-in-itself' (an *objective* fact because of the shared exploitation inherent as a result of the LTV) becomes 'a class-for-itself' (Marx, 1885 [1976]). By this, Marx meant a class with a *subjective* awareness of its social class position; that is, a class with 'class consciousness'— including its awareness of its exploitation and its transcendence of 'false consciousness'. As Hickey (2006) explains:

> Crises provide the opportunity for transition from the oppressive and exploitative, competitive and alienating conditions of the order of capital to a realm of human freedom in which humanity as a whole, through a radically democratic structure, engages collectively in satisfying its needs, ordering its priorities, and constructing new needs and aspirations to strive for, and challenges to overcome.

It should again be stressed that while this scenario is *always* a possibility, it should never be seen as a *certainty*.

Common objections to Marxism and a Marxist response[7]

Marxism is contrary to human nature because we are all basically selfish and greedy and competitive

For Marxists, there is no such thing as 'human nature'. Marxists believe that our individual natures are not ahistorical givens, but products of the circumstances into which we are socialised, and of the society or societies in which we live or have lived (including crucially *the social class position* we occupy therein). While it is true that babies and infants, for example, may act selfishly in order to survive, as human beings grow up they are strongly influenced by the norms and values that are predominant in the society in which they live. Thus in societies that encourage selfishness, greed and competitiveness (Thatcherism is a perfect example) people will tend to act in self-centered ways, whereas in societies that discourage these values and promote communal values (Cuba is a good example) people will tend to act in ways that consider the collective as well as their own selves, the international, as well as the national and local. As noted above, Marx (1845) [1976] argued that '[l]ife is not determined by consciousness, but consciousness by life'. Unlike animals, we have the ability to choose our actions, and change the way we live, and the way we respond to others. Hence, in capitalist society, the working class *is* capable of transcending false consciousness and becoming 'a class for itself' (Marx, 1847 [1995]), as well as 'a class in itself' (Bukharin, 1922 cited in Mandel, 1970 [2008]), that is to say, pursuing interests that can ultimately lead to a socially just society. Socialism does not require as a precondition that we are all altruistic and selfless; rather, as Bowles and Gintis (1976, p. 267) argue, the social and economic conditions of socialism will facilitate the development of such human capacities.

Some people are naturally lazy and won't work

Unlike utopian socialist Henri de Saint-Simon, who believed that we are 'lazy by nature' (Cole, 2008, pp. 15–17), Marxists would argue that laziness, like other aspects of our 'nature', is most likely acquired through socialisation too, but even if it is not, we can still choose to overcome our laziness. In a socialist world, there are sound reasons to work in order to create cooperative wealth. Whereas in capitalist societies, a surplus is extracted from the values workers produce, and hived off by the capitalists to create profits, under socialism everything we create is for the benefit of humankind as a whole, including us as individuals. Thus the only incentive for most workers under capitalism: more wages (an incentive which is totally understandable, and indeed encouraged by Marxists, because it ameliorates workers' lives and lessens the amount of surplus for capitalists) is replaced by a much more worthwhile incentive: the common good.

Why shouldn't those who have worked hard get more benefits in life?

Again this viewpoint is a product of capitalist society, based on selfishness. If everything is shared, as in a socialist world, we all benefit by working hard. No one needs to go short of anything that they need for a good life. In capitalist societies, needs are created by advertisers working for capitalists, and many of these (excessive amounts of clothes, or living accommodation beyond our personal requirements) we do not really *need*. Indeed, excess possessions in a capitalist world where most of the population has nothing or next to nothing is obscene. Moreover, while people are starving and there are food riots breaking out across the world, the fact is, given the world's total resources, there is no world food shortage overall, and there is more than enough food produced to supply everyone with a decent diet (Molyneux, 2008, p. 13). The grotesque nature of capitalism is revealed *par excellence* at the time of writing (summer, 2011), where workers in the UK and the US are being told that they must make massive sacrifices because of the current crisis in capitalism, while at the same time massive war campaigns involving billions of dollars are squandered in imperialism's never-ending 'war on terror'.

Marxism can't work because it always leads to totalitarianism

Marxists have learnt from Stalinism, which was, in many ways, the antithesis of Marxists' notions of democratic socialism. While not in any way condoning Stalinism, part of the reason for its totalitarian nature is that socialism was attempted in one country, whereas Marx, and a number of Marxists at the time (notably Trotsky), believed that, for it to work, socialism must be international. This meant that the Soviet Union, being isolated, concentrated on accumulation rather than consumption. Alone in a sea of capitalist states, the economy was geared to competing economically and militarily with the rest of the world, with workers' rights taking a back seat. I am not claiming that this direction for the Soviet Union was *inevitable* and there are no inherent reasons why these mistakes should be made again. To succeed, socialism needs to be democratic. Indeed, as Jonathan Maunder (2006, p. 13) reminds us, whereas previous exploited classes, such as the peasantry, could rise up, seize lands and divide them up among themselves, workers cannot, for example, divide a factory, hospital or supermarket. Thus if workers do seize control of such institutions, they can only run them collectively. As Maunder (2006, p. 13) concludes: '[t]heir struggles have a democratic logic that can lay the basis for a different way of running society.'

Genuinely *democratic* socialism, where elected leaders are permanently subject to recall democratically by those who have elected them, is the best way to safeguard against totalitarianism (this concept, a central plank of democratic socialism, is in fact enshrined in the 1999 constitution of the Bolivarian Republic of Venezuela in the form of a Recall Referendum. This means that Venezuelan voters have the right to remove their president from office before the expiration of the presidential term). While capitalist political systems are *formally* democratic, representative democracy, for example, in the United States and Britain, amounts in effect to a form of totalitarianism. In these countries, citizens can vote every five years, having in reality a choice (in the sense of who will actually be able to form a government) of two or three main, totally pro-capitalist parties, who then go on to exercise power in the interests of neoliberal global capitalism and imperialism, with little or no regard for the interests of those workers who elected them. There are, of course, some restraints on what they can get away with (minimum wage and European human rights legislation in Britain, for example), and importantly, the balance of class forces and the strength of working-class resistance (e.g. Hill, 2009).

Someone will always want to be 'boss' and there will always be natural 'leaders' and 'followers'

As argued above, Marxists believe in true democracy. If a given individual in socialist society wants to exploit others, s/he will need to be controlled democratically and subject to permanent recall. Under capitalism, if people feel they are 'born to be followers' rather than leaders, this is most like to be due to their social class position in any given society and to their socialisation (see above). Under socialism, there will be more chance for all to take roles of responsibility if they want. Under capitalism, certain people are educated for leadership positions in the society, while others are schooled to be exploited members of the working class (Bowles and Gintis, 1976).

It is impossible to plan centrally in such a hugely diverse and complex world

In a socialist world, local, national and international needs will need to be coordinated fairly and efficiently. Given modern technology, this is easier now than ever before, and will become more and more so as technology continues to develop. Under capitalism, technology is harnessed to the creation of greater and greater surplus value and profit. In a socialist world, technology would be under the control of the people for the benefit of the people as a whole; for universal human need rather than global corporate profit.

Someone has to do the drudge jobs, and how could that be sorted out in a socialist world?

Technology already has the potential to eliminate most of the most boring and/or unpleasant jobs. Some of those that remain could be done on a voluntary rota basis, so that no one would have to do drudge jobs for longer than a very brief period (utopian socialist Charles Fourier had a similar idea—see Cole,

2008, pp. 17–20).Voluntary work under capitalism in the public sector abounds, and there is every reason to assume that such work would flourish much more under socialism.

Socialism means a lower standard of life for all

World socialism will only lower the standard of life for the ruling classes.There will not, for sure, be the massive disparities of wealth apparent in our present capitalist world. There will, of course, be no billionaires and no need for a (parasitic) monarchy. If the wealth of the world is shared, then there will be a good standard of life for all, since all reasonable needs will be met, including enough food (as noted above by Molyneux (2008, p. 13) enough already exists). To paraphrase Marx (1875 [1996]), the principle will be from each according to his or her ability, to each according to his or her needs.

Socialism will be dull, dreary and uniform, and we will all have less choice

This is a popular misconception related to the experiences of life in former Stalinist states such as the USSR, and the former states of Eastern Europe. Life under socialism should be exciting, challenging and globally diverse, as different countries develop socialism to suit their own circumstances, but with a common goal. The intensively creative (world) advertising industry (now in private hands), when under public control could be used for the common good, for example, to increase awareness of the availability of free goods and services (health promotion, universal lifelong education, public transport, advances in medical care and so on). We do not need the excessive branded products common in capitalist societies, and created by different capitalist firms to increase profits.A cursory glance at the website of one well-known supermarket in Britain revealed a total of over 60 different butters/margarines. It is not necessary for Western consumers to have this degree of 'choice' when most of 'the developing world' eats its bread without spreads. Moreover, in many cases, the ingredients in the vast array of products will be very similar, while the huge amount of unnecessary plastic packaging clearly adversely affects the environment (see Cole, 2008, Chapter 7).

A social revolution will necessarily involve violence and death on a massive scale

It is, in fact, capitalism that has created and continues to promote death and violence and terror on a global scale. Inequalities in wealth and quality of life cause death and disease in capitalist countries themselves, and the capitalist West's underdevelopment of most of the rest of the world and the aforementioned massive disparity in wealth and health has dire consequences (Hill and Kumar,

2009; Hill and Rosskam, 2009). In addition, imperialist conquest historically and contemporaneously unleashes death, terror and destruction on a colossal scale. Stalinism, and other atrocities, committed *in the name of,* but not in the spirit of socialism, also shares this guilt, but as argued above, there is no inherent reason why the historical perversities of Stalinism need to be repeated. As far as the violence entailed in future social revolution is concerned, as argued earlier, social revolution is not predicated on a *violent* overthrow of capitalism. As I have argued elsewhere (Cole, 2008, pp. 78–79) socialism is a majoritarian process, not an imposed event that is not dependent on violence. It is, of course, inconceivable that a world social revolution would involve no violence, not least because of the resistance of the dominant capitalist class. However, there are no reasons for violence to be a strategic weapon. Anyone who has ever attended a mass socialist gathering (e.g., the annual *Marxism* event organised by the Socialist Workers Party in Britain (http://www.marxismfestival.org.uk/)) can attest to the fact that violence is not, in any way, an organising tool of the socialist movement. Mass violence is the province of world capitalism.

Moreover, as far as terrorism is concerned, Marxists oppose it unreservedly. Terrorism is reactionary, in that it diverts attention away from the class struggle. It militates against what Leon Trotsky has described as self-organisation and self-education. Trotsky favoured a different resolution to the revenge desired by many who subscribe to terrorism. As he put it:

> The more 'effective' the terrorist acts, the greater their impact, the more they reduce the interest of the masses in self-organisation and self-education . . . To learn to see all the crimes against humanity, all the indignities to which the human body and spirit are subjected, as the twisted outgrowths and expressions of the existing social system, in order to direct all our energies into a collective struggle against this system—that is the direction in which the burning desire for revenge can find its highest moral satisfaction.
>
> (Trotsky, 1909)

The working class won't create the revolution because they are reactionary

It is a fundamental tenet of Marxism that the working class are the agents of social revolution, and that the working class, as noted above, needs to become a 'class for itself' in addition to being a 'class in itself' (Marx, 1847 [1995]). It is unfortunately the case that major parts of the world are a long way off such a scenario at the present conjuncture. It is also the case that successful interpellation and related false consciousness hampers the development of class consciousness and the move towards the overthrow of capitalism. Britain is one example where the ruling class has been particularly successful in interpellating the working class (see Cole (2011) for a discussion).

To take just one example, in the UK general election of 2010, the vote for socialist parties was totally insignificant, and if interpellation was resisted, it was resisted more by a minority who voted for the very right-wing UK Independence Party (UKIP) and the fascist British National Party (BNP). The 2010 UK election resulted in a hung parliament; that is, no political party with an overall majority. The three unequivocally pro-capitalist parties fared as follows: a little over 36 per cent of voters voted for the Conservatives, 29 per cent for New Labour, just over 23 per cent for the Liberal Democrats. About 12 per cent voted for others (this last figure includes nearly 2 per cent for the BNP and over 3 per cent for UKIP, the two most popular parties after the three main parties).

Elsewhere, however, there are examples of burgeoning class consciousness, witnessed, for example, by developments across South America, notably the Bolivarian Republic of Venezuela (see later in this chapter) and in Bolivia. It is to be hoped that, as neoliberal global imperial capitalism continues to reveal and expose its essential ruthlessness and contempt for those who make its profits, class consciousness will increase and the working class will one day be in a position to overthrow (world) capitalism and to replace it with (world) democratic socialism.

Perhaps it should be pointed out here that Marxists do not idolise or deify the working class; it is rather that class's structural location in capitalist societies that interests Marxists. Once the working class has become 'a class in itself' it becomes the agent for change. Moreover, the very act of social revolution and the creation of socialism mean the end of the very existence of the working class as a social class. As Marx and Engels (1845) [1975] put it:

> When socialist writers ascribe this world-historic role to the proletariat, it is not at all . . . because they regard the proletarians as *gods*. Rather the contrary . . . [The proletariat] cannot emancipate itself without abolishing the conditions of its own life. It cannot abolish the conditions of its own life without abolishing all the inhuman conditions of society today which are summed up in its own situation.

Marxists just wait for the revolution rather than address the issues of the here and now

This is manifestly not the case. Marxists fight constantly for change and reform that benefit the working class in the short run under capitalism (for example, Marxists are centrally involved with work in trade unions agitating for better wages) with a vision of socialist transformation in the longer term (increasing class consciousness in the unions is part of this process). As Marx and Engels (1847 [1977], p. 62) put it, referring to members of communist parties:

> The Communists fight for the attainment of the immediate aims, for the enforcement of the momentary interests of the working class; but in the

movement of the present, they also represent and take care of the future of the movement.

The choice is not between life in the neoliberal global capitalist world or a return to Stalinism, but between the anarchic chaos of capitalism and genuine worldwide democratic socialism. There is a burgeoning recognition that this is the case from the mass global movements against globalisation and in the growing anti-neoliberal politics throughout Latin America, from the Bolivarian Republic of Venezuela to Bolivia, from Argentina to Brazil.

Marxism is a nice idea, but it will never happen (for some of the reasons headlined above)

Bringing Marxism to the forefront is not an easy task. Capitalism is self-evidently a resilient and very adaptable world force and interpellation has been very successful. However, as noted above, Marx argued that society has gone through a number of different stages in its history: primitive communism; slavery; feudalism, capitalism. It is highly likely that in each era, a different way of living was considered 'impossible' by most of those living in that era. However, each era gave birth, in a dialectical process, to another. Thus, though it may be extremely difficult to imagine a world based on socialist principles, such a world *is* possible if that is what the majority of the world's citizens come to desire and have the will to create.

Marxists need to address the obstacles full on. As Callinicos (2000, p. 122) has argued, we must break through the 'bizarre ideological mechanism, [in which] *every* conceivable alternative to the market has been discredited by the collapse of Stalinism' whereby the fetishisation of life makes capitalism seem natural and therefore unalterable and where the market mechanism 'has been hypo-statized into a natural force unresponsive to human wishes' (p. 125). Capital presents itself 'determining the future as surely as the laws of nature make tides rise to lift boats' (McMurtry, 2000, p. 2), 'as if it has now replaced the natural environment. It announces itself through its business leaders and politicians as coterminous with freedom, and indispensable to democracy such that any attack on capitalism as exploitative or hypocritical becomes an attack on world freedom and democracy itself' (McLaren, 2000, p. 32). However, the biggest impediment to social revolution is not capital's resistance, but its success in heralding the continuation of capitalism as being the only option. As Callinicos puts it, despite the inevitable intense resistance from capital, the 'greatest obstacle to change is not . . . the revolt it would evoke from the privileged, but the belief that it is impossible' (2000, p. 128). Given the hegemony of world capitalism, whose very *leitmotif* is to stifle and redirect class consciousness, and given the aforementioned reactionary nature of certain sections of the working class, restoring this consciousness is a tortuous, but not impossible, task. Callinicos again:

Challenging this climate requires courage, imagination and willpower inspired by the injustice that surrounds us. Beneath the surface of our supposedly contented societies, these qualities are present in abundance. Once mobilized, they can turn the world upside down.

(2000, p. 129)

As we hurtle into the twenty-first century, we have some important decisions to make. Whatever the twenty-first century has to offer, the choices will need to be debated. The Hillcole Group expressed our educational choices as follows:

Each person and group should experience education as contributing to their own self-advancement, but at the same time our education should ensure that at least part of everyone's life activity is also designed to assist in securing the future of the planet we inherit—set in the context of a sustainable and equitable society. Democracy is not possible unless there is a free debate about all the alternatives for running our social and economic system . . . All societies [are] struggling with the same issues in the 21st century. We can prepare by being better armed with war machinery or more competitive international monopolies . . . Or we can wipe out poverty . . . altogether. We can decide to approach the future by consciously putting our investment into a massive drive to encourage participation from everyone at every stage in life through training and education that will increase productive, social, cultural and environmental development in ways we have not yet begun to contemplate.

(Hillcole, 1997, pp. 94–95)

While the open-endedness of the phrase, 'in ways we have not yet begun to contemplate' will appeal to poststructuralists and postmodernists, for whom the future is an open book, this is most definitely not the political position of the Hillcole Group. Whereas, for poststructuralists and postmodernists, all we have is endless deconstruction without having *strategies* for change (see Cole, 2008, Chapter 5), for Marxists, the phrase is tied firmly to an open but *socialist* agenda. For Critical Race Theorists, there are nonspecific notions of 'ending oppression'. These suggestions are no doubt well intentioned, but they are idealistic in the current historical conjuncture. Like the views of the utopian socialists, the vagaries of CRT do not engage with the nature of the contradictions within capitalism, the dialectic, and with the working-class consciousness needed for revolutionary change. An equitable, fair and just world can be foreseen neither through postmodernism/post-structuralism, nor through the more enlightened and progressive ideas of CRT. For Marxists, as global neoliberal capitalism and imperial hegemony tightens its grip on all our lives, the choice, to paraphrase Rosa Luxemburg (1916), is quite simple: that choice is between barbarism— 'the unthinkable'—or democratic socialism.

Ok, show me where Marxism works in practice

Even if all of the above questions are answered convincingly, Marxists are inevitably asked, 'OK, show me where Marxism works in practice?' I have lost count of the number of times I have been asked that question. Since I first visited Cuba many years ago, and up to my trip to Venezuela where I worked briefly for the Bolivarian University of Venezuela in 2006, I tended to reply on the lines of, 'well, I know it's not perfect, but the case of Cuba is in many respects a good example'. However, I am now able to commend developments in Venezuela with far fewer reservations. Elsewhere (Cole, 2011, Chapter 5) I have discussed at length twenty-first-century socialism in Venezuela. Here I will present a summary.

The Bolivarian Revolution

In Venezuela, neoliberal capitalism is not seen as 'inevitable', nor indeed is capitalism itself. In 2010, Chávez described knowledge and education as the first of three forms of power in the revolutionary process, the others being political power and economic power:

> When we talk about power, what are we talking about . . . The first power that we all have is knowledge. So we've made efforts first in education, against illiteracy, for the development of thinking, studying, analysis. In a way, that has never happened before. Today, Venezuela is a giant school, it's all a school. From children of one year old until old age, all of us are studying and learning. And then political power, the capacity to make decisions, the community councils, communes, the people's power, the popular assemblies. And then there is the economic power. Transferring economic power to the people, the wealth of the people distributed throughout the nation. I believe that is the principal force that precisely guarantees that the Bolivarian revolution continues to be peaceful.
>
> (Cited in Sheehan, 2010)

Earlier in 2010, Chávez asserted that, as well as a Christian, he was also a Marxist (Chávez, 2010), describing Marxism as 'the most advanced proposal toward the world that Christ came to announce more than 2,000 years ago' (Suggett, 2010).[8]

While radical social democratic measures in Venezuela (the various missions providing health and education, social justice, social welfare, anti-poverty programmes that have massively reduced poverty and greatly increased educational opportunities; see Cole, 2011, Chapter 5) are exemplary, the innovations are, of course, in themselves classic social democracy rather than socialism, somewhat akin to the policies and practice of the post-war Labour governments in the UK. What makes Venezuela unique, however, is that whereas these British

Labour governments were posing social democracy as an *alternative* to socialism, and, indeed, attempting to fight off attempts by revolutionary workers to move towards socialism, Chávez is presenting reforms as a *prelude* to socialism. These reforms are seen both by sections of the Chávez government and by large sections of the Venezuelan working class[9] as a step on the road to true socialist revolution. At the same time, Chávez is promoting genuine participatory democracy, involving direct decision making by the workers, that is laying the foundations for the socialist project. Thus for Chávez, '[t]he hurricane of revolution has begun, and it will never again be calmed' (cited in Contreras Baspineiro, 2003). Elsewhere, Chávez asserted: 'I am convinced, and I think that this conviction will be for the rest of my life, that the path to a new, better and possible world, is not capitalism, the path is socialism, that is the path: socialism, socialism' (Lee, 2005).

As Victor (2009) argues, one of the biggest achievements of the Bolivarian Revolution is existential:

> a new sense of identity, a new sense of belonging . . . The great majority of Venezuelans feel they are now in control of their own government and destiny—despite the continuous attacks from the oligarchy and its satellites. Now the Chávistas frame all the political discourse and its name is Socialism of the 21st Century.

Socialism cannot be decreed from above. The people discuss Chávez and they support him, but they are aware that they are the motor of the revolution. It is worth quoting Victor (2009) at length:

> For the first time since the fall of the Berlin Wall, a country in the world repudiates the barbaric version of capitalism that has prevailed since Ronald Reagan and Margaret Thatcher, and embraces a new socialism, one that has its roots in the indigenous people's socialism, in Liberation Theology which was born in Latin America, in Humanism, in the inspiration of Cuba, as well as the works of Marx, but not exclusively in European socialism. It is not Stalinism, it is not a copy of what has passed for socialism to date, but Venezuela's own brand infused with the idea that the people are the protagonists of democracy, that the economy should serve people, not the other way around, and that only their active and direct participation in political decision making will free the country from corruption and inequality.

Appendix[10]

Socialism

Marxists do not have a blueprint for the future (see Rikowski, 2004, pp. 559–560; see also Gibson and Rikowski, 2004 and Cole, 2008, pp. 80–81). However, there are certain features that would distinguish world socialism from world capitalism. What follow are just a few examples.

Bowles and Gintis (1976, p. 54) argue that whereas in capitalist societies, the political system is 'formally democratic', capitalist economies are 'formally totalitarian', involving: the minimal participation in decision making by the majority (the workers); protecting a single minority (capitalists and managers) against the wills of a majority; and subjecting the majority to the maximal influence of this single unrepresentative minority.

Under socialism, this would be reversed. The workers would own and control the means of production and would encourage maximal participation in decision making. Public services would be brought under state control and democratically run by the respective workforces. There would be universal free health care for all, incorporating the latest medical advances. There would be no need for private health. There would be universal free comprehensive education for all and no need for private schooling. There would be free comprehensive leisure facilities for all, with no fee for health clubs, concerts, etc. There would be free housing, and employment for all. There would be full rights for women, for the LGBT (lesbian, gay, bisexual and transgender) communities, for all members of minority ethnic groups, and for disabled people. There would be full freedom of religion.[11] There would be no ageism. There would be no war, no hunger and no poverty. Bowles and Gintis (1976, p. 266) capture the essence of socialism as follows:

> Socialism is not an event; it is a process. Socialism is a system of economic and political democracy in which individuals have the right and the obligation to structure their work lives through direct participatory control. [Socialism entails] cooperative, democratic, equal, and participatory human relationships; for cultural, emotional and sensual fulfilment.

Notes

1 For a discussion of utopian socialism, see Cole, 2008, pp. 13–21. My focus is on Europe because the utopian socialists, which Marx and Engels critiqued in their development of scientific socialism (see below), were Europeans. This is not to imply that socialist thought was not occurring elsewhere in the world. Marxism has been accused of Eurocentrism. However, I would argue that one of the major strengths of Marxism is that it is non-Eurocentric. As I have argued elsewhere (Cole, 2008, p. 76), while Eurocentricity may be true of modernism in general, Marxism is not Eurocentric. That this is the case is attested to by the 'fact that many of the most brilliant, prominent, and effective anticolonial activists have insistently pronounced themselves Marxists' (Bartolovich, 2002, p. 15). While accusations of lack of awareness in the North's complicity in the underdevelopment of the South, of Euro-American genocide, and the lack of dialogue between the North and the South are valid when directed at many 'modernists', they also do not apply to Marxism, particularly *current* Marxist analyses, which do engage with such issues. Top priorities for modern-day Marxists include the way in which the economic situation in the South is a direct result of decisions made in the North, particularly

with respect to impoverishment as a result of debt burdens, and the violence practised as a result of the economic and political trajectory of neoliberal capitalism. This is the form of capitalism where the market rules; public expenditure is cut; governments reduce regulation of everything that could diminish profits; state-owned enterprises, goods and services are sold to private investors; and the concept of 'the public good' or 'community' is eliminated (Martinez and García, 2000). Neoliberal capitalism is accompanied by (US) imperialism. Connections need to be made and lessons learned with respect to resistance to US imperialism and Left political and economic developments in countries such as Cuba, and in Latin America (Cole, 2008, p. 76; see later in this chapter for a discussion of twenty-first-century socialism in the Bolivarian Republic of Venezuela).

2 In Marxist terminology, the dialectic refers to contradictions between opposing forces and their solutions. A dialectical conception of history sees societies moving forward through stages of struggle. Thus, out of opposing forces (thesis and antithesis), a new form of society arises (synthesis). This in turn generates a new thesis and antithesis, and ultimately a new synthesis and so on and so on (see later in this chapter for a discussion of the materialist conception of history).

3 The word 'communism' is a greatly misunderstood one. It was used by Marx to refer to the stage after socialism when the state would have withered away and when we would live communally. In the period after the Russian Revolution up to the demise of the Soviet Union, the Soviet Union and other Eastern European countries were routinely referred to as 'communist' in the West. The Soviet Union, founded in 1922, actually referred to itself, following Marx, as 'socialist'. Some Marxists (e.g. Cliff, 1974) have described what became of the Soviet Union and other Eastern European countries as 'state capitalist'. It is ironic that the West falsely designated these states 'communist'. In reality (despite the fact that many had a number of positive features—full employment, housing for all, free public and social services, safety for women to walk the streets at night, and so on), they were undemocratic dictatorships with special privileges for an elite and drudgery for the many. These Eastern European societies were not real socialist states, and were also far removed from Marx's vision of communism. Marx and Engels also made reference to early pre-capitalist social formations—stages of communal living—for example, 'the ancient communal and State ownership which proceeds especially from the union of several tribes into a city by agreement or by conquest, and which is still accompanied by slavery' (Marx and Engels, 1845, p. 46).

4 Terry Eagleton (1991, p. 3) makes a distinction between the term *proletariat* (originally those who served the state by producing children) and the term *working class*. While the former refers primarily to any kind of subservient labour, the latter denoted a position within the social relations of production. However, in current usage, the two terms have become synonymous.

5 'Forcible' does not necessarily imply or involve excessive violence (a charge often levelled at Marxists). Engels, for example, stated: 'if the social revolution and practical communism are the necessary result of our existing conditions—then we will have to concern ourselves above all with the measures by which we can avoid a violent and bloody overthrow of the social conditions' (Engels, 1845 [1975], p. 243). Engels believed that education could play a role in a peaceful transformation of society: 'the calm and composure necessary for the peaceful transformation of society can . . . be expected only from an *educated* working class' (ibid.). While Marxists recognise that violence has been perpetrated on a grand scale *in the name of Marxism*, it is, in fact, neoliberal capitalism that is currently unleashing unabashedly an orgy of violence, hitherto unprecedented, causing masses of avoidable deaths from world poverty and imperialist conquest (for a discussion of Marxism, social revolution, and violence, see Chapter 10 of Cole, 2008).

6 Marx argues that the origins of the capital held by capitalists lie in the forcible seizure of feudal and clan property, the theft of common lands and state lands, and the forced acquisition of church property at nominal price. In other words, capitalism has its origins in theft and continues on the same basis (see Marx, 1887 [1965], pp. 717–33).

7 The following section of the chapter draws heavily on Cole (2009, pp. 115–30).

8 One of the major differences between twentieth- and twenty-first-century socialism is that the latter is not informed by atheism. For example, in Venezuela, revolutionary processes are underpinned by liberation theology. This is a movement within the Catholic Church in Latin America in the 1950s, achieving prominence in the 1970s and 1980s, and which emphasises the role of Christians aligning themselves with the poor and being involved in the struggle against economic, political and social inequalities. In Chávez's view, '[t]he people are the voice of God' (cited in Sheehan, 2010). Chávez is referring to the Venezuelan revolutionary masses. The Venezuelan revolution is also guided by indigenous spirituality (see Motta and Cole (2012) for a discussion of some differences between twentieth- and twenty-first-century socialisms).

9 The Venezuelan working class should not be viewed as constituting a traditional industrial proletariat. Some 60 per cent of Venezuelan workers are involved in the informal economy (street vendors and so on), primarily in the barrios from where Chávez draws his support (Dominguez, 2010), representing another difference between the processes of twentieth- and twenty-first-century socialisms. 'Barrio' is a Spanish word meaning district or neighbourhood. In the Venezuelan context, the term commonly refers to the outer rims of big cities inhabited by poor working-class communities.

10 This Appendix first appeared in Cole (2011, pp. 44–45).

11 Marx's views on religion are well known. As he famously put it: 'Religion is the sigh of the oppressed creature, the heart of a heartless world, and the soul of soulless conditions. It is the opium of the people' (Marx, 1843–44). The editors of the Marx Internet Archive (MIA) (cited with this extract from Marx) explain that in the nineteenth century, opium was widely used for medical purposes as a painkiller, and thus Marx's dictum did not connote a delusionary state of consciousness, but rather a way of easing the pain of capitalism. Although Marx and Marxism have traditionally been associated with atheism, my own view is that this needs amending. While religion, as opposed to theism (belief in a God or Gods that intervene in the world) or deism (belief in a God who does not intervene in the world) has often been and continues to be a form of oppression and conservatism, there have been and are large numbers of people who identify with a religious or spiritual belief who also identify with Marxism or socialism (millions of Roman Catholics in Venezuela, for example). There are also, of course, many Marxists who are atheists or agnostics. Whatever our beliefs or lack of beliefs, it is my view that our energies should be devoted primarily to the creation of equality and happiness on earth. This becomes increasingly imperative as capitalism and imperialism intensify their ravages.

References

Bartolovich, C. (2002) 'Introduction', in C. Bartolovich and N. Lazarus (eds) *Marxism, Modernity and Postcolonial Studies*, Cambridge: Cambridge University Press.

Berki, R.N. (1975) *Socialism*, Letchworth: Aldine Press.

Bowles, S. and H. Gintis (1976) *Schooling in Capitalist America,* London: Routledge and Keegan Paul.

Bukharin, N. (1922) 'Theorie des Historischen Materialismus', *The Communist International*, pp. 343–45.

Callinicos, A. (2000) *Equality*, Oxford: Polity Press.

Chávez, H. (2010) 'Coup and Countercoup: Revolution!', http://venezuela-us.org/2010/04/11/coup- and- countercoup- revolution/, 11 April (accessed 14 April 2010).

Cliff, T. (1974) *State Capitalism in Russia*, www.marxists.org/archive/cliff/works/1955/statecap/index.htm (accessed 6 July 2008).

Cole, M. (2008) *Marxism and Educational Theory: Origins and Issues*, London: Routledge.

Cole, M. (2009) *Critical Race Theory and Education: A Marxist Response*, New York: Palgrave Macmillan.

Cole, M. (2011) *Racism and Education in the U.K. and the U.S.: Towards a Socialist Alternative*, New York: Palgrave Macmillan.

Contreras Baspineiro, A. (2003) 'Globalizing the Bolivarian Revolution Hugo Chávez's Proposal for Our América', www.narconews.com/Issue29/article746.html (accessed 25 July 2007).

Dominguez, F. (2010) 'Education for the Creation of a New Venezuela', Paper delivered at *Latin America and Education, Marxism and Education: Renewing Dialogues XIII*, London: Institute of Education, University of London, 24 July.

Eagleton, T. (1991) *Ideology*, London: Verso.

Engels, F. (1845) [1975] 'Speeches in Elberfeld', *Marx and Engels, Collected Works, Volume 4*, www.marxists.org/archive/marx/works/1845/02/15.htm (accessed 28 November 2009).

Engels, F. (1877) [1962] *Anti-Dühring: Herr Eugen Dühring's Revolution in Science*, Moscow: Foreign Language Press.

Engels, F. (1892) [1977] 'Socialism: Utopian and Scientific', in *Karl Marx & Frederick Engels: Selected Works in One Volume*, London: Lawrence and Wishart.

Gibson, R. and G. Rikowski (2004) *Socialism and Education: An E- Dialogue*, conducted between 19 July and 8 August, at Rich Gibson's *Education Page for a Democratic Society*, www.pipeline.com/~rougeforum/RikowskiGibsonDialogueFinal.htm (accessed 5 December 2009).

Hickey, T. (2002) 'Class and Class Analysis for the Twenty-first Century', in M. Cole (ed.) *Education, Equality and Human Rights*, London: Routledge/Falmer.

Hickey, T. (2006) '"Multitude" or "Class": Constituencies of Resistance, Sources of Hope', in M. Cole (ed.) *Education, Equality and Human Rights* (2nd edition), London: Routledge.

Hill, D. (ed.) (2009) *The Rich World and the Impoverishment of Education: Diminishing Democracy, Equity and Workers' Rights*, New York: Routledge.

Hill, D. and R. Kumar (eds) (2009) *Global Neoliberalism and Education and Its Consequences*, New York: Routledge

Hill, D. and E. Rosskam (eds) (2009) *The Developing World and State Education: Neoliberal Depredation and Egalitarian Alternatives*, New York: Routledge.

Hillcole Group (1997) *Rethinking Education and Democracy: A Socialist Alternative for the Twenty-first Century*, London: Tufnell Press.

Lee, F.J.T. (2005) 'Venezuela's President Hugo Chavez Frias: "The Path is Socialism"', www.handsoffvenezuela.org/chavez_path_socialism_4.htm (accessed 4 May 2007).

Luxemburg, R. (1916) 'The War and the Workers – The Junius Pamphlet', http://h-net.org/~german/gtext/kaiserreich/lux.html (9 accessed July 2008).

Mandel, E. (1970) [2008] 'Bourgeois ideology and proletarian class consciousness', in Leninist Organisation—Part 2, www.international viewpoint.org/spip.php?article 464 (accessed 14 August 2008).

Martinez, E. and A. García (2000) 'What Is "Neo-Liberalism": A Brief Definition', *Economy 101*, www.globalexchange.org/campaigns/econ101/neoliberalDefined.html (accessed 4 April 2010).

Marx, K. (1843–44) 'Introduction to a Contribution to the Critique of Hegel's Philosophy of Right', www.marxists.org/archive/marx/works/1843/critique-hpr/intro.htm (accessed 22 October 2008).

Marx, K. (1845) [1976] 'Theses on Feuerbach', in C.J. Arthur (ed.) *Marx and Engels, The German Ideology*, London: Lawrence and Wishart.

Marx, K. (1847) [1995] *The Poverty of Philosophy*, Loughton: Prometheus Books.

Marx, K. (1859) [1977] Preface to *A Contribution to the Critique of Political Economy*, Moscow: Progress Publishers.

Marx, K. (1875) [1996] *Critique of the Gotha Programme*, Beijing: Foreign Language Press.

Marx, K. (1885) [1976] 'The Eighteenth Brumaire of Louis Bonaparte', in K. Marx and F. Engels, *Selected Works in One Volume*, London: Lawrence and Wishart.

Marx, K. (1887) [1965] *Capital, Vol. 1*, Moscow: Progress Publishers.

Marx, K. (1894) [1966] *Capital, Vol. 3*, Moscow: Progress Publishers.

Marx, K. and F. Engels (1845) [1975] 'The Holy Family', www.marxists.org/archive/marx/works/1845/holy-family/ch04.htm (accessed 27 July 2008).

Marx, K. and F. Engels (1845–46) *The German Ideology*, http://artsci.wustl.edu/~anthro/courses/361/GermanIdeology.html (accessed 16 July 2011).

Marx, K. and F. Engels (1847) [1977] 'The Communist Manifesto', in *Karl Marx and Frederick Engels: Selected Works in One Volume*, London: Lawrence and Wishart.

Maunder, J. (2006) 'Marxism and the Global South', *Socialist Worker*, 17 June.

McLaren, P. (2000) *Che Guevara, Paulo Freire and the Pedagogy of Revolution*, Oxford: Rowman and Littlefield.

McMurtry, J. (2000) 'Education, Struggle and the Left Today', *International Journal of Educational Reform*, 10 (2), pp. 145–62.

Molyneux, J. (2008) 'Is the World Full Up?', *Socialist Worker*, 5 July, p. 13.

Motta, S. C. and Cole, M. (2012) *Constructing Twenty-first Century Socialism in Latin America: The Role of Radical Education*, New York: Palgrave Macmillan.

Rikowski, G. (2001) 'The Importance of Being a Radical Educator in Capitalism Today', Guest Lecture in Sociology of Education, The Gillian Rose Room, Department of Sociology, University of Warwick, 24 May, Coventry: Institute for Education Policy Studies, www.ieps.org.uk.cwc.net/rikowski2005a.pdf (accessed 1 August 2008).

Rikowski, G. (2004) 'Marx and the Education of the Future', *Policy Futures in Education*, 2 (3 and 4), pp. 559–71, http://www.wwwords.co.uk/pdf/freetoview.asp?j=pfie&vol=2&issue=3&year=2004&article=10_Rikowski_PFEO_2_3-4_web_ (accessed 16 July 2011).Rikowski_PFEO_2_3-4_web&id=195.93.21.133 (accessed 18 July 2008).

Salomon, A. (1935) 'Max Weber's Politial Ideas', *Social Research*, 2, pp. 368–84.

Sartre, J.P. (1960) *The Search for Method (1st part). Introduction to Critique of Dialectical Reason*, www.marxists.org/reference/archive/sartre/works/critic/sartre1.htm (accessed 8 August 2006).

Sheehan, C. (2010) 'Transcript of Cindy Sheehan's Interview with Hugo Chavez', 30 March, http://venezuelanalysis.com/analysis/5233 (accessed 1 August 2010).

Suggett, J. (2010) 'Chávez's Annual Address Includes Minimum Wage Hike, Maintenance of Social Spending in Venezuela', http://venezuelanalysis.com/news/5077 (accessed 5 August 2010).

Trotsky, L. (1909) *Why Marxists Oppose Individual Terrorism*, www.marxists.org/archive/trotsky/works/1909/tia09.htm (accessed 8 August 2006).

Victor, M.P. (2009) 'From Conquistadores, Dictators and Multinationals to the Bolivarian Revolution', *Venezuelanalysis*, 4 December 2011, http://venezuelanalysis.com/analysis/4979 (accessed 8 September 2011).

Weber, M. (c. 1915) [1947] *The Theory of Economic and Social Organizations,* New York: Free Press.

Chapter 10

Social class and schooling
Differentiation or democracy?

Richard Hatcher

Social class remains the strongest predictor of educational achievement in the UK, where the social class gap for educational achievement is one of the most significant in the developed world.

(Perry and Francis 2010, p. 2)

If you want to know how well a child will do at school, ask how much money its parents have. The fact remains that, after more than 50 years of the Welfare State and several decades of comprehensive education, family income and wealth is the single best predictor of success in the school system. Of course some children from well-off homes don't do well at school and some children from poor backgrounds succeed, but the overall pattern is clear: social class, defined in terms of socio-economic status, correlates closely with attainment at school.

Inequality in Britain

Britain is an unequal country, more so than many other industrial countries and more so than a generation ago.

(National Equality Panel 2010, p. 1)

The report *An Anatomy of Economic Inequality in the UK* (National Equality Panel 2010) is a detailed analysis of Britain as a divided nation where the richest 10 per cent of the population are more than 100 times as wealthy as the poorest 10 per cent. The explanation for inequality lies in the workings of the capitalist economy and the neoliberal economic and fiscal policies pursued by the Labour government and its Conservative predecessors. Overall, income and wealth have risen, but the rise has disproportionately benefited the highest paid. Pensions and benefits for the poor, and the national minimum wage, have risen much less than the income of high earners, which remains relatively low taxed (Browne *et al.* 2010). As the National Equality Panel report points out, 'for the last 30 years the tax system as a whole (including indirect taxes) has had virtually no effect on income distribution – direct and indirect taxes have taken the same proportion of income from each fifth of households throughout the period' (p. 50). The high level of economic inequality results in a low level of social mobility between the generations. 'The evidence we have looked at shows the long arm of people's origins in shaping their life chances, stretching through life stages, literally from cradle to grave' (National Equality Panel 2010, p. 398; see also Ermisch and Del Bono 2010).

The Conservative–Liberal Democrat Coalition government took office in May 2010. It rapidly implemented a radical programme of spending cuts, tax rises and benefit reductions; £18 billion of welfare cuts between 2011 and 2014 (Brewer 2010) represented the tightest squeeze on 'public service' spending since at least the end of the Second World War (Crawford *et al.* 2011). Most public sector workers' pay is frozen for three years while inflation increases. Local council budgets are cut by an average of 27 per cent in the four-year period between 2011 and 2015, involving cuts in services and loss of jobs, with the most socially deprived authorities facing the biggest spending reductions (*Guardian*, 14 December 2010). It is estimated that 500,000 public service workers will lose their jobs between 2011 and 2015, with a knock-on effect of perhaps as many again in the private sector. Particularly affected are young people, with unemployment among 16- to 24-year-olds rising to over one million.

The largest single saving from the welfare budget has come from the decision to link benefits and tax credits with the Consumer Prices Index (CPI), rather than the Retail Prices Index (RPI), giving a lower measure of inflation. Some benefit cuts particularly hit families with children, including child benefit, the child and working tax credits, and housing benefit; £3.5 billion is being saved in child benefit by freezing it for three years and then means-testing it (Brewer 2010). Another set of cuts particularly affect young people after age 16, including the scrapping of the Education Maintenance Allowance and the cuts in the Connexions service.

The resulting substantial increase in poverty for many and the widening equality gap will have a significant impact on social class inequality in education, which will be reinforced by cuts in school budgets and local authority support service budgets.

In 2011 the government published *Opening Doors, Breaking Barriers: A Strategy for Social Mobility* (HM Government 2011). It contained detailed evidence of inequality in Britain, but that was not accompanied by a strategy capable of tackling the barriers to greater social mobility through reducing income inequality, reversing the savage public sector cuts that impact most on the less well-off, and increasing the downward social mobility of the rich through taxation.

Children and poverty

Of particular relevance to school is the extent of child poverty. A central theme of the Child Poverty Action Group's report *Ending Child Poverty* (CPAG 2009) is the profound negative impact that being born poor has on children. Under the Labour government the number of children living in poverty fell by 600,000, but by 2007–08 there were still 2.2 million children, amounting to 17 per cent of all children, living in households below the poverty line (CPAG 2009). Under the Coalition government both absolute and relative poverty among children and working-age adults are expected to rise as the austerity programme is implemented. 'A baby born to a low-income family from April 2011 will be around £1,500 worse off compared to a sibling born in April 2010' (CPAG 2010). Between 2012–13 and 2013–14 absolute child poverty is predicted to rise by about 100,000, and relative child poverty by about 200,000. The 2010 Child Poverty Act commits current and future governments to reducing relative child poverty to 10 per cent and absolute child poverty to 5 per cent by 2020–21 (Brewer and Joyce 2010). Achieving the goal of eradicating child poverty by 2020 would require a substantial redistribution of wealth towards the poorest families, which would run counter to the neoliberal policies of the Coalition government and those, as the CPAG trenchantly pointed out, of its Labour predecessor:

> One of the most telling critiques of recent economic policy is that we privatised profit in the good times but were left to socialise debt when things went bad. Large and unequally shared profits attract little tax, but still the ordinary taxpayer has been forced to step in to cover losses once things have turned sour. Such a one-sided deal has bred massive and deeply corrosive social inequality in our society. This is no longer acceptable.
>
> (CPAG 2009, p. 4)

Social inequality in education

These massive differences in the economic resources of families have huge consequences for the education of their children. The most common indicator in education of economic deprivation is eligibility for free school meals (FSM). However, the recorded figures of about 17 per cent of primary and 14 per cent of secondary school pupils are an underestimate because many parents do not claim the benefits that signal their eligibility. It also places the large majority of children in the same category of 'non-FSM' and therefore obscures the very wide difference between rich families, middle-income families and those just above the FSM threshold.

British children's educational attainment is overwhelmingly linked to parental occupation, income and qualifications. Social class differences become apparent during early childhood with regard to readiness for school. In some disadvantaged areas, up to 50 per cent of children begin primary school without the necessary language and communication skills (National Equality Panel 2010). During primary and secondary school the gap in attainment between children from poor families and those from more affluent backgrounds continues to widen (Cassen and Kingdon 2007; National Equality Panel 2010). At the end of Key Stage 2, 53.5 per cent of pupils eligible for free school meals reach the expected level (i.e. Level 4 or above) in English and mathematics, compared with 75.5 per cent of pupils who are not eligible (DCSF, 2009a). At secondary school in 2009, only 26.6 per cent of pupils eligible for free school meals achieved five or more A*–C grade GCSEs or equivalent including English and maths, compared to 54.2 per cent of pupils not eligible for free school meals.

Although social class is the strongest predictor of attainment in the school system it intersects in complex ways with gender and ethnicity. Girls tend to achieve better than boys, whatever their class background, and some ethnic minority groups underachieve compared to white students (Perry and Francis 2010). But the lowest-achieving group is white working-class boys (Cassen and Kingdon, 2007). The achievement gap between white students in receipt of free school meals and non-FSM students is more than three times bigger than the gaps between different ethnic groups (Sveinsson 2010).

Is the class inequality gap in education narrowing over time? The attainment gap in GCSE results has reduced in recent years, but only slightly. For example, the proportion of FSM pupils achieving grade A*-C in GCSE English and in GCSE maths has increased at a faster rate than the rest of the cohort. In English the chances of an FSM pupil achieving a grade A*–C rose from 32 per cent in 2004 to 39 per cent in 2008, and in maths from 25 per cent to 35 per cent (DCSF 2009a, b).

Why do poor children on average do less well at school and children from well-off families do better?

What are the processes by which differences in income and wealth among families are translated into differences in educational attainment among children? One obvious consequence concerns differences in families' ability to afford educational benefits such as books, broadband internet access or private tutoring (DCSF 2009a). But there are also powerful cultural factors – class differences in the ways of life of families and communities – which shape children's identities and interact with the cultures of schools in different ways. The policies and practices of schools may serve to challenge and disrupt patterns of social inequality in education, or sustain and reinforce them. How this complex interaction of home and school factors works to shape individual children's experiences of and attainment in school, and therefore what strategies are most effective in tackling educational inequality, is still not fully understood (Kerr and West 2010, p. 15).

The home

Parents transmit, actively and passively, cultural capital to their children: knowledge, skills, values, attitudes and behaviours. Different class cultures of the home tend to generate different forms of cultural capital that are differentially valorised by the school. Middle-class parents are likely to have themselves succeeded in the education system and so provide role models for their children of the causal link between school success and career success. They are more likely to have high educational and career aspirations for the child, more likely to successfully inculcate them in the child, and more likely to foster a self-concept of academic efficacy (Cabinet Office 2008). Low aspirations by working-class parents for their children have been frequently cited as one of the most significant barriers to working-class educational achievement (Perry and Francis 2010; e.g. DCSF 2009c). It is an argument that can easily lend itself to a 'blame the family' deficit model unless the reasons for low aspirations are located in how the class structure of society shapes class inequalities, and therefore class cultures, over generations. The National Equality Panel report concludes that, after taking account of changes in the labour market, 'there is no evidence that rates of relative occupational mobility have changed at all since the early 1970s' (National Equality Panel 2010, p. 324). Of course, many working-class parents have high aspirations for their children, but they may still lack the cultural and material capital to translate them into effective support. For example, middle-class families are more likely to provide a broader awareness of the wider 'dominant culture', in terms of literature, music, politics, art, science, etc. and the sorts of cultural experiences, ranging from shared reading activities to music tuition and involvement in clubs and other activities outside the home, that have significant benefits in terms of success at school (Sullivan 2007).

Class differences in relation to language have a particular importance. Middle-class children have more of the linguistic capital that is valorised by the school, in several ways. According to Cassen and Kingdon (2007), a young child in a professional-class home will hear every day more than three times the number of words heard by a child in a home where the parents are of low socio-economic status; parents in such homes also tend to interact verbally with their children less than professional parents. School success depends on the ability to understand and use 'academic' forms of language. The spoken language of the middle-class home is more likely to be linguistically similar in register to that of the school, facilitating learning. Reading and writing are the fundamental skills that determine subsequent school success. It is not simply mastery of the technical skills, it is also the meaning of reading and writing for the child. Homes where children have few books and seldom see their parents reading or writing tend to generate a different orientation to literacy, a different cultural predisposition, from ones where reading and writing, in particular the sorts of texts that demand language skills similar to those required for school success, are everyday activities.

Middle-class parents are more likely to possess instrumental knowledge about how to succeed in the education system: knowledge about how to choose a school; knowledge about how to negotiate with teachers about issues concerning the child's education; knowledge about how to effectively support the child's homework or assessed coursework; knowledge about curriculum choices and their likely subsequent benefits; knowledge about how to apply to university and choose an appropriate course. Their knowledge comes partly because they have succeeded in the school system themselves and partly because of class difference in social capital: the interpersonal relationships, whether close or more distant, which bring educational benefits. Middle-class parents are more likely to belong to social networks that communicate knowledge about educational matters such as advantageous choice of school.

In short, middle-class parents tend to have the knowledge and understanding of the 'rules of the game' of school, and the communication skills, confidence and connections, which enable them to maximise their positional advantage in education (see e.g. Vincent and Ball 2006),

The school

We have noted that the class equality gap actually widens during schooling. What is the role of school itself in this? Does it tend to mitigate educational inequality resulting from external factors, which would otherwise be even greater, or does it actually contribute to the maintenance of inequality? Diane Reay has argued that school 'valorizes middle-class rather than working-class cultural capital' (Reay 2001, p. 334). In consequence, children from middle-class homes are more likely to experience a smooth transition between the class culture of the home and the culture of school, whereas children from working-class backgrounds are more likely to experience disjuncture and alienation (Archer *et al.* 2007). Cultural differences (in, for example, the language of the child and the language of the teacher) may be accompanied by teachers' perceptions of the working-class child and family as 'deficient', and by lower teacher expectations that tend to reinforce class differences. These, compounded by the cumulative experiences of lack of success in school relative to middle-class children, may have powerful negative effects on the pupil identities of children from poorer backgrounds (Perry and Francis 2010, p. 19).

The education policies of the Labour government

During the 13 years of the New Labour government a range of strategies were implemented to tackle social inequality in the school system. They can be broadly classified as:

*   general interventions targeting all schools;
*   interventions that target schools in disadvantaged areas;
*   interventions that target underachieving groups;
*   structural interventions, which target how school systems are organised;
*   'beyond school' interventions, which target neighbourhood and family background factors.

(Kerr and West 2010, p. 18)

General interventions targeting all schools

The dominant paradigm of Labour's education policy was the 'standards agenda', designed to improve schools and raise standards of attainment through a combination of a prescriptive national curriculum, a system of school attainment targets, national tests and examinations, and Ofsted inspections. It also included the national literacy, numeracy and Key Stage 3 strategies (subsequently incorporated into the National Strategies), which provided models for effective teaching that teachers were expected to follow. Some studies showed positive results; many were critical. For example, the *Cambridge Primary Review* (Alexander 2009) argued that 'improvements were "negligible" in primary literacy, and "relatively modest" in numeracy; gains in reading skills were at the expense of children's enjoyment of reading; the emphasis on testing was "distorting" children's experiences of schooling; and that a much bigger gap persisted in England between high and low attaining children in reading, maths and science, than in many other countries' (Kerr and West 2010, p. 30). A review by Tymms and Merrell (2007) of evidence about changes in standards concluded that performance in both reading and mathematics at the end of primary school has 'remained fairly constant' since the 1950s. The extent of improvement has been partly achieved by teachers becoming more adept at teaching to the test, at the expense of a broad and enriching curriculum, which particularly disadvantages children from poorer backgrounds who cannot rely on the compensation provided by the 'curriculum of the home'. Gillborn and Youdell (2000) provide evidence of 'triage' within schools, discriminating against low-performing and disproportionately poorer pupils by concentrating resources on boosting borderline pupils to reach threshold grades in SATs tests and GCSEs.

The 'standards agenda' encouraged differentiation. Pupil grouping by ability increased, including in primary schools, as a result of government pressure (DCSF 2009a). Because of the greater likelihood of low attainment among pupils from deprived backgrounds, grouping pupils by ability inevitably results in overrepresentation of these pupils in the bottom groups. The authors of the book *Learning without Limits* (Hart *et al.* 2004) have explained how it functions as a mechanism of social selection. Government policy conceptualises children's learning in terms of scores, levels and targets, and this has had a profound effect on how teachers conceptualise the abilities of children.

> The act of categorising young people by ability reifies differences and hardens hierarchies, so that we start to think of those in the different categories as different kinds of learners with different minds, different characteristics and very different needs.
>
> (p. 29)

One important way in which the fixed ability template affects teachers' thinking is that it creates a disposition to accept as normal, indeed inevitable, the limited achievement of a significant proportion of the school population.

(pp. 28–29)

Differentiation in pupil grouping results in a differentiated curriculum that functions as a process of social selection by means of negative discrimination – giving less to those who have less. Hoadley (2008), researching the reproduction of inequality through a comparison of teaching in middle-class and working-class classrooms, found that 'orientation to meaning' was 'the crucial variable associated with social class' (p. 76). In the working-class school learning was structured by a series of fragmented tasks rather than, as in middle-class contexts, a coherent conceptual trajectory. '*In the working-class context, learners were learning to name the world; and the middle-class context, learners were learning to categorize the world*' (p. 75, emphasis in original). Hoadley's findings echo Jean Anyon's (1981) pioneering empirical research and are congruent with research carried out in France by Bernard Charlot and his colleagues, and discussed in the second edition of this chapter (e.g. Charlot *et al.* 1992).

Dunne *et al.* (2007) investigated how schools and teachers seek to maximise the benefits of attainment grouping and mitigate its disadvantages through smaller numbers in lower attainment groups, with teaching assistants and learning mentors providing learning support and customised curricula. But they also found that though the social class composition of low attainment sets was not widely acknowledged by teachers, they tended to stereotype pupils from lower socioeconomic backgrounds as low-achieving and to allocate them, irrespective of prior attainment, to lower sets, where pupils are at greater risk of exposure to reduced teacher expectations, disruption and loss of self-esteem (Dunne and Gazeley 2008).

Targeting schools in disadvantaged areas

The Labour government implemented a number of initiatives particularly targeting schools in socially deprived areas, including Education Action Zones (EAZ), the Excellence in Cities (EiC) programme, National Challenge, the Every Child Matters agenda and extended service schools. According to Kerr and West (2010, p. 31), 'the evidence on the impact of interventions which have targeted schools in disadvantaged areas is also quite mixed'. Many of these programmes have now ceased.

Numerous school effectiveness and school improvement studies have attempted to identify the factors that have proved effective in raising pupil attainment, and a number of them have attempted to identify the factors that account for the relative success of some schools serving social deprived areas. The DCSF report *Breaking the Link between Disadvantage and Low Attainment* (DCSF 2009b) claims that 'The highest performing maintained schools, serving some of the most deprived areas . . . have broken the link between poverty and attainment for their pupils' (p. 2). The report summarises 'the main symptoms and causes of the attainment gap for disadvantaged pupils, and the strategies which schools and local authorities can adopt to address them' as follows (p. 23):

Some symptoms and issues	Possible school and LA responses
Cognitive gaps already evident before age five	Children's Centres, support for families and early reading
Weaker home learning environment	Schools working closely with parents
Lower prior attainment at each Key Stage	Personalisation, progress, 'keep up not catch-up'
Harder to recover from stalled learning	Tracking, early intervention, one-to-one tuition
Quality of teaching for children in lower sets	In-school teacher deployment, training
Behaviour, exclusion and absence issues	Behaviour, exclusion and absence policies, SEAL, new curriculum
Aspirations, peer influences, 'not cool to learn'	Positive role-models, active information, advice and guidance policies
Weak family/community networks	School/cluster/LA action to compensate
Narrow experiences and opportunities	Broader curriculum; extended school services
SEN/disadvantage overlap	Ensure SEN policies focus on progress
Gaps are too often an 'invisible issue'	Use new accountability framework

The report proposes a 'Framework for action' (p. 31) comprising five strategies:

Raising visibility and awareness	Head teachers/school leaders to ensure staff take special note of disadvantaged/other vulnerable pupils, and target and track their progress
Early years, parents	Ensure that EY services, and school support for parents, target disadvantage. Focus on home/school interface (e.g. homework, reading, resources)

Targeted support in basics	Ensure teachers know and intervene early for FSM pupils (e.g. 1:1 tuition). Consider redeployment of teachers to support pupils with lowest attainment
Beyond classroom – extended school and other services	Broaden pupils' experiences, raise aspirations, linked issues (health, etc.). Use extended services, and lessons from Extra Mile project, to target disadvantage
School and LA accountability and funding	Use external and self-evaluation to focus on gaps and progress, not just average attainment. Consider deployment of extra resources where most effective.

The official perspective on school improvement has always seen the role of the head teacher as decisive. In that context the Ofsted report *Twelve Outstanding Secondary Shools: Excelling Against the Odds* (Ofsted 2009) focuses on the leadership characteristics of schools that serve disadvantaged communities, have a higher than average proportion of students in receipt of free school meals, have exceptionally good results, and have been judged outstanding in two or more inspections. Their features are categorised under the headings of 'achieving excellence' and 'sustaining excellence'.

> Achieving excellence: having vision, values and high expectations; attracting, recruiting, retaining and developing staff; establishing disciplined learning and consistent staff behaviour; assuring the quality of teaching and learning; leading, and building leadership capacity; providing a relevant and attractive curriculum; assessment, progress-tracking and target-setting; inclusion: students as individuals.

> Sustaining excellence: continuity of leadership; maintaining a strong team culture; continually developing teaching and learning; developing leaders; enriching the curriculum; improving literacy; building relationships with students, parents and the community; no student left behind.
>
> (Ofsted 2009, p. 9)

A report published by the NCSL and the NUT, *Successful Leadership for Promoting the Achievement of White Working Class Pupils* (Mongon and Chapman 2008), found that the leaders' strategies were similar to those used by most successful school leaders: building vision and setting directions; understanding and developing people; designing the organisation; managing and supporting the teaching and learning programme; collecting, monitoring, analysing and using information. Head teachers displayed three characteristics that they call 'intelligences': contextual intelligence; professional intelligence; social intelligence;

and showed four personality traits: self-efficacy; internal locus of control; conscientiousness; rapport (pp. 1–3).

While studies of successful school improvement should not be dismissed, they should, as Coe (2009) argues, be read with a certain scepticism. Many studies rely on teachers' and head teachers' perceptions, which may be biased (there are few accounts of unsuccessful school improvement projects); correlations between improvement strategies and successful outcomes do not necessarily entail causality – other factors may have contributed, including the normal annual fluctuations in student cohorts and attainment levels; and the schools might have improved anyway. If the improvement is real, a list of effectiveness strategies abstracted from their specific context may not result in successful transferability to other contexts (Thrupp and Lupton 2006).

Targeting underachieving groups

Perhaps the most popular of Labour's education policy initiatives aimed at socially deprived groups has been preschool support through the Sure Start Children's Centres, of which 3,500 were open by 2010. Evaluation by the National Audit Office (NAO 2009) showed good progress on one of the four sub-targets, increasing the number of Ofsted-registered childcare places, but the other sub-targets were not met. The number of children in lower income working families using formal childcare decreased rather than increased; 49 per cent of children reached a 'good level of development' at the end of the Foundation Stage, compared with a target of 53 per cent; and there was no reduction in inequality between child development achieved in the 30 per cent most disadvantaged communities and in the rest of England, against a target to reduce the gap by four percentage points. In addition, there was a low level of outreach activity to the most disadvantaged families. There is evidence that Sure Start has improved parenting in the early years and has resulted in improved behavioural outcomes for the children but by age five it has had no impact on their cognitive (reading, writing and maths) test scores (Joseph Rowntree Foundation 2011, p. 10). It may be too early to evaluate the extent to which Sure Start reduces social inequality in children's subsequent school attainment: 'All centres we visited emphasised the difficulty of measuring the impacts of children's centres. Some believe it will take several years to demonstrate significant impacts on children's development' (NAO 2009, p. 29).

Structural interventions

The Labour government attacked the notion of the comprehensive school (itself only partly achieved) and promoted different types of state schools, claiming that 'diversity and choice' were the best way both to raise standards and to reduce inequality. The result was to exacerbate the existing historical divisions within the British school system. However, the evidence revealed that the combination of more supply-side diversity and more choice for parents tended to increase social inequality (Ball 2008).

The Labour government's most radical and controversial structural reform aimed specifically at raising standards in schools predominantly serving areas of social disadvantage has been academies, state schools outside the local authority system run by private 'sponsors'. The evidence demonstrates that academies are no more successful than other schools with comparable intakes and taking comparable exams. The conclusion of the final evaluation of academies commissioned by the government concluded that 'there is insufficient evidence to make a definitive judgement about the Academies as a model for school improvement' (PricewaterhouseCoopers 2008, p. 220). Since then research by the National Audit Office (2010) found evidence of improved performance but as a result of two strategies by academies. First, changing the intake. The proportion of pupils on free school meals in academies between 2002–03 and 2009–10 fell from 45.3 to 27.8 per cent. Improvement was due to more middle-class students: 'it is substantial improvements by the less disadvantaged pupils that are driving academies' improved performance overall' (p. 27). The consequence has been a wider equality gap within academies: 'on average, the gap in attainment between more disadvantaged pupils and others has grown wider in academies than in comparable maintained schools' (p. 6; see also Wrigley 2011). The second strategy has been to enter pupils for non-GCSE exams that have a higher pass rate: 'For later academies, the proportion of entries for GCSEs decreased more rapidly than in other schools, and the proportion of entries to GCSE equivalents in 2008–09 was seven percentage points higher than earlier academies, and ten percentage points higher that comparator schools' (NAO 2010, p. 21).

A more successful structural reform, also often involving innovation in governance, was federations of high-performing and low-performing schools in order to raise standards (DCSF 2009d). A quantitative analysis of performance in 42 schools linked, generally in pairs, in 'performance federations' found evidence of significant improvement in the low-performing school compared to comparable schools (Chapman et al. 2009).

The evidence shows that Labour's strategies for reducing educational inequality had little success. The explanation lies in the contradictions within Labour policy:

> there has been a basic fault line in government policy, where halfhearted efforts to 'narrow the gap' have been grafted onto an inherently inequitable system. Unequal educational outcomes arise out of deep social inequalities. These are compounded by competition between schools, narrowly conceived teaching and learning opportunities, and highly centralised and punitive accountability regimes. Endless initiatives targeting failing schools and underachieving groups will make little difference unless these underlying issues are tackled.
>
> (Dyson et al. 2010, p. 3)

The Conservative–Liberal Democrat government and the marketisation of the school system

Michael Gove, the Coalition government's Secretary of State for Education, stated his commitment to tackling social inequality in the school system in his Foreword to the 2010 White Paper.

> Our schools should be engines of social mobility, helping children to overcome the accidents of birth and background to achieve much more than they may ever have imagined. But, at the moment, our schools system does not close gaps, it widens them. Children from poorer homes start behind their wealthier contemporaries when they arrive at school and during their educational journey they fall further and further back. The achievement gap between rich and poor widens at the beginning of primary school, gets worse by GCSE and is a yawning gulf by the time (far too few) sit A levels and apply to university. This injustice has inspired a grim fatalism in some, who believe that deprivation must be destiny. But for this Government the scale of this tragedy demands action. Urgent, focused, radical action.
>
> (DfE 2010, pp. 6–7)

The key principle of the Coalition's strategy has been to extend supply-side school autonomy.

> Across the world, the case for the benefits of school autonomy has been established beyond doubt. In a school system with good quality teachers, flexibility in the curriculum and clearly established accountability measures, it makes sense to devolve as much day-to-day decision-making as possible to the front line. In this country, the ability of schools to decide their own ethos and chart their own destiny has been severely constrained by government guidance, Ministerial interference and too much bureaucracy.
>
> (DfE 2010, p. 11)

This objective is translated into two sets of policies. One promises all schools more autonomy through being freed from Labour's bureaucratic prescription – the national curriculum will be less detailed, targets will be abandoned, and school inspections eased. The other comprises academies and 'free schools'.

Autonomy and internal school policies

The curriculum

Michael Gove has promised increased autonomy over the curriculum for all schools.

> I want to remove everything unnecessary from a curriculum that has been bent out of shape by the weight of material dumped there for political purposes. I want to prune the curriculum of over-prescriptive notions of how to teach and how to timetable. Instead I want to arrive at a simple core, informed by the best international practice, which can act as a benchmark against which schools can measure themselves and parents ask meaningful and informed questions about progress.
>
> (Gove 2010a)

The Coalition government is currently reviewing the curriculum. It will be slimmed down, but it is unclear as yet what will be its scope and how prescriptive it will be. The promise of greater autonomy has been put into question by signs of increased regulation, including the insistence on a phonics approach to teaching reading, enforced by a new phonics-based reading test for six-year-olds.

The DCSF (2009a) regards a broad and appropriately challenging curriculum as a key element in promoting and sustaining educational achievement. However, research into pupils' attitudes cites the curriculum as a major cause of disaffection, disengagement and truancy (Smith *et al.* 2005). The 'standards agenda' resulted in a narrower curriculum experience for pupils, especially in primary schools, as literacy and numeracy squeezed out other subjects. In secondary schools too there has been a move in recent years from a knowledge-based to a skills-based curriculum. With it comes the danger that skills are counter-posed to knowledge, as Robin Alexander argues:

> The belief here is that skills combine contemporary relevance, future flexibility and hands-on experience: that is, those attributes which knowledge is presumed to lack. [. . .] But to set them in opposition is foolish, unnecessary and epistemologically unsound, for all but the most elemental skills – and certainly those that in educational circles are defined as 'basic skills' – require knowledge.
>
> (Alexander 2009, p. 249)

The emphasis on the acquisition of skills and factual knowledge rather than on conceptual knowledge and the development of wider understanding (Young 2008) discriminates particularly against pupils in lower-achieving groups, who are disproportionately from poorer backgrounds, because teachers adapt their teaching to their perceptions of the child, resulting in less intellectually demanding teaching that restricts pupils' access to the powerful modes of thinking afforded by abstract systems of knowledge and locks them into a cycle of increasing inequality of attainment.

Gove has stated his desire to focus the curriculum on 'core knowledge' (DfE 2010). However, this raises three issues that concern social equality. Two of them are evoked by Gove's statement that:

I'm an unashamed traditionalist when it comes to the curriculum. Most parents would rather their children had a traditional education, with children sitting in rows, learning the kings and queens of England, the great works of literature, proper mental arithmetic, algebra by the age of 11, modern foreign languages. That's the best training of the mind and that's how children will be able to compete.

(*Times*, 6 March 2010)

The first concerns whose knowledge. The 'English baccalaureate' represents a socially selective set of subjects. The exclusion of the social sciences excludes those subjects which have proved capable of motivating lower-achieving students and of enabling them to develop a critical understanding of social justice issues. Second, the traditionalist pedagogy Gove advocates has also proved inappropriate for engaging lower-achieving pupils.

The third issue concerns the construction of new class-differentiated pathways in the curriculum. Gove states in his Foreword to the 2010 White Paper that 'employers and universities consistently express concerns about the skills and knowledge of school leavers, while international studies show that other countries are improving their school systems faster' (DfE 2010). The need for schools to be more effective in producing the 'human capital' that the employers demand in the future labour force is a key driver of government policy. The CBI has set the agenda for government:

First, a continuing and unswerving focus on raising literacy and numeracy attainment [. . .]

Second, greater support for schools and pupils to develop vital employability skills.

(CBI 2010a, p. 8; see also CBI 2010b)

While there is a need for young people with higher level science and maths qualifications, the employers' main concern is for basic skills and employability skills such as problem-solving, team-working and time management for future workers in relatively low-skill, low-qualification, low-paid jobs in sectors such as retail, distribution, care, security and routine administration, which are expanding as a proportion of the economy rather than, as the Labour government's 'knowledge economy' rhetoric predicted, declining (Lawton 2009, p. 5). The Coalition government's *Review of Vocational Education – The Wolf Report* (DfE 2011) echoes this analysis. The labour market is shaped like 'an egg-timer or hourglass, with growth at the top and bottom and shrinkage in the middle, rather than an inverted pyramid with more and more "top" jobs' (p. 35) and 'our largest occupations are, in order, sales assistants, care assistants, general office assistants, and cleaners' (p. 36). *The Wolf Report* rejects the vocationally related qualifications that became common at Key Stage 4 under Labour as being both premature and worthless to employers, and instead proposes a general education to age 16 with English and maths at the centre, supplemented by options, including 'practical' subjects, which should not exceed 20 per cent of the time-table.

A common core curriculum up until age 16 with additional elective options is the most effective appropriate curriculum model for reducing social inequality through premature selection. There is however a danger that provision will be distorted by pressure to stratify curriculum pathways in accordance with the stratified labour market, with results that will inevitably be class-biased. The 'EBac' for the top layer, destined for higher education, itself increasingly hier-archised in class terms. A middle technical layer for whom the new University Technical Colleges (a vocational 14–19 academy) are designed. And for the bottom layer, a basic academic education coupled with what Gove calls 'practical learning':

> I'm absolutely clear that every child should have the option of beginning study for a craft or trade from the age of 14 but that this should be comple-mented by a base of core academic knowledge.
>
> (Gove 2010b)

Marketisation and equality

The Conservative–Liberal Democrat government aims to radically extend the marketisation of the school system, in two ways. First, all schools, primary as well as secondary, are encouraged to become academies, starting with those graded 'outstanding' by Ofsted. Like Labour's academies, they are outside local author-ities, funded directly by government, and they gain more freedom over the curriculum and admissions and more control over staff. The second form of marketisation is 'free schools', fresh-start academies that alternative providers – private organisations and groups of parents and teachers – are allowed to open up, again outside local authorities and funded by government.

What effect will the Coalition government's market-oriented reforms have on social class inequality in the school system? There is relevant evidence from existing cases of marketised supply-side reform in school systems, and in particular from those that the government cites as models: charter schools in the US and free schools in Sweden. In 2009 the OECD published a review of inter-national research on marketisation in school systems by Christopher Lubienski. Regarding attainment, his conclusion is as follows:

> it is far from clear that quasi-market forces such as increased autonomy, competition and choice have led to improved outcomes, which would indi-cate that educational innovations are occurring. Evidence of improved academic outcomes is mixed, and improvements in academic performance may result from factors other than quasi-market incentives – for example,

professional efforts, technocratic knowledge, policy alignments, or funding. If quasi-markets offered some type of elixir for educational performance, we might, over time, expect to see nations with more market-like systems outperforming countries where the state plays a more direct role in educational provision. But it is hardly clear that this is the case.

(Lubienski 2009, pp. 27–28)

The most recent large-scale study of US charter schools was published in 2009 by the Center for Research on Education Outcomes (CREDO) at Stanford University: *Multiple Choice: Charter School Performance in 16 States*. It concluded that

17 percent provide superior education opportunities for their students. Nearly half of the charter schools nationwide have results that are no different from the local public school options and over a third, 37 percent, deliver learning results that are significantly worse than their students would have realized had they remained in traditional public schools.

(CREDO 2009, p. 1)

There have been a number of studies of attainment in Swedish free schools. The most recent is by Bohlmark and Lindahl (2008), who found evidence of only small and temporary positive effects.

While there is little evidence that marketised systems raise attainment, there is substantial evidence that they reinforce patterns of social differentiation between schools. This is the result of two intertwined factors: school selection policies and parental and student self-selection. Lubienski (2009) reports that 'when schools have greater autonomy in quasi-markets competitive incentives cause schools to develop marketing innovations that may effectively exclude segments of the population' (p. 24). He gives the example of US charter schools 'locating in more affluent neighborhoods or using admissions policies to dissuade or exclude more difficult-to-educate students' (p. 24). He identifies the mechanisms: 'many independent schools now require parent or student contracts, volunteer hours, adherence to mission statements, or other means that encourage self-segregation by parents that obscure selection of students by schools' (p. 41).

Some charter schools have undoubtedly achieved above-average results. Students in the Knowledge is Power Program schools, predominantly from poorer backgrounds, achieve significantly higher than their peers in other schools (Educational Policy Institute 2005; Ravitch 2010). But major factors may be the selection of likely high achievers by rigorous interviews of potential parents and a high drop-out rate, especially by those students entering the schools with the lowest test scores (Woodworth *et al.* 2008).

In Sweden one consequence of the advent of 'free schools' is greater social segregation between schools. According to the Swedish National Agency for

Education 'Several previous studies, and statistics, show that choice in the school system has led to a tendency to segregate in terms of pupils' sociocultural background, performance and ethnic background' (Skolverket 2006, p. 51). Wiborg (2011, p. 282), summarising recent research, reports that

> The children from highly educated families gain mostly from education in independent schools, but the impact on families and immigrants who had received a low level of education is close to zero.
>   Regarding the question of segregation, several studies reveal that school choice in the Swedish school system has augmented social and ethnic segregation, particularly in relation to schools in deprived areas.

In an attempt to compensate for social inequality in the school system the Coalition government has introduced a 'pupil premium', attaching additional funding to pupils from disadvantaged backgrounds as an incentive for higher-performing schools, often in middle-class areas, to admit more students from poorer families (presumably by changing their catchment areas or introducing 'fair banding' admission criteria). The premium is only £430 per pupil, in contrast to the £3,000 called for by the charity Save the Children. According to an analysis by the Institute for Fiscal Studies (Chowdry et al. 2010) the premium would need to be very high to sufficiently reduce the disincentive for many schools to attract such pupils, putting at risk their academic attainment and public image. The authors conclude that 'The pupil premium may lead to a small reduction in covert selection by schools but is unlikely to significantly reduce social segregation' (p. 2). Nor is the premium sufficiently large (in fact it may be smaller than some socially deprived schools were previously receiving under local authority positive discriminatory funding formulas) to make a qualitative difference in provision for those pupils most in need.

Conceptions of class

Up until now I have discussed inequality in society in terms of income and wealth, and inequality in education in terms mainly of eligibility for free school meals (FSM). Often in education FSM is used as a proxy indicator for social class, but this drastically reduces the size of the working class to a small per-centage (about 16 per cent) of the population. The most common concept of social class in education policy and research is 'occupational social class'. This is a classification of occupations that since 2001 has normally been based on the National Statistics Socio-economic Classification (NS-SEC) (a reworking of the sociologist John Goldthorpe's class schema), which has eight categories ranging from 'Higher managerial and professional' occupations to 'Routine occupations' and 'Never worked and long-term unemployed'. Education researchers often use the collapsed three-class version of the NS-SEC scale – managerial and professional occupations; intermediate occupations; routine and manual occupations – but omit the intermediate category and define the first as middle class (or in Goldthorpe's term the 'service class') and the last as working class. For example, in his book *Class Strategies and the Education Market: The Middle Class and Social Advantage* Stephen Ball (2003) defines the middle class as Goldthorpe's service class. Similarly Diane Reay utilises occupational class in her research (e.g. Reay 2006). Ball and Reay have been among the most insightful writers on class cultural differences in parents' identities and practices in relation to school, illuminating how middle-class parents seek, albeit some-times with moral dilemmas, to secure positional advantage for their children through choice of school. However, their reliance on an occupational concept of class leads to an implicit but seriously politically debilitating consequence: it poses competition between the middle class and the working class as the class struggle in education.

There are two political implications of this position that need drawing out. The first is this: if the principal issue at stake in education is positional advantage then it is not in the class interests of the middle class to have a more egalitarian school system. Those parents who want to combine greater social equality in education with positional advantage for their own children do so on the basis of moral values but not common class interests. To resolve this dilemma we need not an occupational but a Marxist definition of the working class. For Marx the working class was defined as all those who remain under the economic compulsion to sell their labour power to live (Mandel 1976, p. 47). In the UK this comprises over 90 per cent of the active population. Of course there are big differences between professionals and managers on the one hand and semi-skilled workers on the other, economically, culturally and in the education context, but these are differences *within* this broad conception of the working class. The working class should not be thought of as necessarily homogenous: on the contrary, it is continually being reproduced as a hetero-geneous formation, divided into various class fractions – of age, gender, ethnicity, skill, education, geography, income, etc. – which offer positional advantages to some without being in their class interests. Ball's examples of middle-class parents clearly fall within this Marxist definition of working class. For example, in 'Social justice in the head: are we all libertarians now?' (Ball 2006) the Simpsons are a speech therapist and a civil engineer (made redundant); the Wilkinsons are a senior civil servant and a teacher in a private school.

Goldthorpe bases his division between the middle class – the service class – and the working class on the nature of the employment contract in terms of benefits in addition to salary and of degree of professional autonomy. These may be useful criteria to distinguish class fractions but they obscure the underlying common structural identity of being exploited by capital (indeed, many members of the 'middle-class' fraction may well be more exploited, though less oppressed, than semi-skilled workers in terms of the surplus value they produce).

The second political consequence of posing the middle-class quest for posi-tional advantage in education as the class struggle in education is that it obscures the *real* class struggle in education, which is between the dominant class in society, the ruling class, and the inclusive working class as I have defined it, comprising the vast majority of the population. For example, Reay says:

> Within the educational system almost *all the authority remains vested in the middle classes.* Not only *do they run the system*, the system itself is one which valorizes middle rather than working class cultural capital
>
> (Reay 2006, p. 294, emphasis added)

It is true that the state system valorises middle-class cultural capital, but it is not true that the middle classes run the system. It is the ruling class, as the major employers and owners of big capital, which exercises determining power over government education policy, as it does over the state as a whole (while sending their own children to private schools, comprising 7 per cent of the school population but gaining a quarter of all advanced level examination passes and over half the places in the 'top' universities: Dorling 2010). The state school system does not just function to reproduce the advantages of the middle class over the working class. It has a more fundamental purpose, which is to help to reproduce the conditions of existence of capitalist society as a whole. In this context the principal function of the school is to produce the sorts of future workers that the capitalist economy needs. It is these capitalist interests that the Coalition government is enforcing today and that Tony Blair articulated when he said:

> Education is our best economic policy . . . This country will succeed or fail on the basis of how it changes itself and gears up to this new economy, based on knowledge. Education is now the centre of economic policy making for the future.
>
> (Blair 2005)

A Marxist perspective on class focuses not on static categories of income and occupational distribution but on the dynamic reproduction and evolution of the social system as a whole. It enables us to understand the class interests driving policy and to develop an integrated analysis of the *political economy of education* – the *production* of capital in the form of the production of stratified future labour power – and the *cultural politics of education*: social inequality in education as the consequence of the *circulation* of capital in the form of unequal distribution of income and wealth. In Ball's analysis the state is dominant but the ruling class is absent and the source of the dynamic of policy in the economic imperatives of capital is left unexplored.

This is not to imply that the relationship between the economy and education is unproblematic: a simple matter of correspondence. Nor that the school system has solely a labour market function. Governments also have a concern for social inclusion and meritocratic equality of opportunity in education, for reasons of social cohesion, ideological legitimacy and electoralism, but it is always subordinate to the economic imperative and to the determination of governments of whatever political complexion to eschew reforms that might undermine the privileged position in education of 'middle-class' families and thereby lose their electoral support. School also has an important ideological function: governments attempt to shape and set limits to what can be taught in the curriculum. Finally, the Coalition government's policies, building on New Labour's foundations, are also designed to expand the economic function of the school system in the capitalist economy in a different sense, as a market for profit for edubusiness.

There is an alternative

It is possible to draw the conclusion that the weight of social class inequality in society is so great that schools can do little to counter it. Many teachers and educationists have rejected this pessimistically determinist view and offer an alternative based on the principle that all children have the capacity to learn, even in a profoundly economically unequal society. Hart *et al.*'s (2004) starting point is that the core idea is not children's and young people's 'ability' but their 'transformability', the potential for learning capacity to be transformed. They speak of the need 'to find ways of making connections between school learning and the students' worlds, to find ways to make learning meaningful, relevant and important to them' (2004, p. 168). They explain that while ability-focused teachers 'attempt simply to match tasks to what they see as salient differences between their students',

> Teaching that seeks to foster diversity through co-agency is concerned not with match but with connection, achieving a genuine meeting of minds, purposes and concerns between teachers and young people. [. . .] Tasks and outcomes are deliberately left open, or constructed in such a way as to offer choice of various kinds, so that young people have space to make their own connections [. . .]
>
> . . . the teachers project themselves empathetically into young people's minds and try to imagine, in relation to any particular set of curricular concerns and intentions, what will seem accessible, worthwhile and interesting from young people's point of view.
>
> (Hart *et al.* 2004, p. 183)

The student needs to be able to use 'school knowledge' to organise understandings and actions in order to further his or her own meanings and purposes. All learning must start from problem situations, that is to say situations which have a meaning for the student, which pose a problem, which demand the elaboration of ideas to resolve this problem, and which lead effectively to the mastery of rigorous concepts and language. The solution is not a diluted curriculum restricted to popular experience, but one in which 'academic' knowledge and popular experiences and meanings are interwoven and mutually and critically illuminate each other, so that 'school knowledge' infuses and informs the purposes and actions in the life-worlds of children and young people.

Terry Wrigley has shown how language is central to bridging academic and everyday forms of knowledge. In his book *Another School is Possible* he argues that 'The real issue is how to connect language [. . .] with experience, in ways that restore voice and agency to the learner' (Wrigley 2006, p. 91). He draws on Bruner's distinction between two ways of knowing: narrative (storytelling) and the logico-scientific method (academic language).

> My argument is that improving access for marginalised young people requires grounding theoretical knowledge in lived experience, but as a road towards theoretical understanding, not its avoidance [. . .] narrative styles can be more accessible than abstract academic language, and hold together effective and cognitive dimensions, but there are advantages to consolidating and critiquing the knowledge gained by a narrative by using more formal academic discourses.
>
> (Wrigley 2009, p. 73)

Schools tend to trap learners who are struggling with abstract learning in work that is abstract but cognitively simple, instead of developing activities that 'root challenging ideas in experiences and richer forms of representation', providing 'opportunities for teachers to scaffold the learner's language from descriptive/narrative to more abstract theoretical discourses, and from colloquial to formal registers' (Wrigley 2009, p. 74).

This conception of knowledge informs the case studies in Apple and Beane's (1999) book *Democratic Schools*.

> Rather than being lists of concepts, facts and skills that students master for standardized achievement tests (and then go on to forget, by and large), knowledge is that which is intimately connected to the communities and biographies of real people. Students learn that knowledge makes a difference in people's lives, including their own.
>
> (Apple and Beane 1999, p. 119)

Their case studies demonstrate that a curriculum which brings together 'school knowledge' and the real-life experiences and concerns of students is capable of enabling them to construct a meaningful problem-solving relationship to knowledge (see also Queensland's 'productive pedagogies' model: Hayes *et al.* 2006). One promising approach to this is the RSA's *Area Based Curriculum*, which aims to build on the resources already present within local communities:

schools [. . .] could play an important role in tempering the segregation and competitive isolationism that could result from increased marketisation of schooling (potentially exacerbated by the coalition government's move to allow high achieving schools to become academies, and the expansion of the Free Schools model). The Area Based Curriculum approach contests the dominant view of parents as simply the consumers or clients of education services, and also of parents as the only local stakeholders that should engage with schools. The involvement of a broader community in the creation and enactment of curriculum could anchor the curriculum more securely in the local area and community and allow that wider community to act in the interests of all children in a local area.

(RSA 2010, p. 18)

Socially critical teaching and education for emancipation

Social class in education is not solely about reducing inequality of attainment. Education is about the whole person, it is about helping children and young people to understand the world, and to develop the values, knowledge, skills and personal qualities to be able to act in it to change it for the better. There is a tradition within working-class education, stretching back to the early nineteenth century, of education providing 'really useful knowledge' as a means towards social emancipation.

> Really useful knowledge involved, then, a range of resources for overcoming daily difficulties. It involved self-respect and self-confidence which came from seeing that your oppressions were systematic and were shared. It included practical skills, but not just those wanted by employers . . . Really useful knowledge was also a means to overcoming difficulties in the long term and more comprehensively. It taught people what social changes were necessary for real social ameliorations to occur.
>
> (Johnson 1983, p. 22)

In *Democratic Schools* Michael Apple and James Beane (1999, p. 19) say, 'Our task is to reconstruct dominant knowledge and employ it to help, not hinder, those who are least privileged in this society'. One of their case study schools is Central Park East Secondary School, a public school in a poor district of New York. Its curriculum is based on the principle of critical enquiry, embodied in five questions:

- How do you know what you know?
- From whose viewpoint is this being presented?
- How is this event or work connected to others?

- What if things were different?
- Why is this important?

(Meier and Schwarz 1999, p. 35)

Many teachers are taking advantage of the opportunity to develop socially critical learning in their classrooms from a social justice perspective. For example, *Remaking the Curriculum* (Fautley *et al.* 2011) records how two English secondary schools developed a cross-curricular thematic approach to the curriculum in Year 7. Here is an account of a lesson by Debra Kidd, a drama teacher in one of the schools.

> I gave the group a piece of testimony from a child named Ashique – a child labourer in Bangladesh. 'My name is Ashique. I am eleven years old . . .' Ashique recounts how he, his father and his three brothers work up to 18 hours per day in brick kilns for very little return. He understands that the family is in debt to the owner of the kilns – he mentions the fact that his father borrowed money. His testimony is factual and bare. He does not speak of his feelings except to say that he once went to school and 'liked it' but that he was removed by the kiln owner.

> The group were asked to work out what we knew to be true about the situation, and to draft two questions they would like to ask. In all cases, one of the questions was 'Why did Ashique's father borrow the money?' [. . .]

> We quickly learned that Ashique's father Mohammed had borrowed the money to pay for medical treatment for his daughter, but there were other questions to be answered. How long will it take to pay off the loan? Why do the boys have to work? How do they feel? All of these questions were subsequently explored by developing dramatic explorations of Mohammed's increasingly desperate attempts to secure money for his daughter. [. . .]

> Gradually, the group 'discover' that Mohammed's fate is not down to stupidity but to the social conditions he lives in. We look at the data on LEDCs [Less Economically Developed Countries] – infant mortality rates, literacy rates, doctors per capita etc. and understanding dawns.
>
> (Fautley *et al.* 2011, pp. 37–38)

This lesson led to students discussing goods they have bought, such as trainers, which might have been made by child labour in poorer countries, and what might be the effects of boycotting them.

Lessons like these raise the question of how 'critical' is socially critical pedagogy? How does it conceptualise the object of its critique? To what extent can it go beyond developing a critical understanding of specific issues within capitalist societies and enable pupils and students to develop, in ways appropriate to their age, a critical understanding of capitalism itself, and how it pervades and shapes every aspect of social life including their own identities?

In the 1970s and 1980s teachers began to raise issues of 'race' and gender in the classroom, exploring how they worked themselves out in the lives of their students and what their roots were in the structures and cultures of society. They achieved a radical reform of the curriculum and the culture of teaching, which still resonates in schools today, in spite of decades of neoliberalism. Little comparable curriculum innovation took place about issues of social class oppression and exploitation, yet they are even more salient and urgent today, in the context of a deep economic recession, widening inequality, and overtly conflicting class interests. If this is what is dominating the lives and futures of the children and young people in schools, what is the responsibility of teachers? To remain silent is to collude in injustice by depriving our pupils of the knowledge and conceptual tools they need to make sense of the world, leaving them vulnerable to racist and other reactionary explanations. Teaching about class, like 'race' and gender (with which it is often intertwined), is as vital and appropriate in the primary school as it is in the secondary school, whether deconstructing the presentation of class in stories or television programmes, making visible class conflict in history, enquiring how work is organised, what work produces, and how the products and profits of labour are distributed, or exploring class in the contexts of pupils' own lives and the communities they live in.

Engaging in socially critical teaching is a question of professional perspective and principle that depends on the extent to which teachers recognise that critical pedagogy is integral to the teacher's role; and the extent to which they develop the confidence, knowledge, and skill to try out ways of teaching about class and other social justice issues from a radical perspective and get positive feedback from their students. The new government's claim to be restoring professional autonomy to schools offers a window of opportunity now for teachers to explore new approaches to teaching and learning and develop a curriculum that meets the needs of both reducing social class inequality in attainment and helping the development of a critical understanding of social class in society.

Finally, there is one other aspect of social class and school that I have not mentioned: the effective exclusion of the working class (as I have defined it, though especially, but not exclusively, those not in the 'middle-class' fractions), from the decision-making processes in education, whether at school, local authority or national levels. The imposition of academies by the Labour government regardless of popular campaigns of opposition was a case in point (Hatcher 2009, 2010). The bypassing of local education authorities by the Conservative–Liberal Democrat government's academies and free schools policies will further reduce the democratic accountability of the school system. Tackling social class inequality in the classroom has to be complemented by pressure outside the classroom to open up new possibilities for popular participation in educational decision-making in order to change the economic and education policy contexts in which schools work (Hatcher 2011).

Note

1   This raises the question of how we define and distinguish sexuality and sexual orientation. For the purposes of this and the chapter that follows, we regard sexual orientation as a fairly narrow concept relating to where an individual's sexual attraction lies, which is usually regarded as being in either the same, other or another gender. Our argument progresses by demonstrating that orientation is often that basis for categorising individuals and discrimination against them. However, sexual orientation is but one part of sexuality that we regard as the totality of expression, experience, attitudes, values, beliefs and behaviour that go to make up identity as a sexual being.

References

Alexander, R. (ed.) (2009) *Children, their World, their Education (The Cambridge Primary Review)*. Abingdon: Routledge.

Anyon, J. (1981) Social class and school knowledge. *Curriculum Inquiry* 11(1): 3–42.

Apple, M.W. and Beane, J.A. (eds) (1999) *Democratic Schools*. Washington, DC: Association for Supervision and Curriculum Development.

Archer, L., Halsall, A. and Hollingworth, S. (2007) 'University's not for me — I'm a Nike person': urban working-class young people's negotiations of 'style', identity and educational engagement. *Sociology* 41(2): 219–37.

Ball, S.J. (2003) *Class Strategies and the Education Market: The Middle Class and Social Advantage*. London: RoutledgeFalmer.

Ball, S.J. (2006) *Education Policy and Social Class*. London: Routledge.

Ball, S.J. (2008) *The Education Debate*. Bristol: The Policy Press.

Blair, T. (2005) 'Education and regeneration', Speech at Sedgefield, 18 November.

Bohlmark, A. and Lindahl, M. (2008) *Does School Privatisation Improve Educational Achievement? Evidence from Sweden's Voucher Reform*, IZA Discussion Paper No. 3691. Bonn, Germany: Institute for the Study of Labor.

Brewer, M. (2010) *Cuts to Welfare Spending, Take 2*. London: Institute for Fiscal Studies.

Brewer, M. and Joyce, R. (2010) *Child and Working-age Poverty Set to Rise in Next Three Years*. London: Institute for Fiscal Studies.

Browne, J., O'Dea, C. and Phillips, D. (2010) *The Distributional Impact of Labour from 1997 to 2010*. London: Institute for Fiscal Studies.

Cabinet Office (2008) *Aspiration and Attainment amongst Young People in Deprived Communities*. London: Cabinet Office.

Cassen, R. and Kingdon, G. (2007) *Tackling Low Educational Achievement*. York: Rowntree Foundation.

CBI (Confederation of British Industry) (2010a) *Fulfilling Potential: The Business Role in Education*. London: CBI.

CBI (Confederation of British Industry) (2010b) *Ready to Grow: Business Priorities for Education and Skill*. London: CBI.

Chapman, C., Muijs, D., Sammons, P., Armstrong, P. and Collins, A. (2009) *The Impact of Federations on Student Outcomes*. Nottingham: NCSL.

Charlot, B., Bautier, E. and Rochex, J-Y. (1992) *École et savoir dans les banlieus . . . et ailleurs*. Paris: Armand Colin.

Chowdry, H., Greaves, E. and Sibieta, L. (2010) *The Pupil Premium: Assessing the Options*. London: Institute for Fiscal Studies.

Coe, R. (2009) School improvement: reality and illusion. *British Journal of Educational Studies*. 57(4): 363–79.

CPAG (Child Poverty Action Group) (2009) *Ending Child Poverty*. London: CPAG.

CPAG (Child Poverty Action Group) (2010) *The Cuts: What they Mean for Families at Risk of Poverty*. London: CPAG.

Crawford, R., Emmerson, C., Phillips, D. and Tetlow, G. (2011) *Public Spending Cuts: Pain Shared?* London: Institute for Fiscal Studies.

CREDO (Center for Research on Education Outcomes) (2009) *Multiple Choice: Charter School Performance in 16 States*. Palo Alto, CA: Stanford University Press.

DCSF (Department for Children, Families and Schools) (2009a) *Deprivation and Education*. London: DCSF.

DCSF (Department for Children, Families and Schools) (2009b) *Breaking the Link between Disadvantage and Low Attainment*. London: DCSF.

DCSF (Department for Children, Families and Schools) (2009c) *The Extra Mile: How Schools Succeed in Raising Aspirations in Deprived Communities*. London: DCSF.

DCSF (Department for Children, Families and Schools) (2009d) *Your Child, your Schools, our Future: Building a 21st Century Schools System*. London: DCSF.

DfE (Department for Education) (2010) White Paper, *The Importance of Teaching*. London: DfE.

DfE (Department for Education) (2011) *Review of Vocational Education – The Wolf Report*. London: DfE.

Dorling, D. (2010) *Injustice: Why Social Inequality Exists*. Bristol: Policy Press.

Dunne, M. and Gazeley, L. (2008) Teachers, underachievement and social class. *British Journal of Sociology of Education* 29(5): 451–63.

Dunne, M., Humphreys, S., Sebba, J., Dyson, A., Gallenaugh, F. and Muijs, D. (2007) *Effective Teaching and Learning for Pupils in Low Attaining Groups*. London: DCSF.

Dyson, A., Goldrick, S., Jones, L. and Kerr, K. (2010) *Equity in Education: Creating a Fairer Education System*. Manchester: Centre for Equity in Education, University of Manchester.

Educational Policy Institute (2005) *Focus on Results: An Academic Impact Analysis of the Knowledge Is Power Program (KIPP)*. Virginia Beach, VA: Educational Policy Institute.

Ermisch, J. and Del Bono, E. (2010) *Education Mobility in England*. London: Sutton Trust.

Fautley, M., Hatcher, R. and Millard, E. (2011) *Remaking the Curriculum*. Stoke-on-Trent: Trentham Books.

Gillborn, D. and Youdell, D. (2000) *Rationing Aducation: Policy, Practice, Reform, and Equity*. Buckingham: Open University Press.

Gove, M. (2010a) 'Seizing success'. Speech at National College for Leadership of Schools and Children's Services' Annual Leadership Conference, Birmingham, 17 June.

Gove, M. (2010b) 'Vocational education'. Speech to Edge Foundation, 9 September.

Hart, S., Dixon, A., Drummond, M.J. and McIntyre, D. (2004) *Learning without Limits*. Maidenhead: Open University Press.

Hatcher, R. (2009) Setting up Academies, campaigning against them: an analysis of a contested policy process. *Management in Education* 23(3): 108–12.

Hatcher, R. (2010) Local government against local democracy: a case study of a bid for Building Schools for the Future funding for an Academy. In Gunter, H. (ed.) *The State and Education Policy*. London: Continuum.

Hatcher, R. (2011) The struggle for democracy in the local school system. *Forum*, 53(2): 213–224.

Hayes, D., Mills, M., Christie, P. and Lingard, B. (2006) *Teachers & Schooling Making a Difference*. Crows Nest, NSW: Allen & Unwin.

HM Government (2011) *Opening Doors, Breaking Barriers: A Strategy for Social Mobility*. London: HM Government.

Hoadley, U. (2008) Social class and pedagogy: a model for the investigation of pedagogic variation. *British Journal of Sociology of Education* 29(1): 63–78.

Johnson, R. (1983) Educational politics: the old and the new. In Wolpe, A.M. and Donald, J. (eds) *Is There Anyone Here from Education?* London: Pluto Press.

Joseph Rowntree Foundation (2011) *Response to the UK Government's Tackling Child Poverty and Improving Life Chances: Consulting on a New Approach. Submission by the Joseph Rowntree Foundation*. York: Joseph Rowntree Foundation.

Kerr, K. and West, M. (eds) (2010) *BERA Insight: Schools and Social Inequality*. London: BERA.

Lawton, K. (2009) *Nice Work If You Can Get It: Achieving a Sustainable Solution to Low Pay and In-work Poverty*. London: Institute for Public Policy Research.

Lubienski, C. (2009) *Do Quasi-markets Foster Innovation in Education? A Comparative Perspective*. Education Working Paper No. 25. Paris: OECD.

Mandel, E. (1976) Introduction. In Marx, K., *Capital* Vol. 1. Harmondsworth: Penguin.

Meier, D. and Schwarz, P. (1999) Central Park East Secondary School: the hard part is making it happen. In Apple, M.W. and Beane, J.A. (eds) *Democratic Schools*. Buckingham: Open University Press.

Mongon, D. and Chapman, C. (2008) *Successful Leadership for Promoting the Achievement of White Working Class Pupils*. Nottingham: NCSL/NUT.

NAO (National Audit Office) (2009) *Sure Start Children's Centres*. London: National Audit Office.

National Equality Panel (2010) *An Anatomy of Economic Inequality in the UK*. London: Government Equalities Office.

Ofsted (Office for Standards in Education) (2009) *Twelve Outstanding Secondary Schools: Excelling Against the Odds*. London: Ofsted.

Perry, E. and Francis, B. (2010) *The Social Class Gap for Educational Achievement: A Review of the Literature*. London: RSA.

PricewaterhouseCoopers (2008) *Academies Evaluation: 5th Annual Report*. London: PricewaterhouseCoopers.

Ravitch, D. (2010) *The Death and Life of the Great American School System*. New York: Basic Books.

Reay, D. (2001) 'Finding or losing yourself?': working-class relationships to education. *Journal of Education Policy* 16(4): 333–46.

Reay, D. (2006) The zombie stalking English schools: social class and educational inequality. *British Journal of Educational Studies* 54(3): 288–307.

RSA (2010) *The RSA Area Based Curriculum: Engaging the Local*. London: RSA.

Skolverket (the Swedish National Agency for Education) (2006) *Schools Like any Other? Independent Schools as Part of the System 1991–2004*. Stockholm: Skolverket.

Smith, C., Dakers, J., Dow, W., Head, G., Sutherland, M. and Irwin, R. (2005) A systematic review of what pupils, aged 11–16, believe impacts on their motivation to learn in the classroom. In *Research Evidence in Education Library*. London: EPPI-Centre, Social Science Research Unit, Institute of Education, University of London.

Sullivan, A. (2007) Cultural capital, cultural knowledge and ability. *Sociological Research Online* 12(6): www.socresonline.org.uk/12/6/1.html (accessed 12 July 2011).

Sveinsson, K.P. (2010) The white working class and multiculturalism: is there space for a progressive agenda? In *Who Cares about the White Working Class?* London: Runnymede Trust.

Thrupp, M. and Lupton, R. (2006) Taking school contexts more seriously: the social justice challenge. *British Journal of Educational Studies* 53(3): 308–28.

Tymms, P. and Merrell, C. (2007) *Standards and Quality in English Primary Schools over Time: the National Evidence* (Primary Review Research Survey 4/1). Cambridge: University of Cambridge Faculty of Education.

Vincent, C. and Ball, S.J. (2006) *Childcare, Choice and Class Practices: Middle-class Parents and their Children*. London: Routledge.

Wiborg, S. (2011) Learning lessons from the Swedish model. *Forum* 52(3): 279–84.

Woodworth, K. R., David, J. L., Guha, R., Wang, H. and Lopez-Torkos, A. (2008) *San Francisco Bay Area KIPP Schools: A Study of Early Implementation and Achievement. Final Report*. Menlo Park, CA: SRI International.

Wrigley, T. (2006) *Another School is Possible*. Stoke-on-Trent: Trentham Books.

Wrigley, T. (2009) Rethinking education in the era of globalization. In Hill, D. (ed.) *Contesting Neoliberal Education*. Abingdon: Routledge.

Wrigley, T. (2011) Rapidly improving results: penetrating the hype of policy-based Evidence. In Gunter, H.M. (ed.) *The State and Education Policy: The Academies Programme*. London: Continuum.

Young, M. (2008) *Bringing Knowledge Back In*. Abingdon: Routledge.

Index